CALIFORNIA
The Politics of Diversity

FOURTH EDITION

David G. Lawrence
Westmont College

Australia • Brazil • Canada • Mexico • Singapore • Spain
United Kingdom • United States

THOMSON

★

™

WADSWORTH

Publisher: Clark Baxter

Executive Editor: David Tatom

Development Editor: Heather Hogan

Assistant Editor: Rebecca Green

Editorial Assistant: Cheryl Lee

Technology Project Manager: Michelle Vardeman

Marketing Manager: Janise Fry

Marketing Assistant: Kelley McAllister

Marketing Communications Manager: Nathaniel Michelson

Project Manager, Editorial Production: Candace Chen

Creative Director: Rob Hugel

Art Director: Maria Epes

Print Buyer: Lisa Claudeanos

Permissions Editor: Stephanie Lee

Photo Researcher: Terri Wright

Copy Editor: Prachi Chandola

Illustrator: International Typesetting and Composition

Cover Designer: Garry Harman

Cover Photo: Mark Downey/Getty Images

Text and Cover Printer: Webcom

Compositor: International Typesetting and Composition

Printed in Canada

1 2 3 4 5 6 7 09 08 07 06 05

Thomson Higher Education
10 Davis Drive
Belmont, CA 94002-3098
USA

For more information about our products, contact us at:
Thomson Learning Academic Resource Center
1-800-423-0563
For permission to use material from this text or product, submit a request online at
http://www.thomsonrights.com.
Any additional questions about permissions can be submitted by e-mail to thomsonrights@thomson.com.

Library of Congress Control Number: 2005904462

Student Edition: ISBN 0-534-60234-7

Contents

Preface

During the process of researching and writing this fourth edition of *California: The Politics of Diversity,* I jokingly told friends and colleagues that this would be the "Arnold Schwarzenegger" edition. Indeed, the recall election of 2003 and the election of a movie action hero as governor captured the nation's attention and California's imagination. To be sure, voters were in the mood for a change and had soured on Gray Davis-era government as usual in the Golden State. During the recall initiative drive, State Librarian Emeritus Kevin Starr wrote that, "as an ecumenical society of cutting edge creativity in the private sector, California cannot afford to behave like a banana republic as far as its state government is concerned."

In his post-election rhetoric and actions, the new reform-oriented governor promised to shake up state government. Nothing would be the same. As I moved from chapter to chapter, Arnold Schwarzenegger was making his unique mark on the initiative process, elections, interest groups, the legislature, and the budget, to name just a few highlights. Indeed, it appeared his imprint would affect the breadth of state government more than many recent governors. Yet, by early 2005, *Los Angeles Times* columnist George Skelton exclaimed, "California has hit rock bottom. State governments don't get any worse, anywhere." He was referring to a study of all 50 state governments by *Governing Magazine.* In the estimation of that highly regarded journal, California earned a near-the-bottom-of-the-stack C- for the quality and management of its government. Justifications for that poor grade included a continually flawed budget process, neglected infrastructure needs, and a ubiquitous initiative process that robs elected officials of their policy making responsibilities. The challenges of governing the nation's largest state go well beyond whoever is governor, Skelton concluded.

Text Features

In my humble estimation, *Governing Magazine*'s assessment of California government affirms the approach used in this book. In short, governing California is less about leadership—as important as that is—and more about two broad phenomona: diversity and a variant of pluralism we call hyperpluralism. In all four editions, we have tried to show two things: (1) how demographic, cultural, economic, geographic, and political diversity affects how politics actually works in California; and (2) how that diversity expresses itself in political hyperpluralism—the view that California politics is exceedingly pluralistic. That is, the exercise of political power in California is a highly competitive tug-of-war between ideologies, institutions, policymakers, political parties, interest groups, and voters. So many groups now compete and the political system is so complex, governing of any sort is most challenging. Much of the time, power is thinly scattered, not just unevenly scattered. Even charismatic actors turned governors must cope with this truth.

As with many California political scientists, my own teaching assignments have included both California politics and American government. The fourth edition continues to apply important political science and American government concepts to the California experience. Devoting three chapters to public policy, it remains the most policy-focused general California government text on the market.

Pedagogical Features

California continues to offer numerous pedagogical features that help students learn. Each chapter includes:

• a consistent perspective that really makes sense to today's students

• an attractive and functional two-column design that aids in reading

• "In Brief" boxes and outlines which survey forthcoming content

• a conclusion that revisits key points and ties them to book themes

• key terms that are italicized in the text and referenced by page number

• study questions that help students review and apply chapter content

• extensive endnotes that provide opportunities for further reading and research

• Infotrac references that create, in effect, a California politics reader

• carefully selected charts, tables, photos, and cartoons that underscore key points

• "California Voices"—boxes that feature the insights of voters, political activists, governors, and novelists such as John Steinbeck and Frank Norris.

• end-of-chapter Internet web sites that encourage further exploration

• "Did You Know" boxes that feature interesting facts related to chapter topics

Revision Highlights

The fourth edition of *California: The Politics of Diversity* retains an organizational format familiar to many political scientists who teach American government courses. Its student-friendly writing style reflects my view that important ideas should be intelligible ones, especially in an undergraduate textbook. In terms of substance, the fourth edition involves cover-to-cover revisions reflecting the latest developments in California politics. They include:

• Coverage of the 2003 recall election and Governor Arnold Schwarzenegger's first years in office

• Updated coverage of women's issues, Latino power, and gay rights

• A new profile of Proposition 71, the stem cell research initiative

• An analysis of California's role in the 2004 presidential election

• Revised analyzes of California's ongoing budget problems

• New public opinion data from the state's top polling organizations

• The latest cutting-edge research on demographic, economic, voting, and immigration trends

• Helpful comparisons with other states (in terms of state spending, taxes, population growth, and higher education tuition costs)

Supplements

As a Thomson Wadsworth text, *California* offers a number of attractive supplements that aid both professors and students; they consist of the following resources:

• An e-bank and online instructor's manual with test questions and other helpful instructional tips

• Infotrac® College Edition. This online university library lets students explore full-length articles from hundreds of periodicals. When students log on with their personal ID, they will see immediately how easy it is to search, read, and print out articles from the last four years. Periodicals include *State Legislatures, U.S. News and World Report, The Economist,* and *Campaigns & Elections.*

• The Wadsworth Political Science Resource Center (http://politicalscience.wadsworth.com). This site includes information on all Wadsworth political science texts including California politics. The Resource Center contains information on surfing the Internet, links to general political sites, a career center, election updates, monthly news online, and a discussion forum.

Acknowledgments

Textbook writing is a team effort. It involves many more people than a title page would suggest. I am indebted to several teams. The first is uniquely mine. From my own years in and around state and local politics, I must credit the many practitioners who have shared their political insights with me—former city council colleagues, internship supervisors, classroom speakers, journalists, and countless Sacramento Legislative Seminar panelists. Fellow board members of the California Center for Education in Public Affairs provide constant stimulation. I am also grateful to colleague Richard Burnweit, whose own expertise and keen eye aided the revision process, secretary Ruby Jeanne Shelton, and student researchers Christin Fletcher and Andrew Leighton. As always, my wife and best friend Carolyn exhibited patience and provided needed encouragement. I am grateful.

A second team consists of the good people at Thomson Wadsworth who provided helpful direction, assistance, and encouragement. They are publisher Clark Baxter, executive editor David Tatom, development editor Heather Hogan, assistant editor Rebecca Green, associate production project manager Candace Chen, editorial services manager Ben Kolstad, production editor Mona Tiwary, permissions editor Stephanie Lee, marketing manager Janise Fry, advertising project manager Nathaniel Michelson, photo researcher Terri Wright and technology project manager Michelle Vardeman. Professor Dianne Long (California State Polytechnic University, San Luis Obispo) authored the instructor's manual and test bank.

A third team consists of the political scientists who reviewed all or some of *California* along the way. They include:

Theodore J. Anagnoson (California State University, Los Angeles), Michele Colborn Harris (College of the Canyons), John H. Culver (California Polytechnic State University, San Luis Obispo), Robert L. Delorme (California State University, Long Beach), Lawrence L. Giventer, California State University, Stanislaus, Drake C. Hawkins (Glendale Community College), Peter H. Howse (American River College), Stanley W. Moore (Pepperdine University), William W. Lammers (University of Southern California), Dianne Long (California Polytechnic State University, San Luis Obispo), Marilyn J. Loufek (Long Beach City College), Edward S. Malecki (California State University,

Los Angeles), Donald J. Matthewson (California State University, Fullerton), Charles H. McCall (California State University, Bakersfield), Steve Monsma (Pepperdine University), Eugene Price (California State University, Northridge), Donald Ranish (Antelope Valley College), Alvin D. Sokolow (University of California, Davis), Richard S. Unruh (Fresno Pacific University),

Linda O. Valenty (San Jose State University), and Alan J. Wyner (University of California, Santa Barbara).

As helpful as these veteran colleagues were, I take full responsibility for the end product.

David Lawrence

PART ONE

Foundations of California Politics

California, more than any other part of the Union, is a country by itself. . . .
—James Bryce, 1888

As we consider California in the early years of a new millennium, almost everything is and has been said about the state and its politics. In Part 1, we step behind the dire predictions or the rosy forecasts, depending on whom you want to believe, and shed some light on why California politics works the way it does. Part 1 establishes a conceptual foundation for understanding the core reasons for conflict in the public square we call California.

Chapter 1, "Explaining California Politics," presents two general ways of analyzing politics in the Golden State. First, diversity, a recurring theme throughout the text, describes the state itself—its land, regions, resources, people, and economic base. Second, familiar theories in American political science help describe how the state's diversity translates into its politics. Although no single theory best describes California politics, hyperpluralism comes close.

Chapter 2, "California's Political Development," uses the concepts of political culture and political development to survey California's political past. In many ways, California's political present is not only informed by its relatively short history as a state but is dictated by it. California's stages of political development build on each other—to understand that building process helps explain why modern Californians and their political institutions exercise power and make policy the way they do.

Chapter 3, "Constitutionalism and Federalism," marks and discusses the outer limits—legal and political—that affect California politics. First, the state constitution establishes a wide assortment of rules that simultaneously limit government and yet empower it to act. Second, California's role in a larger federal system places politics and policy making here in a larger national context. Third, geographically speaking, California is on the edge of the nation—facing the Pacific Rim and Mexico. This position gives the state both opportunities and challenges. In particular, California's porous border with Mexico and its dependence on the federal government to police it increasingly affect politics inside the state.

CHAPTER 1

Explaining California Politics

In Brief

In this introductory chapter, we survey the big picture of California politics. Many observers claim that the Golden State is no longer the land of milk and honey, yet it continues to draw newcomers from the four corners of the earth. Why the differences in perception? The answer is in both, the diversity of California and how it is governed. This chapter will cover these two subjects.

The state's very diversity has been its strength. The land varies from temperate coastal plains to rugged mountain ranges; from lush agricultural valleys to barren deserts.

People divide California into several regions, but these divisions seem to be a matter of perception. Some divide the state into North and South; others see multiple and diverse regions. California is rich in resources, especially water and desirable climate. Moving the state's water supply around has increased the usability of the land. Throughout its history, waves of people have moved to and around California seeking a better life. These factors have resulted in a diverse economy—one of the world's largest.

How political scientists explain U.S. politics in general helps us understand California

3

politics in particular. To answer the question "Who governs?" four theories have emerged. Democratic theory says the people do, usually through elected representatives. Elite theory claims the upper classes exercise power and influence beyond their numbers. Pluralist theory contends that groups compete for power and policy advantage. Hyperpluralism, an emerging theory, contends that so many groups now compete and the political system is so complex that governing can become most difficult.

Although these theories seem incompatible, each helps to explain aspects of California politics. Evidence of hyperpluralism in California is growing. The outcome is a state of many paradoxes.

Introduction

If you think about it, the state of California and theme park roller coasters have much in common. People flock to both—enduring congestion in the process and experiencing the exhilaration of both ups and downs. In the Golden State, the highs include better jobs, economic opportunities, and living conditions than people could only have imagined back home, whether they are from Missouri or Mexico. People envision California as a place where these dreams can come true. The lows include periodic recessions, occasional droughts, smog, crime, crowded freeways, and unaffordable housing.

Some Californians endure the lows to appreciate the highs, but others find California, like the roller coaster, a bit too much. They flee the state for Washington, Oregon, Nevada, Colorado, and beyond. Or, they move within the state, seeking a calmer ride. As a whole, Californians' confidence in the future of the state can vary remarkably from year to year (see Figure 1.1).

Polling data confirms this roller coaster analogy. Pollster and analyst Mark Baldassare observed what he calls the yin and yang of California political life—"we might call it the New Economy meets the New Demography." That is, the economic optimism shared by many Californians at the turn of the new century was tempered by signs of trouble such as congestion, pollution, and increasing economic inequality; compounding the problem

was a widely shared distrust of government. "Californians, by and large, did not believe that government had the ability to handle problems or that it even had their best interests at heart."[1] Within a few years, economic pessimism replaced optimism while many policy problems festered and political distrust grew. The confluence of these trends and attitudes in part led to the 2003 recall of Governor Gray Davis and the election of optimistic political neophyte and action movie hero Arnold Schwarzenegger. By mid-2005, his own public support appeared to wane. As Californians search for the good life, however they define it, they will need to adjust to the state's growing demographic diversity. A state senator summed it up succinctly: "We Californians have an opportunity, the necessity, the responsibility to realize our great challenge . . . the promise of a multicultural democracy in the global economy."[2]

As far as California is concerned, this search began centuries ago. In the 1500s, Spaniards desired to find and explore a mythical island of *California*. Writer Garci Ordonez de Montalvo described this place as rich in "gold and precious stones"; its people were "robust of body, with strong and passionate hearts and great virtues." As for government, the queen "had ambitions to execute nobler actions than had been performed by any other ruler."[3] Wealth and good intentions—what a combination! No wonder California has been called not only a state, but a state of mind.

Centuries later, California's official state motto captures that mythic search: "Eureka"

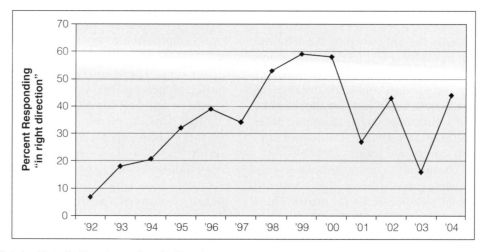

FIGURE 1.1   How Californians view California

When pollsters ask, "Do you think things in California are generally going in the right direction, or do you feel things are seriously off track?" Californians' responses can vary significantly within a 10-year period.

Question: In your opinion, to what extent do these data affect perceptions of governmental institutions and policymakers?

Source: Successive surveys of *The Field Poll* and the Public Policy Institute of California's *Statewide Survey* (August, 2004). Note: Results are based on representative statewide samples of about 1000 California adults. The sampling error ranges from ±3.2 to 4.5 percentage points.

(I Have Found It). The motto itself refers to the real gold many sought and some actually found. But symbolically, it refers to a host of images emanating from California: perpetually sunny days (advertised every year by Pasadena's Rose Parade); hope and opportunity; a chance to start over; plus gorgeous scenery and people to match (says Hollywood).

Chapter 1 introduces two approaches to understanding California politics. The first is the state's remarkable diversity. The second is a set of theories political scientists use to explain aspects of American politics generally. These two broad approaches (diversity and theory) are revisited throughout the book.

How Diversity Explains California Politics

California always has been a compelling place. Few observers write about it without describing its physical diversity, and fewer still ignore its politics. To understand this huge state, one must understand how its public sector works. Political scientist David Easton defined *politics* as "the authoritative allocation of values for a society as a whole."[4] Politics occurs within the context of a *political system*. In our federal arrangement, there are 50 state systems and one national political system. These systems reflect ongoing patterns of human behavior involving control, influence, power, and authority. The process of making public policy, deciding "who gets what, when and how,"[5] exists within the context of a larger environment. The *political environment* is a set of social, cultural, economic, and physical attributes that inform and limit how politics is done. To begin this study of California politics, we must examine California's diverse environment—the land and regions of the state as well as its resources, people, and economy.

LAND

Diverse is truly the only word to describe the physical geography of California. The state's diversity is made possible in part by its sheer size. California's length covers the distance between New York City and Jacksonville, Florida. The nation's third largest state in square miles (behind Alaska and Texas), California supports a rich variety of terrain.

Coastal communities enjoy moderate, semi-arid Mediterranean weather in the South and wetter, cooler weather in the far north. Thick forests including the Giant Redwoods occur in the North. In fact, 40 percent of the entire state is forested. The naturally barren South has been made less so over the years by farmers and gardeners alike. Numerous mountain ranges crisscross the state. The defining North/South range is the Sierra Nevada. Admired by naturalist John Muir, this magnificent mountain range is home to world famous Yosemite National Park and the giant sequoia trees. Farmers and urban residents to the west and south of the mountains depend on the Sierra's snowpack for year-round water supplies, the lifeblood of any arid state. Less imposing coastal ranges help define the attractive but expensive environments around such places as Santa Barbara, Carmel, and Santa Cruz.

The transverse ranges, those mountains that lie in an east/west direction, once defined the limits of urbanization and, to some people's minds, the boundary between Northern and Southern California. The Los Angeles Basin (surrounded by the Sierra Madre, Tehachapi, Santa Ana, San Gabriel, and San Jacinto ranges) once kept its poor air quality to itself. But urban growth and automobile proliferation have spread smog over the mountains to communities on the other side (Palm Springs and Lancaster, for example) and locales as far away as the Grand Canyon in Arizona. The increasingly smoggy Central Valley supports some of the most productive agriculture in the world.

REGIONS

The configuration of the land influences how people settle on and use it—leading to regional differences. These differences are partly a matter of perception. Consider the idea of Northern and Southern California, the most familiar division of the state. People know Northern California for San Francisco (called simply "The City"), wineries, the redwoods, heavy water-consuming crops such as rice, and mountain resorts such as Lake Tahoe. They identify Southern California with its warm days, wide beaches, automobile culture, show business, Latino roots, and, of course, smog. Some suggest that these two regions are actually two states divided by water. The North has it, the South wants it, and the North knows it. These North/South differences are deeply rooted. In 1859, less than a decade after statehood, the legislature voted to split the state in two, but the U.S. Congress disallowed it. Occasional efforts to divide California have surfaced ever since. The most recent efforts, in the 1990s, aimed to divide the state into either two or three states. These efforts seem motivated not only by classic regional differences but by the mounting problems faced by a unified California—economic uncertainty, budget woes, population growth, and demographic diversity. In an advisory vote in 1992, voters in 31 counties considered a two-state proposal; it passed in 27—mostly northern counties. Although these efforts are doomed to failure, they do underscore intense regional divisions in the state. Pundits have long since divided California from north to south into Logland, Fogland, and Smogland.

Perceptions aside, California is really a state of many regions. Different observers have divided the state into anywhere from 4 to 14 distinct regions. Each is markedly different from the others based on geography, economy, populations, political behavior, and public attitudes.[6] Public opinion surveys of 4 regions—Los Angeles County, the San Francisco Bay

Area, the Central Valley, and the Orange County/Inland Empire region—document a number of differences. Los Angeles and Bay Area residents are more liberal than residents elsewhere, especially those in the Central Valley. For example, Central Valley residents are more opposed to affirmative action, illegal immigration, and environmental regulations than their counterparts elsewhere. Based on these surveys, analyst and pollster Mark Baldassare believes these regional differences make it difficult for Californians to unify and see themselves as members of one state. Indeed, "The major regions are drifting further apart at a time when there is a need to reach a statewide consensus on social, environmental, land use, and infrastructure issues."[7]

RESOURCES

In addition to regional perceptions, a state's natural resources affect its politics. Ironically, California's most important resource is its most precious—water. One simply cannot underestimate what the availability and redistribution of water has meant for the Golden State. As writer Carey McWilliams once noted, "The history of Southern California is the record of its eternal quest for water, and more water, and still more water."[8] The entire state has been called a "hydraulic society," and it is easy to see why. Water has transformed parched land into the nation's salad bowl and fruit basket. Water has enabled imaginative people in a semiarid climate to control vast amounts of land or merely turn their own yards into tropical and subtropical gardens. And most important, dams, canals, and aqueducts have channeled water from the North to the South, allowing millions of people to live where nature alone could support very few.

California's overall climate is itself a resource and has directly and indirectly caused the state's phenomenal growth. Americans have always been lured to California because of its weather. Years ago, winter exports of citrus and newspaper ads in the Midwest created a "Garden of Eden" image, which served as a magnet. Asked why he charged $200 an acre for seemingly worthless land, flamboyant speculator Lucky Baldwin retorted: "Hell! We're giving away the land. We're selling the climate."[9] Doctors would recommend California's milder climate to patients suffering from respiratory and arthritic ailments.

California's climate also has fostered elements of California's economy. Early movie producers found weather predictability helpful in shooting outdoor scenes. The films themselves became subtle advertisements for the Golden State. Farmers discovered that, given enough water, several harvests per year were possible. Developers and contractors found they could get away with cheaper, less weather resistant construction. Employers concerned with working conditions and living conditions for themselves found California an inviting destination. California's climate also fostered recreation-oriented "live-for-the-weekend" lifestyles. Much leisure time can be spent outdoors—beach activities, snow skiing, fishing, water sports, camping, biking, hiking—the list is endless. Even at home, many Californians create their own micro-lifestyles, replete with expansive patios, pools, spas, barbecues, and gardens.

All this has resulted in a subtle attitude found in the Golden State. Just as people thought they could change their destiny by moving to California in the first place, many believe they can engineer their destiny once they arrive. As Cartoon 1.1 implies, Californians seek what they call the "good life" despite hindrances of all sorts. They expect their state and local governments to deliver policies fostering and protecting a certain quality of life. They become disillusioned and angry when policymakers fail to meet those expectations. As we noted earlier, in 2003 voters angered over the state's budget crisis—the complexity of

CARTOON 1.1   The good life

Question: How do you define "the good life" in California in light of these periodic misfortunes?

Source: Gary Brookins, *Richmond Times–Dispatch.*

which was difficult to explain or comprehend—focused their ire on Governor Gray Davis and recalled him from office.

PEOPLE

California's resources have encouraged waves of human settlement. In short, diversity and growth characterize the demographics of California. As in the past, the state attracts immigrants from all over the world. Furthermore, they are settling throughout the state. Mexicans were never limited solely to Los Angeles barrios; nor the Chinese to their Chinatowns. But the ethnic and geographic diversity of today's Californians is astounding. Iranians, Indians, Sri Lankans, Haitians, Koreans, Salvadoreans, Vietnamese, and others are moving to and throughout California in large numbers. California's population currently is growing at a rate of 1,400 per day. By 2000, no racial group or ethnic group constituted a majority of Californians. This trend can be seen in Table 1.1.

California's first dwellers were widely dispersed Indians living off the land in small communities. As peaceful peoples, they were no match for the succession of more aggressive Spanish, Mexican, and Anglo-American settlers. Primarily due to disease imported from these settlers, they and their cultures were driven to near extinction. The Spanish, as elsewhere, treated Mexican California as a colony to be conquered, civilized, and exploited, not necessarily to be populated with Spaniards.

By the time of Mexican independence from Spain in 1822, the province of *del norte* was populated by the remaining Indians, a few Spaniards, Mexicans, and the offspring of mixed marriages between various groups. Like their predecessors, contemporary Mexicans come to California seeking prosperity. Be they citizens, resident aliens, or undocumented workers, many Latinos work in the agricultural, manufacturing, and service sectors of the state's economy. Due to continuing immigration and relatively high birthrates, they

TABLE 1.1 Californians at a Glance

Group	Percentage of State Population		
	1990	2000	2025*
White	57	47	33
Hispanic	26	32	42
Asian and Pacific Islander	9	11	18
Black/African American	7	7	7
Other/Multiple[a]	—	1	<1
Native American	<1	1	<1

Source: California Department of Finance, Demographic Research Unit, 2000.

Notes: California's population was 29,760,021 in 1990 and grew to 33,871,648 according to the 2000 Census. Projections (*) suggest the state's share of Hispanics will continue to grow; its share of whites will continue to shrink. [a]The 2000 Census allowed individuals to self-report other races/ethnicities including mixed or multiple races.

Question: To what extent are these changes already evident where you live?

have become a sizeable cultural and socioeconomic force in the state. Latinos, numbered nearly 12 million in 2003 or 33 percent of the entire state population. Their numbers are not limited to Southern California as old images would suggest. For instance, the 2000 Census revealed that the Latino population of Monterey and Tulare Counties was 47 and 51 percent, respectively. Latinos have been known for low voter turnout, in part because many of them are not yet citizens or are too young to vote. Yet a growing number of Latinos have been elected to public office. In 2004, there were several California Latinos in Congress, including two Latina sisters, Loretta and Linda Sanchez. Both Cruz Bustamante and Antonio Villaraigosa attained the State Assembly speakership, and Bustamante won the lieutenant governorship in 1998—the first Latino elected to statewide office since 1871. There are now 28 Latinos in the state legislature. Former legislator Art Torres has chaired the State Democratic Committee. Both population data and electoral returns suggest that Latino political influence will grow in the future but that the rather diverse Latino community may not behave as a monolithic political force.[10]

The Gold Rush of 1849 began what is known as the "American era." This provincial-sounding term refers to the successive waves of Euro-American citizens who moved to California from other parts of the United States. Within a year after gold was discovered at Sutter's Mill in 1848, roughly a third of the state's population was digging for gold in "them thar hills." Many with gold fever never intended to stay but did. Others not only stayed but sent for their families to join them. Population figures tell the story. In 1840, Californians numbered about 116,000, including 110,000 to 112,000 Indians. Two decades later, they numbered 380,000 including only 30,000 Indians.

A second population rush followed completion of the transcontinental railroad in 1869. That last spike, joining the Central Pacific and Union Pacific Railroads in Utah, linked California both physically and symbolically with the rest of the nation. For urban Americans, the lure of open space "out West" actually made possible a newly emerging dream in the late 1800s—a single-family house on a single-family lot. But why California? For one thing, the Southern Pacific Railroad had received more than 10 million acres of Southern California land as a construction incentive. Through shameless hucksterism and discounted train tickets, developers and the railroads lured many midwesterners to the Golden State.

Later, the mass production of automobiles allowed others to bypass trains altogether on their way to sunny California.

In the 1900s, additional waves of Americans moved westward to seek various employment opportunities. Beginning with Summerland near Santa Barbara in 1920, the discovery and drilling of oil led to new jobs and still more land speculation. The Depression-era jobless and Dust Bowl refugees (many were called Okies and Arkies for their home states of Oklahoma and Arkansas) came to California in search of any opportunity they could find. John Steinbeck's *Grapes of Wrath* fictionalized the real misery of these migrants and what they hoped for in California (see California Voices). World War II brought numerous Americans to California for training and war production efforts. Soldiers and sailors who had never been west of the Mississippi River were stationed briefly in California on their way to the Pacific theater. Many of them vowed to return to California—for keeps—and they did. In 2004, white non-Hispanic Californians numbered over 16 million, or nearly 47 percent of the overall population. As Table 1.1 projects, these percentages are destined to decline in the long term.

The war effort in California provided unprecedented employment opportunities for African Americans, many of whom migrated from the South. Their population in California grew 272 percent in the 1940s alone! In 2003, most of California's 2.2 million African Americans lived in the state's large metropolitan areas. As elsewhere, they have suffered racial discrimination and many lag behind other groups in education and income. Benefiting from the civil rights movement, former black officials include the late Los Angeles Mayor Tom Bradley; Lieutenant Governor Mervyn Dymally; Superintendent of Public Instruction Wilson Riles; and two former Assembly Speakers, Willie Brown and Herb Wesson. Janice Rogers Brown is an associate justice of the California Supreme Court. Still others include various state legislators, members of Congress, judges, and numerous county and city officials. In 2003, African Americans constituted only 6.2 percent of California's overall population. Because of modest birthrates and even movement out of California, black political clout may be lessened in the future.

A succession of other minorities entered California over the years. Notable have been California's 3.9 million Asian Americans including those of Chinese, Japanese, Filipino, and Korean descent. Many Chinese were brought to the state during the Gold Rush or to work on railroad construction gangs. By 1870, nearly 150,000 of them were treated as virtual slaves by their employers. During economic downturns, they were considered as excess labor and had to retreat to their Chinatowns for protection and security. The Chinese population of California numbered more than 981,000 in the most recent census.

Japanese Californians numbered about 229,000 according to the most recent Census. Between 1900 and 1920 they increased from 10,000 to 72,000 and, to the dismay of whites, gained control of 11 percent of the state's farmland. Four years later, the U.S. Congress reacted by halting further Japanese immigration. After Japan attacked Pearl Harbor in 1941, Californians of Japanese descent, including American citizens, were moved to relocation camps. Branded temporarily as "enemy aliens," Japanese Americans rose above this wholesale discrimination and economic dislocation to become successful both educationally and economically.

Filipinos are the largest Asian group, slightly outnumbering Chinese Americans with about 919,000 people. Yet they do not command the economic influence of either the Chinese or the Japanese in California. The Vietnam War resulted in an influx of southeast Asians to California. Few Vietnamese were in California in 1970. The 2000 Census counted more than 447,000. Some have achieved material success in the Golden State, but others work at poverty

CALIFORNIA VOICES

Steinbeck on California

"I like to think how nice it's gonna be, maybe, in California. Never cold. An' fruit ever'place, an' people just bein' in the nicest places, little white houses in among the orange trees. I wonder—that is, if we all get jobs an' all work—maybe we can get one of them little white houses. An' the little fellas go out an' pick oranges right off the tree."

Question: To what extent are today's visions of California like or unlike those of Steinbeck's Depression-ravaged characters?

SOURCE: John Steinbeck, *The Grapes of Wrath* (New York: Viking Press, 1939), 124.

---

wages in Southern California sweatshops. Korean Californians number about 346,000.

Ethnic diversity in California also translates into language diversity. The 2000 Census revealed that an impressive 40 percent of Californians speak a language other than English in the home, the highest percentage of any state. In general, children speak English more fluently than the adults in these homes.

What does all this racial and ethnic data tell us? While other parts of America have historically thought of diversity in biracial (black and white) terms, describing the people of California is much more complex. In fact, according to journalist Steve Scott, "California is on the leading edge of a national redefinition of racial diversity, one which acknowledges that race is no longer merely a 'black and white' issue."[11] Some observers ask—Will this multiethnic and multiracial mix we find in California lead to a divisive, Balkanized politics that emphasizes difference over unity? It depends. Aside from race-based policies such as affirmative action, services to illegal immigrants, and bilingual education, research suggests that California's Asians, blacks, Latinos, and whites agree more often than not on a wide range of issues.[12] To the extent Californians view public life in similar terms, they embody what writer O. Henry once said of the state, "Californians are a race of people; not merely inhabitants of a state."[13] Furthermore, as you will see shortly, the "politics

of diversity" in the Golden State is only in part a function of ethnic and racial diversity.

ECONOMY

To the state's geographic and demographic diversity can be added economic diversity. To understand the politics of any state, knowing its economy is essential. Business and politics are closely intertwined. State and local policies can have an impact on economic growth generally, particular economic sectors, and even individual businesses. The economy in turn provides the financial base for state and local policies. California's modern economy has four characteristics—postindustrialism, change, diversity, and a two-tier structure.

1. *Postindustrialism.* California's economy is *postindustrial,* meaning it is characterized by a large service sector, economic interdependence, rapid change, innovation, and advanced technology. As a general rule, traditional manufacturing has lagged behind services and trade, in numbers of workers. This is especially true as some manufacturing job growth moves overseas. Today's postindustrial service economy includes technology, education, research, finance, insurance, and real estate. The sleek buildings, professional office "parks," and shopping malls dotting suburban California epitomize this sector. It also includes both wholesale

and retail sales of groceries, clothing, and other consumer items. To many Californians, fast food franchises and technology firms symbolize (if not oversimplify) postindustrialism.

2. *Change.* California's economic history has been one of constant *change.* The Gold Rush encouraged a "rush" of workers. The expansion of railroads (including the invention of refrigerated rolling stock), plus government-financed water projects, secured agriculture as an economic mainstay. The discovery of oil attracted still more workers and fueled the state's emerging automobile-oriented transportation system. World War II spawned a military-industrial complex, which anchored the state's manufacturing sector. Finally, the technological revolution laid the groundwork for the service-based economy described earlier. Economic change is manifested in other ways. To the extent California businesses depend on exports to Asia, those businesses depend on robust economies in Asia and suffer when those economies suffer. Change has also meant increased international competition. Asian nations have become major competitors in numerous industries, and Mexico's border towns have lured U.S.- and foreign-owned assembly factories called *maquiladora.* California's workers are changing too. The state's labor force is older, more ethnically diverse, and more female than once was the case.

3. *Diversity.* California's economy is richly *diverse.* The sheer size of California's economy (the sixth largest in the world) would suggest diversity. Although less than 2 percent of California's workers are in agriculture, the state is the nation's top producer of more than 50 crops and livestock commodities. The state ranks first among the 50 in international trade. Governors and mayors alike travel abroad to promote trade with California. Geographically, the state is a Pacific Rim "nation" dependent on international investment and trade opportunities. In recent years, economic diversity has been tinged with economic uncertainty. In the early 1990s, factory closed, moved to other states, or transferred or outsourced some operations "offshore" to cheaper labor markets. The federal government closed over two dozen military bases and cuts in defense and aerospace spending hurt large numbers of the state's military contractors. California's economy surged in the late 1990s but reversed course in the early 2000s. Counterbalancing these trends has been an expansion of small companies across the state.

4. *Two-Tier Structure.* Lastly, California's economy has a roughly *two-tiered structure.* In terms of the workforce, the top tier or layer consists of highly educated, well-paid employees in high technology, knowledge-intensive businesses. Included are the fields of education, medicine, communications, law, finance, real estate, transportation, and government. The bottom tier consists of those working in low-paying, low-status service jobs found in retail outlets, the tourism industry, agriculture, and marginal manufacturing concerns. The top tier has enjoyed rising income in recent decades; the bottom tier has actually experienced a precipitous drop in income, especially among male workers. As a result, there is a growing income disparity between these two tiers, especially among male workers. The bad news is that recent influxes of low-skill immigrants have widened the gap still further. The good news is that low-wage workers gradually improve their economic status over time as they gain skills, experience, education, and aptitude in English.[14]

How Political Theory Explains California Politics

As important as it is, a state's political environment alone (land, regions, resources, people, and economy) does not explain its politics. Politics deals with very complex sets of human relationships involving influence and power.

To understand the complexity of politics, theories help explain who governs and why. But not all political scientists can agree on a single theory. As a result, alternative theories have emerged, which we will briefly explore and apply to California politics.

DEMOCRATIC THEORY

According to traditional democratic theory, the answer to "Who governs?" is "All of us," in a sense. Two forms of democracy exist. *Participatory democracy* envisions rule by the many as described by the ancient philosopher Aristotle. *Representative democracy* suggests rule by the few on behalf of the many. In a representative democracy, policymakers may negotiate and compromise with each other but are influenced and ultimately controlled by the electorate. In his *Second Treatise on Civil Government* (1689), political philosopher John Locke viewed this relationship as a "social contract [theory]—the view that the consent of the people is the only true basis of any sovereign's right to rule." The Framers wrote the U.S. Constitution partly with democratic practices in mind. They assumed a collective good existed and that elected representatives could ascertain the common will of the people. Contemporary political scientist Robert Dahl believes an ideal democratic process must meet five criteria relative to the people—equality in voting, effective citizen participation, enlightened understanding, final control over government's agenda, and inclusion (the application of rights and laws to everyone).[15] When we refer to democratic theory in the U.S. context, we mean representative democracy.

American democratic theory also includes the states. The Founders believed states would be major players in a democratic form of government. Alexander Hamilton was convinced that Americans would feel a greater sense of attachment and obligation to their respective states than to a central government ("The Federalist No. 17"). James Madison believed that the states would have many more functions and responsibilities ("The Federalist No. 45").

Democratic theory partly explains California politics, especially its political ideals. The preamble to the state's Constitution reads: "*We, the People* of the State of California, grateful to Almighty God for our freedom, in order to secure and perpetuate its blessings, do establish this Constitution" (emphasis added). It contains the state's own "bill of rights" and establishes various institutions of government that, on paper, are responsible to the electorate. Furthermore, voters have the power to adopt their own legislation (initiatives), approve or disapprove various laws passed by the state legislature (referenda), and remove elected officials between elections (recall). They can do all this on a statewide basis and in their respective communities.

Traditional democratic theory advances political ideals better than it explains political reality. A representative democracy assumes greater citizen interest than often is the case. In California, the politically disinterested and economically weak are clearly disadvantaged. The political equality presumed by democratic thought is largely missing. The result is the emergence of a *two-tier polity* in California. According to columnist Dan Walters: "the most likely political scenario for California . . . is of dominance by an affluent, politically active overclass using its position to protect its privileges against the larger but weaker underclass."[16] He would ask, "Where is the "common good" between the haves and the have-nots?" Democratic theory, then, needs to account for the relationship between government and wealth, the persistence of unequal subgroups in the polity, and what, if any, common ground exists between the haves and the have-nots.

ELITE THEORY

Other theories also attempt to explain the origins and exercise of power. According to elite theorists, all societies naturally divide into two

CARTOON 1.2   California haves and have-nots
Question: Will this cartoon be even more true in the future than it was in 1992?
Source: © 1992 Paul Duginski.

classes—the few who rule and the many who do not. Political power inevitably gravitates to the few out of necessity, what Robert Michels called an "iron law of oligarchy." As political scientist Harold Lasswell once put it, "Government is always government by the few, whether in the name of the few, the one, or the many."[17] Some elites consist of corporate owners and other wealthy persons who exercise political power directly or control those who do on their behalf.

As with democratic theory, elements of elite and class politics can be seen in California. Historically, one corporation, the Southern Pacific Railroad, wielded significant power. The "Big Four" (Leland Stanford, Collis Huntington, Charles Crocker, and Mark Hopkins) were successful businessmen. Controlling a virtual political machine, they shaped the state's early commerce, land development, and overall growth. Through his control of land and water, *Los Angeles Times* owner Harrison Gray Otis helped engineer Los Angeles's growth more profoundly than any city council could have. Elites abound in modern California. Some individuals continue to hold substantial power. For example, with little public notice, J. G. Boswell parlayed a Central Valley farm into a multinational agriculture-based empire through business savvy and political influence.[18] Yet, most elites today operate as groups. The state's media exercise considerable influence through major television stations and a small handful of newspaper chains. Among the most influential groups in Sacramento are large corporations or clusters of them, such as the California Manufacturers Association. The California legislature routinely provides tax incentives and other benefits to power economic interests. Because they are frequent campaign contributors, when these groups speak, policymakers listen. Recent initiatives, presumably the political tool of ordinary citizens, have been sponsored and funded by major economic interest groups. For instance, well-funded Indian tribes and Las Vegas casinos spent a staggering $100 million on a 1998 gaming initiative. In stunning contrast to the distant past, Indian tribes that own lucrative gaming casinos appear to be the newest political elites in California.

Californians themselves sense the power of elites and distrust the results. According to one recent survey, 64 percent of respondents thought that the state government was "pretty much run by a few big interests looking out for themselves" instead of for the benefit of all Californians.[19]

As compelling as elite theory sounds, it, too, cannot fully explain California politics. The influence of the Big Four was ultimately broken in the Progressive era. Today, many California businesses of all sizes compete for power—reducing the influence of any single one. Some initiatives remain downright populist and anti-elitist. For instance, in 1988 voters pointedly ignored the views of the otherwise influential insurance lobby when they approved Proposition 103 in hopes of lowering auto insurance rates. In the late 1990s, they rejected tobacco interests and raised the cigarette tax. In short, because elites exist does not necessarily mean they win on, or even care about, all issues. California's elites tend to husband their resources for issues they regard as most important.

PLURALIST THEORY

Pluralist theory tries to correct aspects of both democratic and elite theory. Electoral majorities, a cornerstone of democratic theory, are something of a myth, given voter apathy. According to political scientist Robert A. Dahl, "On matters of specific policy, the majority rarely rules."[20] Pluralists admit that groups are controlled by elites but observe many groups having access to, competing for, and sharing power. No single group dominates all the

time. In many ways, American politics *is* group politics—a fluid process of competing interests winning or losing, rising or falling, as they seek to influence transitory issues. Interest group politics is readily observable at all levels of our political system. Pluralism's critics, though, argue that the push and pull of pluralist politics does not explain the inherent and systemic inequalities that persist in American life. Furthermore, interests must be organized; some perfectly legitimate interests, such as children or the homeless, rarely organize.

Pluralism is an attractive option for students of California politics. If you look up "Associations" in the Sacramento Yellow Pages, you will be amazed at the breadth of interest groups in the state's capital. Group-inspired lunch hour rallies are a common sight on the Capitol steps. Proposition "wars" now feature dueling initiatives sponsored by opposing groups. Increasingly, ethnic groups are creating *multicultural pluralism* in California politics.

But not all politics in California can be labeled group politics. First, structural features of California's political system (its constitution and institutions) to some extent limit group power. Second, group competition alone does not explain the occasional rise of policy entrepreneurs—individuals who make a substantial difference, such as anti-tax crusader Howard Jarvis, three-strikes proponent Mike Reynolds, bilingual education opponent Ron Unz, and tobacco tax advocate and Hollywood director Rob Reiner. Third, pluralism seems to suggest a satisfactory equilibrium among competing groups. But how does one explain policy indecision, delay, or paralysis—what is often called gridlock?

HYPERPLURALISM

Elements of truth in these three theories may suggest what Dahl calls an "American hybrid,"[21] but a nagging problem remains. All three presume governing does in fact occur. Yet some observers claim that no one "rules" effectively anymore. State governments, California included, lurch from fiscal year to fiscal year. In a sense, recent budget crises serve to magnify the ongoing challenge of governing in the Golden State. In addition, initiatives sponsored by some organized interests, once passed, are challenged in court by other groups. Some political scientists call this state *hyperpluralism.* In this view, power is thinly scattered, not just widely or unevenly scattered as previous theories would suggest. The exercise of political power has become a highly competitive tug-of-war between institutions, policymakers, political parties, numerous interest groups, and voters.

Political scientists who hold this view are both describing a variant of pluralism and making a judgment about government's performance. They admit that the American system was intended to check power, not merely facilitate it. But they also believe checking power is different from preventing its exercise at all. Hyperpluralism seems increasingly helpful in explaining how aspects of American politics work. In explaining California politics, it is downright compelling. Let us consider it in more depth.

How Hyperpluralism Explains California Politics

There is ample evidence of hyperpluralism in American politics, and in California politics in particular—individualism in political life, a growing diversity of group interests and cultures, the changing nature of majoritarian politics, and "built-in" or structural conflict. These components of California hyperpluralism are somewhat intertwined and dependent on each other.

THE CONSTANCY OF INDIVIDUALISM

Individualism is a hallmark of American life, and it is nothing new. In the 1830s, French observer Alexis de Tocqueville correctly defined

American individualism as "a calm and considered feeling which disposes each citizen to isolate himself from the mass of his fellows and withdraw into the circle of family and friends; with this little society formed to his taste, he gladly leaves the greater society to look after itself."[22] Recent scholars have observed the popularity of individualism among "middle Americans" and believe it exists at the expense of commitment to a larger community.[23] Individualism is a key tile in the mosaic of California politics. The proliferation of interest groups, the pursuit of leisure, gated communities, private security systems, solitary rush hour commutes, and widespread gun ownership—a do-it-yourself law enforcement, of sorts—all suggest dependence on self rather than on society to fulfill both needs and wants. In a sense, even low voter turnout in California elections reflects individualism in a culture where political participation is considered optional and even unimportant. The emphasis on individualism is not entirely consistent. As writer Joan Didion reminds us, California's historic dependence on federal spending for water projects, highways, and defense contracts is "seemingly at odds with the [state's] emphasis on unfettered individualism that constitutes the local core belief...."[24]

A DIVERSITY OF INTERESTS AND CULTURES

One aspect of hyperpluralism is the range of interests various groups bring to public life. The most fundamental interest is in civic life itself, what is called civic engagement. Here the ethnic and racial diversity of California is not evident in voting or in other activities associated with public life—signing petitions, attending meetings, writing officials, making campaign contributions, attending rallies, and doing political party work. Research findings indicate that those Californians who are white, older, more affluent, homeowners, and more highly educated evidence the highest levels of civic engagement. Relative to their numbers in the population, whites are overrepresented in virtually every political activity we associate with civic engagement.[25] Politically speaking, those Californians who have the greatest say are not those who arguably have the greatest needs.

Of those groups that do engage in community and public life, many represent relatively narrow viewpoints or advocate relatively narrow agendas. Some even define themselves and behave politically in terms of one single issue—giving rise to what has been called *single-issue politics*. When public problems are viewed in such narrow terms, policy solutions seem obvious and clear cut, but only to the group espousing them. This leads such groups to hold their views with more determination and to communicate them with greater assertiveness. Some behave as grievance groups, out to correct negative treatment by the larger society. All this has increased group conflict in California and has decreased the potential for broader intergroup consensus. Absent a broader consensus, policymakers find that supporting certain groups has a price—the wrath of other groups.

At a deeper level than group politics, California has experienced a growing number of ethnic and other-based cultures. The most rapidly growing group is the Latino population, but Asian groups are growing as well. The politically dominant white or Euro-American culture in California is gradually receding. One survey detected nearly 100 distinct ethnic groups in California. But multiculturalism is broader than ethnicity. "Gay pride" parades and "life chain" marches by abortion foes reflect cultural differences based on gender, sexual orientation, religious belief, and other nonethnic value systems. As we saw earlier, California's various regions to some extent reflect different cultural values. When the diversity of California cultures is coupled with the group behavior just described, the result is a diversification of California's *social structure*,

not just its politics. Public officials are torn between the demands of California's newer, immigrant dominated groups and those of older, white, largely middle-class voters.

FADING MAJORITARIANISM

Another evidence of hyperpluralism is the changing nature of *majority rule*—a major principle of American politics. The nation's Founders thought that, in a representative democracy, elected officials would seek the common good agreeable to a functioning majority. In California politics, a single public interest and a single majority seem to be endangered political species. In a sense, "minorities" already rule in the Golden State. On a statewide basis, a relatively small number of individuals and groups set legislative agendas and determine which issues make it to the ballot. A relatively small percentage of Californians who qualify to vote actually register to vote; an even smaller percentage turn out on election day; and only a *simple majority of those* determine election outcomes. In numerous California cities, there is no single ethnic majority. Ironically, while majority rule means less and less, some political ground rules in California require *supermajorities* to enact public policy. The state legislature must approve the annual budget by a two-thirds vote, and similar majorities are required for voters to raise taxes or amend the state constitution. Such numbers are often difficult to achieve.

STRUCTURAL CONFLICT

One reason California voters decide issues directly is that interest groups that sponsor initiatives want to bypass a cumbersome policy process in Sacramento. Many Californians, ready to assess blame for the results of that process, choose to replace their elected officials or limit their terms of service. Term limits have been increasingly adopted at the local level and have been applied to state legislators and constitutional officers thanks to Proposition 140 (1990).

Are elected politicians to blame? California's political structure itself invites political conflict. First, the state's Constitution in effect predestines a horizontal power struggle between the executive, legislative, and judicial branches. While praised as a necessary "checks and balances" feature of our form government, it does foster political and policy conflict. Second, by dictating certain roles for local government, it guarantees a vertical power struggle between the "locals" (cities, counties, and special districts) and the state itself. Third, allowing voters to directly make policy and even restructure government further complicates matters. According to journalist Peter Schrag, the result has been "an increasingly unmanageable and incomprehensible structure of state and local government that exacerbates the same public disaffection and alienation that brought it on."[26]

California: The Ironies of Diversity

In this introductory chapter, we have surveyed California's rich diversity, the theories that help explain its politics, and the hyperpluralism that is increasingly evident. As California becomes increasingly diverse and hyperpluralistic, several ironies have emerged. First,

compared to other states, California has become both policy innovator and laggard. Over the years, it has "led the way" with such measures as Proposition 13 (which reduced property taxes) and "Three Strikes, You're Out" legislation (which imposed lengthy sentences for three-time felons). Years ago, its investment in freeways was the envy of other states. Yet by the mid-1990s, California ranked forty-ninth in per capita state spending on highways. California's visionary 1961 master plan for higher education (which provided the structure for the state's community colleges and four-year universities) was imitated across the nation. Yet recent spending on education has not kept pace with the state's growth. In 1961, California ranked twelfth in average per-pupil spending; in 2001, it ranked thirty-second, having been nearly fortieth a few years earlier. While enrolling more higher education students than 24 other states *combined*, in 2000–2001 California ranked only thirty-eighth in per-student support of higher education.

Second, the policy generosity of California's electorate and its government is cyclical, contested, and occasionally ambivalent. Consider budgeting. As diverse as California's economy is, the state's dependence on inherently volatile sources of revenue such as the income tax can significantly alter budget priorities. As tax revenues from stock options and capital gains fluctuated, mirroring the fluctuations in the stock market and technology sectors, California's state budget experienced both record

---

Did You Know ... ?

Based on 44 factors ranging from median household income, crime rates, infant mortality rates, and education success to the annual number of sunny days, Morgan Quitno Press ranks the "livability" of all fifty states.

In 2005, California ranked only thirty fifth. New Hampshire was first and Mississippi last.

Question: In your opinion, why do so many Californians rank their own state higher than this publisher does?

SOURCE: *State Rankings, 2005* (Lawrence, KS: Morgan Quitno Press, 2005). Available online at www.morganquitno.com.

Did You Know . . . ?

In response to the 2000 Census, 1.6 million Californians indicated that they were of two or more races. Of that number, more than 94,000 indicated that they were of three or more races.

Question: In the future, will racial categories be more difficult to keep distinct in California?

SOURCE: U.S. Census Bureau; 2000 Census Redistricting Data.

---

surpluses and record deficits—all within barely five years. Of necessity, spending commitments rise and fall accordingly. In terms of civil rights, policy generosity is tempered with ambivalence. For example, a growing number of Californians oppose discrimination against gays and lesbians but many of those still prefer not to sanction gay marriage itself.

Third, while policy paralysis often grips Sacramento, policy progress can be found closer to home. The state's 478 cities have developed entrepreneurial ways to raise needed revenue. Numerous counties have increased sales taxes to pay for transportation projects once thought to be the state's responsibility. Those Californians who can afford to (the upper tier) are buying services their state or local government cannot afford or will not provide. Some have augmented meager public recreation programs with those of private groups. Some install their own security systems; others live in condominium or planned unit developments where neighborhood "quality of life" decisions are made by homeowner associations, not city councils. They transfer from troubled public schools to private ones or they resort to homeschooling.

What does the bottom tier do? They rely on government programs despite the cuts, live by their wits, or simply do without.

Conclusion

The California portrayed in this chapter is of immense proportion. The challenges facing the most populous state in the Union are abundant to be sure, as they always have been. The capacity and potential for California governments to address these challenges is and always has been great. Its political system reflects a state that "is ever Californianizing: searching for what it is and for what it wants to be."[27] Political scientists search for theories to explain why California functions the way it does. While no single theory or approach will suffice, both the state's diversity and its hyperpluralistic political system seem useful in explaining California's current state of affairs.

As a subject of study, California politics is both fascinating and challenging. Due to term limits and demographic shifts, it is also ever changing. As you read this book, you will discover why.

KEY TERMS

politics   (p. 5)

political system   (p. 5)

political environment   (p. 5)

diversity   (pp. 5–12)

postindustrial economy   (p. 11)

economic change   (p. 12)

economic diversity   (p. 12)

REVIEW QUESTIONS

1. Identify the ways in which diversity explains California politics.
2. Describe the various regions of California.
3. How have water and climate affected the state's growth?
4. What demographic groups have come to California and why?
5. Describe the four keys to understanding the state's economy. What makes it two tier in nature?
6. Survey the four theories political scientists use to describe power and influence in American politics. Illustrate each theory with California examples.
7. In what ways does hyperpluralism seem particularly apt in describing California politics?
8. Discuss and illustrate California's ironies of diversity.

WEB ACTIVITIES

California Home Page
(www.ca.gov).
A good starting point, this site will take you in many different directions regarding life and politics in the Golden State.

California Department of Finance, Demographic Research Unit
(www.dof.ca.gov/HTML/DEMOGRAP/ Druhpar.htm)
This "single official source of demographic data for state planning and budgeting" provides helpful information on population growth, change, and diversity in California.

INFOTRAC® COLLEGE EDITION ARTICLES

For additional reading, go to InfoTrac® College Edition, your online research library at http://www.infotrac.thomsonlearning.com

California's Recall

Is California Back?

Race and Activism

NOTES

1. Mark Baldassare, *A California State of Mind: The Conflicted Voter in a Changing World* (Berkeley: University of California Press, 2002), 1.
2. Quoted in Al Martinex, "Can We All Get Along?" *California Journal* 29 (January 1998): 10.
3. Quoted in Andrew F. Rolle, *California: A History* (New York: Crowell, 1969), 34.
4. David Easton, *The Political System* (New York: Alfred A. Knopf), chap. 5.
5. Harold D. Lasswell, *Politics: Who Gets What, When and How* (New York: McGraw-Hill, 1938).
6. Hans P. Johnson, "A State of Diversity in California Regions: Demographic Trends," *California Counts* (San Francisco: Public Policy Institute of California, May 2002).
7. Mark Baldassare, *PPIC Statewide Survey: Californians and Their Government* (San Francisco: Public Policy Institute of California, July 2001), 13.
8. Carey McWilliams, *Southern California: An Island on the Land* (Santa Barbara: Peregrine Smith, 1946, 1973), 183.
9. Quoted in Joseph S. O'Flaherty, *Those Powerful Years: The South Coast and Los Angeles, 1887–1917* (Hicksville, NY: Exposition Press, 1978), 23.
10. Gregory Rodriguez, "The Latino Century," *California Journal* 31 (January 2000): 8–14; Anthony York, "From 'Sleeping Giant' to 'Incredible Hulk'?" *California Journal* 35 (June 2004): 40–44.
11. Steve Scott, "Reality Votes," *California Journal* 29 (January 1998): 25–26.
12. Zoltan Hajnal and Mark Baldassare, *Finding Common Ground: Racial and Ethnic Attitudes in*

California (San Francisco: Public Policy Institute of California, 2001).

13. Quoted in Stephen Birmingham, *California Rich* (New York: Simon and Schuster, 1980), 13.

14. Legislative Analyst's Office, *California's Changing Income Distribution* (Sacramento: Legislative Analyst's Office, August 2000). Marla Dickerson, "State's Workers Making Progress," *Los Angeles Times,* June 10, 2002.

15. Robert A. Dahl, *Preface to Democratic Theory* (Chicago: University of Chicago Press, 1956), 124.

16. Dan Walters, *The New California: Facing the 21st Century,* 2nd ed. (Sacramento: California Journal Press, 1992), 20.

17. Harold Lasswell and Daniel Lerner, *The Comparative Study of Elites* (Stanford, CA: Stanford University Press, 1952), 7.

18. See Mark Arax and Rich Wartzman, *The King of California: J. G. Boswell and the Making of a Secret Empire* (Cambridge, MA: Public Affairs, 2003).

19. Mark Baldassare, *California in the New Millennium: The Changing Social and Political Landscape* (Berkeley: University of California Press, 2000), 47.

20. Dahl, 124.

21. Dahl, chap. 5.

22. Alexis de Tocqueville, *Democracy in America, Vol. II* (J. P. Mayer and Max Lerner, eds.) (New York: Harper and Row, 1966), 477.

23. See Herbert J. Gans, *Middle American Individualism: The Future of Liberal Democracy* (New York: Free Press, 1988); Robert N. Bellah, et al., *Habits of the Heart: Individualism and Commitment in American Life* (Berkeley: University of California Press, 1985).

24. Joan Didion, *Where I Was From* (New York: Alfred A. Knopf, 2003), 23.

25. Karthick Ramakrishnan and Mark Baldassare, *The Ties That Bind: Changing Demographics and Civic Engagement in California* (San Francisco: Public Policy Institute of California, 2004).

26. Peter Schrag, *Paradise Lost: California's Experience, America's Future* (New York: New Press, 1998), 12.

27. Kevin Starr quoted in Carey McWilliams, *California: The Great Exception* (Santa Barbara: Peregrine Smith, 1949, 1979), xviii.

C H A P T E R   2

California's Political Development

In Brief

Chapter 2 focuses on the political culture and development of California. Understanding the variety of political subcultures found in California (traditionalistic, moralistic, and individualistic) helps to put in context the political and policy challenges facing the state today. California's political history is a progression of developmental stages: unification, industrialization, welfare, and abundance. Historic events and a succession of political and economic leaders have shaped each stage.

In the unification stage, Spanish and Mexican control gave way to what has been called an American era, which included statehood and the development of a constitution. The industrialization period featured the famous Gold Rush, the rise of the Southern Pacific Railroad, the development of water resources, the discovery of oil, and impacts of World War II. The politics of welfare was noted for economic growth, progressive policies, and visionary leadership. During the politics of abundance period, growth and prosperity continue but some Californians question whether the state is beginning to choke on its own success. At the end of the chapter, we consider whether the politics of abundance will continue indefinitely into the future and how the politics of diversity affects those perceptions.

Introduction

Why is California different from New York, besides its tendency to elect actors as governors? Both states have large, diverse populations, complex economies, megacities, huge state budgets, and geographic variety (seashore, mountains, farms, forests, etc.). Although Californians struggle to obtain water and New Yorkers do not, the similarities are there. Yet, Californians and New Yorkers know their states are different— and in profound ways. Political scientist Daniel Elazar calls these variations the "geology of political culture."[1] A primary difference stems from how they grew and changed as political and cultural identities. Chapter 2 surveys aspects of California's past that help explain its current political system. This process of growth and change is called "political development." The focus will be on the development of California's political system and its impact on both political culture and modern policy making.

THE IDEA OF POLITICAL CULTURE

To understand the stages of political development found in California, we need to briefly examine the concept of political culture. *Political culture* is the product of historical events, migration and settlement patterns, and the presence of various social groups. It refers to *the shared beliefs, values, customs, and symbols of a society that affect how the society governs itself.* Political culture helps explain the policy choices made within political systems and why those choices vary between political systems.

Although in many respects the United States reflects one broad political culture, Elazar has identified three distinct political subcultures: traditional, moralistic, and individualistic.[2] Although the descriptions of each are largely impressionistic, they do help explain why some states are so different from each other. The *traditional* political subculture is characterized by the dominance of a small, self-perpetuating, paternalistic ruling elite, and a large, compliant nonelite. Its goal is to maintain the established social and economic order, rather than to provide wide access to the political system or initiate new policy. According to Elazar, this subculture had its historic roots in the preindustrial agrarian South.

The *moralistic* political subculture emphasizes a public-spirited citizenry dedicated to the common betterment of all its members. Widespread participation is both valued and expected. Dedicated, selfless, incorruptible public officials strive toward an assumed "general welfare." Politics is a high calling, not dirty work. Nonpartisanship is preferable to party politics. Government intervention in both the economy and society furthers the "public interest." Elazar believed this subculture grew out of the religious values of Puritan New England.

The *individualistic* political subculture emphasizes the goals, aspirations, and initiative of private individuals or groups. Government exists to serve and facilitate these interests. Policy making is transactional, a process of bargaining between self-interested individuals and groups. Public officials represent not only these people but their own personal interests as well. The private citizen's attitude toward government is: "Stay out of my way, let me do my thing, or at least help me do it." Elazar traced this subculture to the mercantile centers of the Eastern seaboard.

As more people immigrated to the United States and Americans already here migrated West, the features of these three subcultures moved and mingled as well. Historically, each of these three subcultures has played an important role in California's political development; elements of all three still exist. The patron-client relationship between California's Indians and the Spanish and Mexican mission padres exemplified the traditionalistic subculture. But, as migrants poured into the state in the 1800s and 1900s, they brought with them the values of all three subcultures. Traditionalists migrated from Mexico and the South into Southern and Central California. Moralists moved into Southern California from the Midwest. Individualists came from the East Coast to Northern California.[3] For a time, these newcomers brought subcultural distinctions to each region. But, in-state migration, the passage of time, suburbanization, and media influences have combined to blur these differences. Yet, elements of all three still persist and have played important roles in California's political development. Although Elazar once thought that the Golden State was primarily moralistic, an arguably persistent individualistic subculture helps account for the state's hyperpluralistic politics.

THE IDEA OF POLITICAL DEVELOPMENT

Political development refers to the growth and change that occurs within political systems. Political scientists view this term differently. Some think it simply refers to government's increasing capacity to manage its affairs and respond to demands placed upon it. Others suggest it means the extension of democratic practices including increased citizen participation and greater sensitivity to the ideals of equality. That view is understandable given the world in which we now live. Still others view political development as what happens when societies become more complex, their labor more specialized, their groups more divided, and their social structures more differentiated.[4] Many

political systems in the Western world have proceeded through distinct stages of political development: (1) unification, (2) modernization, (3) welfare, and (4) abundance.[5] These stages do not have neat beginnings and endings; they merge into each other.

Do states have their own stages of political development? To some extent. To be sure, the states together form a national political culture. Also, the nation's founding documents such as the U.S. Constitution have steered each state's political development in similar directions. Yet, the subsystems we call states entered the union at different times and are distinctly different in terms of the people they attracted, the economies they established, and the political practices they developed.

To view California's political history as its political development allows the student of California politics not only to understand the state's history but to interpret it as well. Author Theodore White once observed, "California politics squirm with a complexity and intrigue that defies reasonable analysis."[6] Not really. Larger than most nations, California has passed through all four stages of political development. To be sure, today's abundance does not affect all parts of the state and its people in equal measure. To analyze the present and anticipate the future, we must first make sense of the past—the goal of this chapter.

The Politics of Unification

During an early *unification* stage of political development, the primary function of government is making a society into a state. Government needs to establish its own central role, guard against early disunion and develop a network of viable local economies. Early California from Native American times through the Gold Rush and statehood embodies this stage.

The West Coast has been a population magnet since prehistoric times. Archaeological evidence suggests nomadic peoples from Asia once crossed a land bridge (now the Bering Strait) through Alaska and down the coast some 25,000 years ago. Native Californians were the eventual products of these early migration patterns. They were gatherers and coastal fishermen. Spanish missionaries observed no pottery making, metallurgy, reading, or writing. In terms of language, there were at least 22 linguistic families and 135 regional dialects. No more than 1,000 Indians spoke any single dialect. Native Californians were peaceable, nomadic, and needed little or no government. Because they lived "lightly on the land," they did not develop even a primitive technology. They resisted change, as well-meaning missionaries discovered, but were not resistant to European diseases and violence, which decimated their numbers.

The first nonnative visitors to California were European explorers who sailed California's coastal waters in the 1500s. They included Juan Rodriguez Cabrillo, Bartolome Ferrelo, and Sir Francis Drake. In 1579, Drake claimed the area north of modern-day San Francisco as Nova Albion (New England) 41 years *before* the Pilgrims touched shore at Plymouth.

SPANISH "RULE"

Spain colonized Mexico in 1519 but did not extend its reach into Alta California until 1769. Governor Gaspar de Portola and Father Junipero Serra established a European settlement and Franciscan mission at San Diego. The missions (eventually numbering 21 and stretching from San Diego to Sonoma) were religious and evangelistic outposts intended to convert the Native Californians to Christianity and more "progressive" (European) lifestyles. As a colonial power, Spain promptly built military bases (*presidios*). Nearby civilian towns (*pueblos*) accommodated modest population growth. Local economies and primitive local, albeit colonial, governments grew up around these settlements. At the height of their influence, the Spanish numbered no more than 3,000

people spread thinly along the California coast from San Diego to Sonoma. The relationship between the two groups was *patron-client* in nature: where the ruled (Native Americans) supported or at least obeyed the rulers (military and church authorities) in exchange for relative security and safety. We should not exaggerate the governing influence of the missions: only 20,000 out of 400,000 Native Californians worked and lived under mission authority.

Colonial governments are extractive in nature. They remove from the colony what the mother country finds either useful or valuable. They may unify the colony, often by force, but do so for their own political or economic purposes. Spain saw no need to "unify" Alta California. To the responsible viceroy in Mexico City, California was "out of sight, out of mind." Spain's inattention allowed economic competition between the missions and the presidios and pueblos to spill into open conflict. An understandable cause was Spain's preoccupation with the balance of their crumbling empire. For whatever reason, Spain passively allowed California to develop into a prize worth fighting for (see California Voices).

MEXICAN "CONTROL"

After years of Mexican frustration and Spanish inattention, Mexico obtained its independence from Spain in 1821. Ironically, the gold-hungry Spanish government abandoned Mexican California, unaware of the rich gold deposits to be discovered only a few decades later. California was now Mexico's colony—a distant and not too important province in Mexico's federal system. Concerned with solidifying its power base and unifying the rest of Mexico, the central government in Mexico City paid even less attention to California than did Spain. Feuds between the presidios and the missions and between the fledging regions of California continued unabated during this Mexican era.

One act of unification during this time was to reduce the role of the church, which in

CALIFORNIA VOICES

Shaler on Spanish California

The Spaniards have, at a great expense and considerable industry, removed every obstacle out of the way of an invading enemy; they have stocked the country with such multitudes of cattle, horses, and other useful animals, that they have no longer the power to remove or destroy them; they have taught the Indians many of the useful arts, and accustomed them to agriculture and civilization; and they have spread a number of defenseless inhabitants over the country, whom they never could induce to act as enemies to those who should treat them well, by securing to them the enjoyments of liberty, property, and a free trade which would almost instantaneously quadruple the value of their actual possessions; in a word, they have done everything that could be done to render California an object worthy of the attention of the great maritime powers: they have placed it in a situation to want nothing but a good government to rise rapidly to wealth and importance.

SOURCE: William Shaler, *Journal* (1804).

California meant the vast mission enterprises developed under Spain. The Mexican government secularized the missions and distributed their massive land holdings to government loyalists.[7] Individuals could obtain 48,000 acres grants while some influential families were able to accumulate *ranchos* as large as 250,000 acres. Many places familiar to Californians today derive their names from these ranchos. The myth of an idyllic, rural California persisted from the rancho period on. According to historian John W. Caughey, "With the rise of the ranchos, pastoral California reached its romantic zenith. Cattle roamed over a thousand hills. Horses became so numerous that they were hunted down to save pasturage for cattle."[8] The ranchos are long gone but some modern Californians continue the myth by developing "ranchettes" complete with horses, even in suburban communities. Less affluent residents move to inland areas in search of a more rural or possibly "pseudorural" lifestyle.

Another development during this period had nothing to do with Mexican policy. A gradual but steady trickle of rugged Euro-Americans found their way to California. These intrepid individuals included whalers, trappers, mountaineers, and adventurers. While some remained on the "wild side," others turned to farming and married into landholding Mexican families. Simply getting to California from the rest of the United States was a feat. After the adventurers proved it could be done (even the Donner party had survivors), more Americans arrived. Most of these travels were peaceful. Not so with Lieutenant John C. Fremont who led several military expeditions into California. A "Bear Flag Revolt" ensued between the *Californios* (native-born, Spanish-speaking Californians) and the American settlers, aided and abetted by Fremont and his associates. The symbol was a flag portraying a grizzly bear with the inscription: "California Republic." It remains the state flag today. A feeble effort by President James Polk in 1845 to purchase California for $40 million was rejected as an insult by the Mexican government.

Mexico's lax control ended with its defeat by the United States in the Mexican American War of 1848. Physical remnants of California's Spanish and Mexican past are everywhere from red-tile roofs to local fiesta celebrations. Mexico did not appear to exercise a unifying influence but, during its interim control, Mexico introduced several governing patterns that would become part of California's constitution.

Also, both Spain and Mexico left behind a traditionalistic political subculture. Vestiges of it remain today if one considers the relative powerlessness of California's newest immigrants and how they are treated by public officials, and the anxious voters they represent.

STATEHOOD

The unification stage of political development was completed with California's admission to the Union. To the Americans, California came to represent a logical stepping-stone in meeting the nation's "manifest destiny." By the end of the war, Mexico "sold" not only California but also Nevada, Utah, and portions of Wyoming, Colorado, New Mexico, and Arizona, reducing its own land area by half. This $15 million bargain was known as the Mexican Cession. The 1848 Treaty of Guadalupe Hidalgo concluded the war, ceded California to the United States, and granted U.S. citizenship and all its rights to the conquered peoples. Private property rights, important to the wealthy *rancheros*, were maintained. California was now a U.S. territory under temporary military control.

The United States, despite its euphoric westward expansion and sense of mission, did not bring unification to California instantly. Its fragmented governance structure was based on a now-collapsed Spanish system of presidios. Furthermore, the bits of gold found by James Marshall on the American River only nine days before the treaty was signed would bring anything but peace to America's newest possession. The news of gold in the Sierra foothills first reached other Californians who quite literally dropped what they were doing to stake their own claims. These reports spread like wildfire across the nation. Colonel Richard Mason, the military governor of California, reported the discovery to President James Polk sending along 230 ounces to prove his point—"I have no hesitation in saying there is more gold in the country drained by the Sacramento and San Joaquin rivers

than will pay the cost of the war with Mexico a hundred times over."[9] Polk mentioned the discovery of abundant gold in his December 1848 annual message: "Now that this fine province is part of our country, all of the States of the Union... are deeply interested in the speedy development of its wealth and resources."[10] Ostensibly, he was trying to sell the Congress on locating a branch mint in California. What he sold was California itself. Professional advertisers could not have done a better job of it.

THE 1849 CONSTITUTION

A very important instrument in unifying a civil society is a constitution. This basic law provides general vision, establishes rights, creates political structures, and places limits on power and those who claim it. Theoretically it is a contract between the government and the governed as well as a covenant among society's members.

California's first constitution was the result of a constitutional convention held in the fall of 1849. The process was a curious mixture of elitism and pluralism. All 48 delegates were relatively young men. Thirteen had lived in California for less than one year. The nonnative Californians came from 13 other states and five other nations.[11] The goal of unification remained a challenge. Differences between Northern and Southern California promptly emerged. Closer to their Mexican roots, Southern Californians preferred territorial status thinking that would give them the best of both cultures. Northern Californians generally favored statehood, sent a majority of the delegates, and eventually controlled the convention.

The convention produced a hybrid document that borrowed heavily from Mexico, Iowa, and New York (a number of delegates came originally from those states). It blended several theories of governing. The Constitution began with a lofty, unifying preamble, and a strong "bill of rights," reflecting democratic ideals. The idea of checks and balances (and the potential for structural gridlock) was found in a plural executive (a governor and several statewide officers) and a bicameral (two-house) legislature. Reflecting Mexican practice, it established a four-tier judicial system of elected judges. As elsewhere, suffrage (the right to vote) was limited to white males. Due to the *Californios*, the document was to be printed in both English and Spanish; so were all future official documents. The Constitution won overwhelming voter approval in November 1849 and on September 9, 1850, Congress admitted California as the thirty-first state. California was to remain slavefree, a condition not applied to other ceded Mexican territories. At that moment, unification, to the extent California would ever experience it, was complete. The Mexican era ended; the North American era began.

In spite of its shortcomings (people demanded a new constitution only 30 years later), California's unifying document was considered a model worth imitating. Argentina's 1853 constitution was inspired by it. Argentinean Juan Bautista Alberti observed, "Without universities, without academies or law colleges, the newly organized people of California have drawn up a constitution full of foresight, of common sense, and of opportunity."[12]

The Politics of Modernization

This sense of opportunity led to *modernization*, the next stage in the process of political development. This is a time when new political leaders emerge, a statewide economy is forged, and the political masses become fully incorporated—becoming the polity of the state. Government's purpose is to encourage economic modernization or industrialization. During this stage, California became a magnet of opportunity and a destination for those seeking jobs or simply a better way of life. Historic benchmarks during this stage were the Gold Rush, the rise of the Big Four, the industrialization of agriculture, and the consequences of World War II.

THE GOLD RUSH

Discovery of gold created the mining frenzy as noted earlier. In retrospect, gold did not change California; the rush for it did. For a time, the population doubled every six months: from 9,000 in 1846 to 264,000 six years later. Seemingly overnight, a heavily Latino California become 80 percent Euro-American. The newcomers were primarily young, single men from every state in the Union, and from as far away as Europe and China. A spirit of entrepreneurialism merged with hard labor and racism. Chinese immigrants were allowed to mine the gold but not own rights to it. Policing the mining towns was rough business. Committees of vigilance—*vigilantes*—often used violence to quell violence. While a few found the gold they sought, many more found unprecedented opportunities of other types. One luckless miner found he could make more money selling pants to other miners; his name was Levi Strauss.

Those who stayed created a new base for California's emerging economy. In effect, the Gold Rush jump-started the state's second stage of development by adding instant diversity to California's population. It created numerous spillover effects (planned or unplanned consequences), such as heightened demand for goods and services. In turn, new demands for transportation improvements created still more opportunities for future entrepreneurs. The cultural change would be profound. According to writer J. H. Holliday: "In one astonishing year [1848–49] the place would be transformed from obscurity to world dominance . . . from a society of neighbors and families to one of strangers and transients; from an ox-cart economy based on hides and tallow to a complex economy based on gold; from Catholic to Protestant, from Latin to Anglo-Saxon."[13] Lastly, it created a worker base consisting of individuals with steely nerve to take a risk, not just on gold, but on California itself. Caughey thought the most important consequence was psychological: "the willingness to believe that the fabulous could be realized."[14] At least that was true for the new dominant majority, the Euro-Americans.

THE BIG FOUR

Four Sacramento merchants dared to believe that "the fabulous could be realized." Their actions furthered the economic growth of the state while making each of them very rich. As we noted, some Americans brought an individualistic political subculture to California. These men personified it. Their eventual political influence and abuse of it unleashed a political reform movement still felt today. Mark Hopkins, Charles Crocker, Collis Huntington, and Leland Stanford responded to the post-Gold Rush demand for improved transportation by forming the Central Pacific Railroad in 1861. Huntington was well connected in Washington, D.C. and served as the group's lobbyist. His efforts paid off. Congress designated this company responsible for the western portion of the ambitious transcontinental railroad and gave it both land and loans to begin construction. However, that was not enough. Stanford became governor and, in a move that would likely violate conflict of interest laws today, obtained additional loans and subsidies from the state legislature.

Because California developed or industrialized so rapidly in contrast to the rest of the West, the Big Four anticipated demand for plenty of transportation within the state. They acquired small railroad companies throughout California. One such acquisition was the Southern Pacific Railroad (SPR), the future namesake for the entire system. Eventually, they controlled 85 percent of the state's rails. This elite became a monopoly and behaved accordingly. By varying freight rates, they rewarded their friends and punished their enemies. This was not just laissez-faire capitalism

at work. Local governments, desiring rail service and all its economic blessings donated right-of-way property as well as cash (euphemistically called "subsidies"). The land grab was substantial. For every mile of track, SPR would receive up to 12,800 acres from the public domain. When San Bernardino refused their demands, the Southern Pacific retaliated by establishing nearby Colton, the site of a new depot. If shippers tried to move their goods along the coast by steamship, the Big Four would simply buy the steamship line and reset rates. As with other monopolies, Southern Pacific rates were higher than necessary, angering growing numbers of Californians. Frank Norris's 1901 novel, *The Octopus*, was a chilling and transparent description of how the SPR operated in the state (see California Voices).

Fearing that popular resentment might lead to state regulation, the Southern Pacific established a Political Bureau, a forerunner of the modern political action committee (PAC). Unlike today's PACs, which operate primarily in Sacramento, the Political Bureau was active at all levels of government. It controlled not only incumbent legislators but also party conventions and candidate nominations. In 1877, Stanford wrote Huntington, "The legislature elected I think is a good one and I apprehend less trouble [for example, rate control legislation] from it than from any preceding legislature for the last ten years—not a single unfriendly senator elected."[15] Others regarded that same legislature as the most corrupt in California's brief history.

As politically successful as the Big Four were, they could not cope with a national depression in the late 1800s that left many out of work. The unemployed blamed the railroads for importing poorly paid Chinese laborers who competed with whites for nonrailroad jobs. One such worker, the fiery Denis Kearney of San Francisco, helped found the radical Workingmen's Party. He was anti-Chinese and anti-Big Four. His incendiary rhetoric was prophetic given the reforms that would sweep the state

CALIFORNIA VOICES

Norris on the Southern Pacific

The clerk brought forward a folder of yellow paper and handed it to Dyke. It was inscribed at the top "Tariff Schedule No. 8," and underneath these words, in brackets, was a smaller inscription, "Supercedes No. 7 of Aug. 1."

For a moment Dyke was confused. Then swiftly the matter became clear in his mind. The Railroad had raised the freight on hops from two cents to five. All his calculations as to a profit on his little investment he had based on a freight rate of two cents a pound. He was under contract to deliver his crop. He could not draw back. The new rate ate up every cent of his gains. He stood there ruined.

"Good Lord," he murmured, "good Lord! What will you people do next? Look here. What's your basis of applying freight rates anyhow?" he suddenly vociferated with furious sarcasm. "What's your rule? What are you guided by?"

S. Behrman emphasized each word of his reply with a tap of one forefinger on the counter before him. "All—the—traffic—will—bear."

SOURCE: Excerpted from Frank Norris, *The Octopus: A Story of California* (New York: Doubleday, Page and Co., 1904), 348–350.

---

in future decades: "The reign of bloated naves is over. The people are about to take their own affairs into their own hands...."[16]

Ironically, the same voters that elected a railroad-controlled State Senate also authorized the calling of a constitutional convention—one noted for its anti-railroad temperament. Original state constitutions seem to need revision within several decades and California was no exception. In California's case, the 1878–1879 convention coincided with economic troubles, anti-railroad fervor, and worker radicalism. The revised constitution literally banned the employment of the Chinese—"aliens who are or may become vagrants, paupers, mendicants, criminals, or invalids with contagious or infectious diseases...."[17] Numerous anti-railroad regulations were imbedded into the constitution to prevent their easy removal. The delegates naively established a railroad commission, thinking such a regulatory body would be insulated from Big Four pressure. On the contrary, the commission "proved as clay in the hands of the great corporations."[18] Furthermore, occasional regulatory victories were often voided by economically conservative courts. A popular political cartoon of the

day entitled "The Curse of California" symbolized not only the power of the Big Four but also the elite theory of politics described in Chapter 1 (see Cartoon 2.1).

Changes in the larger political environment gradually lessened the influence of the Big Four and the massive company they left behind. Their political power was a house of cards based on a monopolistic rate structure and lack of competition. But in the 1880s, when a competing southern transcontinental railroad emerged (the Santa Fe), ensuing rate wars ruined their monopoly. As more towns obtained railroad service, local rivalries waned and company control was no longer necessary. Further industrialization of California would depend less on parochial, intrastate concerns and more on national and international forces. As new transportation routes crisscrossed the state, political subcultures gradually merged. The railroads helped to both unify and industrialize the Golden State.

WATER

A third factor in the modernization of California was water. This commodity affected both

CARTOON 2.1   The "Curse of California"

Edward Keller's "The Curse of California" was published in *The Wasp* on August 19, 1882, and is regarded as the most influential political cartoon in California history. Keller employed the often-used octopus symbol to caricature the political and economic reach of the Big Four. *Source:* Courtesy of the Bancroft Library, University of California, Berkeley.

agriculture and urbanization in the state. A growing interstate network of railroad routes plus the advent of refrigerated rolling stock allowed the nation to enjoy an increasing variety of fruit and vegetables. The early padres, and later farmers, found California's geography could accommodate at least some crops, anytime, anywhere in the state. This led not only to highly specialized farming but also a demand for adequate water. Specialty crops increased a farmer's return per acre but only if there was a sufficient, continual supply of water. The state's endless cycles of wet and dry years produced a yo-yo economy from a grower's perspective.

The Great Drought during the 1860s spurred local irrigation efforts, especially in the great agricultural valleys of California. Instead of isolated farmsteads as found in the Midwest, California farmers settled in colonies. This allowed, and in fact, required them to cooperate on various water projects. These efforts included the diversion of water from the state's major river systems, rivers fed from a permanent snowpack in the Sierra Nevada.

The late 1800s and early 1900s witnessed numerous efforts to increase the volume and dependability of water. The Wright Irrigation Act of 1887 authorized the formation of local water irrigation districts, precursors to modern-day water districts. From that point on, the agricultural sector, in partnership with the state and federal governments, pursued the construction of dams, well, canals, reservoirs, catchment basins, and aqueducts to move water ever farther from its source. In 1908, Los Angeles engineer William Mullholland and business leaders Harrison Gray Otis and his son-in-law Harry Chandler (successive publishers of the *Los Angeles Times*) spearheaded an effort to construct an aqueduct from the Owens River, east of the Sierras, to the San Fernando Valley. Carey McWilliams labeled their actions "water imperialism" because this project eventually sucked dry a previously productive agricultural valley.[19]

The federal government played a major role in later water projects. In 1933, Congress appropriated start-up funds to initiate the Central Valley Project after a $170 million state construction bond went unsold. This effort to conserve, divert, and redistribute the Sacramento and San Joaquin rivers turned family farms into agribusinesses. Three years later, the federally financed Hoover Dam was completed, thereby creating Lake Mead. This massive effort to tame the mighty Colorado River garnered agricultural water for the Imperial Valley and still more water for Los Angeles. In addition, it produced huge amounts of electrical power as well, an additional prerequisite for urban growth in Southern California. Subsequent statewide water plans simply added to the patchwork of projects and confusing laws that constitute water policy in California. During this industrialization period, California would become one of the world's great "hydraulic societies," as Donald Worster put it.[20] Migrant workers during the Depression and later would provide the necessary labor required of industrialized agriculture.

OTHER MODERNIZING FACTORS

The impact of the Gold Rush and visionary water planning were only two features of California's modernization. Several others deserve mention:

Oil

"Black gold" was discovered in various parts of Southern California between 1900 and 1940, creating new economic opportunities. Unlike California's farmers and their crops, the oil companies faced tremendous obstacles shipping crude to distant out-of-state markets. They became vulnerable to overproduction and the vagaries of local demand within California. Producers of crude searched for various shipping methods, including ocean-going tankers and pipelines. Pipeline companies

© Security Pacific Collection/Los Angeles Public Library.

PHOTO 2.1   The war effort in California
California played a critical role in World War II. Here, the Los Angeles
shipyard is the scene of stepped-up wartime construction.

and oil producers became political adversaries. Eventually, the state regulated pipelines as common carriers (much like railroads); oil producers privately agreed to control production and set prices. They sought legislative help on occasion to maintain this balance.[21] By the 1990s, advanced refining facilities could supply both California and nearby markets. Oil helped to diversify California's mushrooming economy. Like yellow gold, early discoveries of black gold produced ripple effects—land speculation and further population growth. It became still another magnet drawing both job seekers and environmentalists concerned about oil-generated pollution.

World War II

A second event that propelled California's industrialization was World War II. As noted in Chapter 1, the Great Depression drove people hoping for a better life to California. The nation's war effort, though, dwarfed Depression era migration. Nearly 2 million people came to or through California to work in defense plants, neighboring communities, or military bases (see Photo 2.1). A transportation network (thanks to the railroads) and plenty of water (thanks to the water visionaries) made wartime growth possible. California's location on the Pacific Rim during a war with Japan made wartime growth inevitable. True, the military-industrial complex had a foothold in California long before World War II, with the establishment of the aircraft industry. But the war accelerated its growth and its impact on the urbanization of the state.[22]

After the war, nearly 700,000 men were discharged in California; many of whom decided to call California home. They furthered the blending of political subcultures in the state. The war itself fostered a pro-business climate. The thirst for defense contracts, "federal gold," continued after the war and helped to forge an alliance between big business and big labor. Political moderates of both parties were elected to continue economic growth brought on by the war. By the 1990s, remnants of wartime California remained visible, including numerous military bases that had never closed after the war. The closures of some of these "surplus" facilities were met with anguish by public officials and neighboring communities alike.

The Politics of Welfare

Political development's third stage is the *politics of welfare*. In this stage, government's task is to shield the citizenry from hardship, manage a smooth running economy, improve standards of living, and assist the less fortunate. It takes an industrial base to afford these activities.[23] In California, several factors influenced this stage of development: the Progressive Movement, the Depression, and the leadership of two governors, Earl Warren and Edmund G. (Pat) Brown. Combined, they represented the state's moralistic political subculture on a grand scale.

THE PROGRESSIVE MOVEMENT

Although California's role as a modern welfare state came after World War II, the foundation for welfare politics was built earlier. California's

version of the nationwide Progressive Movement, led by Governor Hiram Johnson (1911–1917) eliminated the overbearing political influence of the railroads and stressed political individualism and nonpartisanship (see Chapter 4). Progressive reforms weakened political parties by requiring many officeholders to run as nonpartisans. The result was a nonpartisan public spirit to accomplish shared policy goals.

California experienced tremendous economic growth prior to the Depression as people poured into the state, lured by an increasingly diverse economy. Economic growth heightened people's economic expectations, soon be dashed by the Depression. The Progressives in effect created a leadership vacuum by allowing voters to make decisions previously reserved for elected representatives. On a more subtle level, they increased the *expectation* of greater participation by the masses. This in turn fueled mass demand for more services and greater benefits.

THE GREAT DEPRESSION

The Depression itself accelerated demands for public assistance to those crushed by economic hardship (see Photo 2.2). In 1934, novelist and socialist Upton Sinclair became the Democratic nominee for governor. His platform, End Poverty in California (EPIC), combined the goals of tax reform and public employment. Some voters, especially senior citizens, became Sinclair enthusiasts; big business labeled him a radical, a crackpot, and even a communist. Republican Frank Merriam won. Four years later, the same year *Grapes of Wrath* was published, Democrat Culbert L. Olson, won the governorship. Although he served only one term, he too developed ambitious policies to aid those untouched by progress in California.[24] What really helped California was the New Deal, which converted good intentions into actual assistance. The Works Progress Administration

Library of Congress, Prints & Photographs Division, FSA/OWI Collection, LC-DIG-fsa-8b29516

PHOTO 2.2 Migrant mother
This 1936 photo of a migrant pea-picker and her children outside Nipomo, California, became a famous symbol of the Depression nationwide.

(WPA) funded projects from Shasta Dam and the Golden Gate Bridge to lesser-scale schools, libraries, and hospitals. Through what Kevin Starr calls the "therapy of public works," California seemingly built itself out of the depression.[25] These Depression-era experiences suggested that Californians would support an array of policies to improve living conditions *if* they were proposed by competent, moderate, progressive leaders. Wartime California produced those leaders.

EARL WARREN

World War II expedited the welfare era by pumping even more federal expenditures into the state's economy. Politically, it helped produce a coalition of business and labor dedicated to one common goal: a healthy economic future for California. Elected in 1942, Governor Earl Warren was just the leader this coalition needed. During the campaign, Warren, a progressive Republican, rejected incumbent

Governor Olson's partisan pleas: "I am, as you know, a Republican. But, I shall make no appeal to blind partisanship, or follow any other divisive tactics."[26] He was so bipartisan, he took advantage of a Progressive era reform called cross-filing to run on both party tickets in 1946. He won a third term in 1950, the only California governor ever to do so, and was a contender for the Republican presidential nomination in 1952. He resigned in 1953 when President Dwight D. Eisenhower appointed him chief justice of the U.S. Supreme Court.

During Warren's tenure as governor, California made great strides in education and various social programs. In some respects, Warren continued a moralistic political subculture advanced by the Progressives. His social reforms included more generous old-age pensions, broadened unemployment insurance, improved medical care, and progressive labor legislation. Prison and mental hospital reform were top priorities. He used his enormous popularity to push a progressive agenda through a Republican legislature. A massive freeway-building program was launched in 1947, financed through increased gasoline taxes. No wonder President Harry Truman once said of Warren, "He's a Democrat—and doesn't know it."[27] His one major legislative defeat was compulsory health insurance, an issue that would resurface some 40 years later.

Growing state services in the Warren years meant a growing bureaucracy. State employees swelled from 24,000 in 1943 to 56,000 in 1953. An expanding economy made this growth affordable. A 50 percent population increase during this period made it necessary. Consistent with his "leadership, not politics" views, Warren hired experts rather than political cronies to run these growing state agencies. In the spirit of Progressivism, he appointed nonpartisan "committees of experts" to examine policy issues and propose policy recommendations.[28] Historian Robert Glass Cleland credited the state's economy for all this policy vigor: "The war and postwar booms gave Warren only

problems of prosperity to solve."[29] In fact, Warren was able to spend liberally *and* maintain a "rainy day" fund—a feat that seems quite unthinkable in contemporary California.

Lieutenant Governor Goodwin Knight succeeded Warren. While more conservative than Warren, he adopted many of his predecessor's policies. California had become a relatively generous social welfare state, the populace supported that development and politicians of both parties knew it. An implicit social contract was in place. California was to represent continual prosperity; government's job was to bolster and assure that prosperity. A political consensus was in place that would last for several decades.

EDMUND G. (PAT) BROWN

In 1958 Democratic votes finally caught up with Democratic registration trends and Pat Brown succeeded Knight as governor. Like Warren, Brown had been state attorney general and had avoided overly partisan election campaigns. He too avoided close ties with his own party. Under Brown's leadership, the state's Water Project was funded, providing the infrastructure to move vast amounts of water from the mountains to the growing Bay Area and Southern California cities. School and university enrollments mushroomed, as well as requisite school construction, reflecting the state's continued growth.

In 1959 Brown called for a master plan for higher education. This plan allocated different tasks to the University of California, the state colleges, and the junior colleges (as they were called then). Access to higher education by all Californians became part of the state's implicit social contract. Brown continued Warren's progressive welfare policies—an agenda he called *responsible liberalism*. In the area of civil rights, he pushed through the legislature various antidiscrimination measures and a Fair Employment Practices Commission to enforce them. Brown oversaw massive public construction projects including new college campuses, public schools, and a thousand miles of additional freeways. Brown was fortunate in that the freeways were largely funded by the Federal Interstate Highway Act of 1956. The state also became the regulator of air quality and the consumer's protector.[30] Responding to population and economic growth, public officials could not have imagined future growth that later Californians would no longer be willing to accommodate.

By 1966, unrestrained population growth, increased taxes, urban congestion, growing pollution, university campus unrest, farm worker strikes, and the 1965 Watts riot took their toll on Governor Brown. According to journalist and biographer Lou Cannon, "Many Californians who had previously voted Democratic blamed their grievances on government and no longer believed that they lived in the Golden State of their dreams and memories. California was a state hungering for reform and a new sense of direction."[31]

Brown's successor was actor, liberal-turned-conservative, citizen politician Ronald Reagan. He spelled out his sense of direction in his January 1967 inaugural address: "The cost of California's government is too high. It adversely affects our business climate....We are going to squeeze and cut and trim until we reduce the cost of government."[32] Reagan soon learned that his "cut and trim" hyperbole was difficult if not impossible to implement. Most state spending was the product of legislative statutes or federal regulations, not gubernatorial wishes. Promising to cut government waste and "clean up the mess at Berkeley"(student protests were commonplace), Reagan did make substantial cuts in higher welfare, mental health, and higher education. Nevertheless, the overall state budget doubled (from $5 billion to $10.2 billion) during his eight years in office. He even signed into law a major tax increase when the budget necessitated it and the state's first-ever income tax withholding plan. His pragmatic conservatism also marked his years as American president (1981–1989).

The Politics of Abundance and Beyond

Ironically, responsible liberalism can produce negative reactions, even by those it helps. True, the standard of living had increased in California through both public and private spending. The state had moved into the *politics of abundance*. A growing economy provided the taxes to fund a social welfare state and a plethora of services Californians had come to expect. These policies were *majoritarian* in nature: the majority both paid for them and received their benefits. For instance, low-cost public higher education was available to every resident regardless of need. These policies not only were widely supported, they attracted still more people to the Golden State.

But when does growth become too much of a good thing? By the 1960s, many Californians were asking that question. Growth had funded their favorite programs but had also replaced orange groves with endless housing tracts and fueled freeway congestion, air pollution, and overcrowded parks and schools. Although many effects of growth are privately generated, Californians sensed that "politics as usual" was somehow to blame. Responsible liberalism apparently had become irresponsible. A succession of governors including Reagan would try to reverse the politics of growth, especially governmental growth, that had characterized the state's history. California entered an era of lowered expectations. Reagan's successor and Pat Brown's son, Jerry Brown (1975–1983), declared "small is beautiful" and claimed Californians were living in an "era of limits," hardly the language his father would have used. Jerry Brown had rejected the bipartisan growth consensus of the Warren-Brown era. George Deukmejian succeeded Brown (1983–1991). As Reagan did, Deukmejian championed free enterprise, claimed government was the problem, not the solution, and rejected most tax and spending increases. When the Democratic

CARTOON 2.2 Entering California
In 1975 cartoonist Dennis Renault captured the "era of limits" rhetoric of Governor Jerry Brown. To Californians used to the leadership of Governors Earl Warren and Pat Brown, the politics of the 1970s and 1980s did seem to be characterized by lowered expectations. *Source:* Dennis Renault, *Sacramento Bee.*

legislature allowed him to, he pared back the state's regulatory activity, especially that opposed by business.[33]

Political leaders in the 1970s and 1980s heeded Californians' pleas to preserve the "abundant state." If government was the problem, cut off its lifeblood—in a word taxes. Some of these tax limits were self-imposed by elected officials in the annual budget process. Others, like Proposition 13 (which drastically cut property taxes), were imposed by voters led by policy entrepreneurs like Howard Jarvis and Paul Gann. The state's middle-class voters have always been a powerful, albeit fickle, influence on the political process. Buffeted by raging inflation and tax increases in the 1970s, they sincerely believed government revenue could be cut without reducing the services they enjoyed.

While governmental growth slowed down, the state's population growth did not. By the late 1990s, observers were conflicted over the future of Abundant California. Given the constant drumbeat of population growth (1,000 plus per day!), would there continue to be enough abundance to go around? This was a fundamental policy dilemma for Deukmejian's successor Pete Wilson (1991–1998) and subsequent governors, Gray Davis (1999–2003) and Arnold Schwarzenegger (2003–). The 2001 electricity shortage due to, among other things, growing demand and inadequate supply, underscored this point. Nancy Vogel's observations in 1991 seem equally instructive today: "[G]one is [Earl] Warren's cornucopian sense of California. Where Warren dreamed of a garden cottage for every new 'settler,' as he called them, his successors in Sacramento see smog-choked suburbs. Where Warren welcomed migrant musclepower to develop 'latent resources,' today's leaders fear depletion of those resources."[34]

Today, Californians seem conflicted over the state's future as a place of abundance. While some resources are finite by nature (water, air), others are simply perceived to be scarce. For example, there is plenty of land for housing and commerce in California but it may not be where people prefer to live or do business. Still another perception is that public resources are themselves limited or finite; that the State of California, despite its wealth, can no longer afford previously high levels of public services. This view is shared by those who prefer the forced scarcity of low taxes and those who contend that constant population growth makes traditional policy making and

generous spending unsustainable over the long term. Still others view California's current stage of political development—no matter what one calls it—as a series of clashes, not only of competing political interests, but of diverse political and ethnic cultures. They question whether there is any longer a single public interest acceptable to most Californians. More optimistic observers believe that even a highly diverse, constantly growing California will continue to offer hope and prosperity to succeeding generations regardless of wealth or ethnic background.

Conclusion

When British ambassador Lord Bryce visited California in 1906, 2 million people inhabited the state. He asked: "What will happen when California is filled by 50 millions of people and its valuation is five times what it is now? There will be more people—as many as the country can support—and the real question will be not about making more wealth or having more people, but whether the people will then be happier or better than they have been hitherto or are at this moment."[35]

Roughly 34 million people later, his question remains compelling. The bipartisan pro-growth consensus that built California's social and physical infrastructure has collapsed; no alternative consensus has taken its place. The reason appears to be a change in the very political culture of the state. As noted in Chapter 1, the gap between the state's haves and have-nots is growing larger. The moralistic and individualistic political subcultures, which have historically lived side by side in California, seem at war with each other. Individualism may be winning. The state's upper tier, wanting to maintain the abundant state as they define it and remember it, readily participate in California's political system. Meanwhile, the lower tier, which participates to a lesser extent in effect seems to be asking: "Where is the moralistic political subculture when *we* need it?" As political analyst Sherry Bebitch Jeffe notes, in terms of government of, by, and for the people, "the 'people' of California and the 'voters' who make up its electorate are two very different groups."[36]

Caught in the middle, California's policymakers have exercised the "politics of caution." They face certain wrath from some constituents regardless of the policy and budget choices they make. Even Arnold Schwarzenegger was forced to confront this political fact of life as he retreated from some of his reform proposals. The consequence for most public officials is to do little that is bold or significant, especially if it means more or higher taxes. Earlier, we attributed this policy paralysis to an increasingly diverse and hyperpluralistic political system. In Chapter 2 we add to the equation a pattern of political development characterized by individualism and a move toward abundance experienced by many but apparently not all Californians.

KEY TERMS

political culture   (p. 23)

traditional, moralistic, and individualistic
   subcultures   (p. 23)

political development   (p. 24)

politics of unification, modernization, welfare,
   abundance   (pp. 24–39)

presidios and pueblos   (p. 25)

1849 and 1879 Constitutions   (pp. 27–28, 30)

patron-client relationships   (p. 25)

Gold Rush   (pp. 28–29)

Big Four   (pp. 29–30)

Southern Pacific Railroad   (p. 29)

Black gold, federal gold   (pp. 32–33, 34)

Progressive Movement   (p. 34)

responsible liberalism   (p. 36)

majoritarian policies   (p. 37)

era of limits   (p. 37)

REVIEW QUESTIONS

1. Describe Elazar's three political subcultures. How do they apply to California?
2. Describe political history as a process of political development. Define the four stages of political development used in this chapter.
3. Why are Spanish "rule" and Mexican "control" in quotes?
4. Describe the real impact of the gold rush.
5. Why were the Big Four so powerful and so resented?
6. How did California become a great "hydraulic society?"
7. What effects did World War II have on California's political development?
8. Describe the bipartisan growth consensus characterized by the governorships of Warren and Brown.
9. Describe the politics of abundance and why some Californians worry that it will not continue.
10. What do you think will be the next stage of California's political development and why?

WEB ACTIVITIES

California Historical Society (www.calhist.org)
The Golden State's official historical society provides historical data and numerous links to statewide and local resources.

INFOTRAC® COLLEGE EDITION ARTICLES

For additional reading, go to InfoTrac® College Edition, your online research library, at http://www.infotrac.thomsonlearning.com

California Becomes a State of the Union

Gold Rush Legacy

Reagan's Rise

NOTES

1. Daniel Elazar, *American Federalism: A View from the States*, 3rd. ed. (New York: Harper and Row, 1984), 122–123.
2. Elazar, *American Federalism*, chap. 4.
3. Ibid, 124–126.
4. Various theories of development are summarized in David E. Apter, *Introduction to Political Analysis* (Cambridge, MA: Winthrop, 1977), chap. 15.
5. A. F. K. Organski, *The Stages of Political Development* (New York: Alfred A. Knopf, 1965).
6. Quoted in Gladwin Hill, *Dancing Bear: An Inside Look at California Politics* (Cleveland, OH: World Publishing Co., 1968), 4.
7. Secularization in this context meant converting the missions into parish churches (which they continue to be to this day), reducing the power of the friars, and releasing mission land for nonmission uses.
8. John W. Caughey, *California: A Remarkable State's Life History* (Englewood Cliffs, NJ, 1970), 114.
9. J. S. Holliday, *The World Rushed In: The California Gold Rush Experience* (New York: Simon and Schuster, 1981), 48.
10. James Polk, "Fourth Annual Message, December 5, 1848" in *Messages and Papers of the Presidents, Vol. V* (New York: Bureau of National Literature, 1897), 2,487.
11. Paul Mason, "Constitutional History of California," *Constitution of the State of California (1879) and Related Documents* (Sacramento: California State Senate, 1973), 75–105.
12. Caughey, *California*, 215.
13. Holliday, *World Rushed In*, 26.
14. Caughey, *California*, 191.
15. Ward McAfee, *California's Railroad Era: 1850–1911* (San Marino, CA: Golden West Books, 1973), 157.
16. Carl Brent Swisher, *Motivation and Political Technique in the California Constitutional Convention 1878–79* (New York: De Capo Press, 1969), 12.
17. Article XIX, "Chinese," 1879 Constitution.
18. Ibid., 112.
19. Carey McWilliams, *California: The Great Exception* (Santa Barbara: Peregrine Smith, Inc., 1949, 1979), 106.
20. Donald Worster, *Rivers of Empire* (New York, Pantheon Books, 1985).
21. Mansel G. Blackford, *The Politics of Business in California: 1890–1920* (Columbus, OH: Ohio State University Press, 1977). See chap. 3: "The Oil Industry."
22. For an extensive analysis of the "metropolitan-military complex" in California, see Roger W. Lotchin, *Fortress California 1910–1961: From Warfare to Welfare* (New York: Oxford University Press, 1992).
23. Organski, *Stages of Political Development*, 12.
24. See Robert E. Burke, *Olson's New Deal for California* (Berkeley: University of California Press, 1953).
25. Kevin Starr, *Endangered Dreams: The Great Depression in California* (New York: Oxford University Press, 1996), especially Part IV.
26. Quoted in David Lavender, *California: Land of New Beginnings* (New York: Harper and Row, 1972), 397.
27. Quoted in Hill, *Dancing Bear*, 100.
28. G. Edward White, *Earl Warren: A Public Life* (New York: Oxford University Press, 1982). See especially chap. 4, "Governing: Office Holding and Policy making."
29. Robert Glass Cleland, *From Wilderness to Empire: A History of California* (New York: Alfred A. Knopf, 1959), 419.
30. For more on Brown's record, see Martin Schiesl, ed. *The California of the Pat Brown Years: Creative Building for the Golden State's Future* (Los Angeles: The Edmund G. "Pat" Brown Institute of Public Affairs, 1997).
31. Lou Cannon, *Governor Reagan: His Rise to Power* (Cambridge, MA: Public Affairs, 2003), 9.
32. Quoted in James J. Rawls and Walton Bean, *California: An Interpretive History* (New York: McGraw Hill, 2003), 458–459.
33. David Kutzman, Teresa Watanabe, and Arnold J. Hamilton, "The Terminator: Deukmejian Dismantles the State's Regulatory System," *California Journal* 19 (February 1988): 85–88.
34. Nancy Vogel, "Is California Bursting at the Seams?" *California Journal* 22 (July 1991): 295–299.
35. Quoted in Dan Walters, *The New California: Facing the 21st Century*, 2nd ed. (Sacramento: California Journal Press, 1992), 7.

CHAPTER 3

Constitutionalism and Federalism: The Perimeters of California Politics

In Brief

California is a nation unto itself. The most populous state in the union, its economy dwarfs those of all other states and most nations. The state's political development is checkered with unique individuals, groups, and circumstances both historical and contemporary. Yet when California became the thirty-first state, it joined a preexisting nation, a nation with its own constitution and emerging political institutions and traditions. Ever since, California has affected and been affected by the nation as a whole. In recent years, it has been increasingly affected by its neighbors, especially Mexico.

In Chapter 3, we will focus on several perimeters or outer limits that affect California politics. First, we examine California's constitution as a rulebook to which policymakers, institutions, and voters must conform. California's constitutional development helps explain why its core document or rulebook is similar to or different from those of other states. It also helps to explain why some political fragmentation is essentially structural in nature. Second, we discuss California's role in affecting national affairs and public policy. In doing so, we examine the successive stages of federalism as they relate to California and how Californians attempt to exercise influence in Washington. The chapter concludes by surveying how California's own borders create policy challenges not faced by most states.

Introduction: Rules and Boundaries

Western democracies place certain limits on governments. Some of these limitations may be rules that dictate how and under what circumstances power can be exercised, policy made, and by whom. State constitutions and local governing charters contain such rules. Other limitations take the form of boundaries that demarcate territorial jurisdiction. These are legal borders beyond which influence wanes and power means little. National and state borders as well as city, county, and special district lines mark off the legal reach of most public policy efforts. From a state perspective, constitutions and federalism are the *perimeters of politics*—the outer limits that in effect contain the scope of political power.

State Constitutions as Rulebooks

Political scientists call the idea of limited government—government operating within certain rules—*constitutionalism*. American constitutionalism as derived from, among others, English political theorist John Locke (1632–1704). He believed that rights of the people and limits on those who govern them should be spelled out in a "social contract." Natural rights and rules governing the relationship between the people and government would occupy higher legal ground than ordinary laws (statutes passed by legislatures). In fact, the validity of those laws would be measured against the constitution. Accordingly, changing a constitution should be more difficult than changing an ordinary law. Furthermore, any such change should be made by the people themselves.

Locke's views on governance (including the idea of separation of powers) deeply influenced the Framers of the U.S. Constitution. They were largely successful in limiting the document to basic fundamental law and to only 8,700 words. It would be the "Supreme Law of the Land," superseding the Articles of Confederation. With revisions, the colonial constitutions became state constitutions in 1789. Despite their regard for Locke, the Framers rejected his idea of constitutional change by "the People." They believed in a republican form of government in which representatives were chosen only by qualified voters and made decisions on their behalf. Ordinary citizens never voted on the original document and have never directly ratified its amendments.

America's constitutional history actually predates the U.S. Constitution. Those 13 original colonies possessed extensive governing charters reflecting their respective political cultures. Later states brought with them comparable experiences and traditions. Because the founding elites in each new state generally understood what limited government and civil liberties meant, and what basic institutions were necessary to govern, state constitutions were destined to look alike in many respects. Yet they were never intended to be clones of the federal document. For better or for worse, they would reflect not only those beliefs shared by American society as a whole but also the culture, traditions, and unique attributes of each state.

Over the years, some reformers have viewed state constitutions as jumbles of unnecessary trivia. They have sought both to strengthen governmental power and to eliminate what they consider unnecessary clutter. In their view, a state constitution should contain only basic, fundamental law. As several California political scientists once put it, a constitution should be "brief, clean, and unambiguous . . . [expressing] a philosophy of government that has been thoroughly discussed and represents the consensus of thought." Still others believe constitutions are political documents; living, breathing expressions of policy conflict, not policy consensus. Constitution writing is "a struggle between competing groups of people who try to get as many of their ideas and interests as possible expressed in law, so the resulting document represents compromises between numerous groups."[1] State constitutions reflect policy victories and defeats, not just compromise. Even the rules of the game reward one group over another.

California's Constitution

California's current constitution is over 54,000 words in length and has been amended over 500 times, second only to Alabama. Some of the document's most interesting provisions are certain amendments, which will be discussed shortly. Yet the basic framework for California's government was established in the 1800s by two separate conventions producing two distinct constitutions.

The 1849 Constitution provided the basic structure of state government and a 16-section Declaration of Rights. Slavery was banned. Married women were granted separate property rights, the first such guarantee found in any state (see Figure 3.1). Certain policy directions were also set in this constitution. Provisions for public education were specified in some detail, and income from selected state lands was set aside for a future state university.

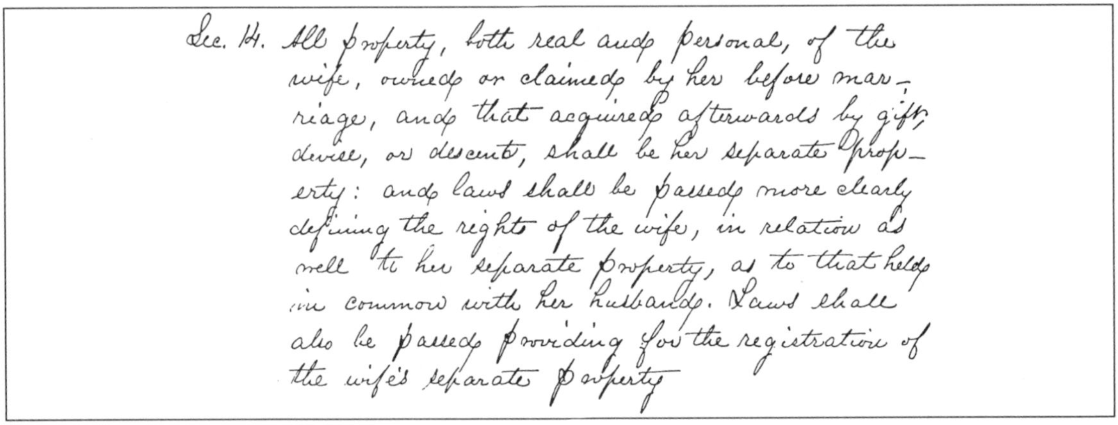
Sec. 14. All property, both real and personal, of the wife, owned or claimed by her before marriage, and that acquired afterwards by gift, devise, or descent, shall be her separate property: and laws shall be passed more clearly defining the rights of the wife, in relation as well to her separate property, as to that held in common with her husband. Laws shall also be passed providing for the registration of the wife's separate property

FIGURE 3.1 Women and the Constitution of 1849

At a time in American history when women were considered legally subservient to their husbands, California's first constitution suggested otherwise. Consider Section 14 of Article 11 (Miscellaneous Provisions) as it appeared in the original.

Source: The Original Constitution of the State of California, 1849: The Engrossed Copy with the Official Spanish Translation (Sacramento: Telefact Foundation, 1965), p. 94.

Public debt of any magnitude was disallowed. This constitution lasted 30 years, longer than many observers thought it would. The voters repeatedly rejected legislative calls for a second constitutional convention. Finally, a second one was held in 1878 amid population growth pressures (a 17-fold increase in only 30 years), farmer/railroad feuds, and the rise of the militant Workingman's Party. Many Californians thought constitutional reform would solve these problems.

The delegates to the 1878 convention generally represented three opposing interest groups: large financial interests (banks, corporations, and large landowners), farmers (opposed to the Southern Pacific Railroad (SPR) and the tax system), and urban workers (alienated by both big business and the influx of Chinese). After 157 days of hard bargaining, they adopted the document on a 120–15 vote; on May 7, 1879, California voters ratified it.

The new constitution was three times longer and more detailed than the old one. Over the years, it has grown still further just as the state has. In the modern paperback version published by the California State Senate, the U.S. Constitution is included. The California Constitution's index alone is twice the length of the entire U.S. Constitution! Over the years, many original provisions have survived intact. Others have been slightly revised. Entire new sections have been added, and other sections have been reorganized.

WHAT IT CONTAINS

California's constitution illustrates features common to all state constitutions.

Duties of Government

It reflects the particular obligations of state government overall and necessary institutions such as the governor, legislature, and judiciary. Since local governments are really subdivisions of the state, the constitution must spell out their duties and powers. Therefore, extensive sections of California's constitution deal with cities, counties, special districts, and school districts.

Mistrust of Politicians

California's constitution, like those of other states, has reflected historic mistrust of elected officials. This mistrust has been aimed at legislators as well as governors. In the 1800s, the state legislature had been widely regarded as corrupt. During several early sessions, the legislature was dubbed the Legislature of 1,000 Drinks and the Legislature of 1,000 Steals. As a result, its powers were sharply delineated. For instance, the 1879 document enumerated 33 instances in which the legislature was *prohibited* from passing laws. Governors have not been spared either. California's constitution requires the governor to share power with separately elected executive officers—the lieutenant governor, attorney general, secretary of state, treasurer, controller, insurance commissioner, and school superintendent plus numerous boards and commissions.

Group Benefits

Typical of other state constitutions, California's has conferred particular advantages or imposed various regulations on interest groups. Numerous provisions address corporations generally and a host of specific groups including financial institutions, the legal profession, the alcoholic beverage industry, churches, contractors, utility companies, the fishing industry, farmers, realtors, and transportation providers. One recent example is Article 4, Section 19, the provision that permits and guarantees gaming rights of California's Indian tribes. Although the constitution does not exactly mirror hyperpluralism as we use the term, any and all groups with requisite political power can use it to garner benefits for themselves or deny them to others.

Money

California's constitution addresses taxation and finance in detail. Tax policies embedded in this document are used to promote a plethora of interests—charitable groups, orchards and vineyards, historical preservation, nonprofit hospitals, the elderly, renters, homeowners, museums, and veterans. Unlike the federal government, state constitutions usually limit the amount of debt states and their subdivisions can incur. In California, the original 1879 state limit of $300,000 remains, but Article 16 of the Constitution allows numerous exceptions that provide ample room for policymakers to borrow considerably more.

Clutter and Trivia

Like other states, California's constitution is filled with clutter and trivia. This minutia must have seemed important at the time it was enacted. For instance, today's public school teachers can be grateful that the state's constitution prevents their annual salaries from dipping below $2,400![2] In the early 1900s, the length of boxing matches and rounds was specified (12 rounds and 3 minutes, respectively). The 1849 ban on dueling remained in the constitution until 1970, long after people stopped dueling. A Cold War–era amendment banned subversives (those wishing to destroy the government) from holding office or receiving tax exemptions.[3] In a post–Cold War world, this provision will seem more and more a relic of the past. Occasionally the voters eliminate such provisions, but others remain simply because they are politically irrelevant. They do no harm, so why spend the energy removing them? More important, some constitutional trivia remains because trivia is relative in a pluralistic society; what is undue clutter

to one group may be economic survival to another. Even trivia represents hard fought political conflict, winners and losers, and historical events in the life of a state. In a sense, it is pluralism at work.

Change

California, like other states, allows its basic document to change. Three methods are available. First is a *constitutional convention*. The legislature, by a two-thirds vote, may call for a constitutional convention. The last such convention was in 1878. California has not used this method as frequently or recently as other states. In fact, voters have turned down such convention proposals on four occasions. In the 1960s, the legislature modified this method by appointing a "blue ribbon" constitutional revision commission to study the document and recommend changes for legislative approval and voter ratification. Overall, the revisions that survived voter approval resulted in a briefer, more streamlined document, at least by state constitution standards. In the mid-1990s, a 23-member Constitutional Revision Commission studied the constitution and how government operates under it. After two years of hearings and reports, it proposed a package of constitutional amendments to overhaul and streamline state and local government, but they died in the legislature.

A second method is change by *legislative proposal,* a method common to all states. Individual members of the California Assembly and Senate propose amendments and process them as bills. If two-thirds of their colleagues agree, measures are placed on the ballot for voter consideration. "Housekeeping" changes and more significant policy proposals have resulted from this method. For instance, in 2002 voters approved Proposition 48, a legislative constitutional amendment that reworded parts of Article VI so it would reflect a prior consolidation of state courts. A third method is the

Cartoon 3.1   Davis Recall-"California Fault Line"
Source: Daryl Cagle, Slate.com. Reprinted with permission from Cagle Cartoons, Inc.

initiative, a product of the Progressive era. The initiative allows individuals and groups to bypass the legislature entirely by placing proposed statutes or constitutional amendments on the ballot. In 2003–2006, it takes 598,105 valid signatures (8 percent of the 7,479,311 votes cast in the 2002 gubernatorial election) to qualify an initiative constitutional amendment. Eighteen states allow this method, but no state uses it more than California. Chapter 4 discusses the initiative process in depth.

WHAT MAKES IT DISTINCTIVE

As we have seen, newer states leaned on the older constitutions for framework and language. Structurally, all state constitutions resemble the U.S. Constitution. Yet state constitutions invariably reflect their regional context, dominant political subcultures, historical experience, and subsequent political trends. At this point, I will briefly spotlight several provisions in California's Constitution that are quintessentially "Californian."

Power to the People

As noted earlier, one significant result of California's Progressive movement, under Governor Hiram Johnson's leadership, was the addition of initiatives, referenda, and recall. None of these is provided for in the U.S. Constitution. The *initiative,* allowing voters to directly place constitutional amendments and statutory proposals on the ballot, was approved in 1911. The *referendum* allows voters to approve or reject statutes already passed by the legislature. In 2003–2006, initiative statutes and referenda require 373,816 valid signatures to be placed on a California ballot (5 percent of the votes cast in the 2002 election). The *recall* allows the electorate to remove elective officials between elections. This provision applies to all elective officials at both the state and local levels, including judges. Once thought impossible to accomplish at the statewide level (it takes the signatures of 20 percent of the votes cast in the last gubernatorial election), Governor Gray Davis was recalled in a 2003 special election.

The Right of Privacy

Only eight state constitutions contain a right of privacy, and California is one of them. Even though it is not specifically mentioned in the U.S. Constitution, the U.S. Supreme Court in *Roe v. Wade* (1973) established a right of privacy relative to reproductive choice.[4] California's original "Declaration of Rights" in 1849 did not include privacy. It read: "All men are by nature free and independent, and have certain inalienable rights, among which are those of enjoying and defending life and liberty; acquiring, possessing, and protecting property; and pursuing and obtaining safety and happiness."[5] In 1974, the year after *Roe v. Wade*, California voters replaced "men" with "people," and added "privacy" after "happiness." Although the emerging abortion controversy was not a key issue in its passage, this rewording has been used to support a pro-choice policy in California.

Water

Many states take water for granted, but not those in the West. California's history of drought, coupled with its agricultural potential, virtually required government's attention from the start. Over the years, much water policy has made its way into the Constitution itself. A separate article is simply titled "Water" (Article 10). Overall, these provisions encompass water development and regulation, water rates, riparian rights (rights of those who live next to a body of water), the water policy role of the state, protection of fish, wildlife, and scenic rivers, and needs of specific areas such as the Sacramento–San Joaquin Delta.

English Only

The original 1849 Constitution was clear: "All laws, decrees, regulations, and provisions, which, from their nature, require publication, shall be published in English and Spanish."[6] The constitution itself was handwritten in both languages, reflecting California's two dominant cultures. Possibly due to the influx of Euro-Americans during the Gold Rush, that bilingual requirement was eliminated in the 1879 constitution. Californians have struggled with this issue ever since. By the 1980s, California's biculture was rapidly becoming bipolar (two cultures in conflict and poles apart). In some communities, the influx of immigrants from Asia and elsewhere suggested a multipolar state. Many white Californians were increasingly uncomfortable with the pluralism around them and the bilingual policies that resulted. In 1986, voters overwhelmingly approved Proposition 63, which declared English as the official language of the state. Its purpose was to "preserve, protect, and strengthen the English language."[7] In 1998, they also rejected bilingual education in the public schools by approving Proposition 227. The long-term impact of these measures remains unclear, but they do reflect discomfort with hyperpluralism in the Golden State—an attitude that tells newcomers: "If you want to live and learn in the Golden State, speak English—*our* language."

Proposition 13

In June 1978, California voters approved Proposition 13, a property-tax-cutting measure that fundamentally altered the relationship between the state and its local governments. The media widely portrayed its passage as the opening volley of a national tax revolt. Careful analysis suggests that the revolt was most successful in Western states with initiative provisions, like California.[8] A more subtle effect was that it paved the way for Ronald Reagan's national anti-tax message two years later as he ran for the presidency. Although other states have adopted their own tax cuts in the intervening years, Proposition 13 captured the nation's attention like no other.

From a governing perspective, California's constitution has fostered fragmentation and gridlock in state politics and polic ymaking. The state's governors must share their power with other elected executives. Legislative prerogatives are curtailed or limited. Protections for powerful interest groups are sprinkled throughout the document. The initiative process allows well-funded interest groups and individuals, via the electorate, to share legislative power. California's constitutional clutter actually encourages litigation, as groups seek to determine what a particular provision really means. This increases the policy role of the courts with which the executive and legislative branches must share power.

California's constitution reflects all three political subcultures. Constitutional policies fostering education, water development, and other infrastructure investments, plus checks on corruption, connote a noble view of government characteristic of a moralistic political subculture. The individualistic political subculture (a more negative view of government) seems evident in efforts to curb political power and elevate individual rights. The traditionalistic political subculture (placing the powerful over the powerless) may be evident in a few scattered provisions such as public housing limits (Article 34) and English-only policies.

California and the Nation: The Boundaries of Federalism

California's relationship to the national government, as with other states, has depended on both constitutional language and political practice. As times have changed, so has this relationship. The Tenth Amendment to the U.S. Constitution defines the general relationship that was supposed to exist between all the states and the national government: "The powers not delegated to the United States by the constitution, nor prohibited by it to the states, are reserved to the states respectively, or to the people."

The Founders never thought the national government would dominate the states in domestic policy. On the contrary, James Madison believed that, in most respects, the national government would be subservient to the states: "The State governments may be regarded as constituent and essential parts of the federal government; whilst the latter is nowise essential to the operation or organization of the former."[9] Alexander Hamilton considered citizens' loyalties to be primarily local. If national representatives were tempted to encroach on the states, "the people of the several States would control the indulgence of so extravagant an appetite."[10]

To modern-day Americans and Californians, these arguments seem both idealistic and unrealistic. The Founders simply could not have anticipated the profound changes that would take place in the federal system. Political scientists have grouped these changes into five historic periods.

DUAL FEDERALISM

This is the original pattern of which Madison and Hamilton wrote. From the founding to about 1913, the national government largely limited itself to activities specifically mentioned in the U.S. Constitution (such as national defense, foreign affairs, coining money, issuing tariffs, and maintaining a post office). The states were expected to make policy on domestic matters such as education, welfare, health, and law enforcement. Political scientists called this "dual federalism"; one compared it to a layer cake.[11] California achieved statehood during this dual federalism period. As a young state, it seemed preoccupied with its own political development. With few exceptions, such as aid for the transcontinental railroad, the federal presence in California politics was minimal and indirect.

COOPERATIVE FEDERALISM

As American society became more complex and the Industrial Revolution produced a national economy, the division of labor between the federal and state levels blurred. From 1913 to 1964, a "cooperative federalism" pattern emerged. A national income tax, two world wars, and the Great Depression combined to make both levels active policy partners concerned with health, welfare, transportation, education, crime, and other issues. Political scientists considered the marble cake with its intermingling of layers a better analogy to describe the relationship during those years.[12] During this period, California benefited greatly from federal spending on water projects, New Deal programs, highway construction, and defense contracts.

CENTRALIZED FEDERALISM

"He who pays the piper calls the tune," claims the old adage. As the federal government's capacity to tax and spend grew, it also became more than simply a cooperative partner in policy making. The "feds" (as state and local officials call national level policymakers) gradually established their own goals. President Lyndon Johnson's Great Society legislation in the 1960s epitomized the next stage, centralized federalism.

The rationale was simple: If policy problems are national in *scope*, they must be national in *nature*—requiring a centralized response. People assumed that states could not or would not provide policy leadership or needed funding. From 1964 to 1980, the Tenth Amendment lost so much of its meaning that political scientists were now describing federalism as a pineapple upside down cake.[13] California followed the national pattern—depending on federal grants for everything from highways to health care. Along with these categorical grants came federal conditions and expectations. Control shifted from Sacramento to Washington, D.C. California public officials at all levels developed both an appetite for federal funds and a distaste for the federal conditions or "strings" that were attached. Increasingly, they had to lobby Washington, not just Sacramento, to get more funds and to avoid more strings.

ON-YOUR-OWN FEDERALISM

The 1980s and the "Reagan revolution" partially shifted this centralization pattern. Building on his experience as California's governor, President Ronald Reagan sought to decrease the national government's role vis-à-vis state and local government. He blamed too many federal grant programs for "a maze of interlocking jurisdictions and levels of government [that] confronts the average citizen in trying to solve even the simplest of problems."[14] He hoped to return many responsibilities to the states and, short of that, to simply reduce spending on programs he disliked. As federal budget deficits ballooned in the 1980s, grant cutting also became a deficit-control strategy, not just a way to implement Reagan's philosophy of federalism. Not wanting to fight a popular president, Congress often went along with these plans.

PRAGMATIC FEDERALISM

Today, the relationship between the federal government and subnational governments, including California, has been called pragmatic federalism, "a constantly evolving, problem solving attempt to work out solutions to major problems on an issue by issue basis."[15] In effect, public officials do what they can to solve a particular problem while shifting the burdensome costs of doing so downward to other levels of government. For example, Congress continues to preempt state and local authority over such issues as bankruptcy, environmental policy, transportation, water, and cable television regulation. It also may require states and local governments to implement federal policies without reimbursing the necessary costs. These are called unfunded or underfunded mandates. For example, the 1993 motor voter law requiring states to register voters at motor vehicle and welfare offices initially cost California $20 million in unreimbursed expenses. Some scholars have called this trend coercive or regulatory federalism.

Other federal policies supplement and sometimes supplant California's own policies. For example, the federal No Child Left Behind Act of 2001 (NCLB)—the newest reauthorization of the decades-old Elementary and Secondary Education Act—requires annual testing of all students, "adequate yearly progress" by all states, and state-issued "report cards" publicizing school-by-school data. It also subjects school systems to stiff sanctions if student progress is insufficient, a rule that tends to penalize California's racially mixed or low-income schools. These requirements are particularly challenging to meet in California. Education officials had to mesh NCLB with its own recently enacted education reforms. Furthermore, recent budget crises left school systems with few local and state resources to meet the law's complex and, some say, overly rigid accountability rules.[16]

California state officials often employ coercive federalism relative to local governments. They require local governments to provide various services or adopt various policies without providing adequate resources. In turn, local officials respond by increasing user fees and local development fees. They may also privatize some services, allowing for-profit firms or nonprofit organizations to deliver services in lieu of government. They may also encourage planned unit developments, where homeowner associations, not cities, are responsible for street maintenance.

California in Washington

As with the other 49 states, California seeks to maximize its influence on federal policy making, a process called intergovernmental lobbying.

Compared to less diverse or smaller states, representing California in Washington is more challenging than size alone would suggest. In one notorious case, California's lack of clout once resulted in Congress awarding a federal earthquake research center to New York State rather than to earthquake-prone California.

According to many observers, California does not even receive in federal funds what it is presumably entitled to receive. In fiscal year 2003, the state sent $50 billion *more* to Washington in taxes than it received back in federal spending, making it a so-called "donor" state. Federal spending in the state includes everything from social security, medicare, and medicaid payments to military wages to highway construction. This "balance of payments" problem is largely due to Californians' higher than average personal incomes (resulting in higher taxes paid), a significantly younger population (resulting in fewer social security payments), and a slippage in federal procurement spending.[17] Making matters worse are other federal inequities that disadvantage California. For example, homeland security reimbursements to California do not include related costs of the California Highway Patrol. Furthermore, state officials argue that federal funding does not recognize potential terrorist targets such as the state's ports, transportation facilities, and tourist attractions. The federal government also underfunds some reimbursement programs such as the State Criminal Alien Assistance Program which promises to cover costs of incarcerating undocumented persons. For 2004–2005, that program reimbursed only 9.3 percent of California's related costs.[18]

The reasons for California's relative lack of influence in Washington are numerous and complex. First, the rules of the federalism game have shifted in the last two decades. Earlier, lobbyists in Washington worked routinely with executive branch bureaucrats who controlled the distribution of grant monies. As both funding and federal programs were reduced

Did You Know . . . ?

Did you know that it takes the population of 23 other less populated states to equal the population of California? Those states have a total of 46 U.S. senators to California's two.

in the 1980s, some grant decision making shifted from anonymous bureaucrats to members of Congress. As a result, California lobbyists found they had to influence the very content of legislation, not just "touch base" with grant administrators. This trend put a diverse and conflict-prone state at the mercy of a more diverse and conflict-ridden Congress.

Second, California lacks clout because it is so "distant" from the rest of the nation. According to public administration scholar Beryl A. Radin, "California is 3,000 miles from Washington, D.C., but the state's political culture creates another sort of distance—a tension between the way Californians view their role in the federal system and how it is viewed by others."[19] Despite donor-state data to the contrary, some non-California members of Congress may resent the state's sheer size and potential influence. According to the California Institute for Federal Policy Research, an organization founded to advance California interested in the nation's capital, "some opportunistic legislators from other states may continue to view California as a drain on the federal treasury and as a competitor for the federal dollars they covet. If that perception were ever valid, it certainly is no longer."[20] Washington veterans call this attitude the *ABC syndrome*—Anywhere But California.

Third, California's congressional delegation (two senators and 53 House members) is by far the nation's largest and most diverse. It faces both structural and ideological challenges. Structurally speaking, high-growth states like California are outnumbered in the U.S. Senate, where each state, regardless of size, gets two senators and, accordingly, two

votes (see Did You Know...?). Ideologically speaking, the California delegation includes some of the most liberal and most conservative members in the entire House. Sharp ideological divisions exist not only between Republicans and Democrats but also within both parties. In addition, California's diverse political geography (north/south, coastal/inland, urban/rural) creates diverse agendas within the delegation. While the challenge of uniting this diverse delegation has been likened to herding cats, incumbent-friendly reapportionment in 2001 lessened some divisions and resentments. Also, there have been notable bipartisan efforts on such issues as disaster insurance, skilled worker visas, and criminal alien incarceration funding. As House member Zoe Lofgren (D, San Jose) put it, "I know we're not going to agree on many things. I hope we can at least stand up and fight for our state on funding formulas and places where California is disadvantaged."[21]

Fourth, California is disadvantaged in the way that some formula grants are calculated. These grants are based on complicated formulas taking into account factors like population, income, poverty rates, education levels, and crime rates. California does relatively well with some grant programs (foster care and welfare) but suffers relative to medical care for the poor (Medi-Cal). Governor Arnold Schwarzenegger promised to collect more formula-based funding from Congress but undoubtedly that would be at the expense of smaller states. Furthermore, lawmakers outside California in positions of seniority and committee leadership would need to concur, an unlikely scenario.[22]

Given California's diversity of interests in Washington, several strategies have been employed to maximize the state's political effectiveness. First, growing numbers of the state's public and private interest groups now saturate the federal government with lobbying activity. Dozens of California counties, cities, special districts, and state agencies (including the legislature) are represented in Washington. All three public higher education systems (the community colleges, the California State University, and the University of California) employ registered lobbyists. Second, California's congressional delegation and California-based organizations have been most successful when they have framed their needs in broader terms and looked outside California for support. That is, they build coalitions. The broadest coalitions involve well-established associations such as the National Governors' Association, the Council of State Governments, or the National League of Cities. More narrow ones would involve other western states or border states. Because many issues come and go, California lobbyists must constantly build new coalitions to deal with new policy challenges. Third, California policymakers have discovered that it occasionally pays to downplay California's interests. State agencies have been known to quietly support or oppose a bill in Congress without actually acknowledging its impact on California. Private businesses from California, such as defense contractors and Silicon Valley computer companies, maintain the usual ties with home-district members but rarely coordinate their lobbying efforts.

California and the World: The Politics of Fences

Just as federalism delineates the relationships between California and the national government, there is a need to delineate the relationships between California and nation-states beyond its borders. According to former California Assembly Speaker Robert M. Hertzberg, "In no other era in the history of California have local interests been more directly tied to international concerns."[23] In an article entitled "California's Foreign Policy," James O. Goldsborough argues that "California is in many ways not a state, but a nation."[24] He argues that, as such, it needs and deserves its own foreign policy.

International pressures on the Golden State are primarily twofold. First, California is by far the most popular destination for both legal and illegal immigrants. What made the state attractive to early immigrants makes it attractive today. Second, California's colossal economy—the seventh largest in the world—is increasingly dependent on international trade. As the nation's largest exporter, the state relies on the ability to trade freely with Canada, Mexico, Europe, and its largest trading source—Asia. Much of California's "foreign policy" is related to immigration and trade. Here, the perimeters of California power are likened to literal and figurative fences. The general policy directions, discussed more fully in Chapter 13, have been to heighten fences relative to immigration and lower them relative to trade.

IMMIGRATION

Arguably, there are few fences between California and the world; that has always been so, at least as measured by immigration patterns. According to the Bureau of Citizenship and Immigration Services, immigrants now account for one in four California residents, the highest proportion in the nation. Between 1970 and 2000, California's immigrant population increased five-fold, from 1.8 million to 8.9 million. In 2001, the United States accepted more than 1 million legal immigrants; more than 27 percent of them opted for California. The leading countries of origin have been Mexico (3.8 million), the Philippines (630,000), Vietnam (470,000), and El Salvador (320,000).

© Nic Paget-Clarke / inmotionmagazine.com

PHOTO 3.1 Walling off California
One of three sets of iron walls and fences being developed along the U.S./Mexico border between San Diego, California and Tijuana, Baja California, Mexico.

The impact of legal immigration crisscrosses the state; immigrants comprise at least 10 percent of the population of 36 out of the state's 58 counties. Furthermore, about 40 percent of all undocumented or illegal immigrants (totaling about 2 million) locate in California.

Given the numbers involved, immigration from Mexico receives the most attention by policymakers, the media, and ordinary citizens. Movement across California's border with Mexico is nothing new. Historically, the nation's approach toward Mexican workers, one shared in California, has been called the "flower petal policy": "I need you, I need you not, I need you. . . ."[25] That is, immigrants are welcome depending upon whether the American workforce needs them. For instance, California welcomed Mexican immigrants after the Mexican Revolution of 1910 when Japanese and Chinese workers were unwelcome. During the Depression, people thought Mexicans were taking "American" jobs. But World War II resulted in another labor shortage, and Mexican laborers were welcomed once again. Renewed deportation efforts occurred in the 1950s and early in the 1980s. Although the "I need you not" rhetoric has been common in recent years, in reality Mexican labor has been essential to numerous California industries including garment makers, electronics, furniture manufacturing, food processing, and tourism.

The attraction of *El Norte* to Mexicans is understandable. Mexico's minimum wage at the California border is roughly $4.25 *per day*, compared to California's minimum wage of $6.75 per hour. This disparity has made the United States, and California in particular, economic magnets. Once they arrive and obtain jobs, frugal Mexican American workers often use excess income to support family members left behind.

Did You Know . . . ?

Not all immigrants to California come from Mexico or East Asia. In Sacramento County, the top nation of birth of immigrants in 2001 was Ukraine. In Santa Clara County, it was India.

No wonder Mexico maintains ten consulates in California, more than any other nation.

Federal immigration policy has been to better secure the border, to shore up the fence. Facing the reality of illegal immigrants already here, Congress passed the Immigration Reform and Control Act of 1986 (IRCA). This law created an amnesty program leading to legal residency for more than 3 million foreigners, over half of whom lived in California. About 75 percent of those were from Mexico. One purpose was to unite family members divided only by national boundaries. The children of these newly legalized aliens became fully eligible for any and all government services and benefits. Critics of current policy complain that some immigrants, mindful of the benefits, cross the border in order to give birth in the United States. California has received only a portion of the federal aid intended to cushion the fiscal impact of the IRCA.

In 1994 the Immigration and Naturalization Service (INS) launched "Operation Gatekeeper" to stem the tide of illegal immigrants pouring into California along the San Diego–Tijuana border—the busiest land-border crossing in the world. In 1996, Congress followed up with the Illegal Immigration Reform and Immigrant Responsibility Act. This law increased criminal penalties for immigration-related offenses and authorized the INS to hire more border patrol agents, construct new fencing, and employ new underground sensors and night vision equipment. Furthermore, the law attempted to limit access to certain public benefits even by illegal immigrants, a provision later declared unconstitutional by the Supreme Court. In the years following the terrorist attacks of September 11, 2001,

U.S. Border Patrol budgets and staffing have increased dramatically.

Have these policies secured the California/Mexico border? Apparently not. While the entry of undocumented immigrants has declined along the San Diego-Tijuana border, entry points have shifted eastward into more perilous desert terrain. To cope with these hostile conditions, some immigrants have paid thousands of dollars to borderwise *coyotes* or *polleros* to be smuggled into the United States and eventually to California. Deaths due to dehydration, exposure, and violence have increased. While the border buildup has failed to reduce the flow of undocumented immigrants, it has encouraged longer stays by those who do manage to enter the United States.[26] In 2004, President George W. Bush proposed to offer temporary guest worker visas to millions of undocumented workers if they already had jobs or job offers in the United States. The visas would not guarantee future citizenship. The proposal and congressional variations of it did not seem to garner much support.

Legal immigration presents its own challenges. In recent years, some of California's technology firms have outsourced certain tasks to nations with cheaper labor pools or have replaced highly paid workers at home with lesser paid immigrants.

TRADE

In contrast to immigration, the approach of California and the federal government to world trade has been to lower economic fences. In 1993, Congress passed the North American Free Trade Act (NAFTA) to encourage trade between Canada, the United States, and Mexico.

Over time, it would eliminate tariffs completely and remove many nontariff barriers to trade such as import licenses. Over ten years, it has created the world's largest free trade zone with a combined gross domestic product of $11.4 trillion. Overall, California's trade with Canada and Mexico jumped from $12 billion in 1993 to $26 billion in 2002. In 2000, Mexico surpassed Japan as the state's largest trading partner. NAFTA's specific impact on California varies from industry to industry and locale to locale. The San Diego area was a major beneficiary as foreign companies like Sony and Samsung located there to take advantage of low-wage assembly-line labor south of the border. Four hundred miles north in Santa Cruz County, food-processing plants closed, victims of soaring agricultural imports from Mexico and beyond.[27]

Beyond NAFTA, California has taken action on its own. In the 1980s, it established the California World Trade Commission with offices in numerous foreign capitals. In recent years, an Export Development Office has assisted California businesses as they seek international markets. Also, California officials have collaborated with their Mexican counterparts on a host of border-related issues including air pollution, poultry diseases, and public health concerns. Yet, many observers agree that economic conditions and public policies in other nations, especially Mexico, affect the politics of borders and fences more so than various efforts to improve bilateral relations. According to Harley Shaiken of UC Berkeley's Center for Latin American Studies, "There's no wall that can be built, no conceivable way that can stop Mexican migration if Mexico needs 1 million jobs per year (and it's creating fewer than 500,000)."[28]

Conclusion

California's position relative to the nation as a whole is most interesting. Its political develop-ment has resulted in constitutional provisions both similar and dissimilar to constitutions in other states. California's diversity is mirrored both in its constitution and in the variety of representatives it sends to Congress. Its sheer size makes it the focal point of media attention when voters dramatically alter their constitution. As a result, California can give birth to national political movements through such changes (for example, Proposition 13 and the "taxpayers' revolt").

California's constitutional development reflects American political theory. The state constitution provides the basic elements of representative government—the cornerstone of American political thought. Political elites dominated California's two constitutional conventions and greatly influenced much of its language. Well-organized interests are amply provided for in the document. Yet the constitution allows for widespread group participation and has been partly responsible for the state's political pluralism. It also planted the seeds of hyperpluralism by dividing political responsibility, limiting some governmental powers, and, through the initiative process, compromising the notion of representative government.

California's size and diversity have affected its relationship to the national government of which it is a part. The state is both the automatic recipient of large amounts of federal spending and the source of resentment at the money being spent. But California's interests are so diffuse and its congressional delegation so diverse that the state rarely speaks with one voice, even when doing so would be in its own best interest. Finally, California's relationships with the rest of the world present an ongoing challenge and reflect the politics of diversity. A solid black line on maps, California's border is in reality a porous screen door through which flow workers, families, jobs, and dollars. Efforts have been made to raise the fence in terms of immigration but at the same time lower the fence in terms of international trade.

KEY TERMS

perimeters of politics   (p. 43)

constitutionalism   (p. 43)

Constitutions of 1849 and 1878   (pp. 44–45)

constitutional convention, legislative proposal, initiative   (pp. 46–47)

referendum and recall   (p. 47)

dual, cooperative, centralized, on-your-own, and pragmatic federalism   (pp. 49–51)

ABC syndrome   (p. 52)

Immigration Reform and Control Act (1986)   (p. 55)

Illegal Immigration Reform and Immigrant Responsibility Act (1996)   (p. 55)

NAFTA   (pp. 55–56)

REVIEW QUESTIONS

1. Describe the concept of constitutionalism and illustrate from California's constitution.
2. Contrast the two California constitutions.
3. In what ways is California's constitution much like those of other states? In what ways is it different or unique?
4. California's constitution both planted the seeds of hyperpluralism and over time mirrored the political subcultures of the state. Illustrate this statement.
5. What developments were occurring in California during each stage of American federalism?
6. How has the reduced role of the federal government affected California? Given these conditions, how do Californians represent their interests in the nation's capital?
7. How is California politics impacted by its proximity to Mexico and the Pacific Rim?

WEB ACTIVITIES

The California Constitution
(www.leginfo.ca.gov/const.html)
The Legislative Counsel of California maintains this website, which contains a fully searchable copy of the state constitution. Contrast it to the U.S. Constitution.

The California Institute
(www.calinst.org)
This nonprofit Washington, D.C.–based organization analyzes federal policy as it relates to California and advises the California delegation in Congress accordingly. The site helps you to assess the impact of a particular federal policy on California.

INFOTRAC® COLLEGE EDITION ARTICLES

For additional reading, go to InfoTrac® College Edition, your online research library, at http://www.infotrac.thomsonlearning.com

State Sees Nominal Return on Funds Sent to Washington

NAFTA: A Letdown for California Border Region

Immigration Problems Require Multi-Pronged Approach

NOTES

1. Winston W. Crouch, John C. Bollens, and Stanley Scott, *California Government and Politics*, 6th ed. (Englewood Cliffs, NJ: Prentice-Hall, 1977), 29, 30.
2. See Article IX, Section 6 adopted November 4, 1952.
3. See Article VII, Section 9, originally adopted November 4, 1952.
4. *Roe v. Wade*, 410 U.S. 113 (1973).
5. California Constitution, Article I, Section 1.
6. California Constitution, 1849, Article XI, Section 21.
7. Article III, Section 6, adopted November 4, 1986.
8. See Susan B. Hansen, *The Politics of Taxation* (New York: Praeger, 1983), 233.
9. "The Federalist No. 45," in Jacob E. Cooke, ed. *The Federalist* (Middletown, Conn.: Wesleyan University Press, 1961), 311.
10. Ibid., "The Federalist No. 17," 108, 106.

11. Morton Grodzins, *The American System* (Chicago: Rand McNally, 1966), 8–9.

12. Ibid., 265.

13. Charles Press, *State and Community Governments in the Federal System* (New York: John Wiley, 1979), 78.

14. President Ronald Reagan, "State of the Union Speech, January 26, 1982," *Public Papers of the Presidents, Vol. I* (Washington, D.C.: U.S. Government Printing Office, 1982), 75.

15. Parris N. Glendening and Mavis Mann Reeves, *Pragmatic Federalism: An Intergovernmental View of American Government,* 2nd ed. (Pacific Palisades, CA: Palisades Publishers, 1984), 27–28.

16. EdSource, "No Child Left Behind in California: The Impact of the Federal NCLB Act So Far" (January 2004). (Available at www.edsource. org).

17. California Institute for Federal Policy Research, *California's Balance of Payments with the Federal Treasury FY 1981–2003* (February, 2005). (Available online at www.calinst.org/pubs/ balance 2003.htm/).

18. *Governor's Budget Summary, 2004–2005* (Scramento: Governor's Office, 2004), 207–210.

19. Beryl A. Radin, "California in Washington," in John J. Kirlin and Donald R. Winkler, eds. *California Policy Choices, Vol. 6* (Sacramento: University of Southern California, School of Public Administration, 1990), 280.

20. California Institute, *California's Balance of Payments.*

21. Quoted in Edward Epstein, "House Delegation Tries to Mend Fences," *San Francisco Chronicle,* December 4, 2003.

22. For more on this challenge, see Dana Wilkie, "Can Schwarzenneger Become the Collectinator," *California Journal* 35 (January 2004), 30–34.

23. Robert M. Hertzberg, "Global California: Greater Legislative Participation in International Affairs," *Spectrum: The Journal of State Government* 76 (Fall, 2003), 22.

24. James O. Goldsborough, "California's Foreign Policy," *Foreign Affairs* 72 (Spring 1993): 88–96.

25. Daniel Levy and Gabriel Szekely, *Mexico: Paradoxes of Stability and Change* (Boulder, CO: Westview Press, 1987), 213.

26. Belinda I. Reyes, Hans P. Johnson, and Richard Van Swearingen, *Holding the Line? The Effect of the Recent Border Buildup on Unauthorized Immigration* (San Francisco: Public Policy Institute of California, 2002).

27. Evelyn Iritani, "NAFTA: 10 Years Later," *Los Angeles Times,* January 19, 2004.

28. Quoted in Tyche Hendricks, "Dangerous Border: Border Solutions Remain Elusive," *San Francisco Chronicle,* May 31, 2004.

PART TWO

Political Participation in California

The cure for the ailments of democracy is more democracy.
—John Dewey, 1927

Was Dewey right? Many Californians seem convinced he was; others are quite convinced he was not. California's history of political participation has been one of both inclusion and exclusion. Although there have been times when some groups have been encouraged not to participate, the march of time has been in the other direction. Gradually, more and more people have established the right to participate if not the habit of doing so. Part 2 examines this march toward political participation in the Golden State.

Chapter 4, "Direct Democracy in a Hyperpluralistic Age," surveys the mechanisms for political involvement originally envisioned and developed by the Progressives. Although the tools of recall and referendum were intended as safety valves, the popular initiative has become one of the most important policy vehicles in California politics. Begun as a weapon to curb interest group power, interest groups now use it to augment and even sidestep the Sacramento-based policy process. Today, it can result in either policy progress or political gridlock, depending on the issue.

Chapter 5, "The Political Behavior of Californians," describes the various levels of actual political participation among Californians. "Actual" participation means not only those voting but also those exiting the system (moving elsewhere) and political protest. This chapter also explores why many Californians either cannot or will not vote when given the chance. The chapter also describes the changing nature of partisanship and how it varies across California's political landscape. Although the Golden State can still be divided into two political classes, voters and nonvoters, some traditional nonvoters are participating at greater levels than in the past.

Chapter 6, "Linking People and Institutions," deals with the activities and people who help link ordinary Californians with the major institutions of policy making in the state. Described in detail are the mass media, political parties, elections, and interest groups. The diversity of the state is increasingly represented in the rich variety of media, political party alternatives, frequent and varied elections, and substantial interest group growth. The sum total of all this activity contributes to hyperpluralism.

C H A P T E R   4

Direct Democracy in a Hyperpluralistic Age

In Brief

In a mature representative democracy, voters play a key role in governing. In a very real sense, the "people" are sovereign, yet they do not and never have behaved in a political vacuum. Just as the public officials they elect, the voters themselves are influenced by profound social, economic, and political forces they do not fully understand. Consider these questions: Why does the electorate vote so often in California? How can they throw out elected politicians without waiting for the next election? What

empowers them to directly legislate on policy issues about which they know little or nothing? The average Californian is probably unable to give cogent answers to these questions. Yet that same person would heartily defend all those electoral powers as necessary in a democracy.

In Chapter 4, these questions are addressed first by unraveling the various layers of history that shroud the origins of the typical contemporary California voter. Beginning with political corruption and emerging urban problems during the "politics of modernization," we trace the rise of the Progressive movement in California; describe its continuing presence in modern politics; and examine the hyperpluralistic election system that has resulted. In the end, what emerges is something of a paradox in the Progressive legacy: the same reforms that gave voters ultimate power also have contributed to the policy and political gridlock we observe in California today.

The Impact of Progressivism

It seems Californians are perennially voting, thinking about the next election, or recovering from the last one. They are inundated with more candidate and policy choices than most Americans could imagine. In some respects, Progressive reforms predestined this state of affairs. *Progressivism* was a turn-of-the-century political movement that sought to rid politics of corrupting influences, return power to "the people," and make government more businesslike. The movement both benefited and departed from a populist strain in American politics that distrusted political and economic elites. According to historian Richard Hofstadter, "Populism had been overwhelmingly rural and provincial. The ferment of the Progressive era was urban, middle-class, and nationwide. Above all, Progressivism differed from Populism in the fact that the middle classes of the cities not only joined the trend toward protest but took over its leadership."[1]

The era from about 1900 to 1920 was one of social upheaval and intense political competition among social classes in the United States. The Progressive reformers were in the middle of this upheaval. Across the nation, these reformers were appalled by the political dark side of the industrial revolution. From coast to coast, new immigrant voters were routinely bribed by members of urban political machines. Unelected bosses of both parties easily controlled many city halls and statehouses. Rather than being above the dirt, political parties were rolling around in it.

Preoccupied by the demands of both machine bosses and corporate moguls, local and state legislators neglected the mounting problems faced by cities in the late 1800s and early 1900s—labor unrest, unemployment, poverty, and urban crowding. Political corruption was only part of the story. As urban problems mounted, the machine bosses were poorly equipped to manage the increasingly complex affairs of city hall. In what Hofstadter called a "status revolution," urban professionals, intellectuals, and muckraking journalists joined to expose the incapacity of the machines to govern effectively. The differences between these warring groups were profound. To the typical machine boss, politics was individualistic, the essence of good personal relations. To the Progressives, politics was a moral obligation to efficiently manage public resources for a larger public good.[2] They assumed there was one public and one public good achievable through consensus. According to Lewis L. Gould, the Progressive era introduced a number of underlying themes in American politics we see today: "Government regulation of economic power, the application of scientific ideas to social problems, a concern for the quality and preservation of the environment, and reform of political institutions to make government more effective."[3]

Californians easily equate the Progressive era with the introduction of the initiative, referendum, and recall. Yet across the nation as well as in California, an entire set of other reforms were enacted to inhibit the influence of political machines. They included these:

• *Direct primaries:* The convention system of nominating candidates was easily controlled by bosses. Many states enacted a direct primary that bypassed party organizations. This enabled voters themselves to nominate candidates who would compete in general elections.

• *At-large elections:* At the local level, at-large elections, in which candidates run citywide rather than from a specific district or ward, were instituted to minimize machine control of individual votes. Progressives also hoped voters would adopt citywide perspectives toward governing and policy issues.

• *Nonpartisan elections:* Another reform removed party designations next to candidates' names on ballots. In California, this applied to all local and judicial offices requiring an election. Reformers thought that machine influence would lessen and that endorsements by "good government" groups would gain importance.

• *Merit systems and short ballots:* To further minimize the power of machines, the concept of a civil service was introduced. Government workers would be hired on the basis of merit, not politics. Also, voters would directly elect fewer officials at the local level. In a short ballot system, the few officials directly responsible to the voters would appoint other administrators.

• *Professional management:* Instead of using machines and poorly trained political "hacks" to run local governments, this reform created positions such as city manager, a professional administrator who would ideally be above and apart from politics. Today, most California cities have city managers or city administrators.

Progressivism: California Style

California was a major center of Progressive era activity. By the turn of the century, its politics exhibited many of the problems detested by the reformers. Analogous to the urban political machines elsewhere in the nation, California had its own statewide machine, the Southern Pacific Railroad (SPR). Its brazen

and arrogant exercise of power became an easy target for the Progressives. Elsewhere in the United States, economic problems and social turbulence were blamed on new immigrants from Europe. In California, comparable problems were blamed on Chinese laborers and the railroad that originally employed them.

California Progressivism possessed five characteristics in common with the movement nationwide. *First,* it represented to some extent both the *individualistic and moralistic political subcultures* in California. On one hand, progressive reformers wanted to pursue their own agendas, unencumbered by big business monopolies or selfish labor union influence. They acted as if they were the heirs of the individualistic ideals of the liberal tradition. On the other hand, they possessed a moral sense. As historian George E. Mowry noted, the California Progressive "pictured himself as a complete individual wholly divorced from particular economic as well as class interests. Ready to do justice in the name of the common good, he was, in his own estimation, something akin to Plato's guardians, above and beyond the reach of corrupting material forces."[4] Historian Spencer Olin paraphrased an old hymn title and called them "Onward Christian Capitalists."[5]

Second, Progressivism was *white and middle class.* According to Mowry, "the California progressive leader was a young man, often less than forty years old . . . probably had been born in the Middle West . . . carried a north-European name . . . came of old American stock . . . was, in the jargon of his day, 'well fixed' . . . invariably a member of his town's chamber of commerce . . . until 1900, a conservative Republican."[6] Not just middle class, Progressives were anti-upper class and anti-lower class. In 1908, the progressive *California Weekly* editorialized, "Nearly all the problems which vex society have their sources above or below the middle class man. From above come the problems of predatory wealth. From below come the problems of poverty and of pigheaded brutish criminality."[7]

Third, as with the rest of the nation, it was *urban* in nature. Although California Progressivism capitalized on agrarian unrest, its roots were in the state's emerging coastal cities. By 1910, 60 percent of California's population was urban; almost half lived in San Francisco, Los Angeles, and Alameda counties. In these places, the progressives waged war with organized labor, the Southern Pacific, and in San Francisco, a political machine controlled by Abe Ruef, a boss in the mold of New York City's legendary Boss Tweed.

Fourth, California Progressivism was *nonradical.* Its leaders were small business owners, lawyers, real estate operators, doctors, and journalists. As members of an upwardly mobile middle class, they were class conscious but not out to destroy those classes unlike their own. They sought to reduce the influence of one corporation, not to destroy the corporate idea. They rejected the socialist tendencies and methods of the labor unions, not labor itself. The Progressives sought to clean up government, not restructure it. Sensing even then a splintering of the state into diverse, hyperpluralistic groups, California's progressives, according to Mowry, "sought to blot out not only the rising clash of economic groups but the groups themselves, as conscious economic and political entities."[8]

Fifth, California's Progressives depended on entrepreneurial leadership—those dynamic individuals who could rally relatively unorganized interests against entrenched power structures. For instance, through the influence of wealthy physician John Randolph Haynes, Los Angeles was one of the first cities in the nation to adopt local versions of the initiative, referendum, and recall. Other cities in the state rapidly followed suit. Los Angeles was ripe for this reform. Collis Huntington of the Southern Pacific tried to monopolize harbor facilities in the Los Angeles area and had made numerous enemies in the process.

Another leader was Hiram Johnson, a prosperous San Francisco attorney who had helped prosecute local political corruption. His targets were the political machine headed by Boss Ruef and the railroad machine headed by William F. Herrin, a Big Four crony. A statewide reform group, the Lincoln-Roosevelt League, talked Johnson into running for governor in 1910. In a style reminiscent of Theodore Roosevelt, Johnson campaigned throughout the state by automobile (he boycotted trains for obvious reasons), promising at every stop to "kick the Southern Pacific Railroad out of politics."[9] Johnson and other Lincoln-Roosevelt candidates ran as progressive Republicans and won huge election victories that November.

At the height of their success, the Progressives in California energized state government and institutionalized all the reforms associated with the era. In some ways, modern reform-minded groups such as Common Cause, the League of Women Voters, and the Public Interest Research Group (CALPIRG) have continued the Progressive tradition. They view their own policy agendas as equally enlightened and have used the old reforms such as the initiative process to enact their goals. Twenty-three states eventually adopted the initiative, but no state uses it more prolifically than California.[10]

Selected Initiative Battles in California

Progressive era reforms are so familiar that modern Californians take them for granted. The reform that has become most familiar to voters is the initiative. In theory, the initiative would empower ordinary people to fight entrenched special interests. In reality, it quickly evolved into a weapon readily available to any group willing and able to use it. The individualist political subculture runs deep in California's political development, and it did not take long for individuals and groups to discover how valuable the initiative process could be. For example, in 1924—13 short years after its advent—Artie Samish, then employed by the Motor Carriers Association, used an initiative

PHOTO 4.1   Hiram Johnson Campaigning
Progressive reformer Hiram Johnson on the campaign trail.

to stabilize taxes on bus companies (he later became an infamous lobbyist). By 1939, well-financed interest groups were initiating measures more often than ad hoc reform groups. This trend has continued to the present. Instead of using it as the safety valve it was intended to be, interest groups *and* politicians use it to bypass the legislature. A brief survey of four recent initiatives will demonstrate the evolving role the initiative has played in California's electoral politics.

PROPOSITION 13: GIVE THE MONEY BACK

The first of these initiatives, Proposition 13, is a classic measure rooted in California's real estate market. In the 1970s, California home prices skyrocketed and so did property taxes.

Legislators and Governor Jerry Brown could not agree on how to best provide tax relief. Homeowner frustration mounted. Los Angeles real estate developer and apartment owner Howard Jarvis proposed cutting property taxes by half and curbing their subsequent growth. He formed the populist-sounding United Organization of Taxpayers, which gathered a record 1.2 million signatures to qualify this historic tax reduction measure for the June 1978 ballot. Despite the dire predictions about its potential consequences, Proposition 13 passed with 64 percent of the vote. Nearly every electoral group measured by political scientists supported it. The consequences *were* dire. With property taxes cut by 57 percent, local services were slashed severely. Local governments, especially counties and school districts, became increasingly dependent on state "bailouts" to

> ## Did You Know . . . ?
>
> All nine pages of Article XIII Section A in the California State Constitution are devoted to Proposition 13 and voter-approved revisions of it. This is about the same length as Article I in the United States Constitution detailing the powers of Congress.

fill in revenue shortfalls. The bailouts became an annual feature of the state budget, and, in the process, local government lost a measure of its autonomy. The crowning blow to this autonomy was passage of the 1993–94 state budget, which not only eliminated the bailout but transferred $2.6 billion in local property taxes to the state for education spending.

Another consequence was the so-called Proposition 13 effect. This is how it works: Under "13," a family purchases a subdivision house for $500,000 in 2005, triggering an increase in property taxes to 1 percent of that new figure or $5,000. The people next door purchased a comparable house in 1979 for $60,000; because Proposition 13 limits the annual property tax increase to just 2 percent, their 2006 taxes (not including other levies) would be only $1,024. The 2006 tax disparity between the two similar homes is $4,076. To avoid sizeable jumps in property taxes, it pays to stay put. Because older homeowners tend to move less often than more mobile young families, the latter group is penalized for moving and pays a disproportionate share of the state's residential property taxes.[11] Inevitable real estate turnover and inflation have reduced the impact of this effect to some extent. In 1992, the U.S. Supreme Court, in *Nordlinger* v. *Hahn*, upheld Proposition 13, including this unequal treatment of property owners. Proposition 13 also made it exceedingly difficult to raise most taxes (a two-thirds vote of the people is usually required). It encouraged local officials to approve land use projects that generated sales taxes not controlled by Proposition 13 (see Chapter 12). Lastly, it spawned a generation of political leaders loath to reform the measure or even question its wisdom, at least in public.

PROPOSITION 5: CASINO FEVER

The Super Bowl of recent California initiatives was Proposition 5, which earned 63 percent of the vote in November 1998. A record-shattering $100 million was spent on it by proponents and opponents. With that kind of money, voters endured a blizzard of television spots, radio ads, and mailbox material. Political consultant Alan Hoffenblum speculated that "more people were aware of Proposition 5 than were aware of who was running for governor."

Proposition 5 stemmed from a longstanding dispute between the 40 Indian tribes that run casinos in California and state officials. Federal law allows Native American tribes to engage in whatever gaming activity is allowed by the states in which they are located. The California State Lottery, approved by the voters in 1984, presented a dilemma. Should the state/tribal compacts that govern Indian gambling allow Indians to use whatever machines the state lottery employs? At issue were slot-like video machines that were already in use on some reservations but that the state and federal governments considered illegal.

Proposition 5 required the governor to approve virtually any tribal casino application. No restrictions would be placed on the number of casinos or machines per casino. The contested video slots would be allowed. A tribal-appointed gaming board would oversee security and personnel issues, but ultimate authority for casino operations would rest with the tribe. A federal

CALIFORNIA VOICES

On Proposition 5

Our biggest challenge was to convey that it was OK to be sympathetic to Indians and still vote No.

—"No-on-5" spokesperson Gina Stassi

I felt compassion for the Indians. They've been on the sidelines for so long. This is their chance to get a part of the American dream.

—South Sacramento voter Arselia Santos

Never at any point in California history had 88 tribes ever gathered together in one tribal location to declare their unity on an issue.

—Spokesperson Waltona Manion, on location to film a TV spot

SOURCE: Claudia Buck, "A Gamble Paid Off," *California Journal* 29 (December 1998): 46–57.

law requiring casino profits to be spent on Indian social services and "tribal administration" was unaffected by the initiative.

Proposition 5 backers called themselves Californians for Indian Self-Reliance. They argued that, as sovereign nations, they are morally justified to run their own casinos. Furthermore, casino proceeds have lifted many Indians out of poverty and off of welfare. They accused opponents of a "shameful anti-Indian assault by Las Vegas and its California shills." The opponents, the Coalition Against Unregulated Gambling, were heavily funded by Las Vegas casinos. They consisted of an unlikely collection of interests representing labor, law enforcement, local officials, horse tracks, and Christian fundamentalists. In their view, Proposition 5 sanctioned "unregulated, untaxed, unlimited" gambling.

True, there were lofty, principled arguments about discrimination against Indians, the need for self-reliance, and the evils of gambling. But, at its most crass level, Proposition 5 was a battle between Indian casino money and Las Vegas casino money. In the end, the tribes spent nearly $70 million to accomplish their goal, more than double the $28 million spent by Nevada interests. Individual spending indicated how high the stakes were. One single tribe—the San Manuel—spent more than $27 million and Mirage Resorts, Inc. spent more than $9 million. To initiatives expert

Craig Holman, the lavish spending on Proposition 5 was "a complete contradiction of what the grass-roots initiative process is all about."[12]

PROPOSITION 22: GAY MARRIAGE

PROPOSED LAW

SECTION 1. This act may be cited as the "California Defense of Marriage Act."

SECTION 2. Section 308.5 is added to the Family Code, to read:

308.5. Only marriage between a man and a woman is valid or recognized in California.

This language was the actual text of Proposition 22, a controversial measure on the March 7, 2000 ballot. Those 14 words galvanized both supporters and opponents of gay rights and gay marriage in California. Although the proposition seemed simple enough, the issue it addressed was quite complex.

In an effort to seek societal recognition and fight discrimination, gay rights activists had demanded that gay marriages be given the same legal footing as heterosexual marriages. If they could achieve that in one state, presumably such marriages would need to be recognized in other states. The United States Constitution provides that "Full Faith and Credit shall be given in each State to the public acts, Records, and judicial Proceedings of every other State" (Article IV, Section 1). Concerned about that possibility, Congress passed and President Bill Clinton signed the Defense of Marriage Act in 1996. This law permitted states to not recognize gay marriages performed in other states. By early 2000, 30 states had passed similar laws.

The concerns of the gay community extended beyond the legal recognition of same-gender marriages. They feared that nonrecognition would result in the denial of various rights, including hospital visitations, inheritance, and dependent health insurance.

Prior to Proposition 22, California disallowed the marriage of same sex couples, but customarily recognized as legally valid all marriages occurring outside the state under Article IV. Proposition 22 proponents had become alarmed because Hawaii had come close to recognizing gay marriages and Vermont was on the verge of doing so (it legalized same-sex civil unions in May 2000).

The impetus for Proposition 22 came from California State Senator William "Pete" Knight (R-Palmdale) who had unsuccessfully sought similar limits in the state legislature. Knight's involvement was intriguing in that his own son was gay and his gay brother had died of AIDS. Lining up to support the measure were various religious groups: the Mormon Church, the California Catholic Conference of Bishops, the state Republican Party, and the Hispanic Business Roundtable. Opposed were various gay rights organizations: the American Civil Liberties Union, a number of labor unions, the California Democratic Party, and still other religious leaders. By the end of the campaign, Proposition 22's supporters outspent its opponents by a wide margin—$9.5 million versus $5 million. As usual, much of this money was spent on television advertising.

In the end, Proposition 22 passed with 61 percent of the vote. The only region to oppose it was the Bay Area; they rejected it by a 69–31 percent margin. The statewide margin of support for 22 was even higher than preelection polling would have predicted. Analysts speculated that large numbers of conservatives turned out because of a competitive Republican presidential primary campaign and effective get-out-the-vote efforts by groups like the Traditional Values Coalition.

Gay rights advocates were both disheartened and energized. Some thought they should seek to qualify their own pro-gay marriage initiative. Others thought that they should press their agenda in the state legislature. Most observers predicted that the struggle over gay marriage was hardly over. Polls suggest that fully 81 percent of Californians oppose discrimination based on sexual orientation; 54 percent think that homophobia is morally wrong. In addition, it appeared that younger voters were more concerned about discrimination against gays than were older voters.[13] Gay rights activists became newly energized in early 2004 when, contrary to Proposition 22, San Francisco Mayor Gavin Newsome declared that gay marriages would be viewed as legal in his city. While his unilateral actions were immediately challenged in California courts, hundreds of gay couples wed in the months following his order.[14]

PROPOSITION 71: STEM CELL RESEARCH

In December 2002, State Senator Deborah Ortiz met over dinner with a group of scientists to plot her next move. The state legislature had rejected her bill to commit a few million dollars to studying stem cells. A stem cell is a type of cell found in humans and animals that has the potential to turn into specialized cells capable of reproducing themselves in the body. Because healthy stem cells can replace damaged cells, medical researchers believe that this research can lead to potential cures for all kinds of diseases, including Alzheimer's, cancer, and spinal cord injuries. While public funding was rejected, the legislature did make such research legal in California. At the federal level, President George W. Bush had limited federal funding for embryonic stem cell research. These cells are usually extracted from extra

PHOTO 4.2   San Francisco Gay Marriages
Hundreds of same-sex couples waited in line for hours to apply for their marriage licenses and to say their vows at San Francisco City Hall on Monday, February 16, 2004.

embryos resulting from fertility clinic procedures. Viewing such procedures as tantamount to abortion, some members of Congress wished to criminalize such research. The senator's dinner group envisioned California as a global center for such innovation. But how would a costly effort such as this be funded? Ortiz's answer was simple enough: Take it to the voters. Her dinner companions agreed that the funding vehicle would be a sizeable public bond initiative.

A few months after that initial gathering, a group of parents met at the home of movie director Jerry Zucker and his wife, Janet. Included were Bakersfield developer Tom Coleman and his wife Polly and Bay Area real estate financier Robert Klein. These people differed in faith and politics but what drew them together was the fact that each had a child with juvenile diabetes, one of those diseases that stem cell research might someday cure. That was motivation enough. Ultimately, these concerned, affluent, and politically savvy parents and their allies would lead, organize, and

substantially fund the campaign for Proposition 71—the California Stem Cell Research and Cures Act. The act would create the California Institute of Regenerative Medicine. A 29-member board would oversee the Institute and fund research grants pursuant to its goals.

The road to the ballot box would be a long one. Early polls suggested that such a bond measure could win but narrowly. The polling also revealed that the more likely voters understood the basics of stem cell research the more likely they would be willing to fund it. Drafting the initiative language would be tricky. To assuage the fears of some social conservatives, human reproductive cloning research would be banned. Given a backdrop of state budget deficits, the repayment of the bonds structured to have as little short-term impact on the state's general fund as possible. The total funding necessary for an estimated ten-year effort was researched and discussed. Other initiative language had to address issues of intellectual property, conflict of interest rules, and grant administration. Thirty drafts and eight months later, the final initiative language authorized the state to sell $3 billion in general obligation bonds spaced out at no more than $350 million per year.

The campaign for Proposition 71 benefited from some developments beyond its own control. During the summer of 2004, former President Ronald Reagan died after a long battle against Alzheimer's. His wife, Nancy, had expressed support for stem cell research that could someday cure the illness known to many as "the long goodbye." Media coverage of his passing often included mention of his disease and the promise of such research. By mid-August, long before most voters pay attention to November ballot items, 40 percent of likely voters said they were aware of Proposition 71, a much higher figure than voter awareness on three other health-related measures.

As is the case in presidential election years, the fall campaign for Proposition 72 shared precious political space with the presidential election campaign, congressional races, and numerous other propositions. In October, proponents aired a television advertisement featuring the late actor Christopher Reeve who had become an activist for the disabled after a 1995 horse-riding accident left him paralyzed from the neck down. He asked voters to "stand up for those who can't." Adding to the poignancy of the appeal was the fact that Reeve died six days after filming the ad. Other high-profile endorsements came from actor and Parkinson's disease patient Michael J. Fox as well as Governor Arnold Schwarzenegger.

Opponents of Proposition 71, including many fiscal and religious conservatives, were unable to mount a credible campaign. By election day, proponents had raised over $12 million including large donations from venture capitalists and wealthy individuals including eBay founder Pierre Omidyar and Microsoft's Bill Gates. Opponents raised just $650,000—mere chicken feed in media-dependent California. Proposition 71 won with 59 percent of the vote. By mid 2005, the new California Center for Regenerative Medicine had its 29-member board, president, skeletal staff, and plans to award research grants.[15]

The Initiative Mess

The stories behind Propositions 13, 5, 22, and 71 are typical of many others, and they point to some disturbing trends. Article titles give you a clue: "Initiatives: Too Much of a Good Thing," "Hiram's Folly?" "California Initiatives: Out of Control," "California: The State That Tied Its Own Hands," and "Is This Any Way to Run a State?" Veteran journalist Peter Schrag believes today's initiative process has caused a "seismic shift in the state's political center of gravity."[16] Onetime assembly speaker and San Francisco mayor Willie Brown went so far as to call the initiative process "the single greatest threat to democracy in California."[17]

What has happened to this ultimate tool of the sovereign voter? In terms of democratic theory, there were two faulty assumptions. Before the initiative was instituted, there was *misplaced confidence in legislators as competent representatives.* This assumes that elected representatives will choose decision over indecision; that they will consult public opinion, rather than the preferences of special interests, especially when the two conflict. Consider this question: Are legislators primarily trustees using their own best judgment to represent the broad interests of their constituents or delegates following each and every constituent preference? The classic debate between trustee and delegate functions of legislators usually assumes constituents are voters back home, not the interest groups and lobbyists with whom contemporary legislators have much more contact.[18]

After the initiative process was established, there was *misplaced confidence in the voters as competent legislators.* Admittedly, political scientists do not always agree on this point. Years ago, Lester Milbrath observed, "we should not expect [the average voter] to give a lot of attention to, and be active in resolving issues of public policy. Nor should we expect him to stand up and be counted on every issue that comes along."[19] Political scientist Thomas Cronin takes a more generous view. He suggests that voters approach initiatives cautiously and vote against measures unless they see tangible personal or public benefit. "Voters who do vote on ballot measures do so more responsibly and intelligently than we have any right to expect." He concludes that bad legislation is just as likely to come from the legislature as from the initiative process.[20]

Many observers blame the state's initiative mess largely on how the process has evolved. In many respects, it epitomizes *hyperpluralistic politics in a technological age.* Remember, California is a large, diverse, industrial state with a complex economy and a large, relatively intrusive state government. The initiative was intended to be a powerful, nonpartisan, and infrequently used tool against singular interests. But California has long since passed the stage of one monopolistic interest such as the SPR. Writer Carey McWilliams once called the state capital the "marketplace of California" where competing groups "bid for allotments of state power."[21] Now the initiative process itself has become California's new marketplace where all manner of groups view the initiative as a vehicle to achieve desired policy outcomes. According to political scientist Elizabeth R. Gerber, citizen groups tend to use direct legislation to bring about policy change whereas economic groups tend to use it to block policy change.[22] Furthermore, in an ironic development, the Progressive assumption that initiatives would bypass political parties has proved to be untrue. In fact, research suggests that California's political parties themselves employ ballot measures to promote their own policy views, damage opposing parties, and rally voter turnout. Initiative backers also rely on political parties for endorsements and campaign contributions.[23]

Widespread access to and use of the initiative process has had numerous consequences:

1. *Many ballot measures represent big money, not just good ideas.* A significant feature of the initiative process today is the increased amount of money spent to affect the outcome. In 1984, Scientific Games, the nation's largest lottery ticket manufacturer, spent $2.2 million on California's lottery initiative, claiming it would benefit California's schools. By 1998, more money was spent on ballot initiatives than on all state legislative races combined—more than $100 million. True, many ballot measures require large financial resources but this does not mean that business groups invariably have the upper hand. Consumer, environmental, and public interest groups find the money well spent if a favored regulation or bond issue is approved. To be sure, not all initiative campaigns require heavy spending, and heavy spending does not always ensure victory. Also, some ballot measures are not the subject of heavy campaigning, especially if other ballot items compete for the public's attention. For example, the 2003 gubernatorial recall ballot also featured Proposition 54, an initiative that would have banned the collection of racial and ethnic data by state agencies. The recall itself monopolized the attention of media and voters alike at the expense of 54. It was defeated by a 64 to 36 percent margin.

2. *New policy and process entrepreneurs can emerge,* rivaling the importance and influence of legislative leaders and even the governor. Some Californians are synonymous with measures they have supported or opposed: Howard Jarvis and Paul Gann (property tax cuts), Harvey Rosenfield (auto insurance reform), Mike Reynolds (three-strikes sentencing reform), Ron Unz (bilingual education), and Tim Draper (school vouchers).[24] The initiative process itself has spawned something of an initiative industrial complex. Although it takes only $250 to file an initiative with the Secretary of State, gathering a million-plus signatures to qualify it for the ballot is no job for amateurs. Major firms such as Kimball Petition Management, Discovery Petition Management, and Arno

PHOTO 4.3   Petition Circulator

Question: To what extent do paid petition circulators ("paids" as consultants call them) reflect democracy run amok, as some critics claim?

Political Consulting hire independent subcontractors who in turn employ solicitors to collect signatures. The solicitors receive upwards of $3.50 per signature, especially as signature deadlines near and they may handle as many as ten petitions at a time. Using these firms, it is possible to garner more than 1 million signatures in one month. In fact, 90 percent of all initiatives require professional assistance.[25] Signature gathering specialists are joined by the standard assortment of campaign consultants, media buyers, and public relations firms. As John Balzar of the *Los Angeles Times* once observed, "California's biannual orgy of ballot initiatives is top in the consulting world. . . . Here is a chance to get rich and do battle over the driving issues of the day—insurance, political reform, transportation—all without the distraction of a candidate."[26]

3. *Initiative campaigns increasingly rely on television.* California's television stations do a re-markably poor job covering the policy process in a representative democracy (see Chapter 6). Complicated issues do not lend themselves to short, visually entertaining stories. Lobbyists need not buy commercial time to woo a legislative subcommittee majority. But a "plebiscitarian" democracy is different. Public opinion surveys suggest that television (in the form of news stories and paid political commercials) exerts the most influence on initiative elections but is the least useful information source in deciding how to vote.[27] In the case of Proposition 5, the opponent's ads featured neon casino signs sprouting from the ground and this message: "With the approval of just two politicians . . . , any tribe could buy land anywhere and build a casino." Proponent's ads featured the media-savvy Mark Macarro, Chair of the Pechanga Luiseño Band of Mission Indians. He calmly reassured viewers that the measure was not that extreme and that it would continue the path toward self-reliance.

4. *The initiative process itself is constantly changing.* At one time, groups opposed to a particular measure simply outspent their opponents. This still works. In March 2000, California Indian tribes spent more than $25 million to lock Indian gaming into the state constitution. Opponents spent a paltry $45,000. A second technique has been for opponents of a particular measure to offer a competing measure with alternative provisions, hoping voters will be attracted to it. For example, in 2004 two *dueling initiatives* dealt with the extent to which gaming tribes should expand their operations and contribute to the state in lieu of traditional taxes. Competing measures may represent valid policy alternatives but they also tend to blur issues and confuse voters. Confused voters are often "no" voters, which may be what some initiative proponents intend. The newest technique has been to "campaign against the campaign," in other words blunt a new initiative effort before it gets to the ballot. In 2004, the state legislature passed a compromise workers' compensation reform bill after years of delay and indecision. What prompted action was the prospect of a Governor Shwarzenegger-supported initiative that would have been submitted to the voters had legislative efforts again failed.

5. *Elected officials themselves employ the initiative.* Criticized as damaging representative government, the initiative has actually become another tool of representative government. Statewide officeholders and legislators alike see it as a new route to public policy and electoral popularity. Policy gridlock in Sacramento has driven some policymakers to bypass their own process. The initiative serves a variety of motives. Depending on the situation, it can be an opportunity for minority party members to go around majority party leaders, a policy vehicle for legislative mavericks or outsiders, a platform for higher office, or one more bargaining chip relative to pending legislation.[28] Then-governor Pete Wilson built at least part of his policy agenda around initiatives dealing with illegal immigration, three strikes, and affirmative action (see California Voices). Local officials rarely attempt initiatives but in 2004 sponsored one that would require voter approval whenever the state legislature attempted to reduce state funding to cities, counties, and special districts.

6. *Government's workload actually increases when initiatives pass.* To work at all, many measures require the legislature to fill in the missing details or to establish implementing legislation. For instance, Proposition 20, the coastal protection initiative in 1972, required the appointment, staffing, and funding of a State Coastal Commission and several regional coastal commissions. Proposition 10, a 1998 initiative that raised the cigarette tax by 50 cents per pack (to 87 cents), established a new state commission to supervise newly funded early childhood development and smoking prevention programs. To receive Proposition 10 funding, county-level commissions were to develop their own spending plans. As you can see, initiative-driven governing is an ongoing process.

7. *Many initiatives end up in court.* Initiatives are often poorly drafted, vaguely worded, or patently unconstitutional. A lawsuit is so likely that initiative drafters usually insert severability clauses; if the courts find one section unconstitutional, the balance of the measure survives. In our dual judicial system, initiatives can be challenged in state or federal courts. The results are mixed. Sometimes the courts may carefully remove an offending provision while validating the balance of the initiative. For example, the California Supreme Court upheld Proposition 140, which established term limits for state officeholders, but removed the retroactive elimination of legislative pensions. Some decisions may be more indirect. In 2001, the U.S. Supreme Court sided with federal drug prohibitions and against Proposition 215 by ruling against six of California's medical marijuana clubs.[29] At times, courts take more

---

CALIFORNIA VOICES

The Governor on Initiatives

Appearing outside a Burbank COSTCO store to support workers gathering signatures for a workers' compensation measure, Arnold Schwarzenegger proclaimed: "I'm a hands on governor. I'm out here with a pen. I'm out here with a paper, saying, sign here. I'm not one to sit around in Sacramento and do nothing."

Quoted in David M. Druker and Dana Bartholomew, "Schwarzenegger Stumps for Workers' Comp Reform," *Los Angeles Daily News*, April 12, 2004.

---

drastic action. In 1999, a 6–1 state supreme court majority struck down all of Proposition 5, the 1998 Indian gaming initiative, because it violated a 1984 constitutional amendment that created the state lottery. As noted earlier, Proposition 1A in 2000 inoculated Indian gaming from further interference by placing it in the state constitution. Professor Gerald Uelman believes the "validity of initiative measures will occupy a steadily growing segment of the California Supreme Court docket."[30]

Federal judges and justices are less generous, possibly because they do not face periodic election. For instance, Proposition 187, the illegal immigration measure, stalled in a Los Angeles federal district court as soon as it passed in 1994. The enforcement of Proposition 209 that banned affirmative action programs eventually became law but only after the Ninth Circuit Court of Appeals (which handles cases from California) upheld it. In a pair of 2003 cases, *Ewing* v. *California* and *Lockyer* v. *Andrade,* the U.S. Supreme Court overturned the Ninth Circuit and upheld California's three strikes law.

Clearly state and federal courts play important roles in the initiative process. Although they tend to infuriate initiative zealots, the courts can modify, rewrite, overturn, or uphold challenged initiatives. In effect, they repair faulty provisions or put the brakes on what they consider unconstitutional ones.[31]

Prospects for Initiative Reform

What we have called the initiative mess would be messier still if voters were less selective. As Figure 4.1 indicates, the vast majority of circulated initiatives never qualify for the ballot and voters approve only a fraction of those. Nonetheless, reformers are concerned about the growing reliance on initiatives by citizens and policymakers alike and the problems caused by the troublesome measures that do pass. What then are the odds of reforming the process? Not very good. In the mid-1990s, the California Constitution Revision Commission made three modest recommendations—(1) allow the legislature to rewrite an initiative before it is submitted to the voters; (2) limit initiative constitutional amendments to November elections when voter turnout is higher; and (3) permit the legislature, with the governor's approval, to amend statutory initiatives after they have been in effect for six years. The legislature has not acted on any of these recommendations.

Ordinary Californians appear to be ambivalent regarding the initiative process. Polls suggest they are relatively aware of its shortcomings as described in this chapter. They admit that many initiatives are confusingly worded, unnecessarily complicated, and often represent the concerns of special interests, not the state as a whole. Yet a majority of them believe that initiatives result in better decisions

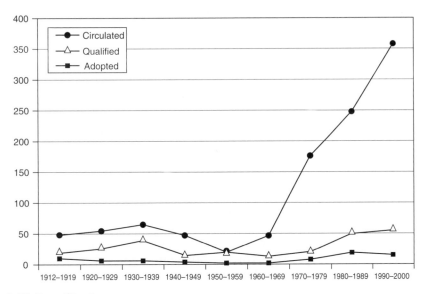

FIGURE 4.1   Initiatives Chart

Initiative Measures Circulated, Qualified, and Adopted. 1912-2000. A growing number of groups and individuals have attempted to use the initiative process to make and influence public policy. But voters are rather selective in what they are willing to adopt.

Question: Why do California voters refuse to adopt most ballot initiatives? Which initiatives have you voted for, against, and why?

Source: J. Fred Silva, (Occasional Paper) *The California Initiative Process: Background and Perspective* (San Francisco: Public Policy Institute of California, November 2000), Figure 2, p. 3.

than those made by the legislature and governor.[32] Support for the current process is shared by voters across racial, ethnic, partisan, and regional divides. All this suggests that significant reform is unlikely.

Progressive Cousins: Referendum and Recall

In contrast to the initiative, two other Progressive era reforms, referendum and recall, are much less utilized. For example, the *referendum* allows voters to prevent a legislative statute from taking effect. There are two kinds of referenda: *petition* and *compulsory*. The petition version is relatively rare. For instance, in 1982, a petition referendum was placed on the statewide ballot to block a legislative decision to build the Peripheral Canal through the Sacramento Delta. The compulsory referendum is more common. All constitutional amendments initiated by the legislature and all bond issues over $300,000 require voter approval. In recent years, bond issues have appeared on nearly every ballot as legislators seek additional revenue for schools, prisons, and highways without raising taxes.

The mechanics of the referendum are simple enough. Compulsory referenda are placed on the ballot by the legislature. The petition referendum is another matter. Within three months of a law's passage, opponents may gather a requisite number of signatures to place the matter on the next regularly scheduled statewide ballot. Certain categories of legislation are exempt: calls for special elections, tax levies, urgency measures, and spending bills.

To be successful, referendum advocates must gather 373,816 valid signatures within 90 days (the figure needed during 2003–2006). In contrast, initiative backers have 150 days to gather the necessary signatures. In short, the rules are stacked against petition referenda.

STATE LEVEL RECALLS

The *recall* allows voters to remove from office state or local elected officials between elections. California is one of 15 states allowing statewide recall; of 60 attempts, the 2003 recall of Governor Gray Davis was the only successful one. In fact, it was only the second gubernatorial recall in American history (the first was North Dakota's Lynn Frazier in 1921). The hurdles to any statewide recall in California are substantial. To place a recall on the ballot, people must gather signatures equal to 12 percent of the votes cast in the previous election for that office (20 percent in the case of a state legislator). Signatures for a statewide recall must come from at least five counties (to prevent undue influence by megacounties like Los Angeles).

The recall of Gray Davis is instructive not only because it occurred but because of how it occurred. Davis's troubles began in his first term (1999–2002). The economic downturn of the early 2000s left voters feeling anxious, pessimistic, and angry. Furthermore, while blame for the 2001 energy crisis was widely shared (botched deregulation by a previous legislature and governor, speculative practices by Enron and other energy traders, government inaction), it was easy to put the blame squarely on Davis. While voters reelected Davis in 2002, they did so with a meager 5 percent margin against businessman Bill Simon. Lost in the campaign rhetoric and prolific spending were the emerging budget issues facing the state. Worse, his January 2003 budget was balanced (as all state budgets must be) with higher taxes, deep spending cuts, plus the usual accounting gimmicks. Californians had not been prepared for such budget pain.

Also in early 2003, antitax gadfly and People's Advocate CEO Ted Costa pushed the idea of recalling Davis for "gross mismanagement of California's finances" and other misdeeds. In no time, a petition drive was underway. But such drives are unfeasible without massive infusions of cash; in fact, the signature drive stalled briefly for lack of needed funds. Over the next few months, U.S. Representative Darrell Issa, a wealthy car alarm magnate and former U.S. Senate candidate, came to the rescue—pouring roughly $1.7 million into the recall drive. The result was the submittal to the Secretary of State's office of an astonishing 1.3 million signatures with more on the way; by the end of the entire recall drive, Davis opponents collected over 2.1 million signatures.

So, the question "Shall Gray Davis be recalled (removed) from the office of governor?" would be on an October 7, 2003 special election ballot. As was the custom in lower level recall elections, replacement candidates would appear on the same ballot. Comparatively low requirements—65 signatures and a $3,500 filing fee—encouraged a small army of candidates to file and indeed they did. By August 8, 135 candidates had qualified to appear on the ballot, leading some pundits to deride the recall as a circus. But media and public attention quickly narrowed to a handful of candidates and, by election day, the most viable candidates were Democratic Lieutenant Governor Cruz Bustamante, Republican State Senator Tom McClintock, and movie star Arnold Schwarzenegger, also a Republican. Early polling and media reporting characterized the recall itself as a foregone conclusion. The entrance of Schwarzenegger essentially altered the dynamics of the campaign. The television media in particular covered his campaign to the virtual exclusion of several others and many aspects of the campaign were framed around him and his governing potential.

In the end, over 55 percent of voters chose to recall Davis and over 48 percent chose Schwarzenegger to replace him. As Figure 4.2

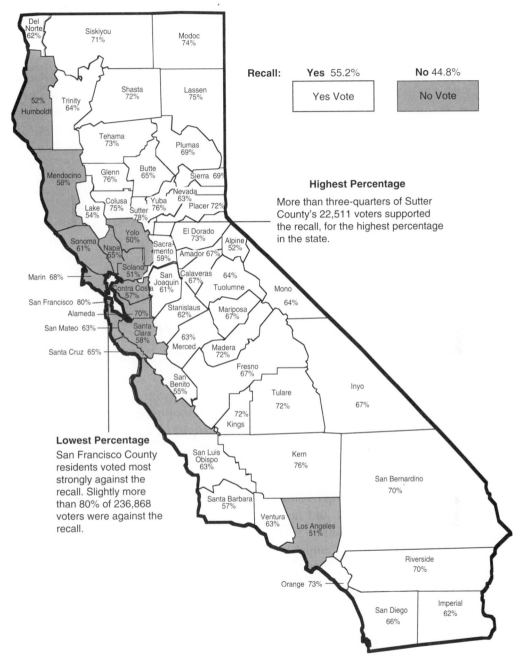

FIGURE 4.2   The California Governor Recall Election: How California Voted

Question: While Governor Gray Davis was unpopular in 2003, he was less unpopular or even supported among some coastal counties. Why?

Source: Los Angeles Times Poll, October, 2003. Figure reprinted with permission from the California Governor Recall Election by Lawrence; © 2004 wadsworth, a division of Thomson Learning, Inc.

indicates, support for the recall was geographically widespread. Recall opponents were concentrated in several coastal counties but even in gargantuan Los Angeles County, only 51 percent of voters opposed the recall. While there has been a great deal of attention devoted to a celebrity governor since the recall, it is helpful to remember that the election was as much or more about recalling Davis as it was about electing Schwarzenegger. Given the confluence of events and the entry of a mediagenic, celebrity candidate, the 2003 gubernatorial recall will likely remain a stunning if rare example of how a statewide recall election works.

A few state legislators have been recalled. Two Republican assembly members were recalled in 1995 when the Assembly was evenly divided between Republicans and Democrats. Mustering enough votes to select a speaker was challenging. In May of that year Los Angeles County voters recalled Paul Horcher after he agreed to support Democrat Willie Brown's continuance as speaker. In November Orange County voters ousted Doris Allen after she cut a deal with Democrats to become speaker, albeit briefly. Republicans regarded both as puppets of power broker Brown. In one notable case, then-state senator David Roberti handily survived a 1994 recall election engineered by gun control opponents, but the effort sapped energy and money from his state treasurer campaign; in the end, he lost that race. Because the recall is a special one-item election, says Roberti, it is "designed for single-issue enthusiasts because they can maintain their enthusiasm and adrenaline ceaselessly."[33]

LOCAL LEVEL RECALLS

Recall is much more common at the local level (as is defeating incumbents at regular elections). A relatively small number of qualifying signatures make it quite feasible indeed. Such recall efforts are often characterized by bitter conflict. What angers local voters enough to recall an official? Most controversies involve unpopular policy decisions, personnel controversies, outrageous behavior, or other local issues. Consider these examples. Latino voters in Bell Gardens ousted four white, "out-of-touch" city council members. Glendora voters removed the mayor and two council members after they fired the city manager and replaced several planning commission members with "cronies." Corruption was the reason South Gate recall organizers targeted several council members. A Santa Barbara county supervisor faced recall over redistricting, a flag salute dispute, and chronic intradistrict feuding. A Taft city council member was forced from office over the firing of a veteran city manager and for "backroom" policy making.

Conclusion:
The Legacy and the Paradox

The legacy of the Progressive era cannot be overemphasized. In fact, it has fostered hyperpluralism. By kicking one group—the SPR—out of politics, Californians invited many other groups into politics. Numerous reforms at both the state and local levels were implemented in those early years. We take many of them for granted today, such as nonpartisan local elections and city managers. Some reforms, such as the referendum, have proved to be rather unworkable. Others, such as the local recall, have truly become the safety valve they were meant to be. The initiative gets the most attention and with good reason. Savvy individuals with enough money can qualify most any pet policy or project for the ballot. But historically, most California initiatives have resulted from interest group activity and, more recently, major policymakers. Progressives defeated one powerful interest group and limited what they considered the negative influence of political parties, as Chapter 6 will attest. But inadvertently, they also strengthened the long-term role of California's interest groups for generations to come.

The process now appears to be a function of hyperpluralism in a technological age. Interest groups participate via initiatives, not just statehouse bills. Truly revolutionary policy can result from this process, but so can policy paralysis. An initiative victory can be whittled away or substantially revised in its implementation. A stunning initiative victory or defeat can actually inhibit further discussion on the policy involved as with Proposition 13. The process has produced more choices and information about them than typical voters can handle. At the same time, it has produced media-centered campaigns that insult voters' intelligence. Yet, for all its faults and abuses, contemporary Californians resist efforts to tamper with the system they have inherited. Voters may well realize that

if they do not understand an issue, in spite of or due to an information blizzard on it, they can simply vote "No."

The initiative process is analogous to true-or-false tests. What voters face at the polls are highly technical issues with uncertain and far-reaching ramifications. Wise policy alternatives come in shades of gray, not black or white. Yet the voters are examined on these complex subjects with up or down decisions. No multiple-choice, fill-ins, or essay questions are allowed. The requirements of direct democracy are such that only the well educated and homework inclined can vote wisely. But a growing number of Californians do not fit that description. As we will see in Chapter 5, all Californians are affected by the state's policies, but a much smaller number actually participate in the system that produces those policies.

KEY TERMS

Progressivism   (p. 62)

Progressive reforms   (pp. 62–63)

traits of California progressivism   (pp. 63–64)

Propositions 13, 5, 22, 71   (pp. 65–70)

policy and process entrepreneurs   (pp. 71–72)

petition management firms   (p. 72)

dueling initiatives   (p. 73)

petition referendum   (p. 75)

compulsory referendum   (p. 75)

statewide and local recall   (pp. 76–78)

REVIEW QUESTIONS

1. What factors explain the rise of Progressivism nationwide? In California?
2. Who were the Progressives, and what did they achieve in California?
3. Describe and illustrate the initiative, petition referendum, compulsory referendum, and recall.
4. How do the initiative cases described here illustrate the pros and cons of the initiative process? Is the process a mess as some believe?
5. Based on this chapter, are recalls a good idea? Why or why not?
6. What larger issues of California politics does direct democracy illustrate?

WEB ACTIVITIES

Initiative and Referendum Institute
(www.dnet.org/initiatives)
As you will see from this site, California is not alone or unique in allowing voters to legislate.

California Secretary of State
(www.ss.ca.gov)
Go to the elections area for progress reports on initiatives currently in circulation. If you want to circulate your own, complete how-to instructions are available.

California Voter Foundation
(www.calvoter.org)
This watchdog and educational group tracks contributions to recent proposition campaigns. Click on "Follow the Money."

INFOTRAC® COLLEGE EDITION ARTICLES

For additional reading, go to InfoTrac® College Edition, your online research library, at http://www.infotrac.thomsonlearning.com

Laws for Sale

Take the Initiative, Please

Referendum Madness in California

NOTES

1. Richard Hofstadter, *The Age of Reform: From Bryan to F.D.R.* (New York: Alfred A. Knopf, 1955), 131.

2. James Weinstein, *The Corporate Ideal in the Liberal State: 1900–1918* (Boston: Beacon Press, 1968), 3.

3. Lewis L. Gould, "Introduction," in Lewis L. Gould, ed., *The Progressive Era* (Syracuse, NY: Syracuse University Press, 1974), 9.

4. George E. Mowry, *The California Progressives* (Berkeley, CA: University of California Press, 1951), 101.

5. Spencer C. Olin Jr., *California's Prodigal Sons: Hiram Johnson and the Progressives, 1911–1917* (Berkeley, CA: University of California Press, 1968), chap. 3.

6. Ibid., 87–88.

7. Ibid., 97.

8. Mowry, *The California Progressives*, 102.

9. Quoted in Olin, *California's Prodigal Sons*, 26.

10. For a historical treatment of direct democracy in California, see John M. Allswang, *The Initiative and Referendum in California, 1898–1998* (Stanford: Stanford University Press, 2000).

11. A still excellent discussion of Proposition 13-related equity issues can be found in Robyn S. Phillips, "Restoring Property Tax Equity," in John J. Kirlin and Donald R. Winkler, eds., *California Policy Choices, Vol. 4* (Sacramento:

University of Southern California School of Public Administration, 1988), 143–169.

12. Quoted in Claudia Buck, "A Gamble That Paid Off," *California Journal* 29 (December 1998), 46.

13. Jennifer Warren, "Gays Gaining Acceptance, Poll Finds," *Los Angeles Times*, June 14, 2000.

14. For more on gay rights, see Bill Ainsworth, "Next Step: Equality," *California Journal* 35 (January, 2004), 6–10.

15. For a Proposition 71 overview and links to various articles on the stem cell research campaign, see UC Berkeley's Institute of Governmental Studies website (www.igs.berkeley.edu/library/htProp71StemCell).

16. Peter Schrag, *Paradise Lost: California's Experience, America's Future* (New York: New Press, 1998), 189.

17. John Balzar, "Brown Labels Anti-Proposition 39 Ads 'Con Jobs,'" *Los Angeles Times*, November 22, 1984.

18. Political scientists regard legislators as *trustees* if they are primarily guided by personal conscience and as *delegates* if they are primarily guided by the wishes of the constituents who elect them.

19. Lester Milbrath, *Political Participation* (Chicago: Rand McNally, 1965), 144–145.

20. Thomas E. Cronin, *Direct Democracy: The Politics of Initiative, Referendum and Recall* (Cambridge, MA: Harvard University Press, 1989), 84–88, 89, 210.

21. Carey McWilliams, *California: The Great Exception* (New York: Current Books, 1949), 213.

22. Elizabeth R. Gerber, *The Populist Paradox: Interest Group Influence and the Promise of Direct Legislation* (Princeton, NJ: Princeton University Press, 1999).

23. Daniel Smith and Caroline Tolbert, "The Initiative to Party: Partisanship and Ballot Initiatives in California," *Party Politics* 7 (2001), 739–757.

24. For a profile of Unz, see Steve Scott, "Gadfly Extraordinaire," *California Journal* 30 (August 1999), 18–22.

25. John Marelius, "Petition Hawkers a Breed Apart," *San Diego Union Tribune*, April 16, 2005.

26. John Balzar, "Consultants: A Political Gold Rush in California," *Los Angeles Times*, June 12, 1989.

27. Mark Baldassare, *A California State of Mind: The Conflicted Voter in a Changing World* (Berkeley: University of California Press, 2002), 212–219.

28. Charles Bell and Charles Price, "Lawmakers and Initiatives: Are Ballot Measures the Magic Ride to Success?" *California Journal* 19 (September 1988), 380–384.

29. *U.S. v. Oakland Cannabis Buyer's Cooperative,* 532 U.S. 483 (2001).

30. Gerald F. Uelman, "Taming the Initiative," *California Lawyer* 20 (August 2000), 50.

31. For more on the courts' role in the initiative process, see Charles M. Price, "Shadow Government," *California Journal* 28 (October 1997), 32–38.

32. Mark Baldassare, *A California State of Mind,* 216.

33. Quoted in Laureen Lazarovici, "The Politics of Recall," *California Journal* 26 (July 1995), 21.

CHAPTER 5

The Political Behavior of Californians

In Brief

Despite the image of a politically involved citizenry, Californians' political behavior, in most respects, mirrors that of Americans in general. Political scientists have categorized the political participation levels of Americans and Californians along a range from uninvolvement to voting and active campaigning. This chapter surveys the diversity of conventional forms of participation and two nonconventional ones—exiting the political system altogether and political protest—all these forms are commonplace in California.

The traits of California voters are discussed as well as the reasons some Californians cannot vote and why qualified voters choose not to vote. Traditionally, Americans have identified with the major political parties, but they do so with greater diversity of motives than once thought. In California, these party identification patterns vary from region to region. Differences emerge between Northern and Southern California and between coastal and inland California. Emerging patterns of political behavior statewide suggest gaps among different groups of Californian voters and nonvoters—a sign of growing hyperpluralism in the state.

California's fondness for initiatives creates the impression that all Californians are reasonably knowledgeable, politically active, and ready to vote on any issue or candidate placed before them. A seemingly constant parade of candidates and policy issues fills their political "space." Yet despite the political demands placed on them, Californians are much like other Americans in their political activity. Only a few are very involved, a larger number vote, and still others choose not to participate in any meaningful way. Yet specific groups of Californians differ from each other in their political behavior. To understand how Californians behave politically, we need to review what political scientists know about generic political behavior. Researchers have collected huge amounts of data, but iron laws of voting behavior are nonexistent. Voting is an individual, private act, and it is also a continuous activity. Electoral attitudes and behavior can and do change. Researchers find voters and nonvoters hard to pin down. Also, voting is only one political behavior among many to measure and analyze. First, we consider the larger idea of political participation.

Forms of Participation in a Democracy

How ordinary citizens participate in a representative democracy has always intrigued political scientists. In recent years, political scientists have identified and categorized the political activities of Americans. *Political participation* consists of individual or group activity intended to exercise influence in the political system. Methods used to exercise such influence are either conventional or nonconventional in nature: that is, inside or outside the norms considered acceptable by the larger society. We will explore briefly these channels of influence.

CONVENTIONAL PARTICIPATION

Political scientists have identified a wide range of civic activities engaged in by Americans. Voting is the most widely shared political activity with 71 percent reporting doing it regularly, followed by joining a political organization (48 percent), contacting political officials (34 percent), attending political meetings (29 percent), and making political contributions (24 percent).[1] Yet political participation is only one measure of community life. Many people participate in voluntary associations that political scientists call "civil societies."

These include service organizations (Rotary, Lions, Soroptimists), youth clubs (Boys and Girls Clubs, Girls, Inc.), and churches, mosques, or synagogues. Many parents are deeply involved in their children's schooling and sports activities. Yet there is growing evidence that many Americans are becoming less engaged with civic life. They may do charity work, but many do not volunteer or work on national, state, local, or neighborhood issues.[2]

These types of political and social behavior do not tell the whole story below the national level. In California, sizable differences in civic engagement and political participation are related to race, ethnicity, language use, and in the case of immigrants, how long they have lived in California. Those Californians who are most active in civic life tend to be white, older, more affluent, more educated homeowners. As Figure 5.1 indicates, they not only vote more frequently than other groups, they participate in other political activities at higher levels as well, such as signing petitions, writing officials, and contributing money. Not surprisingly, the more intensive the activity, the less participation one finds among all groups. To some observers, these are troublesome findings. It appears that low income and minority communities are less likely to be heard in the halls of government or in the prolific use of policy making by way of initiatives.[3]

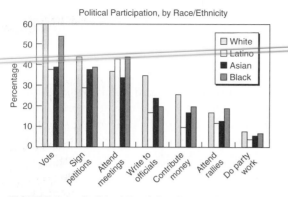

FIGURE 5.1   Political Participation by Race and Ethnicity

Question: What factors might explain the differences in the above graph?

Source: Public Policy Institute of California, 2004.

THE EXIT OPTION

Thus far, we have emphasized voting and other forms of civic participation. But what about those Californians who move from one community to another due to policy dissatisfaction? Those concerns may relate to traffic congestion, gang violence, school issues, or various quality of life issues. Arguably, this is a form of political participation as well, what we call the *exit option*.[4] For example, this form of participation applies to urban Californians who are fed up with crime, smog, and congestion. Given the chance, some may move to Nevada, the Northwest, the Midwest, or anywhere that is more affordable (equity refugees); or they pull their children out of ethnically diverse public schools and send them to less diverse, private ones (ethnic refugees). Some may homeschool their children—the ultimate educational exit option. Demographers monitor this exiting trend in California by analyzing automobile registration data (each driver represents about 1 1/2 persons). For instance, in the early 1990s, many urban Californians were moving to suburbia, rural areas, or beyond—anywhere that was smaller or less dense.[5] By the early 2000s, some of these trends were

reversed. Large numbers of people were migrating to the job-rich counties of Southern California and the Bay Area.

How people respond to political dissatisfaction depends on how invested they are in their communities. Those who are relatively satisfied with a local political system behave constructively—they speak up or express system loyalty in other ways, such as voting. Their level of investment in the community (home ownership, a job, children in school) makes a difference. Low investors more easily opt for political neglect, exiting the system, or even violence. Southern Californians will recall the vivid contrast in the Los Angeles riot of 1992 between rioters on the streets and those who gathered at an African American church for prayer, discussion, and "peaceful protest." Also, the availability of viable alternatives to the status quo determines what dissatisfied people do. For instance, for people to exit an unsatisfactory public school, feasible alternatives need to be either nearby (a neighboring jurisdiction) or affordable (alternative schools).

THE PROTEST OPTION

Extreme levels of community dissatisfaction may result in the use of protest activities—the *protest option*. Sporadic political protest, both violent and nonviolent, has always been a part of America's political heritage. Historically, California has had its fair share. Most of the well-publicized incidents of protest and violence in California have been ethnic in nature. Consider the anti-Chinese demonstrations in San Francisco inspired by the Workingman's Party (1877); union strikes and the union-inspired bombing of the *Los Angeles Times* building (early 1900s); the "zoot suit" riots in Los Angeles (1943); free speech and Vietnam war protests on university campuses (1960s); the Watts riot in Los Angeles following a controversial police arrest (1965); and the 1992 Los Angeles riot (following the acquittal of four Los Angeles police officers accused of beating

PHOTO 5.1   Exercising the protest option

Thousands of California State University students protest proposed higher education budget cuts in front of Governor Arnold Schwarzenegger's downtown Los Angeles office.

Question: Is this form of political participation effective?

motorist Rodney King). In recent years, facing the prospect of significant state budget cuts, numerous groups have "demonstrated" at the state Capitol or state offices in other cities to communicate their views to the governor, lawmakers, or the media (see Photo 5.1). One group calling itself the Earth Liberation Front set fire to numerous Hummer vehicles at auto dealerships to protest their famously low gas mileage.

As forms of political behavior, political protest and violence are difficult to study. Developing a direct cause-and-effect relationship between arson or looting and some conscious political message can be rather speculative. To be sure, protest is a form of political behavior used by groups who lack more conventional resources. These groups, though, may not be able to articulate clearly why they do what they do. In many instances, mob behavior lacks any

civic purpose—it is simply mob behavior. It is fair to say that the connection between protest and violence is tenuous, albeit related. *Not all protest is violent, and not all violence is protest.*

What have we learned about political violence? In studying the Watts riot of 1965, researchers David Sears and John McConahay concluded that urban violence was not only symbolic behavior but, in the minds of rioters, a "functional equivalent" of more conventional forms of participation. Rioters felt they were expressing not only antiwhite hostility but also anger over their own status in the larger society.[6] What about the 1992 riots? Like Watts, there was a precipitating incident in 1992: the acquittal by a nonblack, suburban jury of white police officers accused of beating a black motorist. A widely aired amateur video recorded what many considered to be excessive force.[7]

Paralleling the aftermath of Watts, most observers cited a litany of urban problems and the lack of effective policies to solve them. The 1992 riot did present some interesting twists. Most rioters were African American and Latino men who had not finished high school. Most Latino looters were recent immigrants. Given all the talk of gang violence in Los Angeles, only one in ten of those convicted of rioting in 1992 had gang affiliations.

Voters and Nonvoters in California

To better understand conventional participation and voting in particular, political scientists examine voters (those who show up at the polls on election day or vote absentee) and nonvoters (those who cannot or will not vote). Some Californians are not qualified to vote. Those who are eligible are considered to be the *voting age population* (VAP). For instance, in the 2004 presidential election, California's voting age population numbered over 22 million people and 75 percent of those registered to vote. Another measure of voting is *voter turnout*—the portion of those registered voters who turn out to vote in any particular election, be it in person or by absentee ballot. In the 2004 presidential election, 76 percent of those Californians registered to vote actually did so, the highest percentage since 1980.[8]

WHO VOTES IN CALIFORNIA?

Political scientists want to know not only how many people vote but who votes and what those voters are like. One way to do this is through *exit polls*—polls conducted as voters leave precinct locations on election day. What do California voters look like? Closely examine Figure 5.2, which provides data from an exit poll conducted on November 2, 2004. Some highlights include the following: There

are somewhat more male than female voters. The largest age group is 45-to 64-year-olds. White voters constitute 65 percent of the turnout, a significantly larger percentage than their portion of the population. A majority of voters have at least a college degree. Democrats outnumber Republicans but self-described conservatives slightly outnumber liberals. Moderates of varying degrees constituted 45 percent of California voters. Nearly 60 percent of all voters have household incomes over $60,000. Religiously, the largest group consists of Christian Protestants. An impressive 58 percent reside in Southern California, including Los Angeles County. Lastly, reflecting huge registration and get-out-the-vote efforts, 11 percent of exit poll respondents were first-time voters.

THOSE WHO CANNOT VOTE

The health of representative democracy depends on voting. Yet California and other states have experienced rather high levels of nonparticipation, especially at the ballot box. Nonparticipation takes two forms—*structural nonvoting* (those disenfranchised by the rules) and *preferential nonvoting* (those disenfranchised by their own behavior and attitudes). We will explore both forms.

In our federal system, states administer all elections. "Universal suffrage" does not mean all people get to vote. In fact, states can and do make it difficult and, for some, impossible to vote. California is no exception. Of 35 million Californians in 2004, only 22 million were legally eligible to vote. The other 13 million included people in the following categories:

- Those under 18 years of age
- Noncitizens (documented and undocumented)
- Those who have moved to or within California within 15 days of an election
- Current prisoners and parolees (former prisoners regain their voting rights; those serving

Gender		Party Ideology	
48%	Male	27%	Liberal Democrats
52%	Female	19%	Moderate and conservative Democrats
		10%	Liberal and moderate independents
		5%	Conservative independents
		11%	Liberal and moderate Republicans
		26%	Conservative Republicans
Age			
20%	18–29		
29%	30–44		
39%	45–64		
12%	65 or older		
Race/Ethnicity		**Annual Family Income**	
65%	White	8%	Less than $20,000
7%	Black	15%	$20,000 to $39,999
14%	Latino	18%	$40,000 to $59,999
9%	Asian	17%	$60,000 to $74,999
		42%	$75,000 or more
Education		**Religion**	
43%	Less than college	46%	Protestant
57%	College degree or more	25%	Roman Catholic
		5%	Jewish
Party Registration		**Region**	
45%	Democrats	25%	Los Angeles County
15%	Independents	33%	Rest of Southern California
37%	Republicans	13%	Bay Area
		29%	Rest of Northern California

FIGURE 5.2   California voters: A snapshot

The *Times* Poll interviewed 3,357 voters as they left 50 polling places across California during the November 2004 election. The margin of error for the entire sample is +/– 3 percent. It is slightly higher for some subgroups.

Source: The Los Angeles Times Poll.

jail time for misdemeanor convictions may vote, by absentee ballot, of course!)

• The legally insane (but only upon a judge's formal declaration)

Qualifying to vote is not enough. Individuals must also declare their desire to vote by filing a brief registration form with the appropriate county office (usually a registrar of voters or the county clerk's office). During spurts of ac-tivity before big elections, these forms are available at shopping centers, public buildings, and on street corners. Originally designed to inhibit voter fraud, registration requirements effectively inhibit many Californians from vot-ing (see California Voices). Because one must reregister after every move, highly mobile groups (such as agricultural employees, some construction workers, and college students) find they are unregistered on election day.

Recent surveys suggest that many unregistered Californians are relatively young Latino males with modest levels of income and education. They pay little or no attention to politics or political news. According to pollster and analyst Mark Baldassare, they are "quite oblivious to the election process."[9] The 1993 National Voter Registration Act (called the motor voter law) required states to lower registration hurdles, for instance, by allowing people to register at motor vehicle or welfare offices. By 2004, nearly 14 million Californians had registered or reregistered under the law's provisions. While that seems impressive, some observers believe it has largely benefited those inclined to register anyway. In recent election cycles, Californians have been able to access registration forms online at the Secretary of State's Website. In November 2002, voters rejected Proposition 52, a proposal to allow Californians to register on election day at their neighborhood polling places. This practice is commonplace in Western Europe.

THOSE WHO WILL NOT VOTE

When political scientists, media pundits, and election officials bemoan low voter turnout, they refer to either eligible voters or registered voters who choose not to vote—preferential nonvoters. Only 57 percent of those Californians eligible to vote bothered to do so in November 2004. Why do qualified voters choose not to? The reasons can be divided into personal factors and structural factors.

Personal Factors

Many Californians consider themselves disengaged from government and politics. In a 1998 poll, habitual nonvoting Californians were asked why they do not always vote.[10] Thirty-six percent said they lack enough knowledge to vote. This is understandable. To these people, voting is a daunting task. Primary elections, general elections, special elections, off-year elections, advisory elections— if it is Tuesday, it must be election day, or so

Registration Frustration

The comments of Sylvia Tidwell, a Los Angeles artist, suggest why online voter registration may be a welcome change:

I moved from the Westside to downtown Los Angeles recently and thought that I had to reregister to vote. I didn't anticipate it was going to be this incredible saga. On Oct. 5, I went to the post office. They were out of the forms. They directed me to another post office. On the way there, I passed a Ralph's market to see if anyone doing petitions would have them; they didn't. I then went to a Trader Joe's and there was a petitioner, but he had run out of forms. So I went to the second post office. They had exhausted their supply of forms a week before and said I shouldn't have waited until the last minute. I tried the Robertson Library where a reference librarian said they had been trying to get forms for more than a month, unsuccessfully. . . .

The system has broken down somewhere; these forms are not available to people who want to do their civic duty. People simply cannot register. The very people who have the most to gain from voting are hampered. . . .

If people are frustrated in registering, there is a suppression of enthusiasm and interest. The people who are least resourceful will be less likely to register and later, vote. . . . It promotes voter apathy and perhaps cynicism.

SOURCE: Sylvia Tidwell, "Registration: Testing the Will to Vote," *Los Angeles Times,* October 17, 1998, B15.

CARTOON 5.1   The election was yesterday

Source: Eric G. Lewis

it seems. With some elections being consolidated (municipal, special district, and state), ballots have lengthened considerably. In fact, going to the polls on election day is only the temporary end of a long, information-laden campaign—replete with official voter pamphlets, constant television commercials, political "junk-mail," door hangers, and precinct walkers. Many initiative elections result in information overload for average voters (see Cartoon 5.1). For some, the cost of voting (including the homework involved) is not worth the trouble, especially if the benefit is not clear. Even those who turn out may not vote on every ballot item, a phenomenon called undervoting. For example, in 2004, 16.5 million Californians voted for a presidential candidate but roughly 11 million voted for or against the various statewide propositions farther down the ballot.

Another 24 percent in that survey claimed to be too busy to vote. The better off of these pursue a full routine of activities and feel no need to vote. The less well off are preoccupied with getting or staying employed, holding families together, and simply living from day to day. The least of their concerns is weighing the pros and cons of gubernatorial candidates or proposed constitutional amendments. Still another 16 percent viewed voting as useless. To these politically alienated Californians, voting produces no change so why not boycott elections entirely. Finally, 9 percent said they were "just not interested in politics."[11]

The personal factor of age may also affect voter turnout. Turnout is relatively high among older Californians, but the oldest of them may be too infirm to vote. Many of the youngest voters are less attuned to politics and voting. They have been raised on MTV, view public officials as corrupt, and do not look to government as a problem solver.[12]

Structural Factors

The way the election system is structured also affects voting frequency. Many Californians (as do other Americans) pick and choose elections in which to vote. They tend to think that higher-level elections are more important than lower-level ones. Voter turnout drops successively from presidential to state to local elections. General elections witness higher turnouts than primary elections. The March 5, 2002, state primary recorded the lowest turnout of registered voters ever—34.6 percent. Turnout in separate local elections normally hovers around 30 percent but can go lower. One study showed that where local government elections coincided with presidential elections, those elections experienced 36 percent more turnout than off-cycle, local-only elections.[13]

Other factors also make a difference. Turnout drops in state legislative races where incumbents run unopposed. Special elections (those scheduled outside the normal election cycles) garner fewer voters than regularly scheduled ones. For example, several special elections in 2001 to fill legislative resignations witnessed turnouts of only 14 to 17 percent. When Californians have a chance to vote directly on well-publicized, easy-to-understand issues (initiatives and referenda), political scientists generally believe that interest and motivation to vote increases. For example, the 2003 gubernatorial recall election combined voter anger (at incumbent Gray Davis), a celebrity replacement candidate (Arnold Schwarzenegger), and extraordinary media coverage, resulting in a 61 percent voter turnout—on par with many gubernatorial general elections.

Also, political scientists generally believe that voter turnout tends to increase where candidate races are reasonably competitive and either side has a chance to win. But voter turnout research in California's minority-majority congressional districts—where minority groups constitute a majority of the voting population—alters somewhat this generalization. In those districts where Latinos or blacks were voting majorities, their respective turnouts increased significantly compared to Latino and black turnouts in Anglo-majority districts. Turnout among Latinos was particularly high in Latino-majority districts with Latino Congress members.[14]

Partisan Factors

Political scientists also know that voter turnout varies by political party. The conventional wisdom suggests that Republicans have higher turnouts than Democrats but the 2004 presidential election alone does not bare this out. In that election, Democrats were 43 percent of registered voters; Republicans were 35 percent. Exit polls suggested that Democrats were 45 percent of actual voters; Republicans were 37 percent. When this gap does occur to the benefit of Republicans, it happens in low-turnout elections. When the gap narrows as it did in 2004, both Republican and Democratic candidates must appeal to California's independent voters who comprise 15–17 percent of the state's likely voters.

Regional Factors

All these general explanations apply to California as a whole but not to all parts of the state. Dramatic differences exist between the state's 58 counties. For the 2004 presidential election (when relatively high turnout would be expected), the highest turnout was in Marin County at 89.5 percent; the lowest was Merced County at 59.3 percent. Of those simply eligible to vote, Marin County again experienced the highest turnout at 78.4 percent; Imperial County had the lowest at 42.2 percent. Why the differences? One explanation is that counties with high numbers of Latinos, immigrants, and other low-propensity voters tend to experience lower turnouts than those with lower concentrations of such groups.

What are the long-term trends in California? Even though absolute numbers of voters continue to increase, a gradually smaller percentage of Californians are bothering to register and, once registered, to vote. That is, with the notable exception of 2004. Take a moment

TABLE 5.1 Voter Turnout in California, 1976 to 2004: Presidential Election Years

Year	Adults eligible to register (%)	Turnout of registered (%)	Turnout of those eligible (%)
1976	70.3	81.5	57.3
1980	73.8	77.2	57.0
1984	78.8	74.9	59.1
1988	73.5	72.8	55.5
1992	72.4	75.3	54.5
1996	80.5	65.5	52.6
2000	63.2	70.9	51.9
2004	75.0	76.0	57.0

Source: California Secretary of State.

to study Table 5.1, which documents selected presidential election years when voter turnout was highest. Particularly striking is the long-term decline in turnout among Californians eligible to vote. Is the 2004 turnout turnaround a trend? We must await future elections to know.

Partisanship in California

How citizens participate in the electoral process and why many do not is only part of the picture. Another part includes the various frames of reference citizens use to contextualize their participation. A *frame of reference* is a set of beliefs or observations that gives meaning to ideas and actions. They are "hooks" on which to hang numerous political messages. One of the most important hooks for Americans is political party identification.

Party Affiliation

A *political party* is a relatively permanent coalition that exists to win public offices for its candidates, promote policy positions, and serve as a primary frame of reference for voters.

Party identification is the extent to which citizens affiliate with, relate to, or support a specific political party. Identifiers believe support for a party makes their vote more meaningful. Unlike many multiparty systems elsewhere, the American two-party system presents relatively few choices. Voters respond to that lack by shading or qualifying their partisan loyalties. For instance, the University of Michigan's Center for Political Studies has identified seven distinct categories of partisanship— (1) strong Democrat, (2) weak Democrat, (3) independent leaning Democrat, (4) independent, (5) independent leaning Republican, (6) weak Republican and (7) strong Republican. On a nationwide basis, the center has monitored the weakening of strong identification with either party (called "dealignment"), the erosion of Democratic identification in particular, and the increase of independent voters.

That said, researchers believe people who consider themselves independent often lean toward and regularly vote for Democrats or Republicans. They are not as "independent" as they claim to be.[15] How independent are California voters? Researchers explore this question through various polling techniques. Registration data and exit polls (taken on election day as voters leave polling places) shed some light on independents. In October 2004, nearly 18 percent of Californians listed "Decline to State" under party preference. Exit poll data for 2004 put that number at 15 percent. What motivates this sizeable group of independents? Some polls suggest California independents are more concerned with substantive policy issues than with partisan ideology. While they are relatively moderate in their overall views, they tend to be liberal on social

---

Did You Know ... ?

A composite profile of a California independent would be a white, male, college-educated, 35 year old resident of San Francisco.

---

issues and conservative on fiscal issues. Furthermore, compared to party loyalists, independents are more distrustful of government. All these factors make independents a powerful, but unpredictable, electoral force in California.[16]

The biggest news in recent elections has been the alignment of Latinos with the Democratic Party. Given their status as a minority group and their relatively conservative views on family and social issues, Latinos were once considered "up for grabs" by both major parties. Many observers credit Latinos' recent voting behavior to Republican Party support for Proposition 187 (an anti-immigration measure) and Proposition 209 (an anti-affirmative action measure). These two measures in particular were voting motivators especially for newly naturalized Latinos.[17] Whether or not they officially register as Democrats, Latinos have been voting for Democratic candidates in impressive numbers. Their choices for president have been consistent. In 1992, 63 percent of them voted for Bill Clinton; in 2000, 75 percent voted for Al Gore; and in 2004, 68 percent voted for John Kerry. Whether Latino influence increases in the future depends on whether their citizenship and participation rates match their population growth.[18]

THE PARTISAN GEOGRAPHY OF CALIFORNIA

Generalizations about party affiliation in California can only be understood in the context of the state's diverse geographical regions. Those regions have different voting habits and partisan loyalties. Pollsters often identify five distinct voting regions of California—Los Angeles County, the rest of Southern California, the San Francisco Bay Area, the rest of Northern California, and the Central Valley.

Within Southern California, Los Angeles County remains a Democratic island amid a large and more conservative region. Inner city African Americans remain loyally Democratic; they are joined by lower income Latinos and some urban whites. In 2004, John Kerry garnered 61 percent of the vote there. The rest of Southern California is more conservative, in some places much more so. Although it is more white and middle class than Los Angeles, the surrounding Southland counties have a growing number of Asians and Latinos. In 2004, Southern Californians outside of Los Angeles split their presidential preferences—50 percent for Kerry and 49 percent for Bush. The differences between North and South can be seen by comparing two otherwise similar counties—the Bay Area's Marin County and Southern California's Orange County. Both are affluent, suburban, coastal counties but with substantially different political orientations and subsequent voting behaviors. In 2004, 73.5 percent of Marin County voters opted for Kerry and only 25.5 percent for Bush. In Orange County, only 39.0 percent voted for Kerry while 59.7 percent favored Bush.

Northern California, and especially the San Francisco Bay Area, is more liberal and Democratic than the rest of the state. According to the *Almanac of American Politics*, the Bay Area is overwhelmingly the most Democratic of any metropolitan area.[19] In 2000, Bay Area voters preferred Gore over Bush by a 67 to 27 percent

FIGURE 5.3   California's Presidential Preferences, By County (2004)

Source: California Secretary of State.

margin and, in 2004, Kerry over Bush by a 69 to 29 percent margin. In the 1998 gubernatorial election, 72 percent of them—a larger percentage than any other region—voted for Gray Davis. While his support declined in 2002, several Bay Area counties gave Davis higher margins over Republican Bill Simon than elsewhere in California. Virtually all Bay Area counties rejected the recall of Davis in 2003.

A more recent and telling regional contrast has been between coastal and inland California. Note the contrasts portrayed in Figure 5.3.

This map shows which 2004 presidential candidates won pluralities in each county. Most coastal Californians—and that means most Californians—preferred Kerry over Bush. Voters in portions of the Central Valley and the mountain regions preferred Bush by varying margins. An east/west contrast is also evident in political ideologies. In one 1999 poll, Central Valley respondents reflected more conservative and less liberal viewpoints than Bay Area or greater Los Angeles residents. Only 22 percent of Central Valley respondents claimed to be very or somewhat liberal compared to 30 percent for Los Angeles area and 36 percent for Bay Area respondents. On the other hand, fully 44 percent of Central Valley respondents claimed to be somewhat or very conservative. Only 35 percent of Los Angeles Area respondents and 32 percent of Bay Area respondents agreed.[20] The conservative leanings of Central Valley voters are expressed at the polls. For example, while U.S. Senator Barbara Boxer was winning reelection in a statewide landslide over Republican Bill Jones in 2004, she garnered only 40 percent of the vote in the Central Valley.

California's Electoral Gaps

The political participation patterns we have described must be viewed against a larger backdrop: recent economic and demographic trends affecting both California and the nation. In the early 1990s, columnist Dan Walters predicted that California in the new century would be "a more ethnically complex society, a society of more distinct socioeconomic classes; a more competitive society; a more technologically sophisticated society; an older society, a more harried society; and perhaps, unless a cadre of new civic and political leadership emerges, a society that loses its communal identity and evolves into a collection of mutually hostile tribes."[21] In the late 1990s, his concerns about economic inequality in California remained: "Perhaps we should simply recognize that as California's economy becomes more intertwined with that of the larger world, our society will increasingly reflect the fact that the Earth is not a particularly egalitarian planet."[22]

He was referring to what many call California's "two-tier" society. In Chapter 1, we discussed one aspect of this society—the state's *two-tier economy*. This economy is characterized by a gap between California's rich and poor.

Upper-tier workers have relatively high levels of education, job skills, and experience compared to lower-tier workers. According to one study, this gap is growing not only from rising income among the well off but also from declining income among the less well off. In California, this trend seems to be unaffected by economic downturns (the early 1990s and early 2000s) or upturns (the late 1990s). High levels of immigration account for growing numbers of lower-tier workers, but the study documented growing income inequality among native-born Californians. According to Deborah Reed, the implications for the state are profound. "California has a diverse population with diverse needs and desires for income. When rising income inequality results from growing diversity, our concern may not be with income inequality per se but rather with ensuring that all members of society have the opportunity to achieve economic success."[23]

Is there a comparable two-tier polity? Yes, in the sense that the voting population does not mirror the larger population of the state. This fundamental difference can be expressed in a number of gaps. Most fundamentally is California's *voter/nonvoter gap*. That is, the people who vote appear to be unrepresentative of the entire population of the state. Comparing demographic data and election day exit polls reveals this dichotomy. Consider Table 5.2. In 2004, 65 percent of California voters were white but they constituted only 47 percent of the population. Those who voted had higher levels of education and family income than the overall population. Only 14 percent of voters were Latino, although they constituted 33 percent of the population.

Beyond the voter/nonvoter gap, numerous other gaps characterize the political behavior of Californians. Consider the state's *racial/ethnic gap*. In surveys of likely voters in 2004, six in ten Latino voters were under age 45; six in ten white voters were over age 45. An overwhelming 73 percent of African American voters

94

TABLE 5.2   The California Electorate: Two Tiers or . . . ?

	Voters (%)					
	1994	1996	1998	2000	2004	Population 2004 (%)
Race/ethnicity						
White	81	74	64	73	65	47
Latino	8	10	13	13	14	33
Black	5	7	13	5	7	6
Asian	4	5	8	5	9	12
American	na	na	Na	na	na	<1
Education						
College graduate or more	50	51	54	54	57	32
Family Income						
$75,000 or more		26	33	37	42	32

Source: Various Los Angeles Times exit polls (1994, 1996, 1998, 2000) and Census data.

Question: In the mid-1990s, observers were concerned about a two-tier California (voters versus all other Californians). Given demographic trends, what will California voters look like two decades from now, and how will this affect the two-tier idea?

registered as Democrats; only 7 percent called themselves Republicans. Likely voters with the highest incomes and levels of education are Asian Americans. All this can translate into substantial voting differences. For instance, in November 1996, Californians rejected affirmative action by passing Proposition 209 by a 54 to 46 margin. A substantial majority of whites supported the measure (63 percent) compared to Latinos (24 percent), African Americans (26 percent), and Asians (39 percent). Differences are also evident on less transparently racial issues. In 2004, voters approved a state bond in order to fund stem cell research (Proposition 71). While 56 percent of white voters approved the measure, the percentage of support jumped to 61 percent for Latino voters, 68 percent for black voters, and 72 percent for Asian voters.

Another gap among Californians is a *gender gap*—the margin of difference between the opinions and votes of men and women. In terms of party affiliation, political scientists have observed that more women now side with Democrats than Republicans; the opposite is true with men. Historically, voting behavior in California has reflected this trend but the gap is narrowing. For example, in 1996, 55 percent of women voted for Bill Clinton; only 43 percent of men did—a 12 point difference. By 2004, the difference narrowed; 57 percent of women voted for John Kerry while 53 percent of men did—a four point difference. The gap widened in the Barbara Boxer vote where 62 percent of women voted for her while 55 percent of men did.

Other gaps involve age and partisanship. The *age gap* refers to the fact that, compared to older voters, younger adults express less interest in politics, register to vote at lower rates, are less likely to vote, and less likely to identify with the major parties. The *partisan gap* means that the ideological divide between Republicans and Democrats appears to be widening. This is seen in their respective views on poverty, immigrants, California's economic conditions, gay marriage, and abortion. Contrary to some stereotypes, Republicans now trust the federal government more than Democrats; they also support at greater levels anti-terrorism laws that may restrict civil liberties.[24] This may well reflect their unsurprising support for President George W. Bush.

In years past, some observers expressed concern over these gaps, especially the dominance of affluent whites over the political process. For example, in the early 1990s, pollster Mervin Field proclaimed, "The agenda of the voting elites . . . is obviously demonstrably different than those who do not vote. The more that non-voters become different than voters in color, in class, in attitudes toward life, we create and build threatening pressures which could easily explode and alter for the worse the future course of our precious democracy."[25] Such fears may subside over the long term. First, the overwhelmingly white electorate is becoming less overwhelmingly so. In 1994, whites constituted 81 percent of the turnout; by 2004, it had dropped to 65 percent. Over time, it will decline still more. In numerous California cities, where no racial or ethnic group predominates, this is already the case. Second, while the proportion of white voters is declining, the educational and income level of voters is remaining relatively high (see Figure 5.2). As more ethnic and racial minorities assimilate and enter the middle class, they will to some extent vote as breadwinners and taxpayers, not just as Latinos, African Americans, or Asians. This will also influence party politics. While Latinos often align themselves with the Democratic Party, only a third of them consider themselves to be liberal. According to Anthony York, "Latino voters are a part of the growing group of centrist voters likely to have a moderating effect on both parties in California for years to come."[26]

Conclusion: Divided by Diversity

Recent elections in the United States have prompted observers to wonder if there is a place that represents America's future, electorally speaking. Some have settled on California. According to Adam Goodman, a Republican media strategist, "California more than any other state represents where America is headed. It is as close to being the heartbeat of America as any place in the country."[27] In a sense, California's electorate was destined from the beginning to be diverse. After all, Mexican and American cultures merged to produce early California. A broad electoral consensus in the post-World War II years, based on a less diverse electorate, resulted in bipartisan policies such as new highways and university campuses. These Progressive policies accommodated and encouraged growth. But recent demographic growth patterns have created diverse subelectorates, each with different interests. Those who identify with either major party or no party at all do so for profoundly different reasons. Furthermore, California's various electoral gaps suggest not just pluralistic but hyperpluralistic political behavior. Today, these political behavior patterns seem to be characterized by growing political conflict and competition among increasingly dissimilar groups in the electorate. Electoral consensus seems a thing of the past, and conflict within California's political institutions at times reflects this development. All this may point to a future where no political subculture dominates and where hyperpluralism characterizes how public problems are addressed, or for that matter, ignored. Yet as more groups of Californians earn their piece of the American dream, their similarities may outweigh their differences.

KEY TERMS

political participation   (p. 83)

exit option   (p. 84)

protest option   (pp. 84–85)

voting age population, voter turnout   (p. 86)

exit polls   (p. 86)

structural and preferential nonvoting
(pp. 86–91)

frame of reference   (p. 91)

political party   (p. 91)

party identification   (p. 91)

two-tier economy   (p. 94)

electoral gaps; voter/nonvoter, racial/ethnic,
gender, age, partisan   (pp. 94–95)

REVIEW QUESTIONS

1. Survey the various forms of political participation identified by political scientists. Which forms most aptly describe your own participation in the political system?
2. Why are the exit and protest options exercised by some Californians? Give some examples. Under what conditions might you consider these options?
3. Why do people not register to vote or, once registered, not turn out on election day?
4. Why do sizable numbers of Californians consider themselves independents?
5. How do recent election results underscore trends in voter demographics, turnout, and behavior?
6. Describe the various electoral gaps in California. To what extent are they troublesome for the nation's largest and most diverse state?

WEB ACTIVITIES

Los Angeles Times Poll
(www.latimes.com/HOME/NEWS/POLLS/;
The Field Poll (www.field.com/fieldpollonline/);
and the Public Policy Institute of California
(www.ppic.org/).

These sites feature statewide polling data including the policy views, general attitudes, electoral preferences, and demographic attributes of California's electorate. The Times Poll conducts election day exit polls as well.

California Voter Foundation
(www.calvoter.org/)
Use this site to "follow the money" and to check on recent state and local election results.

California Secretary of State
(www.ss.ca.gov)
Click on "Elections" to locate registration forms, voter registration statistics, turnout data, and past election results.

INFOTRAC® COLLEGE EDITION ARTICLES

For additional reading, go to InfoTrac® College Edition, your online research library, at http://www.infotrac.thomsonlearning.com

No Easy Answer to State's Quest for Relevance

Conflicts in the Coalition: Challenges to Back and Latino Political Alliances

Estimating Voter Choice

NOTES

1. Sidney Verba, Kay Lehman Scholzman, and Henry E. Brady, *Voice and Equality: Civic Volunteerism in American Politics* (Cambridge, MA: Harvard University Press, 1995). 51.
2. Mark Baldassare, *California in the New Millennium: The Changing Social and Political Landscape* (Berkeley: University of California Press, 2000), 34–36.
3. Katherine Ramarkrishnan and Mark Baldassare, *The Ties That Bind: Changing Demographics and Civic Engagement in California* (San Francisco: Public Policy Institute of California, 2004).
4. For an analysis of the exit option and other responses to civic dissatisfaction, see William E. Lyons and David Lowry, "The Organization of Political Space and Citizen Responses to

Dissatisfaction in Urban Communities: An Integrative Model," *The Journal of Politics* 49 (May 1986), 321–346.

5. James W. Sweeney, "Has the Golden State Lost Its Luster?" *California Journal* 23 (March 1992) 131–132.

6. David O. Sears and John B. McConahay, *The Politics of Violence: The New Urban Blacks and the Watts Riot* (Boston: Houghton Mifflin, 1973), 199.

7. Frank Clifford and David Ferrell, "The Times Poll: L.A. Strongly Condemns King Verdicts, Riots," *Los Angeles Times*, May 6, 1992.

8. The benchmark high was a 1964 presidential election turnout in California of over 88 percent of registered voters.

9. Baldassare, *California in the New Millennium*, 31.

10. Mark Baldassare, *The Changing Political Landscape of California: Statewide Survey* (San Francisco: Public Policy Institute of California, September 1998), 22.

11. Ibid.

12. See Noel Brinkerhoff, "Gen X: The Unknown Quantity," *California Journal* 30 (December 1999), 16–22.

13. Zoltan L. Hajnal, Paul G. Lewis, and Hugh Louch, *Municipal Elections in California: Turnout, Timing, and Competition* (San Francisco: Public Policy Institute of California, 2002).

14. Claudine Gay, *The Effect of Minority Districts and Minority Representation on Political Participation in California* (San Francisco: Public Policy Institute of California, 2001).

15. Bruce E. Keith, *The Myth of the Independent Voter* (Berkeley: University of California Press, 1992).

16. For an extended discussion of California independents, see Baldassare, *California in the New Millennium*, 61–80; and David Lesher, "A Decline to State," *California Journal* 33 (February 2002), 8–12.

17. Adrian D. Pantoja, Richardo Ramirez, and Gary M. Segura, "Citizens by Choice, Voters by Necessity: Patterns in Political Mobilization by Naturalized Latinos," *Political Research Quarterly* 54 (December 2001), 729–750.

18. See Jack Citron and Benjamin Highton, "When the Sleeping Giant Is Awake," *California Journal* 33 (December 2002), 42–46.

19. Michael Barone and Richard E. Cohen, *The Almanac of American Politics–2002* (Washington, D.C.: National Journal, 2001), 146.

20. Mark Baldassare, *The Changing Political Landscape of California: Statewide Survey* (San Francisco: Public Policy Institute of California, 1999) (www.ppic.org/publications/calsurvey5/survey 5.ch4.html/).

21. Dan Walters, *The New California: Facing the 21st Century*, 2nd ed. (Sacramento: California Journal Press, 1992), 7–8.

22. Dan Walters, "Research Finds a Two-Tier State," *Santa Barbara News Press*, February 15, 1999.

23. Deborah Reed, *California's Rising Income Inequality: Causes and Concerns* (San Francisco: Public Policy Institute of California, 1999), 2.

24. Public Policy Institute of California Statewide Surveys in 2002 and 2004.

25. Richard Zeiger, "Few Citizens Make Decisions for Everyone," *California Journal* 21 (November 1990), 519.

26. Anthony York, "From 'Sleeping Giant' to 'Incredible Hulk,'" *California Journal* 35 (June 2004), 42.

27. Betsy Streisand, "Where America Is Headed," *U.S. News & World Report*, (December 7, 1998), 24.

Linking People and Policymakers

In Brief

Chapter 6 examines the links between ordinary Californians and the policy institutions profiled in the next four chapters. In a representative democracy, such linkage efforts are essential in making the political system viable and legitimate in the eyes of ordinary citizens.

The mass media link Californians with policy processes primarily through newspapers and television. Newspapers provide substantial amounts of political news and guide public opinion by means of editorials and endorsements. Television has limits unique to the medium but reaches a huge audience in California. Thanks to the Progressives, political parties are weak in California, their powers limited either by law or practice. Supplementing the parties are a host of campaign professionals who, in effect, link voters to candidates. Given the costs of campaigns and the obvious willingness of individuals and groups to make campaign contributions, the role of money in the process is significant. Interest groups may well be *the* driving force in California politics. Groups come in all shapes and sizes, and they use a variety of resources to express their members' policy preferences to policymakers.

Introduction

Chapter 5 examined the political behavior of Californians acting as individuals and groups. We analyzed how they behave in the aggregate (taken as a whole), but the unit of study was the individual participant or nonparticipant. Subsequent chapters examine the formal governing institutions found in California's political system: the executive, legislative, and judicial branches of state government plus numerous local governments. Chapter 6 concerns those activities, processes, and political experts that link individual Californians to those officials and institutions that make policy—what people think of as "the government." In a representative democracy, such linkage institutions build necessary bridges between the governed and those who govern.[1] They help to organize the political attitudes of ordinary citizens (the activity of opinion leaders), frame their political choices (elections and political parties), and both structure and communicate their policy preferences to the government (through interest groups). Linkage institutions help place the policy concerns of citizens on the government's policy agenda.

In a representative democracy (where the people are sovereign but delegate decision making to a relative few), linkage institutions are essential. Power residing in "the people" is only latent (potential but unused) power until people have ways to express it. In California's evolving, complex, and pluralistic society, linkage institutions are the only practical way ordinary citizens can speak or relate to those making policy on their behalf. Even with initiatives, Californians depend on these institutions to structure policy choices.

Political scientist Kay Lawson has identified three types of linkages shared by democratic governments[2]—(1) *Participatory linkage* allows direct citizen participation in government decision making. In California, the initiative, referendum, and recall provide that kind of link.

(2) *Policy-responsive linkage* encourages political leaders to be responsive to the policy views of ordinary citizens. This is done through elections, political parties, and interest groups. (3) *Clientele linkage* often involves political leaders offering specific rewards in exchange for public support. Citizens act as "clients" who "buy" favored services by supporting particular leaders. Interest groups are the dominant clients in California politics.

Scholars of American politics commonly focus on the media, political parties, elections, and interest groups. At times these linkage institutions work smoothly. Both the people and policymakers respectively get what they want and need. Indeed, democratic theory would suggest the two agendas agree much of the time. At other times, though, these linkage institutions may not serve their intended purpose, or they lose meaning to average citizens. When this happens, the ability to govern is affected. Some believe this is the condition of modern California politics. The media may not adequately inform the state's residents. Political parties and interest groups increasingly compete with one another, usually at the expense of the parties. Even during elections, the media and interest groups exercise more power than parties. These developments affect the relationship between those who govern and those who are governed. Chapter 6 describes and evaluates each of these links and the role they play in connecting California's diverse citizenry and its government.

Mass Media

A primary linkage institution in national and California state politics is the mass media. The *mass media* funnel information to large number of people without direct, face-to-face contact. They consist primarily of print media (newspapers and magazines), electronic media (radio and television), and new media

When asked, "Where do you get <u>most</u> of your information about politics?" Californians respond accordingly:

Television	44%
Newspapers	20
Radio	12
Internet	9
Talking to others	8
Magazines	2
Other/Don't know	2

FIGURE 6.1   Political information sources in California

When asked, "How do you get most of your information about politics?" Californians responded this way.

Question: What mix of media do you use to keep up with California politics?

Source: Mark Baldassare. *The Changing Political Landscape of California: Statewide Survey* (San Francisco: Public Policy Institute of California, (October, 2004).

(the Internet). Citizens and public officials alike depend on the media to send and receive messages. Their resulting power is enormous. When he was assembly speaker (the second most powerful office in the state), Willie Brown said, "The press has as much influence on public policy as I have."[3] To underscore his point, consider the fact that media organizations are the only businesses (yes, businesses) constitutionally protected as a check on the government.

In addition to mass media, various *elite media* (those catering to select groups) thrive in California. For instance, the *California Journal,* which covers state politics, personalities, and issues, claims a relatively small but highly influential readership. Numerous political newsletters (*Political Pulse, California Political Week,* and *The Political Animal*) provide timely inside news and gossip considered essential to their subscribers. But their readership is small.

So, on which of these news sources do Californians most rely? In one statewide survey,

television was the most cited source of political news, followed by newspapers and radio. In only six years, newspapers as a primary source of political news dropped from 34 to 20 percent. Nine percent cited the Internet as their primary news source, up from 3 percent six years earlier. (see Figure 6.1). Combined, these media warrant particular attention.

NEWSPAPERS

The rise of California's newspapers parallels the state's political development. Wealthy individuals and families managed the earliest newspapers. One example was James McClatchy of the *Sacramento Bee,* who in the late 1800s worked his way up to editor while gradually purchasing shares in the paper. His heirs gained control of the *Bee* and still own it. He fought for land reform (dividing huge landholdings that had survived statehood) and the transcontinental railroad; he also fought against monopolies and environmentally destructive hydraulic mining. The McClatchy family eventually created an "Inland Empire" of papers in Fresno and Modesto as well as Sacramento. Today, the McClatchy Corporation owns communications properties in six states.

The *Los Angeles Times* was decidedly more conservative than McClatchy's *Bee*. Harrison Gray Otis bought the *Los Angeles Times* shortly after a Southern California railroad project linked Los Angeles to points east. He preached pro-business, anti-union sermons in editorials while hyping the Los Angeles land boom in which he himself had invested. He cooperated with the Big Four, who shared his desire for economic growth, personal power, and enormous income. On the other hand, William Randolph Hearst's *San Francisco Examiner* was decidedly antirailroad and friendly to Progressive reforms. During much of this period, newspapers from San Diego to San Francisco were owned by Republicans and espoused conservative values.

Today, California has more newspapers and newspaper readers than any other state. Yet newspapers across the state have gradually shrunk in number. Many have merged to create "one-newspaper" towns or have been acquired by media chains. For instance, the Copley chain owns the *San Diego Union and Tribune,* Gannett owns newspapers in Palm Springs, Salinas, Tulare, and Visalia, and Knight Ridder owns newspapers in Contra Costa County, San Jose, Monterey, and San Luis Obispo. Larger newspapers own smaller ones, and some chains have diversified by acquiring other media as well while ownership and management have become more corporate in style. Crusading editors like James McClatchy represent a bygone era.

Chains may dominate the newspaper scene, but California is also home to many ethnic minority newspapers. For example, *La Opinion* is the largest Spanish language newspaper in the nation. In Los Angeles, only the *Los Angeles Times* has higher circulation. The media association NCM (New California Media) lists

roughly 400 California-based media outlets including print, radio, broadcast, and online that serve groups including African Americans, Arabs, Armenians, Cambodians, Chinese, Hispanics, and Koreans.

Despite readership declines, many Californians still depend on newspapers for state and local government news. How much knowledge they receive depends on the paper. The *Sacramento Bee* reports state politics heavily because its readers include not only elected officials but thousands of state employees. Sacramento is, after all, a "company town." The *Los Angeles Times* can afford a sizable Sacramento bureau, and their reporting reflects it. But only a small minority of the state's 118 newspapers have Capital-based correspondents. Most newspapers throughout the state depend on wire services (Associated Press) and direct government sources (press releases) rather than doing their own investigative reporting. Coverage of public affairs is a challenge from anyone's vantage point. On one hand, given the competition for space (other news, sports, advertising, and classifieds), public officials find access to newspapers exceedingly difficult, especially in large, metropolitan areas. In Southern California, the *Times* tailors local news with sections devoted to counties such as Orange and Ventura. On the other hand, California's largest newspapers find that presenting political news to multiple jurisdictions and diverse populations is a challenge. The *Times*' Bill Boyarsky confesses, "The hardest part is finding political or other public figures whose names all readers will recognize."[4] Smaller newspapers primarily cover local news, often leaving state politics to larger papers.

Newspapers provide attentive publics with "hard news" about policy issues and policymakers, but how influential are they? Stories appearing only once seem to have little impact on citizens; unfolding stories that run for days on end have much more impact; but often these stories are negative. Such stories usually involve political corruption, mistakes, verbal miscues, or botched public policy. Veteran reporters in Sacramento believe newspaper coverage of state politics has a "harder edge" than it once did. According to the editors of the *California Political Almanac,* "Gone are the times when most of the Capitol's reporters and politicians ate, drank, and caroused together, and neither group judged the other too harshly."[5]

In addition to covering public policy, newspapers endorse candidates and propositions, yet the effectiveness of those endorsements is open to question. Do they really sway public opinion and change voter thinking? Editors think so, but others are less sure. Two conclusions are possible: (1) Given the plethora of today's media, editorial endorsements appear to carry less weight now than in the past. One exception may be local election races (counties, cities, special districts) where other voter cues may be missing. (2) The long-term editorial stance of newspapers appears to be more influential than specific election-eve endorsements. According to journalist and author Peter Schrag, "I don't think any newspaper has any great influence on a quick decision. My feeling is where we make the biggest difference is in setting the climate for the debate."[6]

TELEVISION

The popularity of television has diminished the political influence of newspapers, especially among certain groups. When asked in a 2000 survey where Californians get most of their news about the governor and the legislature, 44 percent of all respondents cited television; for Latino respondents, this figure jumped to 66 percent. Although 35 percent of all respondents listed newspapers as their primary source, only 17 percent of Latinos did.[7] Given its pervasiveness in much of California's political life, television falls far short of its potential as a linkage institution. The reasons are several.

A Visual Medium

Compared to other media, television focuses on the visual. To a news producer, a political story is not inherently interesting unless it is visually interesting. As one television producer admits, his colleagues are interested in "slash, flash, and trash. They want the [story] to bleed, scream and yell."[8] In response, public officials deliberately employ symbols, stunts, or pseudo-events to make their messages visually interesting. For example, at one capitol hearing on the problem of vicious dog attacks, one legislator brought along victims of such attacks. Celebrity witnesses virtually guarantee media coverage of committee hearings that might otherwise go unnoticed. Given his own celebrity status, Governor Arnold Schwarzenegger has staged numerous made-for-media events to publicize his policy agenda. In their defense, policymakers claim they must resort to such measures to inform their constituents and shed light on the state's problems.

Media Bias

Many Americans claim the media is biased, that they treat the news in a partial, unfair manner. Some see an *ideological bias* where the media tend to favor Republicans or Democrats, conservatives or liberals. California journalists think this may be in the eye of the beholder. People want to see a story reported in a predetermined way and find fault if it is not. According to former Associated Press reporter Doug Willis, "Republicans think I am a left-winger and Democrats think I am a shill for a fat-cat publisher. These things balance out."

California reporters do examine what policymakers say and do and compare the differences. According to journalist Steve Scott, "We have a low threshold for hypocrisy." The media also seem attracted to inconsistency and the ironies that abound in politics. For example, journalists found it intriguing that a state senator who pushed Proposition 22—the anti-gay marriage initiative—has a gay son and had a brother who died of AIDS. The fact that a Republican candidate for governor would be accused of groping women was newsworthy, in that the candidate was Arnold Schwarzenegger. But the media was also drawn to the story in light of the Republican Party's pro-family values rhetoric.

Television in particular exhibits a *structural bias*. As a business, television structures news to minimize coverage of government and politics. It tends to focus less on politics and more on human interest stories: entertainment, crime, sports, the weather—anything but politics. For instance, in a survey by the Annenberg School of Communication at the University of Southern California, five large market television stations devoted only .31 percent of local news time to the 1998 primary election for governor. Reflecting on that dismal coverage, television columnist Howard Rosenberg suggested that the only way to attract media attention would be to "have the four leading candidates chase each other on a freeway."[9] Structural bias takes place in the context of fierce competition among stations for ratings and "market share." In addition, television's use of pictures—its primary product—can lead to false impressions. For instance, one study revealed that Southern California stations portray crime in such a way that it over-represents African Americans and Latinos as lawbreakers out of proportion to their actual crime rates.[10]

Sparse Coverage

When television does cover public affairs, the coverage tends to be sparse and shallow. News stories themselves tend to be brief—very brief—due to the inherent limitations of commercial television. The result is a lack of analysis—why events, political or otherwise, happen. For example, one study of California television news showed that violence dominated local news coverage. Furthermore, the emphasis was on the specifics of particular crimes, not on the underlying social conditions that contribute to violence.[11] Coverage of state politics has a similar quality to it, to the extent it is covered at all. Even the governor's State of the State speech cannot be assured live broadcast, even if it coincides with late afternoon newscasts.

Another measure of television news coverage in California is how stations assign reporters. Sacramento-based news coverage had declined significantly from its zenith in the Reagan years—until Schwarzenegger became governor. Some out-of-town television stations vowed to establish or reestablish capital bureaus in the wake of his election but later scaled back their plans. Since state politics coverage is often Schwarzenegger-driven, and he travels widely throughout the state, many stations find a physical presence in the capital unnecessary. Local Sacramento stations still cover state politics and, on occasion, send footage to their network affiliates in Los Angeles and San Francisco. The Northern California News Satellite sells its state politics stories to client stations. Furthermore, the relatively new California Channel allows some 5 million cable households to view floor sessions, committee hearings, news conferences, and other related programming. It has become California's version of C-SPAN for the politically thirsty. In 2002, the state's public television stations partnered

Did You Know ... ?

The cost of operating a television station Capital bureau in Sacramento approaches $1 million per year.

to launch *California Connected,* a periodic weekly hour-long program on policy issues facing the state. Including the addition of more print reporters, the overall presence of the media in Sacramento is larger than it has been in many years.

Given its limitations, why does television news still hold promise as a linkage institution in California politics? In a word, size. The state has about 32 VHF and 77 UHF stations and more cable subscribers than any other state. Ninety-five percent of the state's households own television sets. More important, more than 85 percent of them live in only four media markets—greater Los Angeles, the San Francisco Bay Area, Sacramento, and San Diego. Access to those markets is a precious, costly commodity for public officials, election candidates, and interest groups. The sheer size of the Los Angeles market (reaching more than 50 percent of the state's voters) skews California politics. Statewide candidates from Southern California presumably have built-in advantages if they have had prior media exposure. Candidates from Northern California find they must spend huge amounts of time and money in the Los Angeles and Southern California markets to remain competitive.

In addition, television plays an important linkage role covering elections and crises. They do so through straight news reporting and through the airing of campaign commercials. Political advertising is prolific because it is the only realistic way candidates can reach voters. As a result, candidates often inundate newscast commercial time with messages unmediated by editors, reporters, and producers. The messages get through. Focus group research suggests that Californians are more likely to remember a candidate's television commercials than straight news about the candidate.[12] In covering crises, television has no peer; it has the capacity to provide nonstop news coverage of terrorist attacks, earthquakes, fires, and riots. Regular programming and much commercial time is suspended during such events. Crises in the nation's largest state often attract network attention.

THE INTERNET

Many observers believe the Internet has vast potential to revolutionize U.S. and California politics. In terms of usage, California's households own computers and go online somewhat more than the national average. As we saw, the Internet does not monopolize the political information habits of those households. Currently, the real potential of the Internet is felt most by candidates, political parties, and campaign contributors. For the state's March 2004 primary, there were 263 Web sites representing 48 percent of the 544 statewide, congressional, legislative, and ballot measure campaigns. Not only do these Web sites rally the politically faithful, they are a cost-effective means of raising campaign funds. One California political consultant tells his clients, "If you don't have a Web site, it makes you look like a dinosaur."[13]

How politically important is the Internet? The answer depends on the user. So far, the Internet seems to have attracted already well-informed Californians and political activists. But as a tool of persuasion, it tends to reinforce user views rather than convert undecided voters. According to Republican political consultant Dan Schnur, "The Internet is a proactive medium. With television, you have to make a proactive decision to not watch the commercial. But with the Internet, you have to make an active decision to click, to participate. Base voters of each party are much more likely to do that than the undecided."[14]

Still, Web-based communication is increasingly the norm and seems to be the wave of the future. Most state agencies, all members of the legislature, and many local governments disseminate information and receive feedback by way of the Internet. Furthermore, some initiative entrepreneurs regard the Internet as a promising tool. For example, the March 2000 school voucher initiative drive was launched

---

Did You Know . . . ?

To qualify to vote in California, you may obtain registration materials online by going to the Secretary of State Web site (www.ss.ca.gov/elections/). Click on Elections and Voter Information and proceed as directed.

---

on the Web. Californians may now download voter registration forms. What about registering and even voting online? An Internet Voting Task Force has concluded that "completely replacing today's paper ballots with Internet alternatives, while technologically possible, is not yet practical or fiscally feasible."[15] That said, the 2004 election cycle suggested that the Internet was becoming the driving force behind many campaign practices.

Political Parties

In addition to the media, *political parties* also link citizens to their government. Parties are organized groups that (1) possess certain labels, (2) espouse policy preferences, (3) both nominate and work to elect candidates for public office, and (4) help frame government's postelection policy agenda. In American politics, they are found at all levels—federal, state, and local—though not in equal measure. Political parties come in three forms.[16] The *party in the electorate* refers to voters who hold partisan affiliations; this group was discussed in Chapter 5. The *party in government* refers to partisan elected officials and institutions, such as the legislature, which organize around party labels. These leaders (primarily governors, legislators, and to some extent judges) translate party positions into policy and personify the party in the minds of many voters. The *party organization* means the formal party apparatus: its structure, staff, budget, rules, and processes for achieving its goals. As a linkage institution, we will discuss the party as organization.

POLITICAL PARTIES: CALIFORNIA STYLE

Like the United States as a whole, California has a two-party system. Democrats and Republicans dominate at least partisan elections. But California's system is one of weak parties. To curb machine bosses like San Francisco's Abe Ruef and corporate elites like the Big Four, the Progressives established elements of a weak party system. *Direct primaries* allowed voters themselves to nominate candidates; *cross-filing* allowed the candidates themselves to run as Democrats, Republicans, or on occasion both; and *nonpartisan elections* blurred affiliations of judges and disallowed parties from endorsing or assisting local officeholders.

Over the objections of party leaders, voters in 1996 approved an Open Primary Law (Proposition 198). It created a *blanket primary,* which allowed voters to cross party lines and vote for any candidate, regardless of party label (that is, a registered Republican could vote for a Democratic candidate and vice versa). This innovation enabled more than 1.7 million "decline-to-state" voters a chance to vote for partisan candidates. It also allowed wealthy candidates such as Democrat Al Checchi and Republican Darrell Issa in effect to bypass the party apparatus and wage self-financed campaigns. The blanket primary was employed for the June 1998 primary election and the March 7, 2000, presidential primary. But in late June 2000, the U.S. Supreme Court on a 7:2 vote overturned the law, claiming it violated the First Amendment associational rights of political parties. According to Justice Antonin Scalia, "Proposition 198 forces political parties to associate with . . . those who, at best, have refused to affiliate with the party, and at worst, have expressly affiliated with a rival."[17] In reaction, a new election law permitted parties to allow "decline to state" voters to vote in their respective primary elections if they request to do so. In November 2004, voters revisited the blanket primary issue. Proposition 62 would have opened nonpresidential (state and congressional) primary elections to all voters regardless of party. The two top vote getters regardless of party would compete in the general election. California's presidential primary would be exempt from this requirement unless the political parties opened them voluntarily. In an effort to undercut 62, the California legislature placed Proposition 60 on the ballot, a constitutional amendment that guaranteed that the top vote getter of any party would appear on the general election ballot. Proposition 62 failed with only 46 percent of the vote; Proposition 60 passed with over 67 percent of the vote.

In California's weak party system, Democrats and Republicans control major offices in Sacramento. Their strength in the electorate translates into strength in the government. Based on how successful the parties were in electing governors and legislators, political scientists long regarded California as "two-party competitive" but consistent Democratic victories led them to label California as "modified one-party Democratic."[18] Why the change? After turn-of-the-century reforms, Republicans dominated state politics from 1924 to 1957. Both parties were relatively competitive from 1958 to 1973, and Democrats dominated from 1974 to 1982. Until 1998, voters elected Republican governors and, except for two years, a Democrat-controlled legislature. With the election of Gray Davis in 1998, the Democrats controlled the governor's office and majorities in both the Assembly and the Senate for the first time since 1982. They gained even more legislative seats in 2000 and have controlled the legislature ever since. To be sure, the control of public policy is now shared with Republican Arnold Schwarzenegger.

Minor or *third parties* widen voter choice at least for some voters. What does it take for a third party to be included on a California ballot? Two routes are possible: (1) signing up 77,389 registered voters (1 percent of the total votes cast in the 2002 gubernatorial election), or (2) getting 773,883 registered voters to sign a petition seeking party qualification (10 percent of the total votes cast in the previous gubernatorial election). The first option is relatively easy; the second has never succeeded. To repeatedly appear on the ballot, third parties must maintain a list of 77,389 registered voters or have one of their candidates garner at least 2 percent of the statewide votes cast. In addition to the Democrats and the Republicans, California's officially recognized third or minor parties include the American Independent Party, the Green Party, the Libertarian Party, the Natural Law Party, and the Peace and Freedom Party.

HOW THE PARTIES ARE ORGANIZED

Because the state elections code dictates how California parties are organized, party structures look very similar. California parties do not have precinct-level organizations common in "strong party" states. Therefore, the lowest level is the *county central committee*. Most voters elect these committee members in primary elections without really knowing who they are. These local committees do not "run" local party affairs, have few if any funds to disburse, and must compete for influence with elected officials and unofficial party clubs.

The *state central committee* is the key organizational unit for both Republicans and Democrats. Numbering in the hundreds, its membership is a hodgepodge of party leaders, elected officials, and appointees from the ranks of activist party members. Every two years, state central committee members meet to discuss policy issues, select party leaders, hear elected officials and major candidates speak, "network" each other, and rally the party faithful (see Photo 6.1). Historically, the Republicans

PHOTO 6.1   2004 Democratic State Party Convention
California Senator Barbara Boxer appears before the 2004 Democratic State Party Convention in San Jose to energize the party faithful.
Question: What benefits do conventions like these provide for party members, activists, and officeholders?

have been more cohesive than the Democrats, who divide into official caucuses representing the disabled, women, labor, gays/lesbians, and seemingly every racial/ethnic group in the state. This devotion to group-specific interests has given the party a hyperpluralistic outlook. These party gatherings showcase, for better or worse, the current diversity that exists within both major parties. In the Democratic Party, liberals, moderates, and caucus groups fight among themselves. In the past, Republican Party conventions tended to pit fiscal conservatives against social issue conservatives and pragmatists against ideologues.

The election of Arnold Schwarzenegger has reenergized the California Republican Party and given it a more pragmatic outlook. According to veteran journalist Lou Cannon, Republican Party activists would rather "emphasize

mainstream economic issues on which they largely agree at the expense of social issues on which they differ."[19] Yet as a general rule, party activists regardless of party tend to be more doctrinaire than the public at large. Many are ideologically brittle and lack the ability, willingness, and skill to compromise—traits that are expected of elected officials. Furthermore, because of the geographic diversity of the Golden State, many party activists from interior California have little in common with those from coastal metropolitan areas apart from sharing party labels.

In addition to the state and county committee structures, the political parties in California send representatives to the national committees. Full-time party chairpersons are selected to staff the state central committees. These positions often attract wealthy hyperactivists desiring to rub elbows with elected officials and party donors. Most are unknown to average voters; a notable exception was former governor and now Oakland mayor Jerry Brown who chaired the Democratic Party from 1988 to 1991. As a rule, state party chairs are ineffective spokespersons for the party, but even their election at state party conventions can reveal ideological and issue splits within the party.

SURROGATE "PARTIES"

If political parties are considered important linkage institutions in a representative democracy, what happens in states where parties are destined to be weak? In California, surrogate institutions have been created to replicate strong party functions. For example, a group of moderate Republicans in 1943 formed the California Republican Assembly. Because the group was unofficial, it was not regulated by state law and could endorse candidates. Their endorsement in a congressional race launched Richard Nixon's long political career. Today, this grassroots group claims to be the "conservative conscience" of the state Republican Party and usually endorses social issue conservatives. In 1953, Democrats organized the California Democratic Council (CDC). It helped the party's resurgence after 1958 and launched the career of former U.S. senator Alan Cranston. According to its Web site, it represents "the voice and activism of thousands of community Democrats."

Both these organizations organize into local clubs or chapters, hold grassroots conventions, and provide issue workshops for various party clubs around the state. These surrogate "parties" hold less meaning for the electorate today than once was the case.[20] Nowadays, political action committees, candidate-centered campaigns, and media-driven elections conspire to limit party influence where it matters most: picking candidates and winning elections.

ENDORSEMENT POLITICS

Arguably the most important test of a strong party organization is its ability to control the selection of nominees for public office. Short of hand-picking nominees, parties should at least be able to endorse them. In their quest for nonpartisanship, California's Progressives banned that practice in 1913. Through legislation and party practice, the ban was even strengthened to disallow parties from supporting or opposing preprimary candidates. The surrogates endorse, but few listen. Occasionally, candidates unacceptable to their own parties win primaries. In one notorious case, Democratic voters nominated Ku Klux Klan Grand Dragon Tom Metzger to a congressional seat in San Diego County despite his repudiation by party leaders. In the 1980s, the U.S. Supreme Court intervened in California's party affairs by declaring a state ban on party endorsements unconstitutional. In a case involving San Francisco Democrats, the Court majority argued that such bans violated the parties' rights to spread their views and the voters' rights to inform themselves about candidates and issues.[21]

In 1991 the same Court refused to extend that reasoning to California's nonpartisan elections. Since only 183 of the state's 19,000-plus state and local elective offices are partisan, prohibiting endorsements for nonpartisan offices was a form of censorship, argued petitioner Jerry Brown.[22] (The Court dismissed the case on procedural grounds, leaving open the possibility of future litigation.) California's major parties, despite their newfound power to do so, appear skittish about making endorsements even in partisan elections. Saddled with a recession, even incumbent President George Bush was unable to wrest a preprimary endorsement from the 1992 Republican state convention. California Democrats ceased making endorsements for other reasons. Some prominent Democrats were running against each other due to redistricting while minority candidates were challenging seasoned incumbents. The party did not want to be caught in the middle of these struggles.[23]

If parties cannot or will not endorse candidates, another option is available, namely the use of *slate mailers*—large postcards listing "endorsed" candidates and propositions. Note the quotation marks. In many cases, distributors of these mailers are actually campaign-oriented businesses. Often these mailers have red, white, and blue colors and are designed to look as "official" as possible—as if sent out by the government itself. Their titles sound generic (Voter Information Guide) or may emphasize a particular theme (Official Law Enforcement Voter Guide). Some sound quite official but may be quite misleading. In 2004, the California Professional Firefighters disavowed an unaffiliated paid slate mail operation called Golden State Firefighters. Computer technology makes it easy to target specific groups of voters by region, party, ethnicity, age, or other factors. They even remind voters where their polling place is. Tiny asterisks beside certain names or initiatives indicate which campaigns actually paid to be "endorsed" (see Photo 6.2). What do these mailers cost a campaign? Payments may range from a few hundred dollars for a city council race to $75,000 or more in proposition contests.[24] Because many slate mailers are little more than profitable businesses that offer placements on a first come-first served basis, a Republican candidate may appear on a "Democratic" mailer or the other way around.

Slate mailers took an unexpected turn in 2004. In an unprecedented move by a governor, Arnold Schwarzenegger raised funds to distribute his own slate mailer urging support for or rejection of ten of the measures on the November ballot. (Photo 6.2) Of the ten propositions, the governor's position prevailed on nine. Observers attributed the fate of several of these measures to this mailer. As long as parties remain weak and propositions remain popular, slate mailers will likely remain an attractive electoral tool.

Elections

No matter how weak, American political parties and elections are intertwined, linking average citizens to their government in profound ways. Public officials are to be held accountable periodically for what they do and say. This practice is a key feature of the nation's political culture. Elections are important to policymakers too because they provide some measure of government *legitimacy*. In other words, voters grant officials they choose credibility and authority to act on their behalf. Policymakers occasionally misinterpret their own election victories as *mandates* to do something in particular, especially if they win by wide margins. Aware of the complex factors that determine election outcomes, political scientists tend to discount the mandates so often claimed by election winners.

Californians are peppered with elections. Partisan elections are scheduled for every other even-numbered year. The primary election is the first Tuesday in June, and the general election is the first Tuesday after the first Monday in November. In 2000 and 2004, the state experimented with an early March primary in order to give Californians greater voice in picking presidential nominees. In 2004, lawmakers conceded that the effort failed and returned to the June primary. Nonpartisan elections for judges appear within that cycle as do ballot propositions. Local elections (county, city, special district, and school district offices) may be combined with the primary or general elections or may be scheduled by the local entity for a separate time altogether. As a linkage institution, the election process surely provides California voters with a channel of influence only imagined in many parts of the world.

PHOTO 6.2   Slate Mailer

This 12-page slate mailer was a departure from most mailers. Governor Arnold Schwarzenegger and the Republican Party raised $2 million to send it to about 5 million voters that included many Republicans but also Democrats and Independents. Each mailer included highly-spun descriptions of selected ballot measures, the governor's analysis and a convenient tear-off card with "Arnold's Top Props" for voters to take to the polls.

At election time, voters face an obstacle course. Progressive policies to limit party power also limit their ability to help voters choose. Ideally, direct democracy (initiatives, referenda, and recall) was to put power in the hands of out-of-power groups (groups other than the Southern Pacific). But without strong local party organizations, such groups were either ignorant of or naive about electoral techniques and strategies to reach voters. California's diverse geography, size, and rapid population growth made such electoral efforts all the more difficult. By the Great Depression, voters became more radical, disgruntled, and susceptible to outside forces.[25] All these factors encouraged the rise of campaign professionals who would, in effect, substitute for the parties by linking people to candidates and issues.

CAMPAIGN PROFESSIONALS AND POLLSTERS

California's first political consultants were Clem Whitaker and his wife Leona Baxter who established Whitaker and Baxter in the early 1930s. These two conservatives had close ties to the state's 700 newspaper publishers and helped defeat Upton Sinclair's bid for governor in 1934. One observer believes this particular campaign gave birth to the modern media-centered, professionally managed campaign.[26] Contemporary California is home to all manner of campaign professionals—large and small, liberal and conservative, general and specialized.[27] These people call California the Golden State for the campaign gold that can be mined there. For example, the firm of Winner/Wagner & Mandelbach managed more than $28 million in support of Proposition 5 (the Indian gaming initiative) and stood to net several million of that.[28]

To run a candidate or proposition in California requires a variety of campaign consultants: campaign managers, fund-raisers, media experts, lawyers, accountants, and computer experts. General campaign managers range from solo practitioners (found in smaller communities) to large firms located in Sacramento, San Francisco, or Los Angeles. They advise candidates on all aspects of campaigning, coordinate the use of specialists, and control the technology used in the campaign. Given the cost of campaigning in California, public relations firms adept at fund-raising are a must. They do direct mail or stage expensive dinners featuring "drawing card" celebrities, such as movie stars or recording artists.

Media specialists divide California into media markets, not electoral districts. Because politicians or would-be politicians do not think in those terms, media consultants are essential. They work with candidates and initiative campaigns to produce newspaper advertisements and broadcast commercials. All these media are tailored to specific markets and audiences. Because San Francisco voters are different from San Bernardino voters, appeals are customized based on geographic, demographic, and ideological differences. Candidates use television ads, not only to hype their own qualifications but to criticize opponents. Some are simple "comparison" ads; others are full-blown attack ads. According to one California advertising specialist, "almost all attack ads use flying newspaper headlines superimposed over the worst photo ever taken of the opponent. And, just in case you missed the message, it's reinforced with type at the bottom of the screen and forbidding voice-over."[29]

Lawyers, accountants, and computer experts are also essential. California's campaign finance regulations, a direct consequence of the Watergate scandal in the 1970s, affect campaigns from the governor to sanitary district board member. State regulations require candidates to report campaign spending and to disclose personal income, which in turn requires legal analysis and careful bookkeeping, especially in the larger races. Increasingly, computer software allows campaigns of any size to mange the overall effort; maintain lists of voters, volunteers, and donors; generate correspondence; and compile reports required by California's Fair Political Practices Commission. Webmasters are now essential to create and maintain campaign-based Web sites.

Increasingly, California's campaign professionals work to pass or defeat various initiatives. In these issue campaigns, consultants work closely with coalitions of like-minded interests (business, labor). This trend is understandable. In an era of term-limited state legislators, permanent interest groups believe elections are an increasingly important way to get their issues out before the public. From a consultant's point of view, issue campaigns are more lucrative; there are no spending limits on the "independent expenditure committees" that fund such efforts. Furthermore, issue campaigns are more impersonal; consultants avoid the headaches of candidate emotions and family pressures. As consultant Steve Hopcraft puts it, "Groups don't have a spouse."[30]

Polling specialists ask voters what they think about the issues and the candidates. Any candidate can rely on instinct, letters to the editor, personal mail, or statewide pollsters. Independent statewide polling organizations including the Field Poll, the *Los Angeles Times* Poll, and the polling unit of the Public Policy Institute of California provide a wealth of policy and election-related data. However, from a candidate's perspective, the most helpful polls are tailored to and hired by particular campaigns. For example, *benchmark polls* taken before a campaign begins tell a candidate what issues are important, plus what the voters think of the candidate. *Tracking polls*, taken during the course of the campaign, reveal how the campaign is progressing and whether or not particular strategies are working. *Focus groups* test the reactions of a relative handful of voters to commercials and other political stimuli. All these techniques help pollsters measure the intensity of voter feelings and the impact of candidate messages.

Polls have become so prolific, several polling organizations may cover the same topic during the same week or month. One would think the results would match but often they do not. Different poll findings may be due to exactly when the poll was conducted, differences in question wording and placement, and assumptions about who will turn out to vote. Sample size is a key variable in determining poll accuracy. For example, a small sample of 500 voters statewide would have a margin of error of 4.5 percent. One poll in 2003 indicated that, of 505 respondents, 55 percent favored the recall of Governor Gray Davis. In truth, pollsters were confident that the figure was somewhere between 50.5 and 59.5 percent—hardly an insightful or instructive result.[31]

Do election professionals make a difference in elections? Yes, in certain situations, but less so than many people think. Other factors such as incumbency, issues, and candidate personality play significant roles. Win or lose, consultants appear to contribute to escalating campaign costs. This is a function of consultants raising and spending campaign cash and then taking a percentage of whatever is spent. As one Ohio consultant put it, "Outside California, we call it the Californication of politics."[32]

THE ROLE OF MONEY

In an era where California campaigns seem awash in money, the money itself has become an issue. Former Assembly Speaker and State Treasurer Jesse Unruh once said, "Money is the mother's milk of politics." After assessing the modern role of money in election campaigns, he revised his adage: "Money has become clabber in the mouth of the body politic." Candidates and officeholders complain about escalating campaign costs but seem ready to raise and spend whatever it takes to win. Indeed, Governor Gray Davis raised an average of $1 million a month during his first term in office and Arnold Schwarzenegger doubled that rate during his first months in office. Candidates remind us that television ads and direct mail are costly and previous campaign debts need to be retired. But how much campaign fundraising is enough? It appears no amount is quite sufficient. Regardless of the amount raised, there are ways to spend or allocate every dime. Given the ready availability of campaign funds and the prevalence of safe legislative seats, candidates may not need all they raise, spending the funds on other races or banking unspent funds for future campaigns.

Where do candidates obtain the funds necessary to run? *First,* wealthy candidates are allowed to spend unlimited amounts of their own money. But wealth does not assure victory. For example, in 1994 Michael Huffington spent nearly $30 million of his own money to unseat California Senator Dianne Feinstein, and Al Checchi spent upwards of $40 million seeking the Democratic nomination for governor in 1998. Both lost. *Second,* candidates use direct mail, the Internet, or other means to attract small "grassroots" contributions. Although the amounts may be small, these contributions signal broad-based support. *Third,* to bring in larger contributions, candidates seek contributions from the state's *political action committees.* PACs, the election arms of interest groups, are the largest source of campaign funds for legislative and statewide races. Claiming that they simply want access, PACs commonly contribute to incumbents and to those legislators who control legislation of interest to them. In open seat elections, they may contribute to both sides, assuring some access regardless of who wins. Contributions often come by way of expensive Sacramento dinners, receptions, or other events like golf outings or concerts; legislators often ask $1,000 per ticket or $3,200 to be a sponsor, the legal maximum contribution under Proposition 34. Many of these events coincide with the late-summer end of a legislative session when hundreds of bills of interest to these groups are scheduled for votes.[33] Why Sacramento rather than the legislative districts where voters live? The Capital is where full time legislators spend much of their time and where lobbyists are situated. In fact these mutually convenient Capital fundraisers are called "Third House events."

Contributions to candidate campaigns are strictly monitored in California. The *Political Reform Act of 1974* (Proposition 9) requires disclosure of campaign contributions and expenditures, regulates the organization of campaign committees, limits entertaining by lobbyists, and prohibits conflict of interest by local officials. The *Fair Political Practices Commission* (FPPC) was established to implement this law. Its staff monitors all nonfederal elections, issues advisory opinions, and conducts random audits. It also investigates charges of wrongdoing and fines candidates for missing filing deadlines, submitting inaccurate reports, sending deceptive mailers, and laundering contributions. For instance, in 2001 Governor Gray Davis agreed to pay a $50,000 fine to the FPPC for various campaign finance violations stemming from his 1998 election. Many public officials now think that Act is so complex and the commission so ineffective that a major overhaul is in order.[34]

Although contributions are monitored and reported, they have not been limited in California. Campaign spending continues to climb. State legislators, regardless of party, have resisted campaign finance reforms, thinking they would help challengers. Several initiatives have bypassed the legislature, presenting reforms directly to the voters. Federal courts ruled Proposition 73 (1988) unconstitutional because its spending controls limited freedom of speech and favored incumbents. In 1996, voters approved Proposition 208, a comprehensive campaign reform initiative that limited individual donations to $250 for legislative races and $500 for statewide races.

Court rulings blocked its implementation. In 2000, voters passed still another campaign finance measure, Proposition 34. It set contribution limits so high ($3,000 for legislative races, $5,000 for statewide races, and $20,000 for gubernatorial races) that reformers believe it will do little to alter big-money politics in California. In addition, so-called *soft money* has entered California politics. Political parties are supposed to use these unregulated, unreported contributions for party-building and get-out-the-vote efforts. In fact, they are also used to attack opposing parties, candidates, and views. To get around Proposition 34, interest groups now form their own independent expenditure campaigns that need not conform to the proposition's limits. Like water, campaign money seems to flow around any reform obstacle in its path.[35]

In short, meaningful reform faces numerous obstacles. Incumbents are loath to create a level playing field; the courts think spending limits curtail free speech; and voters reject using tax dollars for campaigning. Some reformers recommend so-called "Clean Money" systems as exist in Maine and Arizona. Under such systems, candidates raise modest amounts of $2-5 contributions, agree to limit overall spending, and obtain full public financing of their campaigns. In the meantime, even reform-minded, term-limited legislators seem to have mastered the art of raising PAC contributions, contributing to a rich candidate's system that favors wealthy contributors and/or wealthy candidates.[36]

CALIFORNIA ELECTIONS AND NATIONAL POLITICS

Elections in California play an increasingly important role in national politics. Four factors help explain this presence.

1. As was noted earlier, voter-approved initiatives often engender similar efforts in other states. Proposition 13 (1978) spawned similar tax-cutting efforts elsewhere. California's rejection of affirmative action in public programs (Proposition 209) encouraged such efforts in several other states. Ron Unz, the primary backer of a successful anti–bilingual education measure (Proposition 227) and Ward Connerly, sponsor of 209, have traveled widely to advise policy activists in other states.

2. California is a significant source of campaign contributions sought by out-of-state candidates. Political consultant Joe Cerrell has characterized the state as a "big ATM in the sky."[37] In the 2003–2004 election cycle, Democrat John Kerry (along with allied groups and the Democratic National Committee) raised more money from California donors than any other candidate has ever raised from a single state for a single election. This was more than former Vice President Al Gore collected nationwide in his failed 2000 presidential bid.[38]

3. California candidates are compelling recipients of out-of-state campaign funds. National PACs join their in-state counterparts and numbers of individual donors join in to swell campaign coffers. Consider U.S. Senator Barbara Boxer. In her 2004 reelection effort, nearly 29 percent of reportable contributions (those over $200) came from out-of-state sources. One of those sources was EMILY's List, a campaign financing group that bundles checks from voters nationwide who support largely liberal and female candidates. Presidential candidates find California a compelling source of primary election campaign funds. Political scientist Nelson Polsby calls this "the Beverly Hills primary" with good reason. While both major parties seek out campaign contributions in California, certain locales are favorites. "For Democrats, Beverly Hills' famous 90210 zip code ranks fourth [nationally] in generosity, with Century City in Los Angeles ranking fifth."[39]

Did You Know . . . ?

In the 2004 election cycle, all California candidates raised an average of $8.78 per voter (based on over 12 million voters).
Source: The Institute on Money in State Politics

4. California's role in the selection of presidential nominees and in the election of presidents is anomalous. Since the state is the source of many convention delegates and by far the largest number of Electoral College votes—55 out of 270 needed to win—one might think candidates would need to devote considerable resources here. Think again, beginning with the primaries. Even though the California legislature frontloaded the primary election by placing it in early March, many other states have done the same thing. In 2004, twenty states held their primaries or caucuses before California's March 2 primary and California shared that date with nine other states. All told, Democrat John Kerry was the presumed nominee before a single Californian voted. Furthermore, California is a daunting place to wage a primary campaign. As *Los Angeles Times* reporter James Rainey put it, California is "too large to buttonhole many voters in person and with TV markets so expensive it can blow a campaign treasury to smithereens."[40] Even cash-rich campaigns find it profitable to spend media funds elsewhere. The California anomaly continues into the general election period. In recent presidential campaigns, public opinion polls have indicated consistent support in the Golden State for the Democratic nominee—Clinton (1992 and 1996), Gore (2000), or Kerry (2004). As a result, Republican candidates—Dole in 1996 or Bush in 2000 and 2004—understandably spent their time and campaign resources where chances of winning were greater. As likely winners in California, Democratic candidates also campaign more heavily elsewhere, especially in those "battleground" states where such efforts could tip the balance.

Interest Groups

Interest groups are a significant force in national and state politics. It would be difficult to overemphasize their power and influence in California politics, both state and local. An *interest group* is a body of individuals who share similar goals and organize to influence public policy around those goals. Their development in U.S. politics was early and immediate. Founder James Madison considered the potential problem of "factions" in America (his term for both groups and political parties) but thought the new republic could control them. By the 1830s, Frenchman Alexis de Tocqueville observed, "In no country in the world has the principle of association been more successfully used or applied to a greater multitude of objects than in America."[41] By the 1950s, political scientists considered the activity of interest groups central to politics. Legislatures basically referee group struggles; victories come in the form of statutes—passed or defeated. The job of government in a pluralistic society is to manage conflict among groups. What strikes political scientists today is the hyperpluralistic expansion of groups and the splintering of interests—a process particularly evident in California.

For ordinary citizens, interest groups provide still another important link to the political system. Multiple memberships are common.

For instance, a local homebuilder is likely to be a member of a local builders group and the chamber of commerce plus several statewide groups, the Building Industry Association, and the Associated Contractors of California. These statewide groups provide the contractor with political access while furthering the broad interests of the building industry: environmental regulations, building code matters, land use controls, and growth policies. But builders are not just builders. They may also be members of churches, health insurance groups, automobile associations, and sporting groups. These interests are also organized at the state level to push their own public policy preferences.

Interest groups have an enormous impact on California politics and clearly contribute to its hyperpluralistic character. The print version of the Secretary of State's official *Directory of Lobbyists, Lobbying Firms, and Lobbyist Employers* used to run nearly 600 pages in length. That is just at the state level. Other groups, including local versions of statewide groups, operate below the state level to sway county governments, cities, special districts, and school districts. For example, local chambers of commerce often have government relations offices that monitor and influence local government decision making from a pro-business perspective.

Interest group development paralleled the political development of the Golden State. By winning the war against the Southern Pacific Railroad (SPR), the Progressives in effect invited other interest groups to participate in California politics. Furthermore, the development of the state's political system coincided with the industrial revolution, the rise of corporate California, and the development of a complex economy. Private sector interest groups multiplied as a result. As the scope of government enlarged, so did the number of government employees. They formed their own interest groups (such as the American Federation of State, County, and Municipal Employees, AFL-CIO). By century's end, an increasingly active state government, spurred by new policy demands and a shrinking federal role, required constant vigilance by an ever-growing corps of interest groups.

CALIFORNIA GROUPS: WHO ARE THEY?

In contemporary California, interest groups are as diverse as the state itself. Together, they resemble the interest group system in the nation's capital. This hyperpluralistic maze of groups can be divided into five categories based on primary interest or motivation:

1. *Economic Groups.* These groups are primarily motivated by money—income, profits, better salaries, or the economic health of a company or trade. In their view, business regulations, tax policies, labor/management issues, access to markets, occupational safety, and environmental rules can mean financial gain or loss. They range from individual companies to trade associations to employee groups. Some of the biggest, measured in lobbyist spending, include the Association of California Insurance Companies, the Western State Petroleum Association, the California Cogeneration Council, the California Manufacturers Association, ARCO, and Chevron.

2. *Professional Groups.* Professionally motivated groups both provide member services and represent group interests in the policy process. They possess economic interests to be sure but are also concerned about the regulation of their profession per se. It is common for the state to both regulate entry into certain professions and oversee their conduct. Notable California examples include the California Teachers Association, the California Medical Association, the California Bar Association, and the California Trial Lawyers Association.

3. *Public Agency Groups.* These groups represent various units of government at the state and local level. Representative are the following:

the League of California Cities, the California State Association of Counties, the California Association of Councils of Government, the California Special Districts Association, the Association of California Water Agencies, and the California District Attorneys Association.[42] At least 85 separate cities hire their own lobbyists. The state even lobbies itself; executive branch agencies routinely defend their own interests at legislative hearings.

4. *Cross-Cutting Groups.* These groups do not fit neatly into other categories even though they share some overlapping interests. Cross-cutting groups attract members from other groups due to social, ethnic, ideological, religious, or emotional ties. Illustrative are the Traditional Values Coalition, Mexican American Political Association, the California Council of Churches, the Sierra Club, and Handgun Control, Inc. Scholars and policymakers alike call some of these groups "public interest" groups because their policy goals are not solely economic or professional in nature. Such groups regard themselves as public interest groups because *they* believe their causes serve a larger public interest or an underrepresented group.

5. *Miscellaneous.* This catch-all category simply means some California groups defy reasonable classification. Where do you place the Americans for Smokers Rights, the California Coin Dealers, the California Equine Council, or California Trout, Inc.? Some groups are ad hoc or single issue in nature: they temporarily organize around a "hot" issue or legislative bill or an initiative. When the issue dies, so do they. Still other groups defy simple classification because they spend only minimal or sporadic amounts of time on public policy matters.

6. *Local Groups.* We should not ignore the many interest groups at the local level in California. Of course, some are local chapters of statewide groups such as the Sierra Club, the Chamber of Commerce, and local teacher

union affiliates. They provide "on the ground" support for statewide policy positions and are available to lobby legislators during frequent district visits. Others are purely local, focusing on issues of local or regional interest. For example, the San Francisco Bay Area interest groups focusing on mass transit issues have included the Bay Area Transportation and Land Use Coalition, People on the Bus, Access BART Coalition, Say NO to BART!, Rescue Muni, Train Riders Association of California, and Marin Advocates for Transit.

As is the case in national politics, the power of California interest groups ebbs and flows depending on economic trends, and whether their interests match the interests of those in power. For example, the California Chamber of Commerce has had extraordinary access to Governor Arnold Schwarzenegger ever since they endorsed him for governor, a political first for the group. His pro-business agenda is in concert with their own. The power of labor unions largely depends on the health of the sectors they represent. The clout of unions representing traditional blue collar trades has fallen as manufacturing jobs have declined in numbers or moved out of state. The newfound power of unions that represent state employees, law enforcement officers, school teachers, and health care workers reflects the growth of those sectors and their claim on public budgets. Consider the fact that public sector unions now contribute more to political candidates than do general trade unions.[43]

People often confuse interest groups with lobbyists. *Lobbyists* are those individuals who represent interest groups in the policy process. In California, they prefer to be called "legislative advocates." All in all, there are more than 1,100 groups or individuals who actually lobby the state government (and are duly registered as lobbyists with the Secretary of State). There are so many of them, they have their own group—the Institute of Governmental Advocates.

Did You Know . . . ?

In 2003, there were nearly ten lobbyists for every California legislator. Lobbyist spending in the state totaled $200 million, more than any other state.
Source: Center for Public Integrity.

HOW INTEREST GROUPS ORGANIZE

Interest groups in California have found there is no best method of organizing to function as linkage institutions. The following patterns are common.

In-House Lobbyists

Some businesses find that policy making so affects their interests that using their own employees is the most effective route to adequate representation. These people are "in-house" lobbyists. For instance, ARCO, Chevron, Allstate Insurance Company, Ford Motor Company, and United Airlines represent themselves in the political process. Some public sector agencies, such as the City and County of Los Angeles, also have their own offices in Sacramento. For good measure, many of these interests hire lobbying firms to augment their own employees.

Associations

Many individual entities join together around common goals. The Sacramento Yellow Pages under "Associations" proves there is strength in numbers. One can almost fill in the blank: The California Association of Nurserymen, Nonprofits, HMOs, CD-ROM Producers, Winegrape Growers, or Suburban School Districts. These are only a handful of the myriad associations found in the capital. Such groups link members to the policy process through numerous meetings, legislative briefings, and newsletters. The larger ones command sub-

stantial resources for lobbying and campaign activity. Because policy priorities are established only at periodic meetings, some associations find it difficult to respond quickly to changing policy developments. Relatively small associations find it economical to contract out even their own management functions.[44]

Contract Lobbyists

Known as "hired guns" in the lobbying world, contract lobbying firms represent multiple clients often in the same general subject area such as education, health, or insurance. For instance, Birdsall, Wasco, and Associates represents more than 20 school districts and other like-minded groups. Examples of large firms include California Advocates, A-K Associates, Advocation, Inc., and Carpenter Snodgrass & Associates. Some contract lobbyists are former legislators, legislative staff members, and administration officials who apply their knowledge of the process and the policymakers involved. Examples include former legislators Philip Isenberg, John Briggs, John Foran, and John Knox, former staffer Cliff Berg, and former Director of Finance Michael Franchetti.

"Brown Bag" Advocates

These modestly funded groups may be associations or individuals. What sets them apart is their lack of the financial resources of the lobbying firms and associations. Large campaign contributions and lavish receptions—tools of the trade for large groups and big firms—are out of the question for groups like the ecumenical group JERICO: A Voice for Justice. Instead, these groups rely on networks of intense believers. For instance, the Children's Lobby (representing child-care providers, educators, and parents) relies on a combination of grassroots activism, a telephone network, and "white hat" issues to provide what clout they have.

WHAT INTEREST GROUPS DO

When interest groups come to mind, the image is of lobbying—testifying at committee hearings or entertaining legislators. But interest group representation is more complex than that. Several tactics are employed to link group members to the political system.

Public Relations

Interest groups want the general public to know that their respective goals are similar. For instance, subtle and not-so-subtle television commercials equate an oil company with a venerated public television series or as protector of the state's wildlife. Numerous companies have "adopted" public school classrooms to further their image in the community and throughout the state.

Supporting Candidates

Once regarded as risky business, interest groups now work both to elect their friends and to defeat their enemies. The development of political action committees has allowed all manner of groups to contribute to legislative campaigns through essentially paper organizations registered with the FPPC. Some cannot afford to contribute (the brown baggers) or legally cannot (government groups, such as the League of California Cities). To hedge their bets, some PACs contribute to both sides, especially in open-seat elections where no incumbent is running. As noted earlier, PACs feel obligated to attend pricey Sacramento testimonial dinners and "legislative briefings."

The money pours in continually whether or not it is an election year. As a result, incumbents often amass huge campaign war chests even before they announce their reelection plans. In recent years, the largest campaign contributors have been medical doctors, trial lawyers, state employees, insurance companies, and bankers.

Influencing Propositions

As noted earlier, interest groups can sponsor or support various statewide ballot measures. Some of these efforts combine altruism with traditional self-interest. For instance, the California Building Industry Association worked closely with the legislature to craft a massive $9.2 billion school facilities bond measure—Proposition 1A. It passed in November 1998 with more than 62 percent of the vote. What was in it for the homebuilders? Lesser known provisions in "1A" included limits on school fees charged to developers and other pro-developer provisions. The builders in turn pumped $2.5 million into the winning campaign.[45] Money and clout do not always persuade voters. In 1998, the tobacco industry outspent its opponents $29 million to $7 million to defeat Proposition 10, a tax hike on tobacco products. It passed, but barely.

Political consultants aid interest groups in this process and sometimes even initiate initiatives. Some have been known to "test market" issues to see whether direct mail would be a profitable tactic. If so, these consultants shop around for interest groups to back them. To fellow consultant Joe Cerrell, these people propose initiatives "so they can make money. It's become a straight business."[46]

Lobbying

Lobbying is what interest groups do to influence policymakers. It includes monitoring legislation, drafting bills for legislators to introduce, testifying at public hearings, and contacting individual members and/or their staff. Lobbyists also pay attention to the executive branch, where agencies issue rules and otherwise implement legislation. Their most important asset is credible, albeit one-sided, information on how a legislative bill or an agency decision will impact their group. Term limits have presented lobbyists with newfound challenges. Influence based on long-time friendships with veteran legislators is disappearing as those veterans leave. According to lobbyist Jack Gualco, with high turnover "You've got to start new every two years."[47] Further discussion on lobbying can be found in Chapter 7.

Litigation

Interest groups often find the courts making policy through interpreting the state constitution, legislative statutes, and administrative rulings. Therefore, in many situations, the most effective method of participation by an interest group is to litigate. For instance, after passage of Proposition 1A, the Indian gaming measure, California's card room operators filed suit to halt its implementation. In 2001, the California Medical Association fought in court new financial disclosure regulations established by the state's Department of Managed Health Care.

If interest groups do not qualify as litigants, they can file *amicus curiae* (friend of the court) briefs to explain their position in court cases. This is done at every level of California's legal system. For example, in 2004, an array of interest groups including Marriage Equality California and Campaign for California Families filed such briefs before the California Supreme Court challenging San Francisco Mayor Gavin Newsome's decision to allow gay marriages in his city.

Conclusion: Competing for Influence

California's linkage institutions indeed connect Californians with their policymakers. The media are daily conduits of political and governmental news, if readers, listeners, and viewers bother to pay attention. During election campaigns, California's television stations link candidates and issue campaigns to voters through paid political advertising. The Internet promises to play an increasingly important role as an emerging linkage institution.

Political parties link partisan voters and their candidates through election activity, but a variety of constraints—legal and otherwise—weaken their efforts to do so. Parties are augmented by "surrogate" parties, for-profit "endorsers," and an army of political consultants who work on behalf of both candidates and issue campaigns. The most formidable competitors to California's political parties are a plethora of interest groups. These groups seemingly represent every agenda, population segment, economic interest, social value, or walk of life in the state. Increasingly, the diversity of the Golden State is mirrored in and represented by these groups. In a sense, California politics today is a hyperpluralistic mix of interest groups clamoring for influence and power.

KEY TERMS

mass and elite media   (pp. 100–101)
ideological and structural bias   (pp. 103–104)
political parties and third parties   (pp. 106–107)
blanket primary   (p. 106)

county and state central committees   (p. 107)
surrogate parties   (p. 109)
slate mailers   (p. 110)
benchmark polls   (p. 113)
Tracking polls,   (p. 113)

REVIEW QUESTIONS

1. Illustrate the concept of linkage with each institution in this chapter.
2. How did newspapers evolve in California?
3. What are television's shortcomings as a linkage institution in California politics?
4. How are the major parties organized in California, and why are they so weak?
5. In what ways are parties augmented by surrogates and slate mailers?
6. In light of this chapter, what advice would you give a potential candidate?
7. Why are campaign professionals important in California's electoral process?
8. Trace the rise of interest groups in California. To what extent do they mirror the diversity of the state and contribute to hyperpluralism?

WEB ACTIVITIES

Fair Political Practices Commission
(www.fppc.ca.gov)
This site describes the work of the FPPC and provides access to all California campaign regulations, conflict-of-interest laws, and enforcement decisions.

Political Parties and Interest Groups
(www.calvoter.org/parties.html and
www.calvoter.org/interestgroups.html)
The California Voter Foundation provides up-to-date links to California's political parties and to many interest groups.

Rough and Tumble (www.rtumble.com)
Updated daily, this site links you to California newspaper articles and columns dealing with state and local government and politics.

INFOTRAC® COLLEGE EDITION ARTICLES

For additional reading, go to InfoTrac® College Edition, your online research library, at http://www.infotrac.thomsonlearning.com/

Effective Slate Mailers

California Governor, Aides Keep Tight Leash on Media Access

Special Interest Groups Press California Republicans, Democrats on State Budget

NOTES

1. Linkage was first coined by V. O. Key, *Public Opinion and American Democracy* (New York: Knopf, 1961), chap. 16.
2. Kay Lawson, *Political Parties and Linkage: A Comparative Perspective* (New Haven: Yale University Press, 1980), 1–24.
3. "Mr. Speaker: A California Journal Interview," *California Journal* 17 (January 1986), 13.
4. Quoted in Susan Rasky, "The Media Covers Los Angeles," *California Journal* 28 (July 1997), 44.
5. A. G. Block and Claudia Buck, *California Political Almanac* (Sacramento: State Net, 1999), 559.
6. Quoted in Bob Forsyth, "Newspaper Editorials: Do They Really Matter?" *California Journal* 22 (January 1991), 31.
7. Mark Baldassare, *Californians and Their Government: Statewide Survey* (San Francisco: Public Policy Institute of California, January 2000), 18.
8. Steve Scott, "Tube Dreams," *California Journal* 30 (May 1999), 29.
9. Quoted in Lou Cannon, "Bleeders Sweeping Leaders Off California TV," *Washington Post*, May 23, 1998, A6.
10. T. L. Dixon and D. Linz, "Overrepresentation and Underrepresentation of African Americans and Latinos as Lawbreakers on Television News," *Journal of Communication* 50 (Spring 2000), 131–154.
11. Lori Dorfman et al., "Youth and Violence on Local Television News in California," *American Journal of Public Health* 87 (August 1997), 1131–1137.

12. Mark Baldassare, *California in the New Millennium: The Changing Social and Political Landscape* (Berkeley: University of California Press, 2000), 40–42.

13. Claudia Buck, "Coming of Age on the Web," *California Journal* 31 (September 2000), 14.

14. Quoted in Sandy Harrison, "Online Campaigning Comes of Age," *California Journal* 35 (May 2004), 29.

15. Secretary of State, California Internet Voting Task Force, *A Report on the Feasibility of Internet Voting* (Sacramento: Secretary of State, 2000). (www.ss.ca.gov/executive/ivote/final_report.htm/)

16. See Frank J. Sorauf and Paul Allen Back, *Party Politics in America,* 6th ed. (Boston: Scott Foresman/Little Brown, 1988), 10.

17. *California Democratic Party, et al. v. Jones, Bill, CA Secretary of State* 99–0401 (2000).

18. Other categories are two-party competition and modified one-party Republican. See John F. Bibby and Thomas M. Holbrook, "Parties and Elections," in Virginia Gray and Russell Hanson, eds., *Politics in the American States: A Comparative Analysis,* 8th ed. (Washington, D.C.: CQ Press, 2004), 86–89. The data used in their analysis predated the 2003 recall of Democratic governor Gray Davis and the election of Republican governor Arnold Schwarzenegger.

19. Lou Cannon, "Riding Herd on California's GOP," *California Journal* 35 (March 2004), 34.

20. Richard Bergholz, "Hard Times Befall Once-Influential Groups," *California Journal* 16 (August 1985), 322–324.

21. *Eu v. San Francisco County Democratic Central Committee,* 489 U.S. 214 (1989).

22. David G. Savage, "Nonpartisan Vote Challenge Voided," *Los Angeles Times,* June 18, 1991.

23. Charles Price, "Political Parties Back Away from Pre-Primary Endorsements," *California Journal* 23 (April 1992).

24. For a negative assessment of slate mailers, see Dan Walters, "Most Voter Slate Cards Aren't Worth the Cardboard They Use," *Sacramento Bee,* November 2, 2004.

25. These factors are described in Robert J. Pitchell, "The Influence of Professional Campaign Management Firms in Partisan Elections in California," *Western Political Quarterly* 11 (June 1958), 278–300.

26. Greg Mitchell, *The Campaign of the Century: Upton Sinclair's Race for Governor of California and the Birth of Media Politics* (New York: Random House, 1992).

27. For a brief history of political consulting in California, see Noel Brinkerhoff, "Consultants and Campaigns," *California Journal* 31 (November 2001), 8–13.

28. Dan Morain and Douglas P. Shuit, "Consultants Strike a Rich Vein," *Los Angeles Times,* October 28, 1998.

29. Bob Gardner, "California Election Folly: Big Budgets; Bad Ads," *Advertising Age* 69 (July 6, 1998), 13.

30. Quoted in Noel Brinkerhoff, "Course Correction," *California Journal* 28 (December 1997), 44.

31. See David Lauter, "Why Poll Results Differ," *Los Angeles Times,* September 12, 2003.

32. Quoted in Brinkerhoff, "Consultants and Campaigns," 10.

33. Robert Salladay, "End of Session Frenzy in Capitol," *Los Angeles Times,* August 18, 2004.

34. Cynthia Craft, "Karen Getman of the FPPC," *California Journal* 32 (July 2001), 22–31.

35. Bill Ainsworth, "Cash Flow," *California Journal* 33 (February 2002), 54–57.

36. Darrell Steinberg, "Campaign Finance Reform," *California Journal* 35 (February 2004), 35.

37. Quoted in Beth Fouhy, "Here Come the Democrats," *California Journal* 34 (March 2003), 40.

38. Lisa Getter, "California Helps Kerry Set Fundraising Records," *Los Angeles Times,* August 11, 2004.

39. Nelson W. Polsby and Aaron Wildavsky, *Presidential Elections: Strategies and Structures of American Politics,* 11th ed. (Lanham, MD: Rowman and Littlefield, 2004), 56.

40. James Rainey, "Delegate-Rich California Has to Share the Attention," *Los Angeles Times,* February 23, 2004.

41. Alexis de Tocqueville, *Democracy in America* (New York: Alfred A. Knopf, 1945), 191.

42. The magnitude of the governmental lobby is revealed in Curtis Richards, "Government Lobbyists: California Spends Millions to Influence Itself," *California Journal* 22 (August 1991), 377–380.

43. See John Howard, "What's Good for Business Is Good for California," *California Journal* 35 (December 2004), 46–50; and John Howard, "California Labor's Big Shift," *California Journal* 35 (November 2004), 7–13.

44. David Goldstein, "Association Management Pros: Does Your Group Need Help?" *California Journal* 21 (August 1990), 395–396.

45. Cynthia H. Craft and Kathleen Les, "School Bonds," *California Journal* 29 (November 1998), 28–35.

46. Quoted in Peter Schrag, *Paradise Lost: California's Experience, America's Future* (New York: New Press, 1998), 211.

47. Quoted in John Borland, "Third House," *California Journal* 27 (February 1996), 30.

PART THREE

Political Institutions in California

Individualities may form communities, but it is institutions alone that can create a nation.
—Benjamin Disraeli, 1866

When we think of "the government," we think of the major institutions in which policymakers work and make decisions. What Disraeli said of the nation can be said of the state. California's political institutions include the state legislature, the governor, an executive branch, and a court system. Because they also make policy on their own or on behalf of the state, local governments are also among the political institutions of California. Although governmental institutions are slow to change, they are living institutions—representing social change and reacting to the political upheaval around them. Part 3 examines the institutions of politics in the Golden State and the political pressures they face.

Chapter 7, "Legislative Politics," describes California's legislature: its history, functions, and processes. In it, we examine why people become assembly members and senators and,

once there, why they have stayed. Also explored is how the legislature organizes itself to make policy and achieve member goals. The chapter concludes with a discussion of lobbying: the process by which interest groups make their policy preferences known. Coloring the whole chapter is the ongoing impact of Proposition 140, a 1990 measure that imposed term limits on the legislature.

Chapter 8, "Executive Politics," examines the office of governor and the executive branch. In California, the governor is the dominant policymaker and possesses a great deal of power, especially in terms of the state budget. Yet in other ways, the governor's power is weakened by having to share it with other statewide elected executives. Each of them is surveyed. The routines of California state policy are managed by about 253,000 employees who constitute the state bureaucracy. They exercise considerable power in their own right and personify California government to many citizens.

Chapter 9, "California's Judiciary," focuses on the state court system and its participants: justices, judges, juries, litigants, and lawyers. It discusses how lawyers become judges and how court decisions are made in both civil and criminal cases. A section on jury justice explores how lay people use their own experiences to make decisions in particular cases. Judges render decisions but also make policy in the process. This policy role allows California judges to both contribute to and break up governmental gridlock found in other governing institutions.

Chapter 10, "Community Politics," surveys the thousands of governing institutions we call local government. The official ones include counties, cities, special districts, and regional governments. The unofficial ones include conglomerations of development called edge cities as well as homeowner associations (in effect privatized neighborhoods). Although these governments vary in nature and scope, combined they provide thousands of Californians with the opportunity to make public policy. Today, these governments are often constrained, even hamstrung, by state-level policy making and by policy problems beyond their reach.

CHAPTER 7

Legislative Politics

In Brief

California's legislature illustrates many of the challenges facing California politics. Increasingly, the legislature also represents the diversity of the Golden State. Once dominated by rural interests and the Southern Pacific Railroad (SPR), its powers were tightly drawn by the Progressives in the early 1900s. After decades of stagnation, the legislature became more professional in the 1960s and, through reapportionment, more reflective of the state's urban growth. Since the 1970s, the legislature has gradually become more partisan

and, on occasion, more deadlocked—reflecting the state's growing diversity of interests. Furthermore, the passage of term limits (Proposition 140) in 1990 has raised serious questions about the long-term policy role of a once-envied institution.

The California legislature performs a variety of functions: policy making, representation, executive oversight, and civic education. Most legislators attain office through a combination of personal initiative and sponsorship by legislative and party leaders. Until Proposition

140, the legislature offered attractive political careers to its members; it still offers opportunities for advancement from one house to another, to statewide offices and Congress, and to influential lobbying positions.

In doing its business, the legislature relies heavily on a handful of leaders, the most powerful being the Assembly speaker. A combination of committees and leadership posts structure the legislative process, one that seems simple on paper but which actually boils with internal politics. Lobbyists provide essential information to members and committees while representing a diversity of interests in California.

Nowadays the California legislature faces a variety of challenges: a growing number of conflicting interests, social change, economic turmoil, and a restive public dissatisfied with the legislature's performance.

Introduction: The Road to Proposition 140

Question: Which state pays its legislators far more than any other state but forces them to leave office as soon as they gain valuable experience?

Answer: California.

Indeed, the California state legislature is an anomaly. It makes statutory policy for the largest state in the Union, incubates political leaders, and is an enviable place to act on behalf of the public interest. It was once regarded as the most professional of all state legislatures and, in many ways, it still is. But today's challenges are sobering. Member tenure is term-limited, campaigns are exorbitantly expensive, and the policy stakes are higher than ever. The legislature is an easy target of criticism. For example, buoyed by higher job approval ratings than the legislature, Governor Arnold Schwarzenegger called his legislative opponents "girlie-men" and threatened to take his policy preferences to the voters if legislators did not approve them.

Believers in representative democracy placed great confidence in legislatures. While admitting the executive would share lawmaking power, political philosopher John Locke viewed legislative power as supreme. American colonial legislatures viewed themselves as mini-parliaments. The Framers assumed Congress would be first among the three federal branches. In the early 1800s, state legislatures were modeled after the Congress and were considered superior to Congress as policy making bodies. After all, states had larger policy responsibilities. But by the late 1800s, state legislatures had fallen into disrepute. British observer Lord Bryce summed up a prevailing attitude: "If [the legislature] meets, it will pass bad laws. Let us therefore prevent it from meeting."[1] By the 1980s, state legislatures had become much more professionalized institutions capable of making effective public policy. Larger staffs, higher salaries, and longer sessions marked this "institutionalization." But by the early 1990s, these trends had backfired. The public began to lose confidence in their legislatures as policy making bodies. Today, state legislatures are undergoing a process of "deinstitutionalization." That is, they are affected more now than ever before by outside forces beyond the control of legislative bodies—public opinion, the media, term limitations, interest groups, and voter initiatives.[2]

California conforms to this trend. Angry Californians passed Proposition 140 in November 1990. As noted in Chapter 4, this initiative limited assembly members to three two-year terms and senators to two four-year terms. The measure also sought to eliminate the legislature's retirement system and severely cut its operating budget. Although the California Supreme Court overturned the retirement system ban for all members, it upheld the balance of 140.[3] The introduction of term limits has shaken the California legislature to its very core, affecting virtually every aspect of the institution. References to it appear throughout this chapter.

California's Legislative History

Criticism of the California legislature is as old as statehood. In fact, the institution has always reflected the state's different political eras. Its history includes the early years, the Progressive era, stagnation amid change, reform, the golden years, and life after Proposition 140.

The Early Years

In the mid-1800s, the state legislature was an amateur body dominated by farmers and beholden to the SPR. People considered the members of the legislature to be dishonest drunks—the legislature of "1,000 steals" or "1,000 drinks." In 1849, it consisted of 16 senators and 36 assemblymen. By the second constitutional convention in 1878, it had grown to its current size, 40 senators serving four-year terms and 80 assembly members serving two-year terms. The combination of frequent elections, part-time politicians, and domination by the SPR's Political Bureau led to a corrupt "political machine" atmosphere and fueled the rise of the Progressives.

The Progressive Era

Under the righteous indignation of the Progressives, Hiram Johnson assumed the governorship in 1911. New constitutional language limited what the legislature could do plus how and when it could do it. Even the number of

days the legislature could meet was specified. The initiative, a reform that would eventually compete with the legislature for policy making power, was instituted. Yet the voters did not support every antilegislature proposal. Between 1913 and 1925, they rejected six referenda to create a unicameral (one-house) legislature—an idea some Californians still favor. During this period, the legislature lost an important political role in appointing U.S. senators due to the passage of the Seventeenth Amendment to the U.S. Constitution in 1913. It required direct election of senators.

Stagnation Amid Change

From the 1920s to the 1960s, California experienced tremendous growth and change. Urban and suburban populations surged as did the economy. The Depression and World War II brought federal programs and dollars to California. The legislature did not fully reflect these changes; in fact, it resisted them. Like the Congress, representation in the lower house (the Assembly) was based on population; in the upper house (the State Senate), it was based on area. No county could have more than one senator (the so-called *Federal plan*). The result was skewed representation. In fact, as late as the 1960s, San Diego, Los Angeles, and Alameda counties claimed half the state's population but sent to Sacramento only one senator each. As a result, rural interests predominated and policy making was factionalized more by region than by partisanship.[4] Meanwhile, interest groups grew in number as the state's economy became more complex. In the process, individual lobbyists such as the colorful Artie Samish gained enormous influence and power.

Reform

In the 1960s, two events led to substantial legislative reforms. First, a legislatively appointed Constitutional Revision Commission (CRC) recommended a series of constitutional amendments allowing the legislature to govern most of its own affairs (such as setting salaries and determining calendars). In 1966, voters approved Proposition 1A by a 3 to 1 margin. Spearheading this effort was Assembly Speaker Jesse Unruh who became something of a nationwide guru for legislative professionalization. Under his leadership, the legislature aggressively pursued a policy agenda apart from the governor's. To this day, an unoccupied desk remains on the Assembly floor to memorialize Unruh's legacy. Second, federal courts ruled against California's "Federal plan" in 1965. Both houses in a state legislature would have to be reapportioned on the basis of "one person, one vote."[5] The post-reapportionment election of 1966 produced immediate change. Compared to the old guard, many new legislators were younger, better educated, possessed more professional backgrounds, and represented more minorities. They also seemed more partisan in their dealings with each other.

The Golden Years

The 1960s and 1970s ushered in still more reform such as the two-year session adopted in 1972. This innovation allowed bills to survive beyond the first year, avoiding time-consuming reintroductions. A robust economy allowed the legislature to spend generously on both public policy and on itself. Staffs and salaries grew steadily. The envy of the nation, the California legislature was rated number one by the Citizens' Conference on State Legislatures in 1973.[6] All was not well, though. Proposition 9 (1974) addressed what the public considered an all-too-cozy relationship between legislators and lobbyists. It limited campaign finances and lobbying practices and disallowed campaign work by state-paid legislative staff. Those elected after Proposition 13 passed in 1978 seemed more rigidly conservative than their veteran colleagues. The breakup of the postwar bipartisan consensus (favoring active government and greater spending) appeared complete.

Inching Toward 140

Voter approval of term limits in 1990 was the culmination of several developments. First, divided government (Republicans controlling the governor's office; Democrats, the legislature) became routine and led to well-publicized policy gridlock. Second, the initiative process increasingly supplanted the legislature as the driving policy force in California. Second, while some voters were gradually "dealigning" from their respective parties (considering themselves to be independents), legislators were becoming *more* partisan in their dealings with each other. Third, the media began to spotlight how campaign funds were raised and spent. Then Assembly Speaker Willie Brown doled out excess campaign funds of his own to loyal colleagues.[7] Members readily sought out service on so-called *juice committees* because industries most interested in those committees would contribute to the committee members' political campaigns.[8] The whole business looked tawdry to ordinary voters. In the wake of several well publicized bribery scandals, the public's general regard for the legislature plummeted.

The Post-140 Legislature

By 1996 and 1998, California had experienced 100 percent turnover in its legislature and the revolving door continues. Proposition 140 has profoundly impacted the legislature in one area after another. Compared to the past, post-140 legislators are younger, and fewer are former staff members. Latinos, women, and those with local government experience have increased in number. Legislative turnover has also resulted in less experienced staff. In addition, power has shifted in various ways. The Senate has gained influence as veteran but termed-out assembly members and staffers join the Senate. Relative to the less experienced legislature, the governor has gained more power. Lobbyists are as knowledgeable as ever but must now work harder to get legislators' attention both in Sacramento and in the members' districts.[9]

What the Legislature Does

Amid all this change, the California legislature still remains at the core of politics in the Golden State. As with all legislatures, its functions are varied. We discuss four broad and overlapping ones: policy making, representation, executive oversight, and civic education.

POLICY MAKING

The first function of a legislature is policy making. California's legislature addresses a stunning variety of policy issues each year. Among the 959 laws that took effect on January 1, 2005, were bills that did the following:

- Increase fees for higher education students

- Place the "Megan's Law" database on the Internet

- Grant domestic partners the same rights available to married couples

- Ban the high-powered .50 caliber BMG rifle

- Permit the sale of hypodermic needles without a prescription

In California, there are three types of legislation: bills, constitutional amendments, and resolutions. *Bills* are proposed statutes (laws at the state level) and can be introduced only by legislators (see Figure 7.1). Even the governor's budget (itself a bill) must have a legislator's name on it.[10] *Constitutional amendments* originating in the legislature require a two-thirds vote of the members and a concurrence of a majority of voters at a subsequent election. *Resolutions* are merely statements representing the collective opinion of one house or both on miscellaneous subjects. They may commend individual Californians, praise a champion sports team, or express a popular opinion on some fleeting issue. The most important bill and most important set of policies the legislature adopts each year is the state budget.

REPRESENTATION

A second legislative function, *representation*, sounds simple enough. In a representative democracy, legislators ideally reflect or act upon the wishes of those who elect them. In reality, representation is very complex and operates on a variety of levels. This is especially true in a diverse and hyperpluralistic state like California.

Geographic Representation

The first level of representation is geographic. Forty senators and 80 assembly members represent the particular interests of their home district. Given the state's diversity, from densely urban districts near the coast to sparsely populated districts in the interior, a multitude of geographic perspectives translate into a multitude of policy perspectives and priorities. Sometimes these differences are manifest in *local bills* that affect only one district. For instance, one local bill aimed to exempt a Downey, California, hospital board from the state's open meeting law. Legislators may also form coalitions with likeminded members based on common geographic interests such as coastal lawmakers do on off-shore oil drilling or Bay Area members do on transportation issues.

Social and Cultural Representation

At another level, legislators often represent the characteristics of constituents back home. Overall, legislators usually approximate their districts in terms of race, religion, or ethnicity. Notice the 2005–2006 profile of the state legislature, especially race, ethnicity, and gender, which is shown in Table 7.1. In recent years, there has been a surge of Latino and female legislators. In fact, in 2003 California ranked second among the fifty states in the percentage of Latino legislators (23 percent); in 2004 it ranked fifth in the percentage of female legislators (30 percent). While legislators arguably seek out the good of California as a whole, they also desire to "represent" their

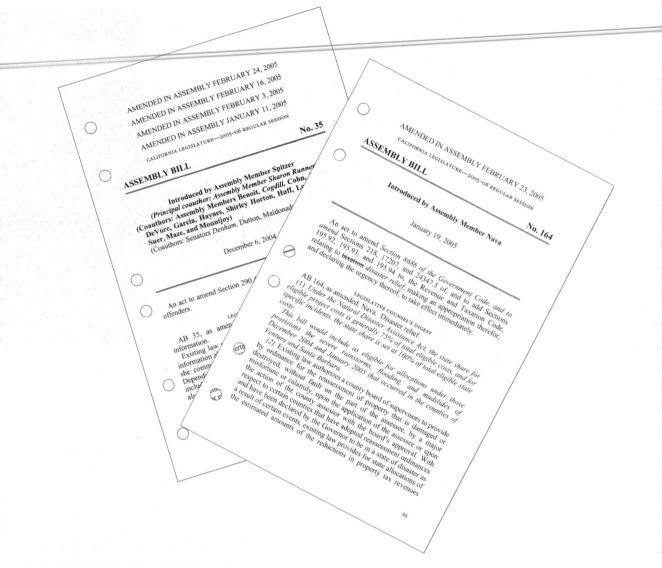

FIGURE 7.1 Typical Bill Cover Page

racial, ethnic, or other affinity group. For example, the Latino and black caucuses are organized around this motivation. California's female legislators are sensitive to family and health issues and consider themselves uniquely qualified to deal with them.[11] Gay members may take the lead on same-sex partner benefits. Yet, compared to their districts, legislators tend to be better educated, more male, more involved in their communities, and more successful in their previous occupations.

Specific Representation

Individual constituents sometimes need specific representation, that is, individual attention. Constituent service, called "casework," is the vehicle through which this function takes

TABLE 7.1 The Legislature at a Glance, 2005-2006

	Senate (40)		Assembly (80)
Democrats	25		48
Republicans	15		32
Women	12		25
Latinas	(6)		(6)
Latinos	5		3
African Americans	2		4
Asian Americans	0		8
Former Assembly Members	36	*Former Senate Members*	4
*GLBT**	0		5

*Gay, Lesbian, Bisexual, Transgendered

Source: *Who's who in the California Legislature (2005–2006)*

place. For instance, many constituents seek help dealing with assorted state bureaucracies such as the Department of Motor Vehicles. Casework often involves little more than researching pending bills or listening to callers vent their frustrations over the telephone. District office staffers, including college and university interns, do the bulk of this work. Occasionally, some policy ideas come from this process, but it usually means troubleshooting for specific constituents.

Functional Representation

Functional representation refers to the specific policy interests and preferences legislators bring to Sacramento. Former teachers, farmers, or city officials may logically gravitate to education, agriculture, or local government committees. Other members may wish to represent key industries in their districts, such as computer technology. As Table 7.2 portrays, the legislature's policy committees are organized around a rich diversity of functional interests. Although constituents may not routinely think in these functional terms, interest groups do. Each committee is monitored by a familiar assortment of interest groups (such as the Aging

and Long Term Care Committee and senior groups).

Perceptual Representation

Legislators themselves perceive their representational roles in different ways. British philosopher and member of Parliament Edmund Burke once distinguished between trustee roles and delegate roles. *Trustees* rely primarily on their own best judgment when voting on legislation rather than the wishes (fleeting wishes, thought Burke) of their constituents who elected them. *Delegates* lean primarily on those constituent wishes and deliberately seek them out. Modern political scientists have added the politico role. *Politicos* combine the two roles depending on how controversial specific issues are locally.[12] For instance, even though he harbored personal reservations about a number of "Three Strikes" bills, imposing long sentences on repeat criminal offenders, then State Senator Leroy Greene concluded he would nonetheless support them. "I'm going to vote for these turkeys because my constituents want me to." These perceptions are not static. One study of the California Assembly suggested that, over time, legislators change their role perceptions. Why? It could be that legislators vote inconsistently or do not think about whether they are trustees, delegates, or politicos.[13]

EXECUTIVE OVERSIGHT

A third function of California's legislature is executive branch *oversight*. The state constitution mandates some of these oversight activities. For instance, the Senate must confirm various gubernatorial appointments to commissions (such as Fish and Game, Public Utilities, and

TABLE 7.2   California's Standing Legislative Committees

Assembly (29)	Senate (23)
Aging and Long-Term Care	Agriculture
Agriculture	Appropriations
Appropriations	Banking, Finance and Insurance
Arts, Entertainment, Sports, Tourism, and Internet Media	Budget and Fiscal Review
Banking and Finance	Business, Professions, and Economic Development
Budget	Education
Business and Professions	Elections, Reapportionment, and Constitutional Amendments
Education	
Elections and Redistricting	Energy, Utilities, and Communications
Environmental Safety and Toxic Materials	Environmental Quality
Government Organization	Governmental Organization
Health	Government Modernization, Efficiency and Accountability
Higher Education	
Housing and Community Development	Health
Human Services	Human Services
Insurance	Judiciary
Jobs, Economic Development, and the Economy	Labor and Industrial Relations
Judiciary	Local Government
Labor and Employment	Natural Resources and Water
Local Government	Public Employment and Retirement
Natural Resources	Public Safety
Public Employees, Retirement and Social Security	Revenue and Taxation
Public Safety	Rules
Revenue and Taxation	Transportation and Housing
Rules	Veterans Affairs
Transportation	
Utilities and Commerce	
Veterans Affairs	
Water, Parks and Wildlife	

the University of California Regents). Both the Senate and Assembly confirm gubernatorial appointments to fill vacancies in constitutional offices. Like Congress, the legislature can remove statewide officeholders and judges through a rarely used impeachment process. General oversight of state agencies is aided by the Joint Legislative Audit Committee. This committee works with the State Auditor to assess the financial practices and performance of various state agencies and programs. For example, one 2004 report criticized a Department of Corrections plan to rebuild the death row complex at San Quentin prison. To maintain its own independence and objectivity, the Bureau of State Audits is itself overseen by another independent group, the Milton Marks Commission on California State Government Organization and Economy (the Little Hoover Commission).

A routinely used oversight tool is the "power of the purse." This term actually refers to several processes. In the *authorization process*, the legislature gives authority for an agency program to exist. In the *appropriation process*, the legislature creates spending authority, thereby allowing the agency to implement the program. Through the annual budget, authorization, and appropriations processes, the legislature can evaluate agency performance and set its own spending priorities. In doing this work, legislative committees hear from executive branch officials as much as private sector lobbyists.

CIVIC EDUCATION

The final function involves the *civic education* of constituents. Legislators are expected to educate people about the legislative process and California politics generally. In Sacramento, they meet with district constituents, students, professional lobbyists, and many interest group members who visit the Capitol. Legislators explain their version of how the process works and why favored legislation is so difficult to pass or afford. On occasion, they (or their staffs) author newspaper opinion pieces. Back in the districts, legislators speak to service clubs and community gatherings, issue press releases, hold "office hours," and confer with local chapters of statewide groups. Each activity provides an opportunity for them to explain the process and their views on policy.

These four legislative functions commingle constantly. A constituent complaint about the Department of Motor Vehicles may lead to a member inquiry about how the department operates. Urban and rural legislators sit side by side on committees, learning to appreciate the geographic diversity they bring to their work. Historically underrepresented groups in the legislature, such as African Americans and Latinos, form their own bicameral caucuses to make social representation more visible and deliberate in the eyes of colleagues. Those more theoretical roles also intermingle. Legislators who think they are "trustees" relative to their districts often behave like "delegates," not of their constituents but of interest groups with whom they more routinely work.

Getting There and Staying There

Why people seek *any* public office is an interesting question to political scientists. Joining a legislature often means giving up one's privacy, normal family life, career continuity, and, for some people, substantial income. What motivates California candidates is especially fascinating. Because being a legislator is a full-time job (and then some, legislators say), a member must maintain two residences, even if one is a small Sacramento apartment. Family dislocation (Where do you put the kids in school? What about a working spouse?) and frequent travel to the district create stresses most Californians can only imagine. What about resuming a career after a term-limited legislative stint? Is that even possible? Yet the price is worth it to many members, who attempt to convert their beliefs into public policy.

RECRUITMENT

The initial decision to run for the legislature is determined by both personal desire and requests by others. Three patterns of candidate recruitment have emerged in California.

Self Starters

Some individuals run for the legislature because they desire to implement policy preferences or begin political careers. They talk themselves into it. Some come from local offices such as school boards, city councils, and county boards of supervisors. They figure they can do as good a job as the legislators they meet coping with state policies and legislative mandates. Other aspiring legislators become interested in the impact of state policy on their own professions. Farmers, doctors, and members of "brokerage" occupations (law, real estate, and insurance) often fit this category. Some gain valuable policy and political experience as staff members in Sacramento or in district offices. Others spend large sums of their own wealth to run for office, claiming independence from special interests.

Sponsorship

Some legislative candidates are sponsored by or recruited to run by others. In California, sponsorship comes not so much from local party officials but from legislative leaders in Sacramento. In recent years, the Assembly speaker and Senate president pro tem as well as partisan caucus staffs have provided both encouragement and campaign funding to promising candidates. This is possible because legislative leaders are able to raise substantial surplus funds well beyond what they need for their own reelection efforts. What do these legislative leaders look for in potential candidates? They generally seek candidates who will be good legislators *and* who will support them in future leadership battles. The ability to win always helps! In contested primaries, these Sacramento benefactors usually wait for a primary winner to emerge and then provide support for a fall general election campaign.

Combination Pattern

In recent years, many legislative races have featured a combination of self-starting and sponsorship. Given the entrepreneurial nature of California politics and the historically weak local political parties, many candidates need self-starter qualities, such as a burning ambition to run and win. Yet these people alone cannot marshal the resources needed to win. Remember, compared to many states,

California's legislature is relatively small: 40 senators and 80 assembly members representing over 35 million people. That translates into huge districts—roughly 875,000 people per Senate district and 437,000 people per Assembly district. No other state legislature has near these per-district populations. Face-to-face voter contact in some districts necessarily gives way to political advertising. Media costs, the largest chunk of any modern campaign budget, are expensive in California. Unless a candidate is wealthy, outside help is essential. Once they are nominated, legislative candidates may be showered with resources including endorsements, party assistance, funding from legislative leaders, PAC contributions, and soft money expenditures.

The Power of Incumbency

Once elected, incumbents enjoy tremendous advantages when running for reelection. They attract the vast majority of PAC contributions, can "draft" staffers as campaign aides, command media attention, and benefit from district-wide name recognition. In primary elections, incumbents often run unopposed as was the case in the March 2004 primary. Of 56 incumbent assembly members seeking renomination, only one faced an opponent, and token opposition at that. On the Senate side, all ten incumbents running in the primary did so unopposed. Interestingly, in the case of presumably competitive open seat primaries—where incumbents are vacating office—few candidates have emerged to run, often only one per party.

WHY THEY STAY: REWARDS OF OFFICE

Given the frustrations of the legislative life in California (hyperpartisanship, gridlock, short tenures guaranteed by term limits, incessant travel, and family pressures), one may wonder why legislators want to stay and hate to leave. What drives them to remain? For instance, why do they run for Senate when their Assembly terms expire? The reasons are several.

Policy Achievement

Given the problems and challenges facing California, finding solutions and crafting statewide policy is a primary goal for many legislators. These members have genuine public service goals and operate in Sacramento and back home with those goals in mind. Serving on just the right committees and moving into leadership positions on those committees are paramount to policy achievers. Post–term limit members bring a sense of policy urgency, knowing they have only a few years to enact their preferences into law. According to former state senator Jim Brulte, if lawmakers want to develop a legacy, they have to get to work immediately.[14]

Material Benefits

Many state legislatures provide poor salaries and working conditions. Not California's. In 2005 an independent citizens commission set members' annual salaries at $110,880, making them by far the nation's highest paid state legislators. That same commission set the annual salaries of the Assembly Speaker, the Senate president pro tem, and the minority floor leader at $127,512; other leadership posts were paid $119,196. On top of that, out-of-town legislators receive a tax-free $138 stipend for living expenses each day their house is "in session." As a result, brief "check-in" sessions are commonplace, even when there is little business to conduct. In a typical nine-month session, that can total another $30,000. Additional benefits include an automobile, cell phone, health insurance, trips to the district, and funds to hire staff and rent office space. Critics call these expenditures unwarranted "perks," but others consider them the normal cost of running the nation's largest state.

Psychic Satisfaction

If legislators do not bring big egos to Sacramento, they acquire them there. They have many staff members to help with policy, research, personal, party, and leadership responsibilities. Members experience other psychic rewards; deference is paid to them by lobbyists, constituents, and virtually everyone they meet. As a former member put it, "an amazing seduction occurs here. When was the last time you rode an elevator where the operator knows your name?"[15]

Careerism, Then and Now

Careerism and political ambition are related. According to political scientists, political ambitions may be discrete (short-term service with return to private life), static (making a long-run career out of a particular office), or progressive (using an office as a stepping stone to still higher office).[16] Until Proposition 140, the California legislature had become known as a hothouse for political careers. The power of incumbency and relatively safe districts assured some job security. By state legislative standards, the pay and perks were good and needed to be because the work was increasingly full time. Considered a dead end in many other states, legislative service in California allowed rapid advancement and rewarded political ambition and policy entrepreneurship. California lawmakers viewed and used their positions as springboards to higher office.[17] Proposition 140 has had an impact on careerism in two ways. For some, it effectively aborts a long-term career as an elected official. For others, it alters the stepping-stone process. In what has been called the term limits shuffle, legislators constantly cast about for other offices—federal, state, and even local—to extend their public careers. Some land appointments to head executive branch agencies or sit on relatively obscure but well-paid boards and commissions. For instance, former legislator Charleen Zettel is director of Consumer Affairs.

The election of Arnold Schwarzenegger as governor could alter legislative ambitions still further. First, in 2004 he suggested that the California legislature return to its pre-1960s part-time status, accusing it of not having enough to do and producing "strange" bills when it did act. While his proposal may have been a playful poke at legislative Democrats, it also may have sparked an initiative battle to de-professionalize the legislature. Second, the governor appeared to back a number of executive branch reforms that would abolish the boards and commissions that have served as well-paid career parachutes for at least some termed out legislators. Chapter 8 addresses these executive branch reform proposals in more detail. Third, he proposed that the task of apportioning legislative districts be removed from the legislature and given to an independent panel of retired judges. As he declared in his 2005 State of the State address: "The current system is rigged to benefit the interests of those in office . . . not the interests of those who put them there. And we must reform it."

HOW THEY STAY: REAPPORTIONMENT POLITICS

To understand reapportionment, you must understand the motives of legislators. Willingness to stay in office is not the same as staying; ask any incumbent who loses a reelection bid. But incumbents generally know what it takes to get elected time-and-time again. More than challengers, they can afford the campaign techniques described in Chapter 6. Also, they fully understand that campaigning is territorial—the very boundaries of a legislative district can spell victory or defeat. How are these boundaries drawn? After each decade, the U. S. Census Bureau counts the population and gathers other demographic data. In a practice called *reapportionment*, the legislature redraws district lines for the U.S. House of Representatives, the State Assembly, and State Senate to reflect population growth and movement within the state. As with other bills, the governor must sign any reapportionment plan. The California

Constitution requires that any plan consider to the extent possible the "geographic integrity" of existing city and county boundaries.

The legislature rarely observes that constitutional guideline because population shifts and communities of interest are not the only factors in redrawing district boundaries. Reapportioning districts for partisan or other advantage is called *gerrymandering*. There are three types: (1) *Partisan gerrymandering* means either "splintering" a district (dividing either Republicans or Democrats among several districts to dilute their strength) or "packing" a district (say, concentrating Democrats into one district to enhance election chances for Republicans in other districts). (2) *Incumbent gerrymandering*, a long-standing one in California, protects incumbents regardless of party. Often called "sweetheart" gerrymandering, this type is sometimes found under divided government conditions. That incumbents protect each other should hardly be surprising. (3) *Racial gerrymandering* has historically been used in the United States to dilute the strength of racial minorities. In recent years, it has been used, often in the South, to concentrate minority voting strength—often ensuring victory for minority candidates. Although this goal may be laudable, the United States Supreme Court has rejected the most obvious racial gerrymanders as a violation of the Fourteenth Amendment's equal protection clause.

When legislators face the task of redistricting, previous reapportionment efforts color their efforts. Consider the 1980s when a Democratic legislature redrew legislative district lines to the advantage of their own party members. Republicans countered with three initiatives challenging the new plans, but the voters rejected them. Eventually, the state Supreme Court upheld the original plan, ruling that the state constitution allows only one plan per decade. Bitter Republicans vowed to prevail after the next census.

By the early 1990s, partisanship was only one factor among many in the redistricting equation.

Growth and ethnic diversity were other factors. The 1980s saw tremendous population growth, especially in interior California. The districts of some entrenched incumbents would have to be substantially redrawn to mirror the addition of more than 4 million new Californians. In addition, a growing number of minorities in California wanted not only a voice in the reapportionment process but also new districts that would increase their voting power. The Mexican American Legal Defense and Education Fund (MALDEF) represented Latino interests and submitted its own redistricting alternatives. At the time, they had the law on their side. The Voting Rights Act of 1965 (as amended in 1982 and interpreted by the courts) required state legislatures to *create* racial and ethnic majority voting districts if at all feasible. Political scientist Bruce Cain called this form of racial gerrymandering the "affirmative action gerrymander."[18] Given the growth of minorities in California, this new priority was bound to conflict with the priorities of incumbents and party leaders.

In 1991, Governor Pete Wilson vetoed several "Democratic" plans submitted by the Assembly and Senate, and legislative Democrats did not have enough votes to override Wilson's vetoes. In the face of this gridlock, the state Supreme Court appointed a panel of "masters" (retired judges) to redraw the districts presumably from scratch, taking into account those legal mandates. The 1992 reapportionment plan they drew and the court approved dealt a stunning blow to many incumbents—forcing some into retirement, others into campaigns against colleagues, and still others into premature stepping-stone races. In the wake of Proposition 140, that reapportionment was truly a bitter pill for California's legislature.

THE 2001 REAPPORTIONMENT

The 2001 reapportionment was an altogether different experience. With little or no debate, the state Senate approved the new maps on

two votes: 38 to 2 and 40 to 0. The Assembly approved the maps on a bipartisan 58 to 10 vote. What happened to the rancor of earlier battles? First, sizeable voting majorities in the Assembly and Senate (50 to 30 and 26 to 14, respectively) gave Democrats a substantial advantage in redrawing the maps; Republicans were at their mercy. Maintaining something of the status quo would be something of a victory for them. Second, although California's ethnic minorities had been growing in the 1990s, plan drafters were unsure if they could eek out substantially more "minority-majority" districts. They were able to maintain and strengthen numerous Latino-majority districts and add a heavily Latino congressional district in Los Angeles County. Several other districts were redrawn in such a way as to benefit Latino electoral chances in the future. The plans seemed satisfactory to Latino incumbents— 23 of 26 Latino legislators supported them. Convinced that more Latino districts could have been created, MALDEF challenged the boundaries of several districts in federal court, but their claim was rejected. A few incumbents complained publicly and privately that their reelection chances or opportunities to seek other offices were doomed. Some had sought to make their *next* seats safe ones. In the end, the 2001 reapportionment process was a classic incumbent protection effort. As a result, it locked in (to the extent redistricting can) Democratic majorities and prior gains made by the state's minorities. It also locked into place, but did not further reduce, the minority status of California's Republican lawmakers (see Figures 7.2a and 7.2b).[19]

Organizing to Legislate

Reapportionment aside, making laws is still the legislature's primary task. Between 4,000 and 5000 bills are introduced during each two-year session of the California legislature. When the great jurist Oliver Wendell Holmes

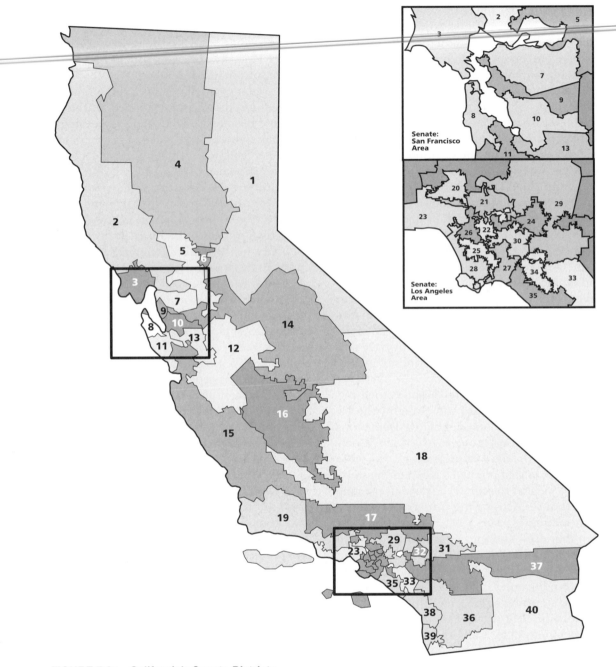

FIGURE 7.2a   California's Senate Districts

Source: Secretary of State's Office, California.

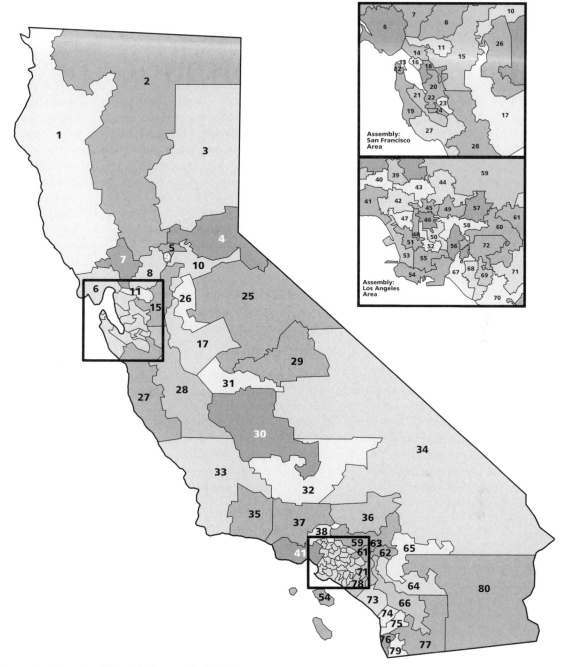

FIGURE 7.2b California's Assembly Districts

Source: Secretary of State's Office, California.

observed that "every opinion tends to become a law,"[20] one might have thought he was commenting on California's legislature. On paper the process of making law seems straightforward enough. In reality, it is complex and fraught with both intrigue and, on occasion, chaos. The members themselves sometimes say, "Never watch laws or sausages being made."

The California Constitution requires a bicameral legislature, consisting of a lower house (an 80-member Assembly) and an upper house (a 40-member Senate). Assembly members serve two-year terms; senators, four-year terms. Under Proposition 140, assembly members are limited to three terms; senators to two. Although both houses behave similarly in many respects, there are differences. The state Senate is more prestigious due to its smaller size and longer terms. Senators tend to be more politically experienced; many gained that experience in the Assembly. Senators can seek still higher office in the middle of their terms without losing their seats—a "free ride." Compared to the Speaker-dominated Assembly, senators are more independent. Each finds publicity easier to attain. As a body, the Senate can more easily challenge a governor by not confirming gubernatorial appointments that require Senate confirmation. Also, the Senate seems quieter and more deliberative than the rough-and-tumble Assembly.

How does the legislature itself organize to do its work? The process in both houses leans heavily on leadership, a committee system, and professional staff.

THE ROLE OF LEADERSHIP

Groups large and small need leaders to manage what they do. Legislatures are no different. In his study of state legislative politics, Alan Rosenthal listed six different leadership tasks: organizing for work, processing legislation, negotiating agreements, dispensing benefits, handling the press, and maintaining the institution.[21] California's legislative leaders perform each of these tasks. The key positions are discussed below.

Assembly Speaker

One of the most fascinating offices in California politics is the Assembly speaker, the pinnacle of what used to be called a "self-inflicted dictatorship." Once elected by the entire Assembly, recent speakers have been chosen by the majority *party caucus*. A party's caucus is its total membership in the chamber when gathered to do business. Speakers sometimes must court minority party votes when majority control of the Assembly is marginal. Speakers balance power and policy—perpetuating their own power while using it to achieve policy goals. In part, this is done by controlling committees: determining the number and titles of committees, assigning all members to committees (with the exception of the Rules Committee), controlling the selection of other leadership positions within the Speaker's party, managing floor action, enforcing Assembly customs, and assigning office space and some staff. When asked why he assigned one first-term critic of his a smelly, windowless, broom closet of an office, then Speaker Willie Brown replied, "I didn't have anything smaller." No wonder he was called the "ayatollah of the legislature." Jesse Unruh was the first Assembly speaker to buttress the role of the office. Under his leadership, the Assembly became a powerful policy making force in state government. Willie Brown occupied the post from 1980 to 1996. He was the first African American to hold the post and served longer than any predecessor.

In 1988, he fought off an attempt to unseat him by a group of moderate Democrats, known as the Gang of Five. After the 1994 elections, when the Assembly was evenly divided between Republicans and Democrats, Brown resigned the post.

Term limits have resulted in a revolving door speakership. Holding the office briefly

were Republicans Doris Allen, Brian Seten-
cich, and Curt Pringle. Recent Democratic
speakers have included Cruz Bustamante (the
state's first Latino speaker and now lieutenant
governor), Antonio Villaraigosa, Robert
Hertzberg, and Herb Wesson. In 2003, Fabian
Nunez, a first term rookie, succeeded Wesson.
While new in the legislature, Nunez was familiar with "The Building," having lobbied the
legislature over the years on immigrant education and labor issues. Nunez hoped that a
longer tenure as speaker would bring "a sense
of stability that the Assembly has lacked."[22]
Nevertheless, term limits pose a fundamental
problem for Assembly speakers. The majority
party must choose between relatively inexperi-
enced colleagues who can serve longer in the
Speaker role or veterans who must leave
within a few years of accepting the post.

PHOTO 7.1 Fabian Nuñez
Speaker of the Assembly

Other Assembly Posts

A number of other leadership posts round out
the legislative elite in the Assembly. The *speaker
pro tempore* is a member of the Speaker's party
and exercises the powers of the Speaker in the
latter's absence. Although this individual is
technically chosen by the entire Assembly, the
Speaker's choice gets the nod. The speaker pro
tem usually presides during floor sessions, allowing the Speaker to mingle with other members. The *assembly majority* and *minority leaders*
are selected from their respective party caucuses. They represent caucus interests on the
Assembly floor; the latter communicates minority wishes to the Speaker. The Assembly Rules
Committee exercises institutional leadership by
selecting many legislative staff, studying legislative rules, and referring bills to committees. Its
nine members include four members each
from the Democratic and Republican caucuses;
the Speaker appoints the chair.

Senate Pro Tempore

In the U.S. Senate, the vice president can
preside and vote in case of a tie, but rarely

performs either function. In the California
Senate, the lieutenant governor has comparable powers but also rarely uses them. Day-to-
day leadership is in the hands of the *president
pro tempore* (pro tem for short). Although the
entire senate votes to fill this post, the majority party invariably chooses one of its own.
David Roberti (D–Van Nuys) occupied the
post from 1980 to 1994, roughly paralleling
Speaker Willie Brown's tenure. In 1994, he
was succeeded by Bill Lockyer (D–Hayward).
When Lockyer resigned to run for attorney
general in 1998, the Democrats picked John
Burton (D–San Francisco). This colorful,
longtime political operator brought passion,
emotion, intensity, and integrity to the job. In
2004, the termed-out Burton was succeeded
by Don Perata (D–Oakland). A former school
teacher, Perata is a Bay Area lawmaker known
for his prowess at deal making and fundraising. On paper, this post appears to be less
powerful than the Assembly speakership. But,
because of longer terms and individual tenures,
the senate pro tem post has been considered

PHOTO 7.2   Senator Don Perata

the second most powerful office in the state. Much of the pro tem's power stems from chairing a five member *Rules Committee*. The other four members consist of two senators from each party caucus. Its powers are comparable to both the Assembly speaker and the Assembly Rules Committee.

THE COMMITTEE SYSTEM

To carry out their policy making responsibilities, modern legislatures must organize into committees—much like Congress does. The committee process recognizes that screening legislation takes specialization and division of labor. California's legislature is divided into numerous committees. Combined, they form a *committee system*: the web of relationships among a number of committees required to enact policy.

Several kinds of committees constitute the committee system in California's legislature. The job of permanent *standing committees* is to process legislation. In other words, they formulate public policy (see Table 7.2 for a complete list of these committees). Members seek assignment to certain policy committees because of former occupations, current policy

interests, or the possibility of receiving campaign contributions. Some women legislators have preferred to serve on committees dealing with human services issues such as children and welfare.[23] We already noted a preference for committees that control legislation of interest to potential campaign contributors—so-called "juice" committees. Examples include the Assembly Government Organization Committee and the Senate Insurance Committee. Apart from election considerations, policy committees give members opportunities to develop policy expertise and address the great and not-so-great issues facing the Golden State.

Several other committees deserve mention. *Fiscal committees* handle bills that require the spending of money. Both houses have appropriations and budget committees devoted to this task. Members seeking power, prestige, or institutional importance covet these assignments. *Conference committees* are convened if the two houses produce different versions of the same bill; their job is to iron out the differences and send unified bills back to both houses for final passage. *Select committees* study various issues facing California with long-term solutions in mind. The Assembly and Senate have almost as many select committees as members—78 in the Assembly and 35 in the Senate. They cover topics ranging from aerospace, horse racing, and wine to California-Mexico relations, gun violence, and mobile homes. About 11 *joint committees* include members from both houses and consider matters of common concern. Examples include fisheries, the arts, and homeland security.

Why all these seemingly extra committees? They can give needed visibility to emerging issues such as border conflicts and school safety. But they also create added chairmanships, opportunities to hire additional staff, and pools of potential campaign contributors.

Not only are there more committees than in the past, many standing committees—the workhorses of the legislature—are larger than ever. The two fiscal committees of the Assembly now have 51 members. One-fourth of the entire Assembly sits on one committee—Water, Wildlife, and Parks. Consequently, scheduling conflicts are commonplace and quorums are illusive. Members often shuttle back and forth between simultaneous committee hearings. According to Jim Knox, executive director of California Common Cause, "The idea of members listening to actual testimony at these hearings has become sort of quaint." As a result, committees are less deliberative than in the past.[24]

THE STAFF

One mark of a professional legislature is a professional staff. Before the California legislature became full time in the 1960s, a few staff offices met its needs for information and analysis: the Legislative Counsel of California (created in 1913 to help draft bills), the California State Auditor (established in 1955 to provide fiscal oversight of state agencies), and the Legislative Analyst's Office (created in 1941 to give nonpartisan advice on fiscal and policy issues). The Analyst's annual *Analysis of*

the Budget Bill can run to nearly 1,600 pages. Over the years, it has developed a national reputation for expertise, solid analysis, and nonpartisanship.[25] In some ways, these offices have been islands of objectivity in a sea of subjective, partisan wrangling. In November 1992, California voters turned down two legislatively sponsored referenda to make the legislative analyst and the auditor general separate and independent offices (Propositions 158 and 159).

As committees grew in number, so did committee staff. In Sacramento, professional committee staff are called "consultants." Given the many policy hats members must wear, the expertise these consultants provide is essential to the committee system. They may earn as much as or more than their elected bosses. In addition to the consultants, each house maintains separate staff to analyze pending bills and to do long range research. Leadership staff assists the house officers for both parties. Party staff assists the respective party caucuses. In addition to secretaries and clerks, both houses employ undergraduate- and graduate-level interns to perform a variety of tasks. Some interns land full-time jobs as a result. More than a few have eventually become legislators.

Proposition 140 affected the legislative staff system in direct and indirect ways. Historically known for their expertise and relative objectivity, many legislative staff became more partisan in recent years. According to some critics, advocacy has overshadowed analysis, and political operatives have eclipsed policy experts. Initially, term limits cut staff budgets; years later they seem to have created a revolving door pattern for staff. According to one veteran staffer, legislative staff work has become "more of a stepping stone to other opportunities, much like the legislators themselves see it."[26] Capitol insiders think this flux in staff will hobble the legislature, but others think staff expansion itself has exacerbated the legislature's problems. To some, armies of staff and reams of paper have replaced policy vision and political fortitude.

The Legislative Process

In truth, passing most legislation requires neither vision nor political courage. Constituents back home could hardly care less about many bills; most are minor changes to existing law, business regulations, and policies affecting the relative few. But all bills, large or small, even the budget bill, must survive the same process. As Figure 7.3 shows, the flow of legislation is quite simple—on paper. An idea for a law can come from any number of sources, such as staff, lobbyists, executive agencies, constituents, and the member's own experience. For example, one legislator decided lasers should not be sold to minors after learning his own son played with one. In the process, he learned what trouble these gadgets can cause. The Legislative Counsel's office drafts the necessary legal language. The legislator who formally submits a bill is its author and is expected to shepherd it through the process; coauthors or cosponsors lend their names as supporters but do little else. In both houses, the respective Rules Committees assign bills to committees for hearings. The very fate of a bill may hinge on which committee hears it. Managing enough votes for a "do-pass" recommendation can be tricky business. A majority of committee members is required regardless of committee attendance when a vote is taken. Given multiple committee memberships, hectic schedules, and the sheer number of bills, simply getting supporters to be there at the right time is a challenge. Ways to kill a bill include assigning it to more than one committee or calling for a committee vote when supporters are absent.

On each house floor, garnering enough votes is equally challenging. Majorities of 41 in the Assembly and 21 in the Senate are required to pass legislation, even if there is only a bare quorum at the time. A two-thirds vote is necessary on the annual budget as well as emergency bills (those taking immediate effect). Yet during floor debate, amendments to the bill may be offered and voted upon by a only a simple majority *of those present*. Because it is so easy (numerically speaking) to amend a bill compared to passing it, floor amendments can be used to substantially modify a bill even to the point of killing it. The process that began in the house of origin repeats itself in the second house. A conference committee resolves interhouse differences. If its members cannot agree with the conference report, the bill dies. If it passes, the governor may sign it (making it law), do nothing (making it law without a signature), or veto it. Like the Congress, a vetoed bill then requires an extraordinary two-thirds vote of both the Assembly and the Senate for it to become law. Even a threatened veto can halt a bill's progress long before it reaches the governor's desk. For example, in 2002 a California Teachers Association–backed bill to give local CTA chapters more power in education decision making was withdrawn by its legislative sponsors after Governor Gray Davis let it be known that he might veto it. In reality, there are many "veto" points or opportunities to say "no" throughout the process. Most bills die somewhere along the way.[27]

Figure 7.3 does not reveal the rhythm of the legislature. The beginning of a term moves rather slowly. By the end of a legislative session (usually late summer), the pace becomes frenetic. At that point, the textbook process becomes fiction as legislators freely amend or completely rewrite ("gut and amend") hundreds of bills without once-essential committee hearings. During the closing days and weeks, some legislators try to slip through local bills (benefiting individual constituents or single groups). Numerous special interest bills are considered during the day while fund-raisers

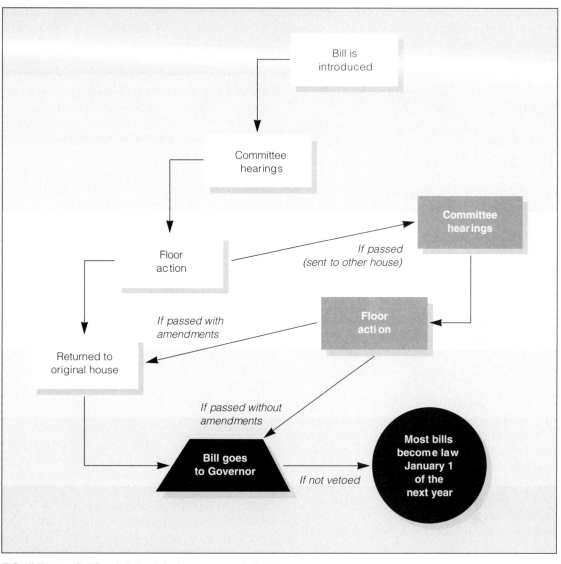

FIGURE 7.3   California's legislative process in brief

Source: Legislative Council of California.

targeting those same interests are scheduled at night. Upwards of 1,500 bills may be considered during those final weeks.

As you reflect on the legislative process in California, remember that the job of the legislature is to both pass and *not pass* legislation. Bills fail for various reasons. Of course, a bill may lack widespread support or be unacceptable to the governor. Schwarzenegger vetoed over 300 bills in his first year as governor. But less obvious reasons also exist. Some members may introduce bills but expend little effort on their behalf. Mere bill introductions may placate some groups or constituents. Legislators may be ambivalent about some bills they feel pressured to author; some bills would make bad law and legislators know it. If a bill dies, a member can breathe easier while blaming committees, the leadership, "special interests," a media blitz, the governor, or whomever for its defeat.

The Third House

In many ways, the legislative process requires lobbying by interest groups. In a representative democracy, interest groups would have to be invented if they did not already exist. Chapter 6 outlined the role of interest groups as linkage institutions in California politics. They organize in different ways to express their policy preferences and serve their members. The professionals they employ to affect the policy process are called *lobbyists*. There are more than 1,100 registered lobbyists in Sacramento who influence the legislative process in six distinct ways:

1. *Making campaign contributions.* Contributing to campaigns is not lobbying per se. But since so many fund-raisers occur in Sacramento, lobbyists are expected to attend. Legislators and lobbyists alike agree that this practice is more used to "buy" access rather than votes on specific bills. Because contributions are made on a year-round basis, lobbyists sometimes make them—and legislators sometimes solicit them—at the same time bills of interest to those lobbyists are being considered. This perceived "pay to play" atmosphere is particularly evident near the end of legislative sessions when fundraising events multiply much like the bills awaiting action. Contributions may also contribute to legislative gridlock. Reflecting on one legislative session, a veteran reporter noted: "Donations did not necessarily buy a bill but donations could purchase a standoff."[28]

2. *Simply being there.* If a physical presence was unnecessary, many groups would locate elsewhere than Sacramento. But because timing is so important in the legislative process, lobbyists need to be on hand to monitor or "watchdog" bills as they proceed through the legislative labyrinth. Being there also includes making friends and establishing numerous contacts with legislators and their staffs. Capitol hallways, elevators, the sixth floor eatery, and members' offices all serve as contact opportunities. Lobbyists may be in hot pursuit almost any time. A veteran lobbyist once noted that, during lengthy committee hearings members "have to go to the bathroom sometime!"

3. *Knowing the process.* Simply being there is not enough. An intimate knowledge of the process as well as the personality quirks of members and staff is essential. Any legislature is a parliamentary labyrinth characterized by a host of written and unwritten rules. The written rules involve the intricacies of the legislative process discussed earlier. Unwritten rules may encompass everything from how members address each other to what they wear. This is why so many successful lobbyists have been former members or staffers.

4. *Providing information.* The most important role a lobbyist can play is giving legislators, committees, and staff accurate, detailed information on a bill, especially its impact on their clients. Lobbyists should be and often are masters of the subject encompassed by a bill. Appealing to common sense logic works especially well on minor bills where other pressures may be absent. On controversial matters, "winning on the merits" is less fruitful. A related technique is the use of a silver bullet—a piece of information that, if made public, would prove too damaging for a bill to survive. If there is opposition to a particular bill, groups often propose amendments to make a bill more acceptable or even harmless. Observers believe term limits will likely increase the informational power of lobbyists and interest groups, the new repositories of institutional memory.

5. *Coalition building.* Many groups believe there is strength in numbers. Accordingly, they develop coalitions with each other to help craft policy, but it takes tenacity for this to succeed. For example, in 2004 counties, cities, and special districts put aside their traditional differences to protect their funding from being raided in order to balance state budgets, an oft-used practice. In doing so, they needed to (1) urge rejection of an initiative (Proposition 65) that they had proposed as a bargaining tool in their negotiations with the legislature and the governor and (2) urge passage of another measure (Proposition 1A) that reflected the agreements they had reached with the legislature and the governor.[29]

6. *Grassroots lobbying.* An increasingly common lobbying technique is the use of *grassroots* pressure. Because legislators of necessity pay attention to constituents back home, grassroots efforts help mobilize them and connect them with their representatives on specific policy issues—even single bills. Modern technology and the presence of term limits makes "farming the membership" both feasible and effective. According to public relations executive Katherine MacDonald, "Grass-roots efforts work more now because new legislators tend to be more grass-roots based and less Sacramento based."[30] As a result, they respond to organized phone call, letter, fax, and email campaigns. A variant of grassroots lobbying is *crowd lobbying.* Members of some interest groups may gather in Sacramento for briefings and to play "lobbyist for a day," as they roam statehouse hallways. The well-heeled stay at expensive downtown hotels, wear business attire, and sport name tags everywhere they go. Others rally on the Capitol steps to voice their views (see Photo 7.3). That said, not all

© AP/Wide World Photos

PHOTO 7.3 Crowd lobbying
Anti-smoking activists gather at the State Capitol.

Question: How effective are these crowd lobbying efforts in contrasts to the permanently situated lobbyists in Sacramento?

constituents are equal or equally significant to legislators. Successful lobbyists know how to cultivate those constituents closest to legislators or how to help their clients become significant constituents worth listening to.[31]

In short the lobbyists, or the third house, represent one point of a legislative triangle. The other two points are legislative committees (both members and staffs) and executive branch agencies (their legislative liaison offices). These triangles or issue networks exist on every subject of permanent interest in state government. They best portray the three-way communication and influence pattern characterizing the legislative process.

Conclusion

Arguably, the California legislature has faced daunting challenges in recent years. This has been due largely to the anger of California voters who passed term limits. In fact, the entire initiative process competes with and even threatens the traditional representative function of the legislature.[32] Future challenges may well center around the state's growing diversity. Although legislatures are intended to represent the people of a state, representation in modern California is no easy matter. As noted, California is becoming increasingly diverse in every sense of the word—culturally, ethnically, socially, and economically. Pluralism is giving way to hyperpluralism. The legislature is increasingly a place where conflicts between diverse groups unfold. Historically, the legislature has best represented the social, economic, and political upper tiers of California—those who can afford to organize. Occasionally, it represents the problems faced by the relatively poor or powerless. In political theory, it is an institution designed potentially to represent pluralistic interests, but, in reality, it most effectively represents the state's elite. For instance, despite revenue declines in the 1990s, business interests received additional tax breaks from Republican and Democratic legislators, ostensibly to create new jobs. Other groups will need to amass political power to match their growing numbers if they are to have comparable clout in the state capital.

Due to Proposition 140, reapportionment, and the newfound electoral clout of women and Latinos, a new generation of legislators has begun to emerge. Some of these newcomers will bring fresh ideas and zeal to "get things done" within their limited terms of office. Others will likely bring inexperience to a complex legislative process. Will they surmount a process that has frustrated so many in the past? Time will tell.

KEY TERMS

Federal plan   (p. 129)

juice committees   (p. 130)

bills, constitutional amendments, resolutions   (p. 131)

trustees, delegates, politicos   (p. 133)

executive oversight   (p. 133)

authorization and appropriation processes   (p. 135)

reapportionment and gerrymandering   (p. 138)

partisan, incumbent, and racial gerrymandering   (p. 138)

party caucus   (p. 142)

assembly majority and minority leaders, speaker pro tem, president pro tem   (p. 143)

standing, fiscal, conference, select, and joint committees   (pp. 144–145)

grassroots lobbying and crowd lobbying   (p. 149)

REVIEW QUESTIONS

1. Briefly survey California's legislative history.
2. Describe the functions legislatures perform.
3. In what ways do legislators perceive their own roles?
4. How are legislative candidates recruited? Why and how do they manage to stay?
5. Describe the power of the Assembly speaker and other leadership posts.
6. Explain how the committee system represents both a diverse state and ambitions of legislators.
7. As a lobbyist, how would you most effectively deal with today's legislature?

WEB ACTIVITIES

California Assembly and Senate
(www.assembly.ca.gov and www.senate.ca.gov)
These sites provide current schedules, district finders, member directories, and links to legislation, various caucuses, and other California government Websites.

Legislative Analyst's Office
(www.lao.ca.gov)
Here you have access to the same policy expertise available to the legislature.

Legislative Counsel of California
(www.leginfo.ca.gov)
This is an excellent gateway site leading you to bill information, state laws, legislative information, and related publications.

INFOTRAC® COLLEGE EDITION ARTICLES

For additional reading, go to InfoTrac® College Edition, your online research library, at http://www.infotrac.thomsonlearning.com

A Better Democracy; Redistricting

Legislative Term Limits: Still a Good Idea?

Arnold Takes on the Gerrymander

NOTES

1. James Bryce, *The American Commonwealth, Vol. 1*, 2nd ed. (New York: Macmillan, 1891), 536.
2. For more analysis, see Alan Rosenthal, *The Decline of Representative Democracy: Process, Participation, and Power in State Legislatures* (Washington, D.C.: CQ Press, 1998).
3. The U.S. Supreme Court ruled term limits for members of Congress (that had also been imposed by Proposition 140) unconstitutional in *U.S. Term Limits v. Thornton*, 514 U.S. 779 (1995).
4. For more on this period, see William Buchanan, *Legislative Partisanship: The Deviant Case of California* (Berkeley: University of California Press, 1963).
5. *Reynolds v. Sims* 377 U.S. 533 (1964).
6. The 50 legislatures were judged on how functional, accountable, informed, independent, and representative they were. See Citizen's Conference on State Legislatures, *The Sometime Governments: A Critical Study of the 50 American Legislatures*, 2nd ed. (Kansas City, MO: CCSL, 1973).
7. See Richard A. Clucas, *The Speaker's Electoral Connection: Willie Brown and the California Assembly* (Berkeley: University of California Press, 1995).
8. See A. G. Block and Stephanie Carniello, "Putting on the Squeeze," *California Journal* 18 (April 1987), 178–180; and Delia M. Rios, "Squeezing the Juice from Committee Assignments," *California Journal* 12 (March 1981), 109–110.
9. This parallels the national experience with legislative term limits. See John M. Carey, Richard G. Niemi, and Lynda W. Powell, *Term Limits in the State Legislatures* (Ann Arbor: University of Michigan Press, 2000).
10. This "author system" is described in William K. Muir Jr., *Legislature: California's School for Politics* (Chicago: University of Chicago Press, 1982), chap. 3.
11. For extensive research on this topic, see Sue Thomas, *How Women Legislate* (New York: Oxford University Press, 1994); relative to California, see the "Women in Politics" issue of the *California Journal* 32 (December 2001).
12. A classic study of legislative roles can be found in John C. Wahlke et al., *The Legislative System:*

Exploration in Legislative Behavior (New York: Wiley, 1962).

13. Kent C. Price, "Instability in Representational Role Orientation in a State Legislature: A Research Note," *Western Political Quarterly* 38 (March 1985), 162–171.

14. Mark Katches, "No More Museum Pieces: The California Legislature is a Whole New Place Since Term Limits Have Swept It Clean," *State Legislatures* 25 (February 1999), 24–27.

15. Quoted in Charles M. Price, "Class of 1992: The Proposition 140 Babies," *California Journal* 24 (April 1993), 36.

16. Joseph A. Schlesinger developed this classic division in *Ambition and Politics: Political Careers in the United States* (Chicago: Rand McNally, 1966), 10.

17. Two related articles on this subject are Peverill Squire, "Career Opportunities and Membership Stability in Legislatures," *Legislative Studies Quarterly* 13 (February 1988), 65–77; and "Member Career Opportunities and the Internal Organization of Legislatures," *Journal of Politics* 50 (August 1988), 726–744.

18. Bruce E. Cain, *The Reapportionment Puzzle* (Berkeley: University of California Press, 1984), 166–168.

19. Carl M. Cannon, "California Divided," *California Journal* 33 (January 2002), 8–14.

20. His dissenting opinion in *Lockner v. New York*, 198 U.S. 45 (1905).

21. Rosenthal, *The Decline of Representative Democracy*, 162–177.

22. Quoted in A.G. Block and John Howard, "The New Assembly Speaker," *California Journal* 35 (March 2004), 44.

23. Although gender differences are not dramatic, men and women do have different policy priorities including committee preferences, according to a multistate study that included the California legislature. See Sue Thomas and Susan Welch, "The Impact of Gender on Activities and Priorities of State Legislators," *Western Political Quarterly* 44 (June 1991), 445–456.

24. See Anthony York, "Capitol Whispers," *Political Pulse* (January 30, 2004).

25. For a profile of head analyst Elizabeth Hill, see Max Vanzi, "Liz Hill: Here Today, Here Tomorrow," *California Journal* 30 (July 1999), 40–43.

26. Quoted in Vic Pollard, "Legislative Staff: Coping with Term Limits and an Unstable Job Market," *California Journal* 25 (June 1994), 16.

27. Some bills follow a tortured path, only to die for lack of a single vote. See William Trombley and Jerry Gillam, "How a Bill Twists in the Wind," *Los Angeles Times*, October 14, 1991.

28. Quoted in James Richardson, "Special Interests Dominate Legislative Session," *California Journal* 21 (November 1990), 528.

29. See Mary Lynne Vellinga, "A Seat at the Table," California Journal 35 (September 2004), 22—27.

30. Quoted in Laureen Lazarovici, "The Rise of the Wind-Makers," *California Journal* 26 (June 1995), 18.

31. For more on legislative strategies of interest groups, see Jay Michaels and Dan Walters, *The Third House: Lobbyists, Money, and Power in Sacramento* (Berkeley: Berkeley Public Policy Press, 2002).

32. For an analysis of the representational challenge faced by state legislatures in general, see Rosenthal, *The Decline of Representative Democracy*.

CHAPTER 8

Executive Politics

In Brief

Administering California's state government is the responsibility of the executive branch; administering that branch and providing overall political leadership for the entire state falls to the governor. In chapter 8, we survey the office of governor, other executive officers, plus a sizable bureaucracy—all of whom compete for power and leadership in the Golden State.

California's post-statehood governors have run the gamut in personality, governing styles and political skills. Most have been forgotten by history, but others have provided uncommon leadership and made a mark on the state through policy entrepreneurship. Governors exercise a variety of duties and powers, including executive powers, budget leadership opportunities, legislative and judicial power, plus roles such as the state's commander in chief and chief of state. They share power and leadership authority with several other separately elected leaders, the most powerful of whom is the attorney general.

In addition to those top posts, California's bureaucracy numbers about 316,000 employees.

They exercise a number of functions common to all bureaucracies, and in doing so, diffuse executive leadership and administration still further. Yet, they deliver state services and personify state government to many Californians.

California's executive branch both mirrors and attempts to govern a diverse state. In the process, it is limited by political and organizational fragmentation that resists efforts to reform it.

Introduction

When Gray Davis ran for governor in 1998, he sported a public resume the envy of most candidates. He had been Governor Jerry Brown's chief of staff, an assembly member, state controller, and lieutenant governor. In fact, the San Jose Mercury News described him as "perhaps the best trained governor in waiting." To that accolade, Davis later responded, "Perhaps?!! I mean, how many offices do I have to hold?" While Governor Davis scored some early successes in education reform, he was hobbled by an energy crisis and major budget problems. Despite unfavorable job approval ratings, unenthusiastic voters returned him to office in 2002, rejecting the Republican's lackluster candidate, businessman Bill Simon.

In 2003, only one year after winning that second term, Davis was ousted in a bitter recall election. If commonplace resume builders like service in the state legislature and in other governmental posts are any measure, Davis was replaced by perhaps the *least* trained governor in waiting—Austrian-born movie star and body builder Arnold Schwarzenegger. During his first two years in office, Schwarzenegger altered the political landscape, cajoled Democratic legislators, centralized executive branch power in his own office, used his celebrity to campaign successfully on behalf of several initiatives, and reenergized California's Republican Party. Even his critics had to admire the seemingly natural skill he brought to the office. During the 2004 election cycle, his devoted followers slapped "Arnold for President" stickers on their car bumpers and suggested that the U.S. Constitu-

tion be amended to allow immigrants—namely Schwarzenegger—to run for president.

The respective experiences of Davis and Schwarzenegger suggest that gubernatorial leadership depends on a fluid mix of many factors—actual job performance, electoral moods, the health of the economy, legislative friends and enemies, formal powers, and structural constraints, partisanship, and one's own personality.

Executive branch politics is both fascinating to watch and complicated to study. State governors perform many of the same tasks American presidents do, but governors usually are out of the national spotlight—usually. The 1992 budget stalemate between Governor Pete Wilson and the legislature occupied the national media for weeks as did Gray Davis' recall and Arnold Schwarzenegger's election. The formal powers of governors, like those of presidents, are not exhaustive. Both must compete for influence in a system full of checks and balances. Political scientist James MacGregor Burns once described presidential power as "essentially the power to dicker and transact."[1] This is all the more true of American governors. Let's examine the political and administrative setting in which California governors operate.

How Governors Lead

The governor operates in a complex pattern of executive leadership. On the one hand, California's governor is at the apex of the political system—more powerful than any other single individual. On the other, the entire executive

PHOTO 8.1 Governor Arnold Schwarzenegger

After a 2005 Capitol steps press conference, Governor Arnold Schwarzenegger heads to a Sacramento restaurant to cheerlead a number of reform measures destined for a special election ballot.

Question: To what extent are these photo opportunities required for governors to lead?

branch exemplifies the themes of this book. It regulates and/or provides benefits to virtually every group or issue in the state, in effect mirroring the diversity that is California. As such, the executive branch (appointed officials, career civil servants, and other workers) represents the state's population. But given how the executive branch is organized and structured, it also exhibits its own form of hyperpluralism: diluted and shared power, politically independent offices and agencies, and many avenues for interest group influence.

Legislators debate policy, help constituents, and collectively pass legislation. Although voters often consider their own legislators political leaders, the legislature's primary role is more to provide representation than to provide leadership. Even the legislative leaders discussed in Chapter 7 provide institutional leadership, not statewide political leadership.

This function necessarily resides in the governorship. But the state's diversity and fragmented political system present numerous roadblocks to leadership.

Experience with colonial governors on the East Coast taught the original colonies a lesson: To prevent autocratic governors, constitutionally weaken their offices. As newer states copied older state constitutions, they also limited gubernatorial power. California did so too, even though it experienced relatively weak colonial governors under Spain and Mexico.

Table 8.1 lists all California governors from establishment of statehood to the present. Three observations are in order. *First,* few early governors are memorable to contemporary Californians. Strong executive leadership was neither valued nor experienced in those years. The most well-known nineteenth-century governor, Leland Stanford, is better known for his

TABLE 8.1 The Governors of California

Governor	Party	Years	Terms
Peter H. Burnett	D	1849–1851	<1
John McDougal*	D	1851–1852	<1
John Bigler	D	1852–1856	1
J. Neely Johnson	A+	1856–1858	<1
John B. Weller	D	1858–1860	<1
Milton S. Latham	D	1860	<1
John G. Downey*	D	1860–1862	<1
Leland Stanford	R	1862–1863	<1
Frederick F. Low	R	1863–1867	1
Henry H. Haight	D	1867–1871	1
Newton Booth	R	1871–1875	1
Romualdo Pacheco, Jr.*	R	1875	<1
William Irwin	D	1875–1880	>1
George C. Perkins	R	1880–1883	<1
George Stoneman	D	1883–1887	1
Washington Bartlett	D	1887	<1
Robert H. Waterman*	R	1887–1891	1
Henry H. Markham	R	1891–1895	1
James H. Budd	D	1895–1899	1
Henry T. Gage	R	1899–1903	1
George C. Pardee	R	1903–1907	1
James N. Gillett	R	1907–1911	1
Hiram W. Johnson	R	1911–1917	>1
William D. Stephens*	R	1917–1923	>1
Friend W. Richardson	R	1923–1927	1
C. C. Young	R	1927–1931	1
James Rolph, Jr.	R	1931–1934	<1
Frank F. Merriam*	R	1934–1939	>1
Culbert L. Olson	D	1939–1943	1
Earl Warren	R	1943–1953	>2
Goodwin J. Knight*	R	1953–1959	<1
Edmund G. "Pat" Brown	D	1959–1967	2
Ronald Reagan	R	1967–1975	2
Edmund G. "Jerry" Brown	D	1975–1983	2
George Deukmejian	R	1983–1991	2
Pete Wilson	R	1991–1999	2
Gray Davis	D	1999–2003	<2
Arnold Schwarzenegger	R	2003–	

*Lieutenant governor succeeded to governorship

+American Party

Question: To what extent and on what basis will recent governors be memorable a century from now?

membership in the Big Four and for the university he founded. *Second,* throughout most of its history, the California governorship has been a rapidly revolving door. Service of less than one term was common among early governors. In 1860, Milton Latham served all of five days! He quit to replace a U.S. senator shot in a duel. Hiram Johnson was the first governor to serve more than four years. He took office in 1911, was reelected in 1914, and resigned to serve in the U.S. Senate in 1917. *Third,* as the table shows, lengthy service as governor is a recent phenomenon. Earl Warren served more than two terms and governors from Pat Brown to Pete Wilson each served two four-year terms. The 2003 recall prevented Gray Davis from serving a second term to which he had been elected. Presumably, eight years gives a governor ample time to form an agenda, exercise leadership, and implement priorities. Ironically, the records of very recent governors suggest that lengthy tenure alone does not necessarily guarantee effective leadership.

The governor's annual salary of $175,000 is among the nation's highest and would seemingly reflect the office's leadership role.[2] In reality, a number of California public employees including public health administrators, top public university administrators plus many local government managers, earn more.

Like other elected executives, California governors do not exercise power in a political vacuum. Borrowing heavily from research on the American presidency, Robert Crew identified five variables that affect gubernatorial leadership.[3] We will apply them to gubernatorial politics in California. They include the governor's personality, political skill, political resources, the overall political environment or context, and strategic considerations:

1. *Personality.* Highly personal factors such as motivation, behavior, and character, affect how governors lead. California governors have possessed diverse personality traits. For instance, Hiram Johnson was tenacious and per-suasive; Earl Warren, competent and well-liked; Pat Brown, confident and active; Reagan, gregarious and surprisingly flexible. Jerry Brown was aloof and philosophical; George Deukmejian, persistent and stubborn; Pete Wilson, tough yet pragmatic. With few close friends and confidants, Gray Davis has been called a "Lone Ranger," a governor short on people skills. Disavowing "politics as usual," Arnold Schwarzenegger brought to the office star power, a desire for action, and an ability to publicly tweak fellow lawmakers. Naturally, the personalities of governors affect how they approach the job, relate to staff and legislators, and communicate with the public.

2. *Political Skill.* California governors need extraordinary political skill to push their priorities through the legislature and the state's bureaucracy. These skills involve working successfully with legislative leaders, political party operatives, the media, and interest groups. For instance, Earl Warren sponsored nonpartisan "town halls"—inviting thousands of concerned citizens to Sacramento during a legislative session. Ronald Reagan mastered the art of sounding ultraconservative (to please his followers) while acting with moderation (in recognition of political reality). Arnold Schwarzenegger innovatively threatened to use the initiative process if the legislature balked at his policy proposals.

3. *Political Resources.* Such resources come from inside or outside the governor's office. Internal resources include the amount of time, information, expertise, and energy a governor has. External resources include party support in the legislature, public approval, electoral margins, and professional reputation. Hiram Johnson could attribute his success to a legislature controlled by fellow Progressives. Republican Pete Wilson possessed the experience and largely moderate political views that have been historically valued by Californians. Gray Davis enjoyed Democratic majorities in the legislature, allowing

him to obtain a number of education reforms. Schwarzenegger faced that same Democratic legislature but his own high public approval ratings (and the legislature's low ratings) became a political asset in dealing with the legislature. By 2005, his ratings dropped as did his clout.

4. *Political Context.* "Context" refers to factors in the external environment that affects a governor's performance. California's economy is one such factor. Depression era governors were hurt by national economic turmoil. Post–World War II governors (Warren, Goodwin Knight, and Brown) took advantage of a growing economy and the taxes it generated. Wilson's first several years were characterized by a persistent recession (the worst statewide economic condition since the Great Depression), sagging revenues, and huge budget deficits. A second external factor is the state's political environment. This includes the electorate's partisan and ideological leanings. It also includes the political era during which a governor serves. Each era witnesses its own governing coalitions, expressions of political culture, and an overall political mood expressed by the public. Public confidence in the future of the state as measured in public opinion polls provides an upbeat political context in which governors can maneuver. Yet in 2004, Schwarzenegger discovered that his own considerable assets could not overcome Democratic leaning legislative districts. Not a single Republican candidate for whom he campaigned won office.

5. *Strategic Considerations.* Given the factors mentioned, each governor must craft a strategy to achieve desired goals. This involves a game plan to deal with the legislature as well as methods to gain interest group and popular support. Previous strategies in California have involved large-scale, ambitious programs such as water projects and the master plan for higher education. Pete Wilson took office espousing "preventative government" programs to reduce the dependence of California's children on government. Arnold Schwarzenegger faced skeptical legislators and continuing budget deficits that narrowed to some extent his policy options.

Timing is an important strategic consideration for governors. Relatively few windows of opportunity exist—times when governors can pursue a policy agenda with some hope of success. These windows are determined by routine political cycles, such as the election calendar and the annual budget process. As with presidents, California governors normally experience brief "honeymoons" of popularity and support early in their administrations. Astute governors take advantage of this phenomenon. For instance, Arnold Schwarzenegger administratively cancelled a controversial car tax increase within minutes of taking office, fulfilling a campaign promise in doing so. Windows of opportunity often close during election years, especially if tax increases are contemplated. Every other year, the entire Assembly is up for election, as is one half of the Senate. During recessions, when revenues cease to grow or even shrink, those windows may never fully open. Since so many policy issues depend on adequate funding, revenue levels themselves open and close windows of opportunity.

The Governor's Duties and Powers

Whether resources are in their favor or not, California governors possess a wide range of duties and powers. In terms of public expectations, their responsibilities to lead the state outstrip their actual, formal powers. The range of powers discussed next are both formal and informal. They stem from both the Constitution and political necessity. They are both visible and invisible to the general public. Some powers the governor must share with the legislature or other executive branch agencies. Others are relatively unchecked by competing forces.

EXECUTIVE POWERS

The governor is first and foremost the chief executive officer of the state. In constitutional language, the "supreme executive power" of the state is vested in the governor. "The Governor shall see that the law is faithfully executed."[4] Although this is much easier said than done, the governor possesses a number of powers to achieve this goal.

Organizing a Personal Staff

The governor's *inner circle* consists of a chief of staff and a variety of assistants called "secretaries," assigned to legislative matters, administration, the press, appointments and scheduling, and legal affairs. Top personal staff members often are veteran associates of the governor.[5] *Their* staffs are often young, energetic, recent college graduates with workaholic schedules. The administrations of Ronald Reagan and George Deukmejian were known for rather hierarchical staff relations (resembling a strict organization chart), whereas Jerry Brown had a relatively loose "spokes of the wheel" arrangement. In this latter style, numerous individuals had relatively free access to the governor. Given Arnold Schwarzenegger's lack of public sector experience, his initial appointments included a number of former administrators under Governor Pete Wilson and staffers from a number of business oriented interest groups. His senior advisor was Bonnie Reiss, a Democrat who was a founding director of Schwarzenegger's All Stars, a group providing after school programs to middle schools.

Making Appointments

Although most of California's 300,000 plus executive branch employees belong to a civil service system, the governor appoints several thousand individuals to various posts. These people include the governor's own personal staff, high-level administrators, various board and commission posts, and judgeships. In addition to running state agencies, governors can accomplish several things through their appointments. First, they can diversify their administrations. For instance, in a departure from previous practice, Jerry Brown named numerous ethnic minorities and women. Second, they can reward their friends and political allies. For example, Davis appointed several Sacramento veterans and former legislators to his cabinet—Gary Hart as his first education secretary and Robert Presley as secretary of the Youth and Adult Correctional Agency. Schwarzenegger made similar appointments. Third, they can extend their own power by appointing like-minded people. Davis went so far as to say that appointees should "think like I think."[6]

Managing the Executive Branch

California governors have their own versions of presidential cabinets. Notice Figure 8.1, an organization chart of the state's executive branch. Wary of the huge number of appointees reporting directly to him, Governor Pat Brown reorganized a plethora of departments into several *superagencies*. Subsequent governors have reorganized a bit, but the superagency structure remains. These agencies include (1) Business, Transportation, and Housing, (2) Environmental Protection, (3) Health and Human Services Agency, (4) Resources, (5) State and Consumer Services, and (6) Youth and Adult Corrections. All these people are part of the governor's *cabinet*, but they are less powerful than their "super" titles would suggest. For instance, within Business, Transportation and Housing are CalTrans, Housing and Community Development, Commerce, and the Highway Patrol. Each operates like a semiautonomous fiefdom, well outside the governor's routine attention span.[7] These agency secretaries, joined by the education secretary and several other departments (Food and Agriculture, Finance, Industrial Relations, and Veterans Affairs) make up the governor's cabinet. These various agency

CALIFORNIA STATE GOVERNMENT - CURRENT ORGANIZATIONAL STRUCTURE

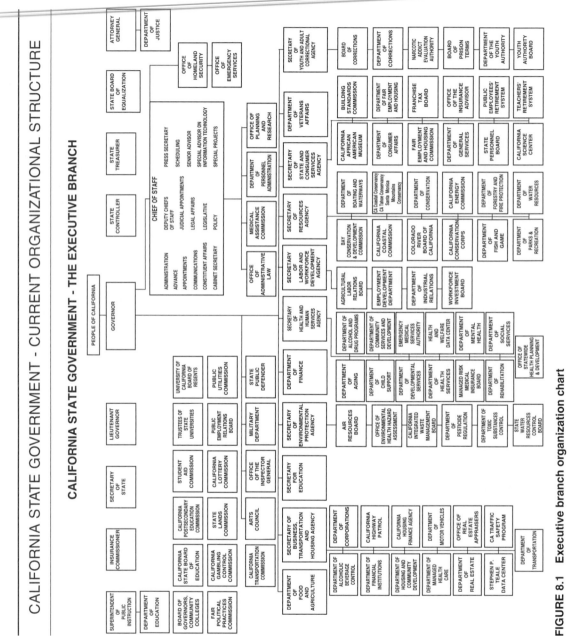

FIGURE 8.1 Executive branch organization chart

Question: Which parts of the executive branch do you think cost the most? Compare your answer with budget data in chapter 11.

heads vary in importance. The director of finance is a crucial appointee, given the governor's budget responsibilities. As a group, the governor's cabinet is less a policy body than a collection of executive branch appointees.

Issuing Orders

The "executive power" of California's governor also includes the ability to take action independent of the legislature. A primary vehicle to do this is the *executive order*. Such orders usually contain this language: "NOW, THEREFORE I, Arnold Schwarzenegger, Governor of the State of California, by virtue of the power and authority invested in me by the Constitution and the laws of the State of California, do hereby issue this order to become effective immediately." For example, days after being sworn in as governor, Schwarzenegger issued an executive order prohibiting state departments and agencies from hiring new employees.

BUDGET LEADERSHIP

Although the constitutional language "supreme executive power" sounds impressive, what requires the governor's constant attention is the state's budget (discussed further in Chapter 11). The California Constitution requires the governor to submit a budget to the legislature within the first ten days of each calendar year. A tremendous amount of preparation goes into the submission of that "budget bill." The state budget is the premier policy statement for California and governors want their priorities reflected in it. The process is twofold. The *internal budget process* (within the executive branch) begins the previous July when the governor, through the Department of Finance (DOF), submits a "budget letter/price letter" to all executive agencies and departments. The budget letter relays the governor's policy priorities, while the price letter contains fiscal assumptions (like the rate of inflation) used to determine budget baselines. During the rest of

the year, departments and the DOF haggle over which figures will emerge in the governor's January budget.[8]

The *external budget process* pits the governor against the legislature. This part of the process is the most visible to the public and clearly the messiest from the governor's standpoint. At this stage, the governor shares budget power primarily with the Assembly Budget Committee, the Senate Budget and Fiscal Review Committee, and the Legislative Analyst's Office. Each has a staff that examines and often second-guesses the governor's figures. When stalemates occur (they often do when revenues and expenditures do not easily match), a parallel group—the "Big Five"—emerges to further haggle over the budget bill. The governor and the two caucus leaders each from the Assembly and Senate form this group.

The Constitution also requires that the legislature enact the budget bill by June 15 and for the governor to sign it by June 30, the last day of each fiscal year. It also mandates an extraordinary two-thirds legislative vote on the budget, an increasingly difficult political feat to achieve. Now and then, budget stalemates occur among the Big Five. July 1 may pass without a budget, and the largest state in the Union is declared "broke." On one occasion, creditors and employees were paid in registered warrants (called "IOUs") until a budget was approved months later. Less publicized conflicts occur regularly. When revenues are down, budget makers argue over where to cut spending; when revenues are up, they argue over new spending ideas versus new tax cuts.

Once a budget is passed, additional spending requests plus new revenue projections require further adjustments during the fiscal year. Although the governor's budget power seems to dissipate during legislative debate on the budget bill, the governor's power over an approved budget is substantial. The most formidable tool the governor has at this point is the *item veto*. This refers to the governor's ability to reduce or reject any item in an appropriations

CALIFORNIA VOICES

A Line Item Veto

"I object to the following appropriations contained in Senate Bill 1113." With that simple declarative sentence, Governor Arnold Schwarzenegger "blue penciled" numerous spending items in the state's 2004–2005 budget. The particular item below deletes $1,265,000 from the Department of Education's budget for local assistance. Notice how he unilaterally reduces the expenditure approved by the legislature and provides his rationale for doing so:

Item 6110-130-0001 –For local assistance, Department of Education. I reduce this item from $10,300,000 to $9,035,000.

I am sustaining $9,035,000 for the Advancement Via Individual Determination program (AVID) to provide training to teachers and school leaders and assistance to schools in implementing this program that helps students prepare for and be successful in college that might otherwise not attend. During better economic times the State was able to fully support a variety of worthy programs. However, due to limited resources in the General Fund, the State is unable to continue to sustain the same level of support.

In making this reduction I encourage districts that currently participate in the AVID program to utilize some of the existing staff development dollars available to them. This budget already includes $957 million for staff development and teacher training programs.

I am revising Provision 1 to conform to this action.

Question: Can you see why U.S. presidents would love to have the line item veto, especially if the legislature was controlled by the other political party?

SOURCE: California State Budget 2004–2005 (accessed at www.dof.ca.gov/)

(spending) bill. Including California, 42 governors, have this power. Notice "California Voices," a portion of a veto message attached to a 2004 budget bill. Here Schwarzenegger deleted $1,265,000 from a teacher training program intended to better prepare students for college admission and explained his rationale for doing so. Item vetoes can add up. George Dukemejian, known in Sacramento as "Governor No," vetoed about 1,700 expenditure items totaling nearly $7 billion during his two terms.

A final word on the governor's budget powers is in order. Many parts of the overall budget are difficult to control. They include separate spending decisions made by voters through initiatives (Proposition 98's funding requirements for education), particular revenues dedicated to certain uses (gas taxes for highway expenditures), or automatic spending increases called COLAs (cost of living adjustments). All these "uncontrollables," as political scientists call them, amount to a significant majority of the entire state budget. They substantially limit the ability of the governor to control spending and, therefore, policy.

LEGISLATIVE POWERS

California governors must deal constantly with the legislature and not just on the annual budget. They must exercise legislative leadership to achieve a host of other policy goals. California's most successful governors, legislatively speaking, were admired and respected by many legislators, utilized bipartisanship, and enjoyed high public approval ratings. But many California governors experienced significant political conflict because they brought profoundly different perspectives to their leadership role.

• *Party Differences:* The most telling source of conflict occurs when the governor is of one major political party and the legislature is controlled by another major party. In recent decades, Republican governors and Democratic legislative majorities have clashed on taxes, welfare spending, and many other issues. In contrast, Gray Davis and legislative Democrats had to temper efforts to impose an activist agenda the public might not support. In light of persistent budget problems, Arnold Schwarzenegger initially appeased both Republicans and Democrats; the former, by opposing tax increases and the latter, by postponing many deep program cuts. In 2004, he became more aggressive and combative in pushing a variety of budget and political reforms. Unified party control does not necessarily connote smooth interbranch relations. For instance, fellow Democrats in the legislature overrode a number of Jerry Brown's vetoes in the late 1970s, and fellow Republicans opposed Pete Wilson's flexibility on tax increases in the early 1990s.

• *Constituency Differences:* At times, differences in perspective between a governor and the legislature can be traced to constituency differences. Legislators represent individual, more homogeneous districts whereas the governor represents the entire state population, as diverse as it is. The needs of the whole state may not square with the constituent views of a particular Assembly or Senate district. For instance, a governor must balance the water needs of the entire state, not just those of farmers or city dwellers, as individual legislators might. Some parts of the state may hunger for economic development and growth; others might resist such growth.

• *Interest Differences:* Legislators are particularly responsive to the views of individual interest groups, as noted in Chapter 7. Governors try to represent the larger "general interest" of the state and, in doing so, seem more willing to step on interest group toes in the process. For example, Gray Davis received a great deal of electoral support (campaign contributions and votes) from labor unions but resisted demands by unionized government workers for substantial pay increases. Arnold Schwarzenegger entered office "beholden to no one" but the public but even he accepted contributions from pro-business groups.

• *Responsibility Differences:* When California legislators want to diffuse blame, they can easily point their fingers to committee chairpersons, legislative leaders, or insensitive fellow legislators from elsewhere in the state. Governors cannot spread the blame for failure nearly as far. If they try, their own leadership ability is questioned. Furthermore, the public tends to lay singular responsibility on the governor. The highly respected Field Poll measures the *governor's* popularity, not each legislator's.

Governors employ several resources in dealing with the California legislature: an overall legislative program, the general veto, calling special sessions, and personal relations. This is how each works.

• *Legislative Program:* Each January, the governor presents a "State of the State" speech, much like the president's "State of the Union" speech. This is an opportunity to fashion a coherent set of policy priorities by which legislation might be evaluated. California governors never command media attention comparable to that received by presidents, though. Many television stations rarely carry more than excerpts of the state of the state speech. In response, governors often stage symbol-laden media events. Recognizing his own unique ability to attract media attention, Arnold Schwarzenegger has staged many such events including the fueling of a hydrogen-powered Hummer, symbolizing his commitment to alternative, clean energy.

• *General Veto:* As noted earlier, the item veto allows the governor power to "blue pencil" a particular expenditure contained in an appropriations bill. A *general veto*, like the president's veto power, allows the governor to reject an entire non-spending bill. In "California Voices" on this page is the text of a general veto by Arnold Schwarzenegger. Here, AB 2832 would have raised the state's minimum wage from $6.67 to $7.75 per hour (the federally required minimum wage has been $5.15 since 1997). Schwarzenegger provides a brief rationale for his opposition to the bill. Over time, these vetoes add up. George Deukmejian exercised the general veto on 2,298 bills during two terms, largely because he governed alongside a Democratic legislature.

• *Special Sessions:* In the past, when the legislature was not in session, governors would call *special sessions* to deal with pressing matters. Since modern legislative sessions are virtually year round, fewer special sessions are needed. But governors still call them now and then. In December of 1989, Governor Deukmejian called one in response to the Loma Prieta earthquake in the San Francisco Bay Area. In late 2003, Arnold Schwarzenegger called a post-recall special session of the legislature in order to address the state's yawning budget gap, including his proposal to float $20 billion in bonds.

• *Personal Relations:* One of the governor's most potent but underrated legislative tools is good interpersonal relationships. For example, Ronald Reagan cultivated the press corps. Earl Warren and Pat Brown were known for their warm relations with legislators, while Jerry Brown and George Deukmejian were more distant and cool. Even members of his own party detested Jerry Brown's spartan lifestyle and unconventional tactics. Also, personal relations can be hampered by policy differences as Pete Wilson discovered in the 1990s. His support for Proposition 140 and Republican-oriented reapportionment plans angered Democrats and his support for certain tax increases angered conservative Republicans. Arnold Schwarzenegger capitalized on his larger-than-life persona by giving legislative leaders coveted personal attention, yet

CALIFORNIA VOICES

A General Veto

To the Members of the California State Assembly:

I am returning Assembly Bill 2832 without my signature.

This bill would raise California's minimum wage to a level that would be the highest in the nation. According to the Employment Development Department, this will increase the costs to California employers by at least $3 billion, and as much as $4.4 billion.

In recent years, the high cost of doing business in California has driven away jobs, businesses, and opportunity. We have launched California's recovery by making our state a more attractive place to do business, so that employers will stay in our state, expand in our state, and create more jobs here.

Now is not the time to create barriers to our economic recovery or reverse the momentum we have generated. I want to create more jobs and make every California job more secure.

For these reasons, I am unable to support this measure.

Sincerely,

Arnold Schwarzenegger

Question: This was one of over 300 vetoes in Arnold Schwarzenegger's first year in office. What larger message do prolific vetoes send to the legislature and to the public at large?

SOURCE: California Governor's Office (www. governor.ca.gov)

calling legislators "Girlie Men" when they opposed his budget proposals.

JUDICIAL POWERS

Gubernatorial power also involves the judiciary or can be essentially judicial in nature. For instance, the governor's appointment power extends to the judicial branch, as explained in Chapter 9. When a vacancy occurs on the California Supreme Court or the Courts of Appeal, the governor makes the appointment. Governors even appoint superior court judges when vacancies occur between elections. These appointments can add up. By the end of Governor Deukmejian's two terms, he had appointed nearly two-thirds of all state judges.

Like American presidents and appointments to the U.S. Supreme Court, governors can leave their imprints on state supreme courts. Deukmejian's appointments were moderate conservatives with pro-business credentials. Jerry Brown's appointments reflected his desire to create opportunities for minorities and to shake up the legal system. His selections included several firsts: Chief Justice Rose Bird (the first woman), Cruz Reynoso (the first Latino), and Wiley Manuel (the first African-American). Once appointed, appellate justices must face the voters. Both Bird, Reynoso, and another justice, Joseph Grodin, were ousted in 1986, in part because they opposed the death penalty.

The governor's purely judicial powers involve *clemency* (or acts of mercy). *First,* the governor may *pardon* an individual convicted of a crime. This means releasing someone from the consequences of a criminal conviction. *Second,* the governor may *commute* or reduce a sentence. *Third,* the governor may issue a *reprieve* (the postponement of a sentence). In the 1990s, Pete Wilson denied capital punishment reprieves to Robert Alton Harris and David Edwin Mason. Gray Davis rejected similar pleas by Jaturun Siripongs (a Thai immigrant convicted of a double murder) and Manuel Babbitt (whose beating of an elderly woman caused a fatal heart attack). *Fourth,* the governor may reverse parole decisions by the Board of Prison Terms, a power only three states grant their governors. For example, in 2004 Arnold Schwarzenegger paroled Rosario Munoz after she served 16 years in state prison for killing her husband's lover. *Fifth,* the governor may *extradite* a fugitive to another state from which the fugitive has fled. Governor Jerry Brown once refused South Dakota's request to extradite Dennis Banks, a militant Native American, fearing he would not receive a fair trial.

A related task is more legal than judicial in nature. Governors largely determine which court cases the state pursues at the appellate level. For instance, Pete Wilson decided to appeal a federal judge's ruling that Proposition 187 (the anti-immigrant measure) was unconstitutional. His successor, Gray Davis, had to decide whether or not to continue the appeal. He was torn. "I have two conflicting obligations. I opposed 187. I personally think it is unconstitutional. I also believe I have certain obligations as the chief executive to support the law."[9] After asking the Ninth Circuit Court of Appeals to mediate the matter, Davis decided to drop the appeal. The most controversial features of 187 were dead.

OTHER POWERS

During times of crisis and public disorder, the governor's role as *commander in chief* of the National Guard (the state militia) comes into play. The scenario usually involves a local riot or disturbance, the inability of local police to restore order, a mayoral request for National Guard assistance, and the deployment of guardsmen to restore order. In 1965, Pat Brown deployed 1,000 guardsmen during the Watts Riot. In 1992, Governor Pete Wilson sent 7,000 guardsmen to riot-torn Los Angeles and, in 1994, a smaller number to Northridge to help with earthquake relief efforts.

Lastly, governors are *chiefs of state.* As such, they greet foreign dignitaries, address interest group conventions, accompany presidents who are traveling in California, cut ribbons on public works projects, and process a huge volume of mail. Schoolchildren write governors assuming they exercise far more power than we have discussed. Consider this one: "Dear Governor Reagan: I wrote you once before about having to go to school on my birthday—and nothing happened. My next birthday is a month away and I am wondering what your plans are. Let me hear from you soon. Jeff."[10] Given the extraordinary demands on his time, Arnold Schwarzenegger carefully rations his chief of state role.

The Plural Executive: Competing for Power

As considerable as the governor's powers are, they are circumscribed in some profound ways. A significant limitation is called the *plural executive*—an array of executive officials with cabinet-sounding titles who are separately elected and politically independent of the governor. Cabinet members in Washington serve at the pleasure of the president and can be removed at any time. California governors can only wish they had that power. Many comparable state office holders are elected directly by the people. This reflects an historic mistrust of gubernatorial power. Although competition for power understandably ensues, a plural executive does not necessarily hinder a governor's leadership role. The duties of some of these elected officials are largely administrative in nature; often independent political power is neither required nor even possible. Consequently, these fellow executives rarely pose a political threat to the governor.

LIEUTENANT GOVERNOR

The least threatening office of the group is lieutenant governor. California Governor Friend W. Richardson (1923–1927) never held the post but sized it up succinctly: "to preside over

the senate and each morning to inquire solicitously after the governor's health." In 1998, former Assembly Speaker Cruz Bustamante won this office by a 53–39 percent margin over State Senator Tim Leslie (R, Tahoe City). In succeeding Gray Davis, he became the first Latino elected to statewide office since 1871. During 2003, he opposed the recall of Davis but nevertheless ran as his replacement on the same ballot; he finished second to Arnold Schwarzenegger with 31.6 percent of the vote. The lieutenant governor's annual salary is $131,250.

Since lieutenant governors consider presiding over the California State Senate a waste of time, and modern governors tend to be quite healthy, what do they do? *First,* they sit on various boards, including the Regents of the University of California, the Trustees of the State University System, and the State Lands Commission. Since this last body regulates over 4 million acres of state lands and supervises on- and off-shore oil leases, the lieutenant governor occasionally can generate media attention. The lieutenant governor also chairs the Commission for Economic Development, an agency intended to attract new business to California. Less significant memberships include the state's Emergency Council, the World Trade Council, and the Commission on Building for the 21st Century.

Second, the lieutenant governor becomes acting governor the minute the governor leaves the state. This is problematic when the two are of opposing parties. For instance, when Democratic Governor Jerry Brown traveled the nation running for president, Republican Lieutenant Governor Mike Curb hastened to appoint a judge before Brown could return. There is an irony then when California governors are mentioned as possible presidential candidates. Incumbent governors can ill afford the absenteeism required to wage a national campaign.

Political speaking, the lieutenant governor is in a "Twilight Zone" of sorts. The responsibilities assigned to the office rarely embrace the great issues facing California. The media all but ignore the office, giving its occupants few opportunities to communicate with the voters who elect them. According to Leo McCarthy: "When I was [Assembly] [S]peaker, I could say something perfectly inane and be quoted as saying something that must be important. As lieutenant governor, I could make a telling comment full of wisdom and have it ignored."[11] The office is a slippery stepping stone at best. In California's history, only six lieutenant governors have become governors. McCarthy repeatedly reached for the governor's office or the U.S. Senate without success, earning the label "perennial bridesmaid." On the other hand, Gray Davis eked a great deal of publicity out of the office and positioned himself well for a successful gubernatorial campaign. Bustamante's poor showing in the recall election delayed and possibly damaged his gubernatorial aspirations. Reformers would like to either abolish this post or, at minimum, require the governor and the lieutenant governor to run on the same party ticket (a requirement in 23 other states). Yet, polls show most Californians favor the status quo.

ATTORNEY GENERAL

In contrast to the lieutenant governor, the state attorney general is quite powerful. Former Attorney General Robert Kenny (1943–46) once quipped: "A smart A.G. could practically take over the state from a dumb governor—if he had a mind to." In fact, the attorney general is the second most powerful position in California's executive branch. This office oversees the state's Department of Justice which employs 5,000 people, including 1,000 attorneys. Historically, the "A.G." has truly been a stepping stone to higher office. Attorneys General Earl Warren, Pat Brown, and George Deukmejian each became governor. Although some have come from legislative backgrounds (Dan Lungren was a congressman and Deukmejian, an assemblyman and state senator), others have been prominent,

politically active district attorneys (Warren, Evelle Younger, and John Van de Kamp). High visibility "crime busters" often become natural candidates for the state's "top cop" position. The position pays $148,750 per year.

In criminal matters, the department conducts investigations, argues all appeals above the trial court level, and nominally oversees local district attorneys and county sheriffs. On rare occasions, the department even prosecutes local crimes if a district attorney refuses to. In 1981, Attorney General Deukmejian stepped in to prosecute Angelo Bueno, Jr., the suspected Los Angeles "Hillside Strangler," eventually winning the case. Los Angeles District Attorney John Van de Kamp had dropped the case for lack of evidence, a decision that haunted him when he tried to run for governor in 1990.

In civil matters, the attorney general and his army of lawyers advise other state agencies and litigate on their behalf. The office's advisory opinions are legally binding until replaced by a court's decision. The attorney general also defends the state in various lawsuits, but is not obligated to do so if the A.G. disagrees with the state's position in a case. For instance, Deukmejian once refused to defend the state's legal positions on state-funded abortions, environmental regulations, and collective bargaining by public employees. Upon taking office in 1999, Democrat Bill Lockyer vowed to aggressively pursue civil rights claims and environmental protection. In 2002, he won reelection over Republican state senator Dick Ackerman with 51 percent of the vote and will be "termed out" of office in 2006.

SECRETARY OF STATE

In terms of discretionary power, the secretary of state stands in stark contrast to the attorney general. Whereas the nation's secretary of state is essentially a minister of foreign affairs, California's Secretary of State is essentially a clerk of records and elections. As archivist, this official maintains all current and historical records.

This $131,250 per-year-post also possesses many election-related duties (preparing and distributing statewide voter pamphlets, processing candidate papers, certifying initiative petitions, publishing election results, and tracking campaign donations and expenditures). Accordingly, the secretary of state decides early in the presidential primary season which presidential candidates to place on the June ballot. In March 1992, Fong Eu retained Paul Tsongas on the ballot months after he quit the Democratic primary race. Later that year, she dropped independent Ross Perot's name from the November ballot after he withdrew as an active candidate. After his famous change of mind, she reinstated him.

Historically, the position of Secretary of State was so routine and devoid of controversy, it was held by a father/son team (Frank C. and Frank M. Jordan) for nearly all of the period between 1911 and 1970. Capitalizing on his famous last name, Jerry Brown won the post in 1970. He used the position to push for campaign reform including the Political Reform Act of 1974, a voter initiative discussed in Chapter 6. Eu, the first Asian American elected to California's plural executive, assumed office in 1975 when Brown became governor; she left in 1994 to become U.S. Ambassador to Micronesia. In 1994, Republican Bill Jones won the post and was re-elected in 1998. Jones championed term limits, the blanket primary, and various voter registration and election reforms.[12] In 2002, he sought the Republican nomination for governor but lost to Bill Simon. In the general election, Democratic assembly member Kevin Shelley faced former assembly member Republican Keith Olberg. Shelley won with 46 percent of the vote.

By 2004, Shelley managed to make the office controversial and the subject of numerous investigations. In particular, he was accused of diverting federal funds from their intended use, hiding improper campaign contributions, and being verbally abusive to his staff. In the midst of several probes, he resigned in 2005. Arnold Schwarzenegger appointed former state senator and moderate Republican Bruce McPherson to fill out his term. The legislature happily confirmed him.[13]

SUPERINTENDENT OF PUBLIC INSTRUCTION

One of the most fragmented arrangements in California's executive branch is the Superintendent of Public Instruction. Several features of this $148,750 per year office set it apart from other statewide elective offices. *First*, unlike other members of the plural executive, the position is officially nonpartisan, reflecting the notion that education and "politics" should not mix. *Second*, the superintendent shares responsibility for the 1200-employee Department of Education with a gubernatorially appointed 11-member Board of Education. *Third*, even though 80 percent of school funding flows through this department, the actual task of education takes place locally in over a thousand school districts. In recent years, an increasingly visible partner has been the federal Department of Education as implementor of the 2001 No Child Left Behind Act. This governance structure has been a perfect formula for policy fragmentation and diffusion of educational responsibility. As Davis' former education secretary, Gary Hart, put it, "Everybody is bumping into everyone else."[14] Consequently, in hyperpluralistic fashion, governors, *their* education secretaries, superintendents, the state board, legislators, educators, and interest groups continually battle over education policy and funding (*see* Chapter 13). In 2002, a legislative veteran in the area of public education, State Senator Jack O'-Connell won election to the post. As his predecessor, Delaine Easton, he vowed to use the position as a bully pulpit for education.

INSURANCE COMMISSIONER

In 1988, California voters "pluralized" still further the executive branch by approving Proposition 103. They authorized auto insurance rate reductions and joined eight other states which have an elected insurance commissioner. Prior to "103," the governor had appointed the commissioner. This is the only office in California's plural executive to have been created by the initiative process. The commissioner heads the state's Department of Insurance, which regulates the insurance industry in California and is paid $140,000 annually. In 1990, state senator John Garamendi became the first commissioner to win election to the post. He returned to the post from private life in ranching and business in 2002. The insurance commissioner enforces the state's insurance code, approves industry mergers, pursues industry fraud, levies fines for insurance wrongdoing, and controls insurance rates. From 1994 to 2002, Republican Chuck Quackenbush held the post. Facing certain impeachment, he resigned in disgrace after diverting and misspending insurance funds intended for Northridge earthquake victims. The Quackenbush scandal raised some larger issues surrounding this post. For years, consumer groups viewed the department as little more than a cheerleader for the politically powerful insurance industry. Making the post elective rather than appointive may have worsened the problem. Most campaign contributions come from insurance industry political action committees, calling into question how supportive the commissioner would be to the interests of insurance companies. In recognition of this dilemma, Garamendi has personally refused such funding but that practice is not legally binding.

FISCAL OFFICERS

While all members of California's plural executive are elected and therefore require campaign funds, the very job descriptions of some of them center around money: collecting it, investing it, and disbursing it to pay the state's bills. These offices are the controller, treasurer, and Board of Equalization.

• *Controller:* As the chief fiscal officer of the state, the controller pays all bills, monitors all state accounts, audits various state and local programs, and earns $140,000 per year. In addition, this official sits on a staggering 63 boards, committees, and commissions, including the Franchise Tax Board (which collects the state's income tax) and the Board of Equalization (which collects other taxes). Gray Davis, who served from 1986 through 1994, used his membership on the State Lands Commission to oppose oil drilling and toxic waste dumping, a popular stance among California's environmentalists. Kathleen Connell served from 1994 through 2002. In 2002, former eBay executive Democrat Steve Westley won a tight race for the post over Republican State Senator Tom McClintock.

• *Treasurer:* If the controller writes the state's checks, the treasurer handles the money while it is in the checking account. Because there is a lag between when revenue is received and when it is spent, the treasurer invests it in the interim. Obviously the goal is to obtain the highest possible interest rates for moneys on deposit. Another important responsibility is to auction state bonds (a form of borrowing discussed in Chapter 11). Because this revenue funds major construction (such as water projects, school construction, and affordable housing) and must be paid back with interest to large financial institutions, the treasurer tries to obtain the lowest possible rates. In 2005, the treasurer oversaw the investment of $53 billion in public moneys and sat on pension boards (including those of state employees and school teachers) that invested roughly $300 billion in the American and global economies. Because the treasurer decides who gets to resell revenue bonds to investors, investment firms have contributed to treasurers' election campaigns, a questionable practice given their economic stake in the office. Nonetheless, New York City, home to many of those firms, does appear to be a predictable campaign stop for state treasurer candidates. Although Jesse Unruh enhanced the powers and clout of this office, it remains a rather slippery stepping stone to higher office. Kathleen Brown (Pat Brown's daughter and Jerry Brown's sister) became treasurer in 1991. She issued numerous bonds approved by the voters for school, prison, water, parks, rail, and other projects as well as helped to end junk bond investments. When she ran unsuccessfully for governor in 1994, she was succeeded by Matt Fong (the adopted son of March Fong Eu). After his failed effort to unseat U.S. Senator Barbara Boxer in 1998, the voters elected former Democratic Party chair and businessman Philip Angelides to this $140,000 post. He won reelection in 2002. Among fellow state executives, Angelides has been one of the few vocal critics of Governor Arnold Schwarzenegger.

• *Board of Equalization:* The last fiscal office in California's plural executive is the Board of Equalization, consisting of four elected individuals plus the state controller, who serves ex officio (without vote). The four are elected by districts, representing over 8 million people each. These four, who earn $131,250 per year, are largely invisible to average Californians, even when campaigning. The Board administers and collects over $40 billion in sales taxes, excise taxes, and fees each year. This organizational relic was placed in the 1879 Constitution to assess Southern Pacific Railroad's (SPR) property, a needed reform at the time. To this day, the board sets the market value for public utilities and railroads and, as a quasi-judicial body hears franchise and income tax appeals. Progressive reformers would be aghast to know that board members often collect substantial campaign contributions from the very utilities they assess. After several scandals, the legislature in 1990 disallowed board members from deciding cases involving major contributors to their own campaigns, a standard the legislature has yet to set for itself. On occasion, it serves as a landing pad for termed out legislators as happened with former assembly member Carole Migden and former state senator Bill Leonard. While critics call this board outmoded, efforts to fold it into the Franchise Tax Board have failed.

California's Bureaucracy and the Politics of Diversity

Any large, diverse state with a complex economy and a comprehensive state government will possess a substantial bureaucracy. California boasts one of the nation's largest. According to the *California Political Almanac,* "There is virtually no aspect of life in California that is not in some way touched by the state bureaucracy and its work force."[15] Over 300,000 employees work for a host of departments, agencies, boards, and commissions. Although this seems like a lot, the ratio of state employees to the state's overall population—a more realistic measure of bureaucratic size—has been declining in recent years. In fact, the number of state employees per 1,000 Californians was consistently higher in the 1970s than it is today in the 2000s.

Several hiring systems govern state employees. About 90,000 are governed by the tenure and hiring practices of the University of California and State University systems. Most of the rest operate under *civil service*—the idea that permanent employees should be hired and evaluated on the basis of merit, not politics. This means competence and expertise rather than political connections and clout. California's civil service system, like those of other states, was modeled after the federal Pendleton Act of 1883 and Progressive era opposition to patronage. The *State Personnel Board* administers the overall civil service system, hears appeals from aggrieved employees or job applicants, and spearheaded the state's affirmative action program before Proposition 209 abolished it.

FUNCTIONS OF BUREAUCRACY

Even the briefest survey of California's bureaucracy demonstrates the magnitude of government and the diversity of its work. About seven out of ten state employees work in higher education, corrections, transportation, 24-hour care institutions, and public safety. The fastest growing group consists of correctional employees, due to a 300 percent increase in the state's inmate population since the early 1980s. At the opposite end of the spectrum, the University of California and the California State University systems in recent years have lost more employees than any other sector of state activity.

The primary purpose of California's bureaucracy is implementation—carrying out policies and laws approved by the legislature and even the voters (through initiatives). Most of the myriad day-to-day activities of bureaucracies are required to implement policy. The following sampling of various state agencies illustrates some of these activities. The Highway Patrol *patrols* state highways and *monitors* school bus transportation. The Department of Alcoholic Beverage Control *licenses and regulates* the manufacture, sale, purchases, possession, and transportation of alcoholic beverages. The State Banking Department *protects* Californians against financial loss at state-chartered banks. The Integrated Waste Management Board *promotes* recycling and composting. The California Department of Transportation *builds, maintains, and rehabilitates* the state's roads and bridges. The Department of Fair Employment and Housing *enforces* the state's civil rights laws that ban various forms of discrimination. The Department of Health Services *manages* numerous health programs. The Air Resources Board *establishes* clean air standards and *researches* anti-smog approaches.

To the extent the various layers of government in California contribute to hyperpluralism, the same can be said about California's bureaucracy. Virtually all state agencies, departments, offices, and boards coordinate their activities with similar local government efforts, or they may actually direct those efforts. Consider just K–12 education. The State

Board of Education selects textbooks for grade levels K–8, develops curricular frameworks, approves local waivers from state regulations, and oversees the credentialing of teachers. The Commission on Teacher Credentialing certifies teacher preparation programs in the state's colleges and universities. The Department of Education communicates education policy to school districts, approves instructional materials, and provides curriculum leadership. Local school districts receive and account for state funds, deliver education per state standards, administer state-designed tests, cope with enrollment growth, and innovate wherever they can.

All these functions have produced mountains of paperwork in the Golden State. No matter where one turns, there are regulations to follow, forms to fill out, and fine print to read. The title of one Little Hoover Commission report on California's bureaucracy summed it up—*Too Many Agencies, Too Many Rules.*[16] Critics of California's bureaucracy would do well to remember this: Given the state's size, complexity, and diversity, California's bureaucracy is bound to be large, complex, and diverse.

POWER SHARING AND CLOUT

California's bureaucracy also shares power with the federal government. Most federal aid destined for the state and even local governments passes through state agencies. Structurally, you can think of these relationships as a fiscal version of a picket fence. For example, the portion of federal gas taxes returned to the state funnels through the Department of Transportation (Caltrans) to various states or local transportation improvements (*see* Figure 8.2). Certain state agencies also share power with local governments. For example, counties actually deliver many state services and have some, albeit limited, discretion over their provision. Administration of welfare programs is one example.

The clout of California's public employees comes not only from what they do but from

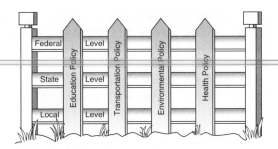

FIGURE 8.2   Picket Fence Federalism in California

Picket fence federalism can be found in virtually every policy area where the federal government provides grants, issues rules, or otherwise impacts the policy roles of state and local governments. For instance, a federal education program involves vertical communication between officials in the federal Department of Education, the California Department of Education, and local school systems.

Source: Reprinted with permission from *America: The Politics of Diversity* by Lawrence. © 1999 by Wadsworth Publishing Company.

their ability to organize. Borrowing labor practices from the private sector, most state employees are organized into more than 20 different bargaining units, represented by 12 unions. The largest is the California State Employees' Association, representing over 140,000 active and retired civil servants. There are also specific unions representing specific professions in state government. For instance, about 25,000 prison guards belong to the California Correctional Peace Officers Association (CCPOA).[17] As union members, state employees deal with many personnel-related issues such as collective bargaining rights, and sexual harassment, plus the administration of pension plans. In 1992, they heavily supported the passage of Proposition 162, which gave public employee pension boards greater power to manage their own affairs. In the past, the legislature occasionally "borrowed" (some say "raided") assets from the pension plans to help balance state budgets. The two largest boards are PERS (the Public

Employees Retirement System) and STRS (the State Teachers Retirement System).

EXECUTIVE BRANCH REFORM

When Arnold Schwarzenegger campaigned for governor, he vowed to "blow up the boxes," that is, reorganize the workings of state government. It made for colorful, Terminator-like election rhetoric but one had to wonder at the time how much he knew of those boxes that constituted the executive branch. If not then, he would later learn that 339 separate boards and commissions shared power with executive branch agencies and departments. He would discover that members of one such group, the California Integrated Waste Management Board, were paid over $117,000 for doing arguably part-time work. As governor, he would witness the legislature create still more of these groups such as the Ocean Protection Council and the Commission on Latino/Latina Affairs. Calling the state government a "mastodon frozen in time," Schwarzenegger appointed a 275-person team—the California Performance Review—to study the executive branch and make recommendations for reform. Their 2,700-page, six-inch-thick report recommended the elimination of over 12,000 jobs, the abolition of 118 boards and commissions, and the streamlining of still other agencies where policy redundancy was routine.

Reform proponents praised the report, the billions of dollars in anticipated savings, and the promise of greater accountability. Critics claimed that the cost savings were exaggerated and that many of the proposals centralized too much power in the governor's office. In response to the findings, the governor pledged to use the report to create a "21st century government for the future of California." "We cannot just chip away at the edges of our state's problems. Sometimes a surgeon has to cut in order to save the patient."[18] Given Schwarzenegger's declining popularity, his diffuse agenda, and the inherent difficulty of bureaucratic reform, significant changes as he envisioned them seem improbable.

Conclusion

The themes of hyperpluralism and diversity emerge from a review of California's executive branch. Executive leadership in California is a diffused phenomenon. Power is shared between the governor, other statewide elected officials, plus a huge bureaucracy. California governors, as elsewhere, can employ a number of resources to enhance their leadership potential. Historians regard Hiram Johnson, Earl Warren, Pat Brown, and Ronald Reagan as gubernatorial giants. They clearly made the most of the power they had. But they governed in a simpler time over a smaller and less diverse California. Today's governors wield substantial formal powers, but even these are shared by the legislature,

a plural executive system, and at times the voters themselves. The office's most singular duties are constitutionally mandated, such as submitting a budget, exercising veto power, and performing various judicial roles.

The vastness of California's bureaucracy in some respects mirrors the diversity of the state itself. As Figure 8.1 suggests, virtually every economic sector and demographic group is represented in and/or regulated by the executive branch. The state's bureaucrats can wield a great deal of power but commonly share it with the judiciary or legislature. Reformers increasingly believe that the gridlock between the executive branch and the other branches is the source of California's governing problems. But given the enduring idea of checks and balances in American politics, others believe gridlock is a price worth paying to avoid unchecked executive and bureaucratic power.

KEY TERMS

political context   (p. 158)

inner circle   (p. 159)

superagencies   (p. 159)

cabinet   (p. 159)

executive order   (p. 161)

internal and external budget
  processes   (p. 161)

item and general veto   (pp. 161–164)

clemency   (p. 165)

special session   (p. 164)

plural executive   (p. 166)

civil service   (p. 170)

State Personnel Board   (p. 170)

REVIEW QUESTIONS

1. Apply Crew's gubernatorial leadership variables to Governor Gray Davis and other recent California governors.

2. Of the governor's duties and powers, which do you think are the most and least important?
3. What advice would you give California governors on how to maximize their budget powers?
4. In what ways does California's plural executive increase political fragmentation and encourage hyperpluralism?
5. If you wanted to use a statewide elective office as a stepping stone to the governorship, which would you seek, not seek, and why?
6. In what ways can California's bureaucracy exercise power independent of the governor? Is the bureaucracy itself a function of hyperpluralism?

WEB ACTIVITIES

Governor's Office
(www.governor.ca.gov)
Aside from a "Governors' Gallery," this site features biographical information, speeches, press releases, executive orders, and volumes

of other information related to the current governor.

State Agencies
(www.ca.gov)

Click on State Agency Index; this will lead you to a stunningly long list of agencies, departments, divisions, boards, commissions, and other state entities. This site epitomizes the scope and diversity of California's executive branch.

INFOTRAC® COLLEGE EDITION ARTICLES

For additional reading, go to InfoTrac College Edition, your online research library, at http://www.infotrac.thomsonlearning.com

Arnold, the Bold; A New California?

It Never Ends, Arnold; California's Broken Government

Massive Battle Looms Over How the State Will Be Run

NOTES

1. James MacGregor Burns, *Leadership* (New York: Harper and Row, 1978), 388.
2. The wealthy Arnold Schwarzenegger returns his salary to the state.
3. See Robert E. Crew, Jr. "Understanding Gubernatorial Behavior: A Framework for Analysis," in Thad Beyle, ed. *Governors and Hard Times* (Washington, D.C.: Congressional Quarterly Press, 1992), 15–27.
4. California State Constitution, Article V, Section 1.
5. These top staff members are occasionally profiled in the *California Journal* and the state's larger newspapers. For instance, two articles on Bob White are Ron Roach, "Chief of Staff Bob White," *California Journal* 22 (January 1991), 17–19; and Richard C. Paddock and Paul Houston, "White Keeps Wilson Machine Running," *Los Angeles Times*, December 16, 1990.
6. Steve Scott, "Rating Gray Davis," 34.
7. This agency secretary's main job apparently is to hype California business. See Caren Bohan, "Carl Covitz: The Businessman as Public Servant," *California Journal* 23 (April 1992), 209–215.
8. For more on the budget process, see Richard Krolak, *California's Budget Dance: Issues and Process*, 2nd ed. (Sacramento: California Journal Press, 1994).
9. Quoted in Dave Lesher, "Davis Faces Deep Dilemma Over Appeal of Prop. 187," *Los Angeles Times*, April 14, 1999.
10. Quoted in Helene Von Damm, *Sincerely, Ronald Reagan* (Ottawa, Illinois: Green Hill, 1976), 162–163.
11. Steve Scott, "Leo McCarthy: One More Into the Breach for a Veteran Politician," *California Journal* 23 (April 1992), 192.
12. For more on Jones, see Bill Ainsworth, "Bill Jones: From GOP Good Ol' Boy to Republican Renegade," *California Journal* 31 (May 2000), 30–33.
13. Robert B. Gunnison, "The Beleaguered World of Kevin Shelley," *California Journal* 35 (November 2004), 28–31.
14. Quoted in Sigrid Bathen, "Who's In Charge?" *California Journal* 28 (June 1997), 16.
15. Block and Buck, *California Political Almanac*, 89.
16. See www.lhcdir/133rp.html/.
17. For a profile of this powerful union, see Noel Brinkerhoff, "Guardians of the Guards, *California Journal* 28 (March 1997), 44–47.
18. Quoted in Peter Nicholas, "Schwarzenegger Vows to 'Make Every Use' of Overhaul Plan," *Los Angeles Times*, August 4, 2002.

CHAPTER 9

California's Judiciary

In Brief

California's judiciary shares power with the legislative and executive branches. As in other states, it is divided into two levels: trial courts and appellate courts. Lower courts handle major disputes and offenses and hold preliminary hearings on more serious matters. Trial courts decide matters of fact; appellate courts matters of law. All cases are either criminal (wrongs against society) or civil (disputes among individuals and/or organizations).

Lawyers who want to be judges must become politically involved. Although all judges

in California must eventually face the voters, most assume the bench through gubernatorial appointment. In a representative democracy, judges need to be both independent and politically accountable—a difficult balance to achieve. Judges are also accountable to professional standards policed by the California Commission on Judicial Performance.

Judges make case-specific decisions as well as public policy. At the trial court level, cases follow a predictable chronology, including various pretrial activities designed to avoid trial, the trial itself, and the sentence or judgment. Appellate justices have the most leeway in making public policy, as recent state supreme courts demonstrate. The judiciary's most visible policy role involves criminal justice, especially cases involving the death penalty.

Although the legal profession does not reflect California's growing ethnicity, judicial policy making in California is influenced by both the state's diversity and its population growth. While carrying out its own policy role, California courts also share power with the legislative and executive branches.

Introduction

News item: A parent in Granada Hills, California, sues a Little League executive after he is told to stop smoking during a game. The parent claims emotional distress.

News item: An attorney sues to ban Oreos because the cookies' trans fats content harms children.

News item: Years after the fact, a customer sues a tattoo parlor for misspelling the word "villain" on his arm. The customer provided the incorrect spelling but considered the parlor at fault nonetheless.

These three actual cases illustrate some broad trends occurring in California and the nation. First, we are a litigious society. Although scholars disagree about whether the frequency of lawsuits is outpacing population growth, they do agree on this: Americans increasingly view all manner of problems in legal terms. Lawyers and laypersons alike assume that for every wrong there must be a legal remedy, usually determined in a court of law. Second, there has been an explosion in the number of lawyers in U.S. society. Of all U.S. lawyers, about one in seven practices in California. In 2005, there were more than 149,000 active attorneys in California; only New York boasted similar figures. More lawyers likely means more lawsuits. Third, the crush of civil and criminal cases has bogged down California's busiest court systems. At any one time in Los Angeles County there are more than 1 million small claims and civil cases in process; resolving many of them can take years.

Despite all the litigation, Californians' knowledge of the legal system is rather spotty. In a State Bar Association survey, 53 percent of the respondents could not identify the nation's Bill of Rights; 48 percent did not know that defendants are presumed innocent until proven guilty; and 68 percent were unaware they had only limited liability if someone used their name to make an unauthorized purchase. Yet 90 percent knew it took a .08 or higher blood alcohol level to be convicted of adult drunk driving; 95 percent realized both parents could be liable for child support; and 95 percent knew husbands could be prosecuted for spousal rape.[1]

Given the role of law in California's political system, what courts, judges, and juries do affects all Californians. The judiciary has always shared power with the legislative and executive branches. Conflict among them is increasingly common. At times it seems judges have the final say; at other times, they seem only to contribute to the policy gridlock occurring in the nation's most populous and diverse state. This chapter examines California's legal system and its policy making role as well as how it is organized and what its participants do.

State Courts in Our Legal "System"

I use the term "legal system" advisedly. The federal Judiciary Act of 1789 actually created a dual system of courts, national and state. The federal courts deal with matters arising from the U.S. Constitution, civil cases involving regulatory activity, plus a relatively small number of criminal offenses. Fifty separate state systems address matters arising from state constitutions, civil matters, and most criminal offenses. State courts handle the vast majority of all court activity in the nation.

California is only one of those 50 systems, but it is not simply a copy of the others. Each state's judiciary reflects to some extent its political culture and history. The independent spirit that characterized California's history was bound to be reflected in its legal system; in fact, its Supreme Court has developed a national reputation for independence from the federal judiciary. Unlike many southern states, which used a "states rights" philosophy to impede federal civil rights efforts, California's courts have viewed independence in progressive terms. The state's "independent-state-grounds" doctrine assumed that when state and federal constitutional provisions are similar, California could interpret those provisions more expansively or liberally. This view, pioneered by the late State Supreme Court Justice Stanley Mosk, expanded individual rights beyond those granted by the U.S. Supreme Court—a doctrine called "independent state grounds."[2] In several celebrated cases, the California Supreme Court struck down the death penalty before its federal counterpart did, rejected the state's method of financing public education (a decision the U.S. Supreme Court has refused to make), and invalidated a citizen initiative that would have banned fair housing laws.[3] This exemplifies *judicial federalism*: the ability and willingness of different court systems to produce potentially diverse, fragmented, and contradictory policy.

California's independent-minded judiciary does not operate in a vacuum. Some people prefer to resolve their legal disputes at the federal level. California has four federal district courts located throughout the state. It is possible for state and federal courts to hear the same kinds of cases (civil rights and liberties), a phenomenon called "concurrent jurisdiction." As a result, Californians can "shop" for the level—federal or state—most likely to give them the desired result. Challenges to voter-approved initiatives are often filed in federal court. Examples include Propositions 187 (immigration) and 209 (affirmative action).

If decisions by the federal district courts in California are appealed, they go to the United States Court of Appeals for the Ninth Circuit. This court is famous for its own judicial independence. In fact, the U. S. Supreme Court has rebuked this circuit court for frustrating California's efforts to execute death row inmates. More than most federal appellate courts, the Ninth Circuit handles cases involving diverse populations and sweeping social changes. The judges themselves admit that California provides them with a variety of cutting-edge issues because of the state's size, diversity, and propensity to pass constitutionally vulnerable initiatives. For example, in 2001 they ruled unconstitutional a petty theft sentence under California's Three Strikes Law. This decision involving the theft of some video tapes was overtuned by the U. S. Supreme Court.[4] Reflecting the region it serves, the Ninth Circuit Court of Appeals has been inundated with immigration cases in recent years.

How California's Courts Are Organized

California's judicial system is the largest in the world, consisting of more than 2000 judicial officers divided into three tiers of courts. These layers divide the judiciary's caseload within the system while allowing ample opportunity for litigants to appeal unfavorable decisions (see Figure 9.1). Let's briefly look at each layer, beginning where most cases start—at the bottom.

TRIAL COURTS

On the lowest rung of the judicial ladder are the state's *trial courts*. These courts are triers

---

California Supreme Court
1 chief justice, 6 associate justices
- Hears oral arguments in San Francisco, Los Angeles, and Sacramento
- Has discretionary authority to review decisions of the Courts of Appeal and direct responsibility for automatic appeals after death penalty judgments

Courts of Appeal
105 justices
- 6 districts, 18 divisions, 9 court locations
- Review the majority of appealable orders or judgments from the superior courts

Superior Courts
1,499 judges, 437 commissioners and referees
- 58 courts, one in each county, with from 1 to 55 branches
- Provide a forum for resolution of criminal and civil cases under state and local laws, which define crimes, specify punishments, and define civil duties and liabilities

---

FIGURE 9.1 California court system

Question: Should death penalty cases go directly to the Supreme or work their way through the Courts of Appeal like other cases?

Source: Judicial Council of California.

of fact; they determine who is right in civil disputes and who might be guilty in criminal cases. Until recently, there were both municipal courts and superior courts. The municipal courts handled minor criminal offenses (punishable by fines or jail time), infractions (fineable violations of state statutes or local ordinances), and civil claims of $25,000 or less. In 1998, the passage of Proposition 220 allowed municipal and superior court functions to merge into the superior courts. All state trial courts are now organized in this manner. In 2002–2003, there were nearly 1,500 authorized judges and over 400 commissioners and referees with authority to act as judges. In addition to all felony and civil disputes, the superior courts serve as family, juvenile, and probate courts. Depending on the county's size, superior court judges either hear a wide variety of cases or specialize in a particular area of the law: juvenile, family,

probate, or criminal. They are paid about $144,000 per year, not including county-funded benefits. At this level, cases may be decided by juries or only judges (*bench trials*). California's *Three-Strikes Law* (which imposes a minimum 25-years-to-life sentence for defendants with two or more prior felony convictions) has significantly increased the workload for some trial courts. In many cases, defendants opt for jury trials rather than guilty pleas. The law requires more time be spent by judges, juries, and staff who record and assess second- and third-strike data. Supporting the judges are professional court administrators who manage court personnel, budgets, and workloads. Because more than 30 percent of criminal arrests in California are illicit-drug-related, many counties have established "drug treatment courts" that combine the standard judicial process with community drug treatment services.

The volume of trial court cases in California is staggering. In 2002–2003, almost 8 million filings were handled by trial courts. There are more criminal cases than civil cases. Although juvenile and criminal felony cases constitute only 13 percent of the total, they consume disproportionate resources due to frequent hearings, motions, and jury trials.

In addition to court consolidation, California's judiciary has experienced other recent improvements. The 1997 Trial Court Funding Act transferred financial responsibility for the trial courts to the state. The purpose of this law was to stabilize and make more equitable judicial services across the state. Chief Justice Ronald M. George called it "without a doubt one of the most important reforms in the California justice system in the 20th century."[5] California has also increased court interpreter services and with good reason. On any given day, more than 100 languages may need translation in the state's courts.

APPELLATE COURTS

District Courts of Appeal hear appeals from superior courts and quasi-judicial state agencies. Unlike superior courts, they normally decide questions of law, not fact. For instance, instead of deciding guilt or innocence in a car theft case, California's 105 appellate justices typically sit on three-member panels to determine if legal procedures were applied properly in that case. (Was the suspect informed of his or her rights? Did the judge instruct the jury properly?) If legal errors did occur, they can order a new trial. Although appeals are common, appellate courts dismiss most of them. At that level, there are no "trials" as such, no witnesses or juries. The justices read trial court transcripts and occasionally hear oral arguments by opposing attorneys. They spend hours in private legal research, not in the courtroom. When they hear cases, they usually sit as panels of three. Because the California Supreme Court also declines to hear most cases appealed to it, appellate court decisions are often final. Appeals rarely involve life-or-death, earthshaking issues. As one California appellate justice put it: "If 90 percent of this stuff were in the United States Post Office, it would be classified as junk mail."[6] In the 2002–2003 fiscal year, the Courts of Appeal processed over 22,000 filings and disposed of 12,543 matters through written opinions. Only 7 percent of those were significant enough to meet official criteria for publication.[7] Appellate justices earn about $165,000 annually; presiding justices earn somewhat more.

SUPREME COURT

The *California Supreme Court* is at the pinnacle of the system. Its purpose is to raise important constitutional issues as well as maintain legal uniformity throughout the state. When it speaks, other courts listen—not only in California but in other states and throughout the federal judiciary as well. Due to heavy volume, this court must be very selective in what it chooses to hear and what it chooses to say. In the 2002–2003 court year, the Supreme Court received nearly 9,000 filings but wrote only 123 opinions. Its seven justices spend most of their time in legal research and opinion writing. They hear oral arguments for only one week of every month they are in session. The court consists of a chief justice and six associate justices. The associate justices earn about $176,000; the chief justice earns about $191,000.

If the Supreme Court is so selective, what kinds of cases is it willing to hear? First, much of its work is civil in nature, reflecting the legal problems of California businesses. Second, all death penalty cases are "automatic appeals"; they bypass the appellate courts and must be heard directly by the Supreme Court. In 2002–2003, the Court considered 27 death penalty appeals and the backlog of such cases is growing. Most of these cases are 10 to 15 years old by the time they reach the court. Some appeals languish because lawyers are unwilling to represent such clients. The paperwork for these

PHOTO 9.1   California Supreme Court Hears Gay Marriage Case in San Francisco.
From left to right: Associate Justices Janice R. Brown, Kathryn Mickle Werdegar and Joyce L. Kennard; Chief Justice Ronald M. George; and Associate Justices Marvin R. Baxter, Ming W. Chen, and Carlos R. Moreno.

Question: How independent from the U.S. Supreme Court should state courts be?

appeals is enormous; numerous motions require the court's attention even before formal hearings take place. Third, some observers believe the widespread use of the initiative in California has skewed the court's workload toward initiative-related litigation, to the neglect of other worthy issues.[8] Examples include affirmative action, term limits, and illegal immigration.

So You Want to Be a Judge

A law school official once said that A-students become law professors, B-students become judges, and C-students become rich! A judgeship is a noble goal regardless of grade point average. Judges earn much less than senior corporate law partners, but the pay is reason-

able; plus, a judgeship offers a level of prestige no law firm can match. A number of steps are required to become a judge. Given the number of judicial officers and attorneys licensed to practice in California (2,000 and 150,000, respectively), only a small percentage will ever achieve this elusive goal.

ENTERING THE PROFESSION

To become a judge, one must first become a lawyer, but this was not always the case. In the past, nonlawyers could serve as justices of the peace, but times have changed. Today, virtually all California lawyers are law school graduates. To practice law, the state constitution requires all practicing lawyers to join the State Bar Association of California, a quasi-official group that oversees the admission and discipline of the state's attorneys. After a protracted conflict with Governor Pete Wilson, the CBA was forced to reform, reorganize, and rebuild itself.[9] Applicants to the bar must pass the state bar exam, considered one of the nation's toughest. The best overall preparation for the exam is law school. California boasts 18 American Bar Association accredited and 16 state accredited law schools plus assorted unaccredited schools and correspondence law courses.

Who employs California's lawyers? A 2001 bar survey revealed that more than 75 percent are in private practice. The rest work in government, private industry, education, or other contexts. As was the case across the nation, the profession historically has been male dominated. U.S. Supreme Court Justice Sandra Day O'Connor graduated from Stanford Law School only to discover that California law firms would only hire her as a legal secretary. That was in the 1950s. Today, about half of all law school students are women. Although 68 percent of the state's lawyers were still men in 2001, the profession is slowly moving toward gender equality.[10]

A major challenge facing the legal profession in California is equal access to legal representation. Two major variables here are race and income. Non white attorneys make up just 17 percent of the bar. Although they represent a third of the population, Latinos constitute only 3.7 percent of the state's attorneys; most of them work for government or in small or solo practices. African American trial judges are few in number, even in California's big cities. Judges and court officials are largely white. Furthermore, the poor experience much less access to legal representation than wealthier Californians. While progress has been made in recent years, California still lags far behind other states in providing legal aid to its poorest residents.[11]

THE RIGHT EXPERIENCE

Few California lawyers are situated to become judges. To be considered judgeship material, lawyers find they need a network of personal, legal, and political relationships. When asked what it took to become a California Supreme Court justice, former Justice Mathew Tobriner said to go to high school with someone who planned to become governor.[12] After law school, most lawyers settle into private practice or work for government. They become involved in a local bar association and may dabble in partisan politics. Attending political fund-raisers helps, and contributing to a governor's campaign helps a great deal. Many judges appointed by recent governors have contributed to their campaigns. One's legal specialty also affects one's chances of becoming a judge. Young lawyers grinding out billable hours for high-powered law firms may find little time, energy, or incentive for politics. Of those who practice criminal law, aspiring judicial candidates are likely to be district attorneys, not defense attorneys.

SELECTION MECHANICS

The formal steps to becoming a judge vary, depending on the court level. All levels in California employ a version of the *Missouri Plan*, which combines both elections and appointments. This hybrid method is based on two assumptions: (1) Fellow lawyers can best assess the attributes of judicial candidates, and (2) in a representative democracy, ultimate accountability to the voters is important, even for judges.

Trial Courts

At the local, trial court level, voters elect judges for six-year terms in officially nonpartisan elections (once again, thanks to the Progressives). Reelection is virtually guaranteed. What lawyer wants to run against a judge, lose, and then face that judge in court? Some judges resign or retire from the bench between elections. When vacancies occur at the trial court level, the governor appoints a replacement, relying on local bar association recommendations and local political allies. Judges themselves can fill some vacancies by appointing commissioners, lawyers who act as judges on a temporary basis. These lawyers gain invaluable experience they can tout if a permanent judgeship opportunity arises.

Although some political scientists refer to judges as "politicians who wear robes," local judicial elections have been staid affairs. Judges raise modest campaign support from fellow lawyers and the business community, but rarely wage the kind of combative election campaigns voters see in other branches of government. There is little or no precinct walking, television advertising, or direct mail flyers. Maybe a few yard signs or newspaper ads. But times are changing. Due to their own campaign inexperience, judges increasingly employ campaign management firms. According to Joe Cerrell, a political consultant specializing in judicial races, judges need professional guidance to avoid "political potholes." Also, California judicial candidates are spending more and more money on their own campaigns. In urban areas, judicial campaigns may cost $200,000 per candidate, even more in the big cities. Because of trial court consolidation, all judges must run on county-wide ballots. Even a simple 200-word candidate statement in a Los Angeles voter pamphlet will cost the campaign $60,000.[13]

Appellate and Supreme Courts

The governor initially appoints all appellate and Supreme Court justices. At the next gubernatorial election, voters answer this question: "Shall Chief Justice Ronald M. George be elected to the office for the term provided by law?" State Supreme Court justices face all California voters. Appellate justices face only the voters in their appellate districts. Once they win election, they serve 12-year terms. If they are filling an unexpired term, they serve only the remainder of the term. Justices rarely face opposition and never particular opponents in these retention elections. Usually voters pay little attention to what judges do, but 1986 was different. In a historic election, California vot-

ers rejected Chief Justice Rose Bird, and Associate Justices Joseph Grodin and Cruz Reynoso, allowing then governor George Deukmejian to appoint their successors. The justices' support for defendant rights and consistent opposition to the death penalty, despite public support for it, fueled a well-organized "anti-Bird Court" coalition. A 1998 effort by anti-abortion activists to unseat two justices was unsuccessful. Chief Justice Ronald George and Justice Ming Chin each raised $700,000 for their retention elections; their opponents raised only $40,000. George garnered 75 percent of the vote; Chin 69 percent.

How appellate or Supreme Court justices are originally appointed is intriguing. Although the governor makes the initial appointment, he shares that power with two other groups. First, the state legislature requires that the State Bar Association's Commission on Judicial Nominees Evaluation investigate nominee credentials and rate their fitness for office. Four grades are possible: exceptionally well qualified, well qualified, qualified, or unqualified. A governor can ignore these ratings but, because so many lawyers are professionally "fit," the commission considers most nominees acceptable. In a notable exception, African American appointee Janice Rogers Brown received an "unqualified" rating by the bar committee, due primarily to her lack of adequate judicial experience. Not only did Wilson appoint her anyway, she won praise by judicial conservatives.[14] In 2005, President George W. Bush elevated her to the U.S. Court of Appeals. Second, a nominee needs approval by a three-member Commission on Judicial Appointments, consisting of the chief justice of the Supreme Court, the attorney general, and the senior presiding justice of the court of appeals. Although this group normally approves a governor's choice, a split vote can embarrass the governor and spell future trouble for the nominee. Both Rose Bird and Cruz Reynoso were approved by 2 to 1 votes, raising public doubts about their fitness.

JUDICIAL DISCIPLINE

As we have seen, voters can, but rarely do, oust sitting judges. Does that mean lawyers and judges can do most anything they want? Not quite. The California Constitution provides for the impeachment of state judges "for misconduct in office."[15] This involves impeachment (an indictment of sorts) in the Assembly and a trial in the Senate. Aside from this rarely used method of judicial discipline, there is a complex system of judicial accountability involving not only the public but the legal profession as well. Judges are held to professional norms and subject to peer review.

Professional Norms

Lawyers learn to think and behave like judges during law school, a process called *judicial socialization*. First, they learn about judicial ethics. For example, judges are not supposed to decide cases in which they have a personal stake. Yet some do. One trial court judge issued an order releasing from custody his own son who had been arrested for drunk driving, an action roundly criticized in the legal community. Second, they learn to appreciate the rule of precedent—*stare decisis*. Judges are expected to make new decisions by relying heavily on previous ones, especially those of higher courts. Third, judges render decisions within certain limits such as sentencing standards, jury instruction rules, and uniform legal procedures. Whereas the general public cares primarily about verdicts, judges are equally concerned with procedures used to achieve verdicts. In a state and nation governed by the "rule of law," procedure is the all-important vehicle through which courts ascertain truth.

Peer Review

What happens when a judge yells at attorneys and their clients? Or calls two juvenile assailants "bitches"? Or takes five months to rule on a routine family law motion? These are the kinds of complaints handled by California's Commission on Judicial Performance. This independent state agency consists of nine members, including judges, attorneys, and lay citizens.

Its primary duty is to investigate charges of willful misconduct by judges. According to a recent annual report, the commission examines a surprising variety of complaints involving judges' on- and off-the-bench behavior. They include offensive courtroom demeanor, disparaging the attorneys present, using a court computer to access adult websites, sexual harassment, and using court resources for personal business.[16] Various versions of a code of conduct have guided judges since 1949. Today's *Code of Judicial Ethics* was adopted by the state Supreme Court in 1996 and revised in 1999. These canons represent a judicial consensus, and all members of the judiciary must comply with them.

Of the roughly 1,000 complaints filed against California judges in 2003, most came from litigants and their families. Only four of those resulted in public disciplinary measures including the removal from office of two judges. Is this a poor track record? Can the judiciary really discipline itself? The answer depends on one's perspective. A substantial percentage of all complaints allege legal error not involving judicial misconduct per se. Moreover, commissioners believe educating judges is more constructive than publicly castigating or removing them. Therefore, they usually send private admonishment letters ("stingers") to judges they have investigated. Only in the very worst cases are there public hearings and media exposure.

The Ballot Box

Although many voters pay no attention to disciplinary matters, they do react to well-publicized decisions they do not like. When judges consistently make decisions outside the broad political beliefs of Californians, sooner or later they may suffer the consequences at the polls. In the

PHOTO 9.2   Ballot box discipline

In 2002 Dana Point attorney John Adams and 10 other write-in candidates garnered more than 67 percent of the vote in their effort to unseat Orange County Superior Court Judge Robert Kline. Days after the filing deadline, authorities had charged Kline with accessing child pornography on the Internet. Even if Kline had survived the run-off election he lost to Adams, a conviction on those charges would require the Commission on Judicial Performance to remove him from office.

Question: To what extent should personal character determine the outcome of judicial elections?

1986 election, three Supreme Court justices were defeated largely due to their adamant opposition to the death penalty; they had reversed 52 of 55 death penalties by early 1986. In some cases, they seemed to stretch reason, at least in the opinion of some Californians. For example, the court majority overturned one death sentence, finding the defendant lacked intent to kill, even though the victim had been decapitated and was missing both hands.

At the local level, unpopular decisions can lead to recall efforts, even though these tend to be unsuccessful. For example, one Los Angeles judge who sentenced a shopkeeper to mere community service for killing a suspected teenage shoplifter spent $300,000 to fend off a recall attempt. She eventually resigned. An Orange County judge who allowed O. J. Simpson to reclaim his two children after his murder acquittal also battled a recall attempt. As a general rule, judges chafe at the notion of strict electoral accountability. Sacramento Superior Court judge Roger Warren echoed the paradox of judicial accountability: "We don't want judges who are totally immune and divorced from real life, and on the other hand we want them to be sufficiently independent so that they can make decisions based on principle."[17]

How Courts Make Decisions

In previous chapters, we examined how legislators and executives make policy and share power. Judges do both as well. But court decisions are different from policy decisions made in other branches. They result from pretrial and trial activity. As elsewhere in the nation, trials in California are based on the concept of *adversarial justice*. Determining truth and justice involves a contest between two conflicting sides. Each presents only information favorable to its side. Judges and juries find the "truth" in and around conflicting claims.

In any California courtroom, the process one sees is rather generic. The steps may vary somewhat depending on whether the case is criminal or civil. Criminal cases involve alleged wrongs against society (murder, armed robbery, and so on). That is why such cases are entitled "*People v.* _____." Civil cases involve disputes between individuals in society (usually involving financial transactions, real estate, personal property, business relationships, family relationships, and personal injuries).

THE CRIMINAL PROCESS

Criminal cases feature numerous steps and decision points. We will examine what happens before, during, and after trials. Throughout the process, an enormous amount of discretion is available to virtually everyone but the defendant.

Pretrial Activity

The first decision is obviously the decision to arrest someone. Police exercise discretion at this point based on their own attitudes, the nature of the crime, the relationship between the suspect and the victim, and department policy. The second decision is the decision to prosecute. Prosecutors, called "district attorneys" in California, make that decision based on the quality of evidence and witnesses, office policy,

and the availability of alternatives such as alcohol education programs. Which charges to file can vary depending on the locale. For example, "junk" crimes such as minor shoplifting and unreturned rental videos are rarely prosecuted in mega-counties like Los Angeles. San Diego prosecutors often return illegal immigrants to Mexico rather than press charges. Poorer counties used to avoid murder filings because they could not afford the massive budgets required to prosecute such cases. State responsibility for trial court funding may rectify this situation at least to some extent.

District attorneys play a dominant role compared to judges or defense attorneys. Contrary to the legal ideal—innocent until proven guilty—courtroom work groups (prosecutors, defense attorneys, judges, and other court officers) operate on an *assumption of guilt*. "If you are there, you are there for a reason," so the reasoning goes. This logic is based less on prejudice than on daily experience. During an *arraignment*, a judge informs the accused of the charges and the legal options available. In a felony case, a *preliminary hearing* determines if there is probable cause to hold a trial. That decision is called an *indictment*. In addition to district attorneys, grand juries sometimes issue indictments. These bodies are citizen boards, selected from auto and voter registration lists. They tend to be used in complex or sensitive cases and when witnesses need protection. Most criminal arraignments are accomplished with dizzying speed given the volume of cases judges must face. When people talk of "assembly line justice," they are usually referring to the arraignment calendar.

Defendants often bypass trials using *plea bargaining*. By pleading "no contest" or "guilty" to lesser charges, they avoid predictable guilty verdicts involving more serious offenses. Judges usually rubberstamp bargains negotiated by prosecutors and defense lawyers. How often does this occur? In 2002–2003, 96 percent of all felonies were disposed of before an actual trial. Without plea bargaining (euphemistically called "case management"), judges and lawyers alike believe the criminal justice process would grind to a halt. In one Los Angeles study, 98 percent of the defendants pleaded guilty rather than face trial. District attorneys, who dominate the process, strike such bargains based on the strength of their cases, the seriousness of the alleged offenses, and defendants' criminal records. In 1982, voters passed Proposition 8 (the Victims' Bill of Rights) in an ultimately unsuccessful effort to curtail the practice. California's Three-Strikes Law has altered plea bargaining significantly. In third-strike cases, defendants who might have once plea bargained a lesser sentence figure "what is there to lose?" and seek a full trial.

The Trial

Criminal trials can be heard before a judge only (bench trials) or a jury made up of one's peers. Sometimes a defendant can choose which type. Bench trials are common for less serious offenses and constitute more than 20 percent of all criminal trials in California. Prosecutors and defense attorneys traditionally have played key roles in the selection of juries. Since justice means "winning the case" to both sides, picking the right jury is essential. The process is both art and science. Jury selection experts believe that identifying prejudices is at the heart of jury selection. Proposition 115, passed in 1990, allows judges to question potential juries exclusively, eliminating repetitious questioning by lawyers. In some counties, judges now handpick all juries. On occasion a trial site is moved due to unfavorable pretrial publicity (a "change of venue"). In the famous 1992 trial of Los Angeles policemen accused of beating African American Rodney King, many legal experts believed the outcome was predetermined when the trial was moved to suburban Ventura County.[18] A jury dominated by whites acquitted the officers. In 2004, the media-saturated Scott Peterson murder case was moved from Modesto to Redwood city.

Misdemeanor trials must begin within 45 days of arraignment, 30 days if the defendant is in custody. Felony trials must begin 60 days after arraignment unless the defense requests a delay. Judges usually grant such requests. Criminal cases thus take priority and force lengthy delays for civil cases, which have no such time constraints. In other words, the old rule of thumb "justice delayed is justice denied" does not necessarily apply to civil cases in California.

The steps of a trial are rather predictable. After opening statements by both sides, the prosecution presents evidence consisting of witnesses and various exhibits. The defense cross-examines the witnesses. The defense makes its case in much the same fashion. As the trial ends, both sides present closing arguments. The judge instructs the jury, if there is one; the jury deliberates and decides guilt or innocence. In felony cases, a 12-member jury is required and its decision must be unanimous. In misdemeanor cases, a smaller jury is possible if both sides agree.

The Verdict and Sentence

After the trial, the judge determines a sentence if the accused is found guilty. Jail and prison terms are set by the state legislature. Generally speaking, judges are guided by a determinate sentencing law that sets finite prison terms and gives judges less discretion than they once had. Within these bounds, judges do have discretion based on restitution to victims, the need to protect society, or other special conditions. For example, they may require juvenile offenders to clean up graffiti, not just pass the time in a Youth Authority facility.

THE CIVIL PROCESS

Most courtroom time is devoted to civil cases—disputes involving individuals, businesses, and government agencies. There are distinctive stages involving pretrial activity, the trial itself, and a judgment.

Pretrial Activity

First, an aggrieved party files a *complaint*. It consists of a specific claim (say someone breaks an ankle in a sidewalk hole) and a proposed remedy (usually a dollar amount to cover medical expenses and possibly pain and suffering). The defendant is informed of the claim and files an answer. The next step is called *discovery*, the gathering of information to prepare for a possible trial. This process can involve *depositions* (oral testimony under oath) conducted by the lawyers involved, *interrogatories* (written questions and answers), and research into various documents and materials. Every effort is made to settle the case before a trial actually begins. Sometimes the process is formal, involving ADR—*alternative dispute resolution*. It takes two forms. Generally speaking, *mediation* is voluntary and *arbitration* is determined by law or by prior agreement. An arbitrator's decision is legally binding. California requires a "mandatory settlement conference" as the trial date approaches. Out-of-court settlements can range from mutual apologies to millions of dollars. To avoid costly and unpredictable trials, many litigants including corporations and celebrities use retired judges who charge up to $10,000 per day for their legal know-how and settlement experience. Some legal experts are concerned about the fairness of this "rent a judge" trend. Since decisions are achieved in private, important settlements escape any public scrutiny. Furthermore, not all litigants can afford those fees. One appellate justice claims the practice "slams the courthouse doors in the face of the poor."[19] With or without private judging, the vast majority of California's civil cases are settled without a public trial.

The Trial

Trials are available for those who cannot or will not settle. The process in court is very similar to the process in criminal trials. In a jury trial, three-fourths of the jury must agree for there to be a verdict.

The Judgment

At the conclusion of a trial, the judge or jury decides whether a wrong was committed, who was responsible, and what damages, if any, should be awarded. Lawyers for the losing side may file posttrial motions asking to set aside or reduce any damages awarded. Judges may reduce damages they think are excessive.

JURIES AND POPULAR JUSTICE

As noted earlier, both criminal and civil cases can be decided by juries. Although juries are charged with deciding questions of fact and reaching appropriate verdicts, these bodies of laypeople do not necessarily research decisions as judges would. Microcosms of the local community, juries have been known to weigh facts selectively or interpret them in light of their own experiences. This has been called *popular justice*. The extreme of this has been called *jury nullification*—when jurors or juries ignore irrefutable facts, judges' instructions, the applicable law, or all of the above. For example, one California jury acquitted flamboyant automaker John DeLorean of cocaine possession, a charge resulting from a sting operation. The jury seemed to think the sting itself was unfair. In a case involving the beating of riot victim Reginald Denny, a jury seemed to regard the *defendants* themselves as victims of mob behavior during the riot. Many Californians felt that O. J. Simpson was wrongfully acquitted of murder by a Los Angeles jury that ignored incriminating evidence. Fearing popular justice by juries, some people who are sued settle cases out of court, paying huge amounts of money in the process. When cases go to trial and defendants have liability insurance, juries may figure they are penalizing the insurance carrier more than the defendant. After all, should not insurance companies have to pay out now and then?

How Courts Make Policy

Courts not only make decisions, they make policy. Public policy is what governments choose to do or not do. Individual policy decisions can be made by a host of public officials, including those in the judiciary. Individual court decisions may not seem like broad policy statements; it depends on which level—trial or appellate.

TRIAL COURT POLICY MAKING

Trial court judges in California as anywhere else are primarily finders of fact. They make public policy in less obvious ways. First, they reflect policy preferences over time in many cases. This is called *cumulative policy making*. Years of decisions in comparable cases reveal certain patterns, which vary from judge to judge. As a trial court judge, former California Chief Justice Malcolm Lucas was labeled "Maximum Malcolm" due to his typically harsh sentences in criminal cases. Second, judges generally reflect community norms. These norms are part of a community's local legal culture. Because these cultures vary from place to place, a form of judicial diversity results. For instance, California's big city judges may decide certain cases differently than would their counterparts in rural communities. Charges of disturbing the peace, loitering, or obvious marijuana use may be treated differently in university towns than in wealthy residential enclaves. Third, trial judges' decisions reflect their own ideological perspectives. For instance, legal norms aside, conservative judges tend to side with insurance companies in claims cases or with management in labor disputes; liberals with claimants and organized labor. This fact is not lost on governors who fill trial court vacancies. For example, Governor Gray Davis preferred jurists who favor the death penalty and a woman's right to choose an abortion. According to law professor Gerald Uelman, "A wrong answer . . . [on these issues] is likely to end the inquiry and the candidate's judicial aspirations."[20]

APPELLATE COURT POLICY MAKING

Unlike trial courts, California appellate courts decide matters of law, not fact. They can confirm, reject, or modify public policy with a single decision. Although guided by *stare decisis* (the rule of precedent), they are not wedded to it. They can enter the "political thicket" of partisan conflict or avoid it. The choice is theirs. When Californians think of judicial policy making, they usually think of the California Supreme Court, and rightfully so. We will consider briefly this court as policymaker under three chief justices: Rose Bird (1977–1986), Malcolm Lucas (1986–1996), and Ronald George (1996–present).

The Bird Court

Rose Bird, a former public defender, presided over a court that viewed itself as change agent and problem solver. Remember, California courts have long assumed their independence from the federal judiciary. The California Supreme Court was a national trendsetter in this regard. In 1955, it ruled that illegally seized evidence could not be used in court. The U.S. Supreme Court agreed six years later. The California court stipulated various rights of accused persons one year before the famous *Miranda* decision did the same nationally. The Bird court was both independent and active. It overturned numerous death sentences, widened opportunities for liability suits, nullified several initiatives, and generally favored environmental protection and the rights of workers, renters, women, and homosexuals. By the early 1980s, the Bird court was so active, one superior court judge exclaimed: "Nothing is sacred any more. . . . It's difficult for trial judges to know what the law is. They change it every 10 minutes."[21]

The Lucas Court

The historic defeat of Bird, Reynoso, and Grodin in 1986 allowed Governor George

Deukmejian not only to name their replacements but to shape the court's future policy role. A succession of appointments by Deukmejian and his successor, Pete Wilson, left the court with only one liberal, Stanley Mosk, a 1964 appointee of Pat Brown. Under Lucas, the court became less activist, less assertive, and less willing to use the state constitution to establish new legal doctrines. That is, the Lucas Court tended to follow the lead of the U.S. Supreme Court rather than forge its own policy and law. In criminal cases, it was reluctant to overturn guilt verdicts. Whereas the Bird Court often found "reversible" errors, the Lucas Court found most errors to be harmless, minor defects that do not endanger the right to a fair trial. Most important, the Lucas Court upheld more than 80 percent of death penalty convictions, in remarkable contrast to the 94 percent reversal rate of the Bird Court. As law professor Clark Kelso put it, "When the voters speak loudly enough, even the judiciary listens."[22]

The George Court

Under the leadership of Ronald M. George, the state Supreme Court has continued many of the trends and policies set by the Lucas Court. Possibly because the court is more diverse than it once was (two women, one African American, one Asian American, and one Latino), it cannot be neatly divided into ideological voting blocks. It seems to align itself into different majorities on a case-by-case basis. The court still retains its independent-mindedness relative to federal law and even state election trends. According to George, "the job would not be worth holding if you had to look over your shoulders to see which way the political winds were blowing."[23] On a procedural note, the George Court has continued another Lucas legacy—verbiage. According to law professor Stephen R. Barnett, the California Supreme Court writes longer opinions and takes much longer to decide cases than does the U.S. Supreme Court.[24] In general, the court's opinions are much longer than those of the U.S. Supreme Court and other states' supreme courts.

CRIMINAL JUSTICE AND PUNISHMENT

The policy role of California's courts is most visible in the area of criminal justice. Coping with endless waves of defendants is a challenge shared by other policymakers, the federal courts, and society in general. California's criminal justice system demonstrates both the diversity of the state and the hyperpluralistic nature of its political system. The state's judiciary has been affected by sweeping social trends, changing sentencing laws, the perennial issue of capital punishment, and the state's investment in new prisons.

Social Trends

In many ways, court cases simply mirror broad social trends. They include changing demographics plus the widespread use of guns and drugs. First, population experts have noticed a rise of young, minority males who statistically contribute more than their fair share of street crime (see Figure 9.2). For example, in 2005, blacks constituted 7 percent of California's overall population but nearly 29 percent of its prison population. Experts attribute this to reduced employment opportunities, residential segregation, the presence of gangs, and the absence of positive role models in minority communities. Despite tough law-and-order, "build more prisons" rhetoric by elected officials, crime rates are largely dependent on these economic and demographic trends.

Second, the widespread availability of handguns and assault weapons also colors the crime picture in California. The statistics are sobering. Over 70 percent of all homicides in the state involve firearms, most of those handguns. More Californians die of gunshots than die in motor vehicle accidents. Gun-related homicides are extraordinarily high among young, urban youth. Although handguns outnumber

Male	93 percent
Race	
White	29 percent
Black	29 percent
Hispanic	37 percent
Other	6 percent
Drug-related offenses	21 percent
Average age	36
Average reading level	Seventh grade
From Southern California	59 percent

FIGURE 9.2   California's prison population, 2005

Question: What larger issues regarding incarceration in California does this prisoner profile raise?

Source: California Department of Corrections, 2005 (www.corr.ca.gov/).

assault weapons, the latter are increasingly used against the police, in drive-by shootings, and by California's gang culture. In short, the state is awash in weapons.[25] In recent years, the state legislature has responded by toughening its ban on certain assault weapons, limiting handgun purchases, discouraging the manufacture of cheaply made handguns, and requiring safety devices for all weapons sold, transferred, or manufactured in California.

Third, drugs and alcohol figure in many of California's criminal cases. Because criminal cases take priority over civil cases, they have in effect swamped the courts. As we noted, the courts have responded by creating so-called drug courts to better manage this aspect of the overall workload of the judiciary.

Sentencing Mandates

California courts are not only impacted by social trends, they must abide by the state's sentencing policies. Traditionally, the state legislature sets sentencing policy. For example,

before 1977, California judges worked with an "indeterminate sentence" policy adopted by the legislature. The idea was that convicts would stay in prison until "rehabilitated" or until the completion of a broadly defined term (say, 1 to 5, or 1 to 10 years). The policy reflected an optimistic view that most convicts could be rehabilitated. The only problem was that "rehabilitated" convicts returned to prisons at alarming rates (a phenomenon called *recidivism*). In 1976, the legislature passed the Uniform Sentencing Act, specifying narrower sentencing ranges within which judges can work. In 1994, California voters altered tradition by passing the state's Three Strikes law. Some scholars have called this reform "the largest penal experiment in American history."[26] Three Strikes made sentencing even more uniform by providing 25-years-to-life sentences for anyone convicted of a third felony, whether violent or not. In recent years, some prosecutors have used the discretion granted them by the law to scale back the number of life sentences they seek in third strike cases. Even though the U.S. Supreme Court eventually upheld the law, critics contend that people are being sentenced too severely for petty crimes such as stealing cigarettes or, in one famous case, a slice of pizza. Defenders say Three-Strikes is fulfilling its intent—incarcerating habitual, repeat felons.[27] Voters must agree—they rejected Proposition 66 in 2004, a measure that would have narrowed third strike-eligible offenses to violent or serious felonies.

California's diverse population seems to have an impact on sentencing decisions. One study concluded that, at almost every stage of California's criminal justice process, whites fare better than African Americans and Latinos. They are more likely to have charges reduced or receive rehabilitative placements versus prison time. Why the disparity? Researchers believe judges tend to follow probation reports, which weigh individual backgrounds in recommending sentences. Since many minorities come from lower socioeconomic backgrounds (a phenomenon associated with higher crime rates to begin with), many have prior records— a major factor in sentencing decisions. Also, whites plea bargain more often than minorities. If they are materially better off, they can more easily afford restitution to a victim, thereby avoiding jail or prison.[28]

Capital Punishment

The ultimate sentence is death. Age-old arguments over both its morality and its effectiveness have characterized its history in California. The penalty has been a political football in recent decades. In 1972, both the U.S. and California Supreme Courts ruled the death penalty unconstitutional due to its capricious and arbitrary use. In the federal case, *Furman v. Georgia*, Justice Potter Stewart regarded the death penalty as cruel and unusual "in the same way that being struck by lightning is cruel and unusual." In a 1973 bill authored by then Senator George Deukmejian, the legislature reinstituted capital punishment, citing the "special circumstances" under which it would be employed (such as killing during a robbery, multiple homicides, and murder of police officers). Thirty-four other states did the same. In 1976, the U.S. Supreme Court ruled in *Gregg v. Georgia* that such efforts to reduce the penalty's arbitrariness were permissible and that capital punishment was allowable where such measures were employed. In 1978, California voters passed an initiative extending those circumstances (the California Death Penalty Law), but, as noted earlier, the Bird Court usually found ways to overturn particular death sentences. Subsequent appointments to the high court have made all the difference. By 2005, there were 635 inmates on death row—more by far than in any other state.

In the 1990s, California resumed actual executions. In 1992, Robert Alton Harris was the first person in 25 years to be executed in California. The gas chamber at San Quentin was the

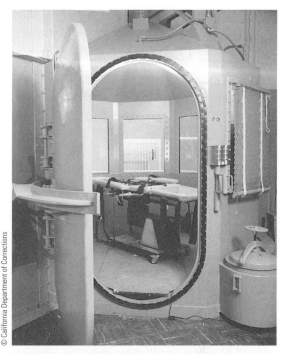

© California Department of Corrections

PHOTO 9.3   California's lethal injection chamber, San Quentin State Prison

Question: To what extent should the imposition of the death penalty depend on different supreme court eras or differences between states?

last stop on a 13-year odyssey of appeals. There have been only 12 executions from 1978 to 2005. Officials allow and the condemned seem to prefer lethal injection. With this method, those slated for execution are strapped to a gurney and injected with a chemical cocktail.

Why are there so many Death Row inmates and so few executions? California houses 20 percent of the nation's death row inmates but accounts for only 1 percent of the nation's executions. While there are limits to endless appeals, allowable appeals are long and costly. One law professor suggests Californians are paying for their own ambivalence about the penalty.[29] Donald Beardslee was executed in January 2005 after serving nearly 21 years on Death Row for the drug-related murder of two young women. Furthermore, the imposition of the death penalty continues to be, as it always has been, dependent on local prosecutorial practice. Because district attorneys in each county decide who is charged with special circumstances offenses, California has "in effect 58 death penalty laws," according to a former Supreme Court justice.[30]

Prison Politics

Unlike their role in death penalty cases, California courts have been relative bystanders in the debate over prisons. For years, California prisons were able to keep pace with a growing state, but no more. Because of demographic factors, the rise of drug-related crimes, tougher sentencing laws, and vigorous prosecution efforts (such as large-scale drug sweeps instead of individual arrests), more people face prison terms. By 2005, more than 163,000 Californians were housed in prison or other correctional facilities. Another 122,000 were on parole. About 60 percent of parolees return to prison for violating their parole, and the reasons are clear. According to one report, they tend to be unemployed substance abusers lacking basic survival skills. As we noted, contrary to public images, most California inmates are incarcerated for nonviolent offenses, such as drug use, property crime, and driving under the influence of alcohol.

Because of these factors, prison construction has become a growth industry in California.

Several bond measures provided funds for new prison construction. Some communities shuddered at the thought of a nearby prison; others relished the prospect of new, well-paid jobs. By 2005, California had 32 prisons, 47 work camps, 12 community correctional facilities, and five prisoner-mother facilities. The cost of warehousing convicts has become enormous. Prison construction can reach $50,000 per bed and annual operating costs per prisoner exceed $35,000. Since 1984, California has built 20 new prisons and experts believe more will be needed in the long term.

Those convicted of lesser crimes or awaiting trial spend time in California's county jails. These facilities are also overcrowded. As Chapter 13 notes, growing numbers of the mentally ill spend time in jail rather than in more appropriate care facilities. The overcrowding is understandable. There is some state funding for local jail expansion, but it is not enough. Other local needs compete for precious county dollars. Furthermore, second- and third-strike inmates stay longer in jail while fighting long prison sentences. As a result of these factors and court-imposed limits on the number of people held at any one time, some jail officials have released nonviolent felons and advised the police to stop arresting low-level offenders. Jail demographics make matters worse. Race-based and gang-related violence, once the norm in state prisons, is increasingly commonplace in county jails.

Did You Know . . . ?

California's gargantuan penal system is the third largest in the world. The largest is that of the People's Republic of China; the second largest is the United States federal prison system.

SOURCE: John Howard, "A New Look at Crime and Punishment," *California Journal* 35 (May 2004), 8.

Prison Reform

The challenges facing California's correctional system are enormous. In recent years, critics have accused the system of the following:

• an archaic administrative structure

• budget overruns and administrative waste

• undue influence by the prison guards union

• prisoner abuse or neglect by those very guards

• shoddy medical care

• dysfunctionally high recidivism rates

• a focus on warehousing prisoners versus re-habilitation

• a gender-blindness that treats female and male prisoners alike.

In response to these challenges, Governor Arnold Schwarzenegger vowed to reform California's $6 billion correctional system, claiming that the "purpose of corrections is to correct." Initial proposals centered on some structural changes (combining adult and youth correctional agencies) but many experts believe that more fundamental reforms will need to address sentencing practices that contribute to the current crisis. Whether the governor can alter the ethics and culture of this vast system is an open question. What is clear is that reform-oriented leadership will need to arise from outside the system itself.[31]

Conclusion

California's judiciary manifests several trends in California politics. First, the legal profession in California certainly does not mirror the state's growing ethnic and cultural diversity. It remains largely white, middle class, and male in membership. To be sure, more women are seeking legal careers and gaining professional strength. Second, in terms of workload, the judiciary is clearly impacted by the state's diversity. Criminal caseloads denote population changes plus widespread use of alcohol, drugs, and guns. Civil caseloads reflect a large, increasingly complex and regulated economy, plus an increasingly litigious society. Third, access to the judiciary is problematic, especially for the poor. Although public defenders, court appointed attorneys, and legal aid clinics provide low- or no-cost legal help, the poor in California do not enjoy the quality and quantity of legal assistance available to the middle and upper classes.

Fourth, in terms of governance, the judiciary carries out some vital functions (such as dispensing case-by-case justice) but also contributes to the "divided government" problem normally associated with the governor's office and the legislature not controlled by the same political party. The courts' role is a two-edged sword. On some occasions, the judiciary contributes to policy paralysis by allowing political struggles to continue for years, even decades, in the courts. The history of capital punishment illustrates this point. On other occasions, the judiciary can break the gridlock between the other two branches, as it has in areas such as reapportionment. Also, interest groups strategically use the courts to achieve policy preferences they could not obtain elsewhere in government.

California's judiciary also reflects political fragmentation and hyperpluralism. Judges themselves are relatively insulated from the electorate, rightly so in their view. Yet they can occasionally feel the pressure and even the wrath of volatile voters. But holding judges accountable is no easy task for voters. Trial court judges share power with policing agencies, courtroom work groups, and juries. On occasion, juries define facts, the law, and justice on their own terms. In making decisions, all judges respond to professional norms, statutory laws, conflicting interest group demands, and their own sociological and political backgrounds. In an age when voters seem to think that political parties make no difference, recent appointments to California's Supreme Court suggest the very opposite.

The policy making role of California's judiciary will continue to be important and on some issues paramount. The courts will always been needed to validate, implement, or repair initiatives proposed by interest groups and passed by the voters. As the federal government continues to shift policy responsibility and accountability to the states, state courts will have no choice but to respond with policies that reflect each state's political culture and environment. California is no different.

KEY TERMS

judicial federalism   (p. 177)

superior courts, district courts of appeal, the California Supreme Court   (pp. 177–180)

Three-Strikes Law   (p. 178)

Missouri plan   (p. 181)

judicial socialization   (p. 183)

Code of Judicial Ethics   (p. 183)

adversarial justice   (p. 185)

assumption of guilt   (p. 185)

arraignment, preliminary hearing, indictment (p. 185)

plea bargaining   (pp. 185–186)

complaint, discovery, depositions, interrogatories (p. 187)

alternative dispute resolution, mediation, arbitration   (p. 187)

popular justice, jury nullification   (p. 187)

cumulative policy making   (p. 188)

REVIEW QUESTIONS

1. How does the dual judicial system help explain judicial independence in California?
2. If you were a California appellate court judge, how would your work day differ from that of a trial court judge?
3. If you were a lawyer aspiring to become a judge, what would you do or not do to reach that goal? How would you be held accountable once you reached your goal?
4. Describe the workings of the civil and criminal process.
5. How do both trial and appellate courts make policy? How has state Supreme Court policy shifted in recent decades?
6. What factors affect who is charged and sentenced in California?

WEB ACTIVITIES

Judicial Branch of California (www.courtinfo.ca.gov)

This site contains a wealth of data on California courts including opinions, procedures, administrative issues, latest developments, and links to other law- and court-related Websites.

California Department of Corrections (www.corr.ca.gov)

To learn more about capital punishment in California, prison populations, or specific prison facilities, this site is helpful.

INFOTRAC® COLLEGE EDITION ARTICLES

For additional reading, go to InfoTrac® College Edition, your online research library, at http://www.infotrac.thomsonlearning.com

California Supreme Court Invalidates Gay Marriages

Private Judges

California Juries Keep Handing Big Losses to Big Tobacco

NOTES

1. Philip Hager, "Poll Finds Wide Legal Ignorance," *Los Angeles Times,* May 2, 1991.
2. For an account of both Mosk's career and this doctrine, see Bob Egelko, "Justice Stanley Mosk," *California Journal* 32 (August 2001), 26–31.
3. The relevant cases were *People v. Anderson,* 1972; *Serrano v. Priest,* 1971; and *Mukley v. Reitman,* 1966.
4. *Lockyer* v. *Andrede,* 538 U.S. 63 (2003).
5. Ronald M. George, *1997 State of the Judiciary Address.*
6. John T. Wold, "Going Through the Motions: The Monotony of Appellate Court Decisionmaking," *Judicature,* 62 (August 1978), 61–62.
7. An appellate opinion is published if it establishes a new rule of law, involves a publicly visible issue, or contributes significantly to legal literature.
8. Preble Stolz, "Say Goodbye to Hiram Johnson's Ghost," *California Lawyer,* 10 (January 1990), 44–45.
9. See Bill Ainsworth, "State Bar in Crisis," *California Journal* 29 (May 1999), 56–58.
10. "Survey Finds Bar Makeup Shifting, But Slowly," *California Bar Journal* (November 2001). Available online at www.ca.bar.org/2dbj/01nov/.
11. California Bar Association, *The Path to Justice: A Five Year Status Report on Access to Justice in California* (California Bar Association, 2002). (Available online at www.calbar.org/).
12. David Balabanian, "Justice Was More Than His Title," *California Law Review,* 70 (July 1982), 880.
13. Bob Egelko, "Judicial Money Race," *California Journal* 232 (May 2001), 36–40.
14. Martin Lasden, "Justifying Janice," *California Lawyer,* 21 (June 2001), 34–38, 75.
15. Article IV, Section 18b.
16. Commission on Judicial Performance, *2003 Annual Report,* (San Francisco: Commission on Judicial Performance, 2003). (Available at http://cjp.ca.gov/)
17. Sheryl Stolberg, "Politics and the Judiciary Coexist, But Often Uneasily," *Los Angeles Times,* March 21, 1992.
18. Henry Weinstein and Paul Leiberman, "Location of Trial Played Major Role, Legal Experts Say," *Los Angeles Times,* April 30, 1992.
19. Ted Rohrlick, "Growing Use of Private Judges Raises Questions of Fairness," *Los Angeles Times,* December 26, 2000.
20. Gerald F. Uelman, "A 'Death-Qualified' Judiciary," *California Lawyer,* 19 (September 1999), 27.
21. Quoted in K. Connie Kang, "Brown's Court Legacy: Crusaders Against Social Injustice," *California Journal,* 13 (September 1982), 311. Another article evaluating the Bird Court is Bob Egelko, "The Court's National Stature Has Waned Under Bird," *California Journal,* 17 (September 1986), 428–433.
22. Quoted in Maura Dolan, "State Court Is Strong Enforcer of Death Penalty," *Los Angeles Times,* April 9, 1995.
23. Quoted in A.G. Block and Claudia Buck, eds., *1999–2000 California Political Almanac, 6th ed.* (Sacramento: State Net), *81.*
24. Stephen R. Barnett, "Report Card," *California Lawyer,* 21 (January 2001), 27–28.
25. John Borland, "The Arming of California," *California Journal,* 26 (October 1995), 36–41.
26. Franklin E. Zimring, Gordon Hawkins, and Sam Kamin, *Punishment and Democracy: Three Strikes and You're Out in California* (New York: Oxford University Press, 2001).
27. Janet Weeks, "Arguing the Third Strike," *California Lawyer,* 19 (December 1999), 39–42, 78–79.
28. Greg Krikorian, "Study Questions Justice System's Fairness," *Los Angeles Times,* February 2, 1996; and Ted Rohrlich, "Blacks, Latinos Get Longer Sentences, Study Concludes," *Los Angeles Times,* June 30, 1983.
29. Rone Tempest, "Death Row Often Means a Long Life," *Los Angeles Times,* March 6, 2005.
30. Quoted in Ted Rohrlich, "Executions: Who Dies and Why," *Los Angeles Times,* April 2, 1990.
31. John Howard, "A New Look at Crime and Punishment," *California Journal* 35 (May 2004), 8–15.

CHAPTER 10

Community Politics

In Brief

Chapter 10 surveys the most diverse set of institutions in California politics: local government. The thousands of local governments in California can be grouped into five types: counties, cities, special districts, school districts, and regional governments, plus privatized versions of local government such as urban villages and homeowners associations. This chapter considers the idea of community and the functions of local governments in those communities. Such governments are limited in their capacity and even in their willingness to govern effectively.

All six types represent diversity and fragmentation in California politics. With each type, we examine how local governments are established and how local officials exercise power.

Also surveyed are the inherent limits of local government, the role of the state in local affairs, and the fiscal and policy problems faced by each type of government. In recent years, all local governments have faced revenue volatility due to voter-enacted tax cuts, reduced aid from the state, and the ups and downs of California's economy. In general, cities are more fiscally healthy than counties.

California's numerous local governments represent a rich diversity of governing styles and institutions, allow ample opportunities for citizen participation in politics, and provide a wide assortment of options for living in community. There is a downside to this diversity however. According to political scientists, the sheer numbers of local governments in California reduce political accountability and undermine the ability of local governments to manage problems, especially those that spill beyond their boundaries.

Introduction

"Divorce L.A. Style" was the title of a Newsweek article on the desire of many San Fernando Valley residents to secede from the City of Los Angeles.[1] By the time of the November 2002 election, two divorce proposals were on the ballot: the San Fernando Valley and Hollywood. "Breaking Los Angeles apart is not the answer," pleaded the mayor.[2] Although both proposals went down to defeat, Rancho Cordova chose to incorporate that same election day, bringing the total number of cities to 478. Several years later, disgruntled residents of the northern portion of Santa Barbara County initiated an uphill battle to split their county in two. In fact, California has been breaking apart into cities and other local governments since becoming a state (see Figure 10.1). Chapter 10 explains these community-level governments.

There are myriad local governments, laid side-by-side and on top of each other across the state. Picture several jigsaw puzzles stacked one on top of each other. That is what local government looks like in the Golden State. Cities, counties, special districts, and various regional governments are the official local governments of California. There are also various "urban forms"—places that look and behave like cities but most definitely are not governed like them.

The two broad themes of this book, diversity and hyperpluralism, are vividly represented in California's local politics. The state's profound diversity plays itself out at the community level. It is in community that people work, pursue various lifestyles, raise families, and educate their children. It is where neighbors do or do not get along, where California's polyglot of racial and ethnic groups live—in harmony or otherwise. From school board meetings to city hall hearings, it is in community that values collide and cultures clash. Communities are where the American notion of individual sovereignty (power in the hands of the individual) rubs up against the need for group norms, responsibility, and expectations. In short, California communities are vivid expressions of a culturally pluralistic, differentiated society. At this level, the struggle for power and control between individuals and groups is constant.

California communities also represent government at its most fragmented level, and are one manifestation of what we call hyperpluralism. Fifty-eight counties, 478 cities, nearly 1,000 school districts, and about 3800 other special districts all present diverse approaches to community governance. During most any weekend drive, a California motorist will encounter (unknowingly in most cases) dozens of governmental jurisdictions; and these do not include a growing number of quasi-governments such as neighborhood homeowner associations. Californians may complain their local governments are ineffective; they can hardly object that there are too few of them. Los Angeles County alone has nearly 500 subdivisions of government.

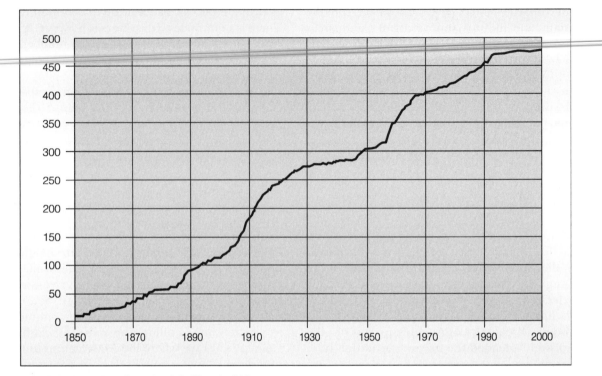

FIGURE 10.1   The Growth of California Cities

Question: What do you think is the local impetus to incorporate, to form cities?

Source: Paul G. Lewis, *Deep Roots: Local Government Structure in California* (San Francisco: Public Policy Institute of California, 1998), p. 23; updated by author.

Across the state, there are so many local governments, that citizens are often unsure which government provides which service and whom to call when a problem arises.

Hyperpluralism also suggests a host of public policy problems beyond the reach of governing institutions. Increasingly, problems facing local officials spill beyond their reach. And funding shortages, an absence of public support, and lack of political will leave those public problems within their reach unaddressed—for years, decades or longer. Local interest groups and regional forces, economic and demographic, usually dictate where growth occurs more than does local government. Furthermore, the growing dominance of the state in local matters has fostered both local dependence on the state and resistance to it.

THE ROLE OF COMMUNITY

The late U.S. House Speaker Thomas P. "Tip" O'Neill once said, "All politics is local." A corollary could well be: "All politics begins at the community level." Local governments in California's communities perform three generic yet important functions: providing services, socializing community members, and managing conflict.

Providing Services

Local governments deliver various goods and services to their residents. These include education, garbage disposal, water, sanitation, building inspection, law enforcement, and fire protection. To some extent each community can determine the mix and quality of services to provide. But most services are either fully expected by local residents (police) or flatly required by the state (welfare). The question, Which level of government, state or local, should pay for what services? has been at the heart of recent budget battles in Sacramento. Those who believe the primary purpose of local government is to provide tangible services tend to think local government should operate as an efficient business.

Socializing Community Members

In addition to services, local governments provide varying degrees of personal attention to community residents. Most newcomers are assimilated into local society; they learn what behavior is acceptable and unacceptable. These norms can vary from community to community or even from neighborhood to neighborhood. For example, simply "hanging out" in one place may be viewed as "loitering" elsewhere. Gang graffiti (called "tagging") may be quietly tolerated in some neighborhoods but vigorously opposed in others (see Photo 10.1). Regulation of behavior by local government is called the "police power."

Managing Conflict

One of the most important functions of local government is managing conflict among people and groups. Some conflicts are essentially arguments over policy such as service complaints,

© AP/ Wide World Photos

PHOTO 10.1 Gang Graffiti/graffiti cleanup
In the Panorama City section of Los Angeles, evidence of gang activity covers a neighborhood phone booth. To control gang behavior, the city imposed a controversial injunction on 100 members of the gang, prohibiting them from carrying pagers, blocking sidewalks, and congregating in public.

Question: To what extent can a city's police power truly curtail some forms of urban behavior?

land use controversies, and budget allocations. Others reflect deep-seated social and cultural divisions in a community—divisions among racial and ethnic groups, rich and poor, home-owners and renters, or newcomers and old-timers. The more heterogeneous a community population or the more a community values extensive political participation, the more visible conflict will be. Such conflicts become political because government is expected to intervene. Political conflict is common in cities of all sizes. The larger cities of California contain numerous and diverse ethnic and income groups. A growing number of California communities no longer contain a single ethnic or racial majority—they are "majority-minority" cities. As many of these groups have become more politically conscious, they have become more politically assertive. To some observers, the multiethnic politics (white, Latino, and Asian) in Monterey Park, California represent what other communities can expect.[3] Small, relatively homogeneous, and presumably peaceful communities encourage political involvement, no matter how small the issue. Both settings require the management of conflict, at times intense conflict.

THE LIMITS OF COMMUNITY GOVERNMENT

Despite expectations that local governments provide all three functions, California communities are limited in doing so. Three limits discussed here are the privatization of development, Dillon's Rule, and the myth of apolitical politics.

Privatization of Development

Historically, California's communities were regarded as economic entities. The growth of these places was dictated by a tradition of *privatism*—an ongoing succession of private economic transactions. The Big Four, land speculators, and private utility companies were the essence of early privatism in the Golden State. To be sure, local government had a role to play, usually accommodating, assisting, and at times subsidizing those private interests. Because many local governments have continued this traditional role, they have remained largely ineffective in controlling private interests when public and private interests clash. How this applies to land use politics is addressed in Chapter 12.

Dillon's Rule

In 1868, shortly after California's admission to the Union, an eminent jurist wrote an opinion which would become a commonplace legal doctrine and a fixture in American federalism. Judge John F. Dillon wrote, "Municipal corporations owe their origin to, and derive their powers and rights wholly from, the legislature. It breathes into them the breath of life, without which they cannot exist. As it creates, so it may also destroy. What it may destroy, it may ...control."[4] The idea that states dominate local governments was adopted by the U.S. Supreme Court, other state courts, and, naturally, state legislatures. In California, this doctrine underlies all state-local relationships. True, the state allows significant *home rule* (a measure of local self government). But Article XI of the California Constitution stipulates local powers and even the very existence of local government. To this day, California communities look to Sacramento for permission to do this or that or to raise revenue—in short, to exercise political power. In turn the state can legally take back both services and revenues. For instance, in the midst of a 1992 budget deficit, the California legislature created an Educational Revenue Enhancement Fund in order to backfill its education budget with local property tax dollars. Local governments have attempted to retrieve that revenue ever since.

Apolitical Politics

A final limit on local self-government in California is the enduring assumption that party politics corrupts governing. As noted in Chapter 4, the Progressives wanted to take "politics" out of government, meaning the corrupting influences of political parties and bosses. Their solutions included nonpartisan, at-large local elections, as well as professional city management. California political scientist Eugene Lee once described the nonpartisanship ideal: "City government is largely a matter of 'good business practice' or 'municipal housekeeping' . . . There is little room for 'politics.' Therefore, it is not necessary to establish organized political competition as suggested by the partisan ballot."[5] The Progressives believed good government meant the efficient provision of various municipal services. They underestimated government's role in reflecting and managing political conflict. Even today, some local officials sincerely believe that an entire constellation of social and political issues are beyond the scope of local government. On the contrary, local governments find they are caldrons of California's diversity—expected to give voice to, address, and even solve the pressing problems faced by various individuals and myriad groups.

California's local governments are both numerous and richly diverse. We now survey the most common local governments in California: counties, cities, special districts, school districts, and regional governments.

Counties

One of the most diverse units of California local government is the *county*. California, as did other states, borrowed the county idea from British local government tradition. Originally, a county was a territory administered by a count. It was both a local government and a subdivision of a central government; counties retain this dual role today. In fact, unless prohibited by the state constitution, the legislature may delegate to counties any task belonging to the state itself.

THE SHAPE OF CALIFORNIA COUNTIES

In many ways, California's 58 counties reflect a bygone era. Consider the map in Figure 10.2. At the time of statehood, California had relatively few large counties. Southern California was one vast desert; much of it still is, as San Bernardino County's boundaries attest. The Sierra foothill counties are elongated and relatively small for a reason. During the Gold Rush, it was thought that miners should be no farther than a day's horseback ride from a county seat where mining claims were filed. Those boundaries remain today.

In the late 1800s and early 1900s, new counties were formed, reflecting population and power shifts plus emerging local rivalries. Giant Mariposa County (encompassing much of Southern California) was subdivided into 12 counties. San Mateo broke away from San Francisco. Farmers and ranchers, fearing the early growth of Los Angeles, helped form Orange County in 1889. The last breakaway, Imperial County, formed east of San Diego in 1907. Despite vast demographic and economic change, the shape of California's counties has remained fixed since 1907. Local political cultures developed and calcified in that span of time, making further boundary changes difficult if not unthinkable. Occasional efforts in recent years to form new counties have failed. For instance, Los Angeles County communities north of the San Gabriel Mountains maintain they have little in common with the greater Los Angeles Basin but have been unable to form their own county.

This static situation has resulted in tremendous differences between modern California counties. Geographically, San Bernardino is the nation's largest (20,000 square miles). It is 200 times larger than San Francisco County, and embraces about 20 percent of the entire state. Los Angeles County teems with over 10 million people (larger than that of 44 other *states*) while tiny Alpine County is home to about 1,200 people. Some counties have experienced

FIGURE 10.2 California's Counties
California's 58 counties come in all shapes and sizes; their boundaries have not changed in more than 90 years despite massive population growth and change.

Question: How would you redraw these boundaries if given the chance?

uncontrolled growth while others have languished in California's economic backwaters. The state expects all 58 to perform similarly as units of government. Yet their resources for doing so vary widely.

THE SHAPE OF COUNTY GOVERNMENT

Legally speaking, there are only two types of counties: *general law* and *charter*. California's 45 general law counties adhere to state law as to the number and duties of county elected officials. Thirteen charter counties are governed by a constitution-like document called a "charter" which replaces some general laws and provides a limited degree of home rule. California's urban counties have charters, and two-thirds of all Californians live in those counties. Both general law and charter counties are the primary units of local government in rural and some suburban areas.

Answering the classic question, Who governs? at the county level is no easy task. Authority and responsibility—in short, power—is widely dispersed and shared among the following decision makers.

Boards of Supervisors

In California, each county's legislative body is the board of supervisors. These boards are de facto city councils for those living outside of cities. Board members serve for four-year, staggered terms. They are elected during primary elections in even-numbered years. If they do not garner a majority of votes (50 percent plus one), a November runoff is necessary. Although the elections are technically nonpartisan, informed voters likely know the partisan leanings of better-known candidates, especially incumbents. Their names sometimes appear on those partisan slate mailers discussed in Chapter 6. In the past, county supervisors were "good old boys"—older white men with business backgrounds. In recent years, more women have become supervisors and in a few counties, they have constituted board majorities. Over the years, service on a board of supervisors has been a stepping stone to the state legislature or other elective posts. Occasionally, the reverse occurs. Los Angeles County Supervisor Gloria Molina served in the state legislature but regarded the county board a promotion. In terms of pay and power, it was. Her colleague, Yvonne Brathwaite Burke, once served in the state assembly and Congress.

Boards adopt county budgets, determine some service levels, and make numerous decisions affecting unincorporated areas. The most contentious policy issues usually surround land use. Although county planning commissions make many land use decisions, supervisors hear various appeals and make final decisions. Where to locate shopping centers, housing projects, or unpopular industries (sometimes called LULUs—locally undesirable land uses) pits counties against cities, neighborhood against neighborhood, and occasionally neighbor against neighbor. Ironies abound. On the one hand, board consideration of a relatively small land use project may fill a room with surly citizens on both sides of the issue. On the other hand, discussion of a multimillion dollar expenditure deep inside a county budget may attract little or no public interest whatsoever. Boards of supervisors hire *chief administrative officers* or CAOs (called county managers in some places) to carry out board policy and administer county routines. Preparing and monitoring annual budgets plus preparing weekly board agendas consumes a lion's share of a CAO's time.

Counties also provide for a variety of other elective officials. Together, they are California's local version of a plural executive. The exact arrangement of these positions varies from county to county. The most common elected officers are district attorneys, sheriffs, various fiscal officers, clerks, and school superintendents.

District Attorney

The lead prosecutor for the county is elected. As noted in Chapter 9, district attorneys can exercise a great deal of discretion in setting prosecution policy in a county. Some have become well known due to the cases they prosecute (Los Angeles' Gil Garcetti and the O.J. Simpson case and Santa Barbara's Tom Sneddon and the Michael Jackson case). Public defenders (who provide defense counsel for the poor) are not elected—making them potentially more dependent on a board of supervisors. District attorneys and public defenders can get caught in political battles between supervisors and judges. Trial court judges respond to state laws and professional norms, yet are funded by the supervisors as well as the state. Arguments between these groups often arise over budget, support staff, and facilities.

Sheriff

The chief law enforcement officer for a county is an elected sheriff. This individual is usually an experienced, professional peace officer. Sheriffs administer an office, numerous deputy sheriffs, the county jail, and in some cases the coroner's office. The coroner conducts inquests of all questionable deaths. County sheriff departments often provide law enforcement services to cities that cannot or will not provide their own police departments.

Fiscal Officers

Several county officials including auditors, treasurers, assessors, and tax collectors, handle the monies counties receive. This means they collect and count it, manage and invest it, and monitor its expenditure. Because their tasks are largely ministerial (administrative in nature with little room for personal discretion), they generate little controversy and few political enemies or opponents. Usually. In 1994, Orange County declared bankruptcy because its treasurer, Bob Citron, invested $1.7 billion of county funds in risky Wall Street securities.[6]

County Clerks

These individuals maintain county documents and records, such as real estate titles and transactions. They also act as voter registrars, supervising elections, and maintaining voter lists. Voters rarely hear from clerks and usually re-elect incumbents.

Superintendent of Schools

In some ways, this position is an oddity in county government. California's county school superintendents often respond to separately elected county boards of education, not boards of supervisors. They do not administer local schools because district-appointed superintendents do that. The offices headed by superintendents provide staff, payroll, training, and other support services to local school districts. Due to economies of scale, they can provide those services more cheaply than many local school districts acting separately. Although the California Constitution Revision Commission recommended that this office be abolished, there is little public concern one way or the other.

Other departments with unelected heads oversee local transportation, land use planning, public health, and welfare. In fact, California's counties play a critical role in administering CalWORKs—the state's version of the federal Temporary Assistance to Needy Families program (TANF) which is discussed in Chapter 13.

CALIFORNIA'S TROUBLED COUNTIES

Governing California's counties is particularly challenging today but some of these challenges are inherent to county government in America. In the 1800s, British observer Lord Bryce observed that American citizens are less attached to county government than other levels: "[The county] is too large for the personal interest of the citizens: that goes to the township. It is too small to have traditions which command the respect or touch the affections of its inhabitants: these belong to the state."[7] Bryce considered counties artificial entities. He could well have been writing about California today. Several developments in recent decades have created substantial pressures for California counties, affecting their identity and their ability to govern at the local level.

Funding Pressures

A significant problem for California's counties is fiscal in nature. Proposition 13, which cut property taxes by half in 1978, also cut the counties' share of that tax (from 30 percent to under 20). Some counties responded by closing libraries or allowing roads to deteriorate. Counties cannot cut just any program, though, because they must administer a variety of state policies (welfare, environmental regulation, and public health policy). The state continues to tell counties what to do by issuing *mandates*. Some of these policy directives are fully funded; others are not. Even if the state later rescinds a mandate, residents can become used to the service it required; cutting it becomes politically unfeasible. As one county association staffer put it, counties have had to fund assorted services with the fiscal equivalent of "band-aids, bailing wire, and bubble gum."[8] In recent years, county officials have urged the state to better fund required services, to fully fund trial courts, and to prevent counties from losing revenue when new cities incorporate.

Issue Spillover

Modern policy problems in California ignore political boundaries. Smog readily moves across county lines, frustrating the ability of any single county to deal with the problem. Region wide population growth has swamped some urban and "urbanizing" counties with traffic jams on obsolete road systems. Some welfare recipients, crushed by housing costs along coastal California, have moved to less expensive areas of the state. This has transferred unanticipated welfare costs to the counties in those areas. Spillover issues affect specific counties differently. One study concluded that there is a positive relationship between program performance and resident income, county revenues, and caseload size. Obviously, those counties that are most affected are those with high levels of poverty, inadequate revenues,

and high caseloads (of parolees, needy children, welfare recipients, and the ill).[9]

Political Responsiveness

In a representative democracy, people expect elected bodies to be responsive to their wishes. This is problematic for county boards. In smaller counties, boards of supervisors are often ideologically conservative and pro-growth regarding development. Even in the face of desperate need, some boards champion a low-tax, low-spending ideology. Size is also a problem. The state requires five-member county boards regardless of population size (San Francisco is a combined city-county with an 11 member board plus a mayor). The Los Angeles board has been called the "five little kings" by critics who believe it is indifferent to the needs of most constituents. Some reformers argue that larger boards in larger counties would allow greater opportunity for minority representation and political responsiveness.

Due to unresponsiveness and other issues, some communities seek to become separate, legally recognized municipalities; that is, they seek to *incorporate*. Often, they are dissatisfied with county services and/or want greater control over land use policies. In some places, this has meant the creation of low density "snob" zoning to keep out poor and working class Californians.[10] Many recent incorporations stem from a local desire for control, image, and identity—those same qualities Lord Bryce observed missing from county government a century ago. The communities that manage to incorporate further drain county budgets by reducing the county's share of property and sales taxes.

Cities

While California has its share of open space, most of its residents are fundamentally urban. Today, more than 80 percent of the state's residents live in cities. California's earliest cities

(San Diego, Los Angeles, Monterey, and San Francisco) were located along the coast, when passage by ship was one of the few travel choices available. Subsequent cities developed along major land transportation routes: roads, railroad routes, and later, freeways. All California cities needed adequate water to develop. Urban giants like Los Angeles and the Bay area shipped it from great distances. Smaller urban areas developed local reservoirs to capture runoff water, tapped into agricultural water projects (like the Central Valley Project), or even built desalinization plants (converting coastal salt water into potable fresh water).

California's 478 cities have developed their own identities through economic specialization. Central Valley cities service surrounding farm areas. Large central cities are home to banking, legal, corporate, and information services. Other cities are manufacturing centers attracting many commuters. Still others in scenic locations (including coastal cities, mountain communities, and California's wine growing regions) attract tourists. Many suburbs are bedroom communities, offering housing and little else. Others have attracted "clean" industry, shopping malls, and opportunities for recreation.

California's cities, including suburbs, defy overgeneralization. Together, they now represent the state's economic and ethnic diversity. For example, Table 10.1 depicts a considerable range in median household incomes among thirteen of California's largest cities. In such places, people sometimes think they live among diversity. Said one Southern Californian: "We have diversity—tract homes and custom homes." In a growing number of cities, no single racial or ethnic group constitutes a majority of a city's residents. These are California's majority-minority cities.

HOW COMMUNITIES BECOME MUNICIPALITIES

If voters in a locale wish to incorporate, they usually initiate such a proposal via a petition. A *local agency formation commission (LAFCO)* studies the possible impacts of the new city. LAFCOs were established in 1963 to foster the orderly development of local government and to prevent urban sprawl. Usually consisting of two city council members, two county supervisors, and one public member, LAFCOs in recent years have been particularly sensitive to the revenue losses counties experience when new cities are formed. After a favorable LAFCO vote, the voters decide whether or not to incorporate. New cities with fewer than 3,500 people must be general law cities. Larger ones can choose which approach to take. Only 108 California cities have their own charters. Some are quite detailed—Los Angeles' newest charter contains ten articles and over 1,000 sections. Like counties, California's general law cities operate under the statutes of the state. For example, the state requires every city to have a reasonably up-to-date general plan—land uses projected for the future.

Did You Know . . . ?

California is a state of sizable cities. Sixty-three of them are 100,000 people or more. Los Angeles is clearly the largest at 3.9 million. The smallest incorporated city is Vernon, with only 96 full-time residents. Because of its 1200 industrial businesses, 44,000 Californians commute there on weekdays.

SOURCE: Demographic Research Unit, California Department of Finance, 2005.

TABLE 10.1 California Cities: Contrasts in Median Household Income

California's Richest Counties		California's Poorest Counties	
San Jose	$70,240	Stockton	$43,857
San Francisco	$57,833	Sacramento	$42,142
San Diego	$47,631	Los Angeles	$40,733
Riverside	$46,755	Santa Ana	$36,968
Bakersfield	$45,791	Long Beach	$36,652
Anaheim	$45,707	Fresno	$36,537
Oakland	$44,129		

Of thirteen major cities in California, San Jose's median household income is nearly double that of Fresno.

Source: U.S. Bureau of the Census, 2003 American Community Survey

Question: How might a community's wealth affect its politics?

"CITIES" WITHOUT "GOVERNMENT"

In the early 1960s, Samuel Wood and Alfred Heller wrote about the *phantom cities* of California. According to the authors, such places are "thickly settled, urban in nature. But they are not cities in the traditional sense of being more or less self-contained settlements controlling their own destinies. They are phantom cities."[11] Included were unincorporated cities (generalized urban growth outside city boundaries), special interest cities ("cities" dedicated to one industry or land use type, like housing), contract cities (jurisdictions which buy some or all of their services often from counties), seasonal cities (recreation-oriented communities which become bustling "cities" only during the tourist season), legitimate cities (but with problems extending well beyond their borders), and regional cities (entire metropolitan areas without effective governments to match). All these phantoms exist today.

A more recent phantom has been so-called *urban villages* or *edge cities*—conglomerations of shopping malls, industrial parks, office "campuses," institutions, and residential housing. Orange County's urban village—the Costa Mesa-Newport Beach-Irvine complex—is considered California's third largest "downtown." In these "post-suburban" communities, a consumer culture predominates.[12] The development of such places rarely coincides with existing governmental jurisdictions. The impacts of urban villages elude cities and other local jurisdictions. Urban villages in Southern California and the Bay area create similar impacts well beyond the reach of traditional cities.

Even at the neighborhood level, a growing number of middle-class Californians live in housing developments governed not by city hall but by *homeowner associations*. Today, about 6 million Californians live in 36,000 such common interest developments. They are set up initially by developers and all homeowners are automatic members. Such groups have boards of directors in turn governed by assorted bylaws and documents called "C,C&Rs" (covenants, conditions, and restrictions). In some respects, these documents are analogous to city charters. No wonder they have been called "shadow governments." Like cities, homeowner groups must obey various state statutes that set certain performance standards in areas like budgeting and insurance. Their powers are both substantial and picayune—from maintaining private streets to dictating window coverings and exterior paint colors (usually beige or the pale equivalent). These powers are largely unregulated by the state; significant disputes are often taken to court. Many associations augment local law enforcement with security gates and alarm systems.

Courtesy of David Lawrence

PHOTO 10.2 A California gated community

In California, gated communities come in all varieties—from exclusive adult communities (as pictured above) to middle-class condominiums to mobile home parks.

Question: Should local governments approve more privatized neighborhoods in California? Why or why not?

Do such neighborhoods foster "cocoon citizens" who flee community life around them, as some critics suggest? While research suggests that CIDs are less diverse than the larger communities that surround them, there is little evidence that these residents have seceded from public life generally. Nonetheless, these "privatopias" could be considered the newest phantom cities in contemporary California.[13]

HOW CALIFORNIA CITIES ARE RUN

Political scientists refer to city governments as either unreformed or reformed. Unreformed cities, unaffected by the Progressive movement, tend to have strong mayors, council members elected by district, and strong partisan influence. Reformed cities adopted many Progressive era practices such as at-large, nonpartisan elections, professional city managers, and weaker mayoral offices. Unreformed governments are most often found in large cities in the Midwest or on the East Coast. Reformed governments are most often found in small cities, suburbia, and in the West, including California.

Most California city governments consist of an elected council plus a mayor elected by the people or chosen by council colleagues. The council hires a city manager, a professional administrator who runs the day-to-day affairs of the city.

City Councils

These local legislatures adopt *ordinances* (local statutes), allocate revenue, determine the extent of public services offered, and make land use decisions. Except for California's largest cities like Los Angeles, city council work is part-time. As with county supervisors, council members used to be primarily white, male and middle class; but political times have changed. City councils today are more diverse—representing a wider range of economic interests, more ethnic minorities, and many more women. Most council members possess a volunteer ethic, a take-it-or-leave-it attitude toward their jobs. Many do little more than respond to city manager proposals. Some are elected on single issues and remain singularly focused. All in all, the primary power of most California city councils is to veto or second-guess the recommendations of professional city managers.

Mayors

California's largest cities have full-time mayors, who often command more public and media attention than their powers would connote. Generally speaking, California mayors are weak—competing with elected councils and myriad commissions often possessing autonomous authority. Political scientist Edward Banfield once suggested the mayor of Los Angeles was "almost too weak to cut ribbons."[14] In fact, Los Angeles Mayor Antonia Villaraigosa shares power with numerous departments, offices, boards, and commissions. Yet big-city residents perceive that mayors run their cities and hold them accountable for policy successes and failures. This is especially true regarding local economies. In the face of

heightened responsibility but limited authority, California's big-city mayors must build coalitions among neighborhood associations, business interests, and other groups. They must be both visionary and results-oriented. As one journalist put it, "With populations that are ethnically diverse and economically divided, California's big-city mayors have their work cut out: rebuilding, reinvigorating, and redefining the future[15] (*see* California Voices).

Voters in nearly 150 cities directly elect the mayor. Many of these cities are medium-sized ones where the mayor's powers are even more circumscribed than those of large-city mayors. Mayors of medium-sized cities often serve as both mayors and council members. Although they preside over council meetings, in many ways they are equal to their council colleagues. They are expected to represent and lobby on behalf of their cities at various state and national meetings. Small city mayors are predominantly council members, often chosen by their colleagues after each election. This is usually the case in California's smaller cities. While they preside at council meetings, they rarely possess a mandate to lead in any meaningful sense. Their mayoral duties are largely ceremonial: cutting ribbons, presenting resolutions to deserving citizens, and speaking at various social functions. When affairs in their cities go well, they rarely get the credit but when community problems arise, they can easily become scapegoats.

City Managers

Professional administrators personify the ideal that "politics" and "administration" can be separated. City managers are directly responsible to the council. Although a growing number have long-term contracts, many city managers can be fired with little notice by a council majority. "Three votes on any Monday night and I am out of a job," said one. A primary responsibility of the manager is to build agendas for council meetings. Between meetings, managers

CALIFORNIA VOICES

Willie Brown on Being Mayor

When he was mayor of San Francisco, Willie Brown compared that role to his prior role as Speaker of the California Assembly in a *California Journal* interview. Here is an excerpt:

It's far easier being speaker of the Assembly than being mayor of this city, and I suspect almost any other city. But particularly this city. The level of political involvement by every person who takes a breath of life in this city is just incredible. I suspect that at birth, instead of receiving a Social Security number, newborns receive membership in a political organization or neighborhood club. And they are expected to begin to participate when they enter their first organized school activities. And it makes for a great, great challenge. Your skills and management and cajoling people into consensus is much more difficult and much more challenging in San Francisco than it ever was in the Legislature.

You also have a lot less flexibility budget-wise. You cannot pay people what they're worth, and you cannot reduce people who are not worth it, if they are al-

ready at a certain level. You cannot assign people to jobs that are comparable and consistent with their talent, nor can you remove people who, if they preceded you, are not talented.

When you see things that you ought to be able to change overnight and you cannot, it is as annoying as hell. One example: the municipal transportation system. You would want to . . . correct it overnight, but it takes three years to get one new rolling stock, one new bus. In the meantime, you have to live with this inadequate, old, antiquated, unreliable equipment as you go about trying to change the system. And that's very frustrating.

Question: Where in California might mayors find the job less challenging?

SOURCE: James Richardson, "His Willieness Speaks," *California Journal* 29 (August 1998): 31–32.

hire and supervise department heads, provide budget leadership, study the city's long range needs, and do whatever else the council wants. In recent years, they have had to devote growing chunks of time to finance. Some develop statewide reputations as fiscal wizards, able to generate revenue from unlikely sources. Contrary to Progressive thinking, good city managers *are* good politicians.

A city manager's ability to get along with a city council is paramount. Council factions often determine a city manager's success. A manager can be too entrepreneurial and dynamic (thereby competing with the mayor and council) or insufficiently dynamic (and therefore ineffective as city hall and community leader). In recent years, the biggest problem managers have faced is how to meet unrealistically high expectations. Council members and voters alike are tempted to think managers can balance budgets painlessly without mak-

ing political enemies whether revenues are up or down. As group diversity and conflict become commonplace in California cities, so does criticism of these career professionals.

Commissions

Although they are easy to ignore, local commissions and boards play important roles in California cities. Large cities have many of them while small cities may have only a few. Some commissions may actually operate harbors, airports, or public works enterprises. Others merely advise or make recommendations to elected policymakers. The most common are planning commissions that advise city councils on land use matters. They can exercise considerable power, as any developer can attest. Other boards provide advice on social services funding, libraries, the arts, and other matters. Service on these boards provides lessons in governing and occasionally that first step toward elective office.

CITIES AND COUNTIES: AN UNEASY RELATIONSHIP

Given the diversity of California's counties, generalizations that are applicable to all are few. But this can be said: For the most part, California cities are in better fiscal shape than California counties. The reasons are clear. *First*, California cities have fewer policy responsibilities mandated by the state such as welfare and public health. As a result, they are unburdened by staggering welfare costs, public health crises, and education tasks. *Second*, cities have more flexibility than counties. County boundaries are fixed, while cities can annex unincorporated land for future development. Furthermore, new cities can form, capturing revenue generated from suburban population growth. For instance, by the time Southern California's Moreno Valley incorporated, its population had swelled to 100,000. Cities can pick and choose what services to provide and at what levels. If they want to provide police protection or garbage collection without maintaining expensive bureaucracies, they can "contract out" for those services. *Third*, cities have more opportunities to raise revenue than counties. When Proposition 13 cut California property taxes, cities sought other revenue sources. Because one cent of the state sales tax is returned to where it was collected, cities began favoring revenue-rich commercial projects like shopping malls, auto dealerships, and "big box" retailers like Costco and WalMart—the *fiscalization of land use*. Although counties could also approve such developments, typical building sites tend to be within city boundaries.

Cities had still other options. Many created *redevelopment agencies* to improve "blighted" areas. The meaning of blight is ambiguous because most any swath of a city could be considered blighted according to California redevelopment law. Such agencies were able to capture the tax increment, the amount of new taxes attributable to new development. Resulting developments included office buildings, in-town malls, entertainment facilities, convention centers, and other mixed-use projects. Counties, too, could create such agencies but had much less urban blight to redevelop.

Revenue flexibility did not exempt cities from the pressures on urban California. The tax base of many cities has been reduced as manufacturing plants close or move elsewhere. Smog, traffic jams, overcrowding, and crime continued unabated across the state. Responding to these problems required a steady stream of new revenue. Cities that bowed to no-growth pressures found some revenue sources such as developer fees drying up. To make matters worse, occasional recessions reduce consumer spending and, in turn, sales tax revenue. In such lean years, California cities, like counties, must downsize, scale back, and trim both services and revenue projections.

Special Districts

They have been called America's "forgotten fiefdoms." There are nearly 30,000 of them across the country; they outnumber cities. California claims about 3,400, not including 989 school districts. Four counties have over 200 of them; most counties have 50–200. They are special districts. Many of them were formed years ago to extend urban services to rural areas.

WHAT MAKES THEM SPECIAL?

While California's special districts together provide 50 different services, 85 percent of them provide only one service. Nearly 450 provide water; another 342 provide fire protection. Other services include community services, reclamation, sanitation, recreation, and even cemeteries (we consider school districts separately). Special districts do what general purpose local governments cannot or will not do. They can assess property taxes, issue bonds, and charge fees that are tied directly to the service provided. Not only do they spend vast sums on these services, they manage budget reserves of roughly $20 billion.

A San Joaquin irrigation district was California's first special district. Created in 1887, its purpose was to provide steady water supplies at predictable prices to area farmers. Since that time, special districts have multiplied in the Golden State. They became attractive to communities that desired a particular service and local control over its provision. Cities and counties rarely resisted, because these districts did not threaten existing political structures or boundaries; they simply added new, noncompeting layers of local government.

California special districts are either *dependent* or *independent*. Dependent ones are actually subdivisions of cities and counties. They commonly fund parking lots or street lighting through separate assessments, which, in effect, insulate a particular service from the larger annual budget battles faced by general purpose governments. City councils and county boards of supervisors provide policy direction. Counties also maintain more general service or maintenance districts in unincorporated communities. These districts sometimes give way to municipal incorporation efforts by residents wanting more home rule than these districts provide. California's 2,300 independent districts are separate legal entities with their own elected boards providing and financing particular services noted earlier.

Special districts epitomize the diversity of local government in California. Some are tiny slivers of government quietly providing a specialized service at modest cost to relatively few people. Others are gargantuan. The Southern California Rapid Transit District and the Metropolitan Water District of Southern California are two of the nation's largest. The latter's jurisdictional tentacles reach to the Eastern Slope of the Sierra Nevada—channeling precious runoff water to 17 million Californians in six counties. Acting as a giant water wholesaler, this district maintains water supplies, determines water rates, establishes mandatory conservation programs, and levies fines against noncomplying client agencies.

THE STEALTH GOVERNMENTS OF CALIFORNIA

The largest special districts are powerful indeed. But most are virtually invisible and in many ways unaccountable to average Californians. They are the *stealth governments* of California. Special districts are governed by elected boards whose members serve rather anonymously. Meetings are poorly attended and are rarely reported in the local media. One cemetery district manager could not recall someone from the public *ever* attending a meeting. Special district elections are often the misnomers of democracy. Challengers are rare and elections are sometimes canceled when no one steps forth. Voter turnout is typically low unless these elections are folded into California's primary or general elections. On occasion, lavish business trip spending makes news, but, in many respects, special districts operate outside the limelight, much like private businesses. No wonder many citizens express a combination of ignorance and apathy regarding these stealth governments.[16]

SPECIAL DISTRICT POLITICS AND PROBLEMS

California's special districts, like cities and counties, have been buffeted by fiscal pressures in recent decades. Those dependent on a portion of the local property tax saw that revenue source shrink after Proposition 13 passed. The creation of redevelopment agencies threatened to siphon off what little property tax was left in some areas. Districts relying on user fees faced fiscal pressure too. How high could rates increase without incurring voter wrath? This question has become increasingly troublesome for water districts during California's periodic droughts. To conserve increasingly scarce supplies, water districts institute mandatory rationing and conservation programs. A perverse irony results. As water use declines, so does fee revenue just when districts need *more* revenue, not less, to meet fixed expenses and develop new water supplies.

Political scientists view the plethora of special districts as organizationally messy—the height of governmental fragmentation. Why should the Bay area have two dozen separate transportation agencies? Why should a patchwork of neighboring water agencies trip over each other providing a commonly scarce resource? Why shouldn't single-purpose agencies have to weigh competing priorities like cities and counties do? Defenders of special districts disagree. To them, special districts foster home rule by providing particular services tailored to particular locales—customized government if you will. Furthermore, most special districts are quite efficient. As one district executive director put it, "We're lean, we're mean, and we do a better job than cities or counties could."[17]

California's special districts are poised to defend the status quo and fight for their share of both political clout and adequate revenue. In Sacramento, they are represented by the California Special Districts Association and numerous specialized groups including the California Association of Sanitation Agencies and the Association of California Water Agencies. Most of California's special districts have successfully resisted elimination, consolidation, or other reforms. A former state senator, Marian Bergeson, has called them "the closest thing to immortality you can get."[18]

School Districts

California's 989 school districts are different enough from other special districts to warrant separate consideration. As a group they, too, exemplify both diversity and hyperpluralism— our continuing themes. They range in size from the mammoth Los Angeles Unified School District with about 700,000 students to several hundred districts composed of single schools. As a group, these districts educate the state's children and youth, a growing segment of the state's population. Increasingly, they serve an ethnic rainbow in California— groups of people from the four corners of the Earth.

Organizationally, school districts reflect the assumption that politics and education can and should be separate. With the exception of Los Angeles (which has a seven-member board), California's local school boards consist of five members. All run on nonpartisan ballots; some are elected at large while others are elected by district. Like other units of government, district-based boards must reapportion every ten years, and have been under pressure to better reflect California's minority groups. Boards typically meet several times a month. Many members receive only minimal fringe benefits. In contrast, the Los Angeles Board members receive $24,000 per year, actually a modest sum given their workload. These boards were once common stepping stones to higher office, especially for women. But, of the ten former K-12 school board members in the 2005–2006 legislature, only four were women.

Professionally trained superintendents head educational staffs—teachers, support personnel, and other administrators. Usually possessing doctorates in education, superintendents prepare board agendas, system-wide budgets, and various policy proposals. While small districts may be "lean and mean," large districts employ huge numbers of administrators, often a bone of contention among lesser paid teachers. Board members and administrators are destined to conflict. Elected board members represent accountability in a representative democracy. They bring to meetings the "common sense" views of parents, taxpayers, and neighbors. By contrast, professional educators bring expertise including educational practices, trends, and jargon that may be foreign to their boards.

Unlike most other special districts, school districts operate under very close scrutiny—by parents, various interest groups, and the state government on which they heavily depend. The state's influence is pervasive. *First*, about 60 percent of school funding comes from state aid (based on ADA—average daily attendance figures). *Second*, California's massive Education Code dictates in surprising detail what districts can and cannot do. *Third*, the state Department of Education also impacts local districts by administering statewide testing of various grade levels in various subjects, influencing curricula, approving textbook lists, and inspecting district performance. The federal government once played a relatively modest role by funding or subsidizing certain programs (such as school lunches) and enforcing various civil rights laws. Now the U.S. Department of Education oversees the No Child Left Behind Act of 2001, a law that holds the states and local school districts accountable to achieve certain educational standards. While requiring highened performance and accountability, the federal portion of the state's education budget was only 13 percent in 2005–2006.

Pressures on California school districts will mount in the future, as we discuss more fully in Chapter 13. Enrollment growth shows no signs of slowing. Education policy will continue to be a battleground involving ethnic, religious, and ideological groups—each demanding their priorities be reflected in the curriculum and in education policy generally. At one level, they must cope with a host of social phenomena such as divorce, juvenile delinquency, drug abuse, and many inattentive parents. At another level, they are supposed to respond to a growing school-age population, parent demands for greater choice, state expectations for reform, ethnic diversity, and the usual assortment of local conflict and controversy.

Regional Governments

The growth that has impacted California's schools has impacted most of its local governments. According to *California Journal*'s Craig Hamley and A.G. Block, "Once quaint and peaceful, many Northern California cities now resemble the mess of smog, water shortages, gridlocked freeways, and overpriced housing that has been the status quo for much of Southern California for years. Resolution of the problem will involve complex negotiations, and some recognition by everyone involved that the old way of parceling out authority no longer solves problems."[19] Thinking in regional terms would be a start, and regional governments already exist in California for that purpose. Californians rarely thirst for regional government. The proliferation of local governments in a region has allowed greater local identity, access to policymakers, opportunity for influence, and insulation from problems faced by nearby jurisdictions. Supporters of regional government point to two models in California: coordination and regulation.

REGIONAL COORDINATION

The coordination model is best exemplified by the state's 22 *councils of governments* (COGs). COGs are like small United Nations, groups of autonomous counties and cities in a region coming together to deal with issues of common significance. The federal government designates them as *metropolitan planning organizations (MPOs)* and requires them to draw up plans for transportation, growth management, hazardous waste management, and air quality. But they usually lack the legal authority to actually implement their plans. COGs also

CARTOON 10.1   LA Unified school district
Eric G. Lewis

provide a forum for the member jurisdictions to communicate with each other. In the past, California COGs received large federal subsidies but in recent years have had to depend on member dues, transportation planning funds, and consulting fees usually paid by member agencies. In addition to the state's required regional councils are 13 regional commissions that focus exclusively on transportation planning and policy.

Of the nation's nearly 700 COGs, SCAG (the Southern California Association of Governments) is the largest—its members include six counties and 127 cities. ABAG (the Association of Bay Area Governments) does planning for a nine-county, 100-city region. Numerous other COGs cover only one county (such as Kern, Humboldt, Fresno, Merced, San Diego, Sacramento, and Santa Barbara). Not only do

COGs lack significant legislative authority, their voting members (county supervisors and city council members) typically and understandably put local interests first. They resist giving a regional agency the power to dictate policy to member local governments. Yet, to the extent knowledge is power, the COGs' ability to issue reports and studies often frames local policy debates. For example, SCAG's conclusion that an Orange County airbase should become a sizeable regional airport stirred local sentiment on all sides of the issue.

REGIONAL REGULATION

Regional agencies employing a regulation model have the power both to write and to enforce various rules and regulations, usually in the field of environmental pollution. For example,

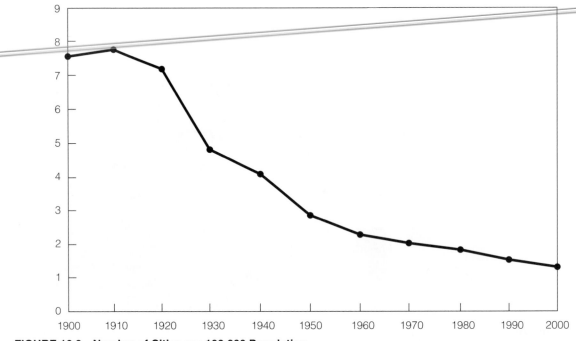

FIGURE 10.3 Number of Cities per 100,000 Population

The graph suggests that California has accommodated population growth by expanding existing cities rather than by creating new ones.

Question: Why do many Californians seemingly prefer to live in larger cities?

Paul G. Lewis, *Deep Roots: Local Government. Structure in California* (San Francisco: Public Policy Institute of California, 1998). p. 23; updated by author.

the San Francisco Bay Conservation and Development Commission can veto any waterfront construction that threatens the bay itself. The Tahoe Regional Planning Agency has similar powers relative to Lake Tahoe. Of the state's 20 air quality districts, the South Coast Air Quality Management District (SCAQMD) is one of the more controversial. As other districts do, the SCAQMD studies problems, writes plans, and then issues rules. Its rules either ban or regulate myriad pollutants such as gasoline components and use, solvents, open burning, animal matter, asphalt, odor nuisances, and "fugitive dust." These region-wide regulatory efforts usually involve complex

trade-offs among various agendas, mandates, and organized interests.[20]

Regional government in California seems to be at a crossroads. Two contrary political forces explain the dilemma. On the one hand, some government officials and business leaders would like to strengthen or require regional approaches to admittedly regional problems. On the other hand, an opposite movement has been growing to empower grassroots groups and strengthen home rule *below* the local government level. NIMBY (not in my back yard) and environmental groups have flourished by opposing land use projects of both local and regional significance. These contrary goals lock horns profoundly in an increasingly diverse and hyperpluralist state.

Conclusion: Diverse Communities, Diverse Governments

California's local governments mirror the profound diversity of the state. Cities and counties come in all shapes and sizes. Special districts, the stealth governments of California, provide single services controlled by unpublicized boards. School districts educate children and youth through high school while the state's 109 community college districts provide similar services to some high schoolers, college students, and adults. Regional governments face the permanent challenge of coordinating other local governments and educating them to think regionally. Private groups, such as homeowners associations, duplicate public governments but avoid (or think they do) the worst social, political, and economic problems at the local level.

Local government fragmentation mirrors a diverse state, but how problematic is fragmentation itself? Experts are not sure. Some governing problems are a function of size; some

jurisdictions are too large or too small. The Los Angeles School District may be too large to serve well its school-aged population. In recent years, reformers have discussed breaking up this behemoth into smaller, more manageable districts—an ideal people seem to support.[21] Other jurisdictions, especially some counties, are so small they cannot afford to provide even basic state-required services.

Is California overly fragmented? The layering of local governments across California's political landscape does seem to create voter confusion and the need for constant coordination. The state's regional governments help, but only help, in addressing local fragmentation. Nonetheless, local government fragmentation seems to be less of a problem in California than elsewhere. According to one study, California has fewer cities, counties, and special districts per capita than the national average. School districts have decreased in number as have the number of cities per 100,000 population (Figure 10.3). The result has been jurisdictional stability in a sea of fiscal, political, and demographic change.[22] A state-level Commission on Local Governance for the 21st Century suggested numerous reforms to address local government fragmentation and accountability issues in California but few have been implemented.

KEY TERMS

privatism   (p. 200)

Dillon's Rule   (p. 200)

home rule   (p. 200)

general law and charter counties
   and cities   (pp. 202–203, 206)

chief administrative officers   (p. 203)

mandates   (p. 205)

incorporation   (p. 205)

local agency formation commissions   (p. 206)

phantom cities   (p. 207)

urban villages, edge cities   (p. 207)

homeowners associations   (p. 207)

ordinances   (p. 209)

fiscalization of land use   (p. 211)

redevelopment agencies   (p. 211)

independent and dependent special
   districts   (p. 212)

stealth governments   (p. 212)

councils of governments   (pp. 214–215)

REVIEW QUESTIONS

1. What are the purposes of and limits to government at the community level?
2. Survey the historical forces that shaped California counties.
3. Why are California counties in trouble?
4. If you wanted your community to become a city, what would you need to do?
5. Describe and illustrate "phantom cities" from the text and your own observations.
6. What do special districts do, and why are they the stealth governments of California? Which ones exist in your home county and could any of them be combined?
7. Describe the two major approaches to regional governance in California.
8. How is local governance in California impacted by diversity and hyperpluralism?

WEB ACTIVITIES

California State Association of Counties (www.csac.counties.org)
Information here includes the counties' lobbying activity, issues of interest to counties, county profiles, and links to 45 specific county Websites.

League of California Cities (www.cacities.org)
The LCC site features legislative bulletins, association news, and links to over 300 city home pages. Look up yours.

INFOTRAC® COLLEGE EDITION ARTICLES

For additional reading, go to InfoTrac® College Edition, your online research library, at http://www.infotrac.thomsonlearning.com

Divorce L.A. Style

Doing It His Way by the Bay

Room to Grow in California's Valleys

NOTES

1. Andrew Murr, "Divorce, L.A. Style': The San Fernando Valley Wants to Secede from Los Angeles. Can This Marriage Be Saved?" *Newsweek* (May 13, 2002): 38.
2. Quoted in Jim Newton, "Mayor Attacks Secession, Urges School Reform," *Los Angeles Times*, April 8, 1999.
3. John Horton, *The Politics of Diversity: Immigration, Resistance, and Change in Monterey Park, California* (Philadelphia: Temple University Press, 1995).
4. Quoted in *City of Clinton v. Cedar Rapids and Missouri River Railroad Co.*, 24 Iowa 455, 475 (1868).
5. Eugene C. Lee, *The Politics of Nonpartisanship: A Study of California City Elections* (Berkeley, Ca.: University of California Press, 1960), 173.
6. See Mark Baldassare, *When Government Fails: The Orange County Bankruptcy* (Berkeley: University of California Press and Public Policy Institute of California, 1998).
7. Lord Bryce, *The American Commonwealth* (London: Macmillan and Co., 1891), 586.
8. Quoted in Noel Brinkerhoff, "The Worst of Times," *California Journal* 28 (September 1997), 18.
9. Legislative Analyst's Office, *California Counties: A Look at Program Performance* (Sacramento: Legislative Analyst's Office, 1998).
10. See Robert Reinbaum, "Climate Right for Creating New Cities," *California Journal,* 18 (October, 1987), 497–499.
11. Samuel E. Wood and Alfred E. Heller, *The Phantom Cities of California* (Sacramento: California Tomorrow, 1963), 43.
12. For a thorough analysis of this phenomenon, see Rob Kling, Spencer Olin, and Mark Poster, eds. *Postsuburban California: The Transformation of Orange County Since World War II* (Berkeley: University of California Press, 1991).
13. Tracy M. Gordon, *Planned Developments in California: Private Communities and Public Life* (San Francisco: Public Policy Institute of California, 2004).
14. Edward Banfield and James Q. Wilson, *City Politics* (Cambridge, MA: Harvard University Press, 1963), 80.
15. Kathleen Les, "Big City Mayors," *California Journal* 32 (April 2001), 21.

16. See Little Hoover Commission, *Special Districts: Relics of the Past or Resources for the Future?* (Sacramento: Little Hoover Commission, 2000). (www.lhc.ca.gov/).

17. Ibid.

18. Quoted in Kevin Johnson, "America's Forgotten Fiefdoms," *Los Angeles Times,* May 26, 1993.

19. Graig Hamley and A.G. Block, "Regional Government: Everyone Wants to Land on Boardwalk," 21 *California Journal* (November 1990), 534.

20. See Wyn Grant, *Autos, Smog, and Pollution Control: The Politics of Air Quality Management in California* (Aldershot, UK, and Brookfield, VT: Edward Elgar, 1995).

21. Louis Sahagun, "Few Hold Positive View of L.A. School Board," *Los Angeles Times,* April 4, 1999.

22. Paul G. Lewis, *Deep Roots: Local Government Structure in California* (San Francisco: Public Policy Institute of California, 1998).

PART FOUR

Public Policy in California

Politics, n. A strife of interests masquerading as a contest of principles.
—Ambrose Bierce, *The Devil's Dictionary,* 1906

lthough definitions abound, public policy is essentially what governments choose to do or not do. The result of Bierce's "strife of interests" is a host of laws, programs, pronouncements, and other activities we call public policy. Part 4 describes public policy in the Golden State. To avoid a disjointed discussion of dozens of major policies in California, I have grouped them into three categories: budgeting policies, policies stemming from growth, and policies stemming from the state's diversity.

Chapter 11, "Budget Policy: The Cost of Diversity," surveys the premier policy statement of any government—its budget. A budget is a projection of what a government will spend and what revenue it will raise in order to do so. The spending categories are a government's priorities. At the state level, California's annual budget is a reflection of its economy to be sure, but more important, it reflects what its policymakers regard as truly important. Surprisingly few policies consume surprisingly large chunks

of the state budget. At the local level, budgets reflect local economies and local priorities, but they are also tempered by state and federal spending decisions. At both the state and local level, budgets represent group conflict in an increasingly diverse state.

Chapter 12, "Policies Stemming from Growth," reviews the persistent population growth that has characterized the state's political development. Some policies, such as the provision of water and transportation infrastructure, actually helped make California an attractive place to migrate to. These policies fostered and accommodated growth. Other policies have been in response to that growth, in particular, housing and a variety of environmental policies. Many local governments have attempted to control growth per se but with mixed results. Recent decades have been characterized by growing political conflict over what to do about population growth and its impacts. No matter what California policymakers choose to do, it seems they will be reacting to continued population growth rather than controlling it.

Chapter 13, "Policies Stemming from Diversity," addresses a variety of issues and policies rooted in the political and cultural diversity of the state. Many policies set group against group and always have. But other policies, once majoritarian in nature, seem to be breaking down into group struggles as well. The abortion debate in California not only parallels the national debate but predates it, pitting different value systems against each other. Education policy in California is fueled by population growth, ethnic diversity, social change, and competition for scarce public resources. These pressures have been felt in the state's colleges and universities as well. California's social programs, including welfare and health programs, represent a hodgepodge of particular policies and a loose partnership between the federal government and the state. Population growth heightens demand for these services but also heightens conflict between two perceived groups: the state's taxpayers and tax spenders. Lastly, immigration policy, although a federal responsibility, has had an impact on California in some profound ways. The result in the 1990s has been a reexamination of the state's generosity toward newcomers, especially those from Mexico.

CHAPTER 11

Budget Policy: The Cost of Diversity

In Brief

One of government's most important activities is to raise and spend money. The state of California and its local governments, like governments elsewhere, develop budgets to do so. These are government's premier policy statements, highly political documents that essentially represent contracts between policymakers and various sectors of society. As with the nation, the basis and context of California budgeting is the state's economy. The Golden State's economy historically has been diverse and continues to be. But economic upturns and downturns can significantly impact the dynamics of the budget process.

The state budget process in California is characterized by historic spending habits, significant input by various executive branch bureaucracies, and control by the governor and legislative leaders. At the local level, executive leadership and outside forces well beyond local control significantly impact budgeting.

California public budgets consist of a wide diversity of revenue. Major state revenues include the personal income tax, the sales tax, corporate taxes, excise taxes, the state lottery, and borrowing. Local revenues include the property tax, aid from other levels of government, miscellaneous taxes and fees, plus borrowing. Where does all this money go? The state spends most of it on the Big Three: education, health and welfare, and corrections. California's counties spend most of their revenue on public assistance and public safety activities. Cities spend most of theirs on public safety (police and fire), utilities, community development, and transportation activities.

In recent years, budgets have been characterized by unpredictable revenues on the one hand and by growing demands for government spending on the other. Stormy budget debates in recent years seem to illustrate an increasingly diverse state whose policymakers can no longer achieve consensus on its arguably most important public policy.

Introduction: Budgeting as Public Policy

"Budget Cuts Deeply, Spares Few." (1992)

"Budget Big on Schools, Jails, Kids." (1998)

"Future Uncertain for Students Seeking Aid." (2005)

These actual newspaper headlines epitomize budgeting in California. Because of its dependence on the condition of the economy, the budget process has a yo-yo quality to it (see Figure 11.1). In economic bad times, there is pessimistic debate over service cuts, denied pay increases, postponed projects, and possible tax increases. In economic good times, there is rosy talk of service expansion, restored funding, pay increases, new programs, and possible tax cuts. But even in the good years, budgeting itself is not easy. The process is cumbersome, party politics infuses deliberations, interest groups clash, and numerous external constraints limit budget options. In Chapter 11 we discuss how and why budgeting in California works the way it does. In the end, we find that *budgeting in California increasingly reflects the state's hyperpluralistic character as increasingly diverse groups make claims on the public purse.* How policymakers respond to those demands is characterized by conflicting interest group goals, the "tribalization" of interest group relations, and a budget process often colored or even paralyzed by the competing demands placed on it.

Before proceeding to budgeting in the Golden State, we need to explain four basic characteristics of public budgets in American politics.

1. Any *budget is simply a plan that specifies what monies will be spent (expenditures) and how those monies will be obtained (revenues).* According to political scientist Aaron Wildavsky, "Budgeting is concerned with translating financial resources into human resources. A budget, therefore, may also be characterized as a series of goals with price tags attached. Since funds are limited and have to be divided in one way or another, the budget becomes a mechanism for making choices among alternative expenditures."[1]

2. As Wildavsky implies, *a government's budget is its premier public policy statement. Public policy* is whatever government chooses to do or not do. Particular policies are laws, programs, pronouncements, and other forms of public decisions. In a sense, "nondecisions" (what governments choose not to do) are also forms of public policy. Where a government chooses to spend its revenue is truly the ultimate statement of its priorities. In a representative democracy, these priorities represent what society deems important and unimportant. Where government obtains its money also represents the allocation of political power—who pays,

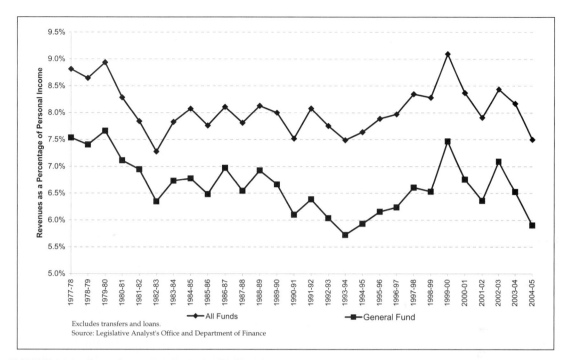

FIGURE 11.1   State Spending Reflects California's Economy

As the economy rises and falls, so does state spending, no matter who is in power.

Question: In what ways, if any, can state policymakers encourage a steady economy in California?

Source: Legislative Analyst's Office and California Department of Finance. Reprinted from California Budget Project (www.obp.org).

who benefits, who wins, and who loses where money is concerned.

3. *Budgeting is profoundly political.* The budget process is where the sentences and paragraphs of this premier policy statement are torn apart, analyzed, and taped back together. In this regard, the budget shapes government around various spending and taxing decisions, consuming policymakers' attention spans, and often dictating what in fact can and cannot be done. Politically speaking, it reflects the state itself. California's state budget, for instance, exemplifies an assortment of phenomena: past budget decisions by policymakers and voters alike, population growth, interest group conflict, and the health of the state's economy.

4. *Budgeting is, in essence, a contract.* Contracts represent agreements and commitments be-

tween two or more parties. Budgets serve as short-term political contracts between various participants in the political process as well as between the voters and their government. At a deeper level, a budget represents a covenant or contract between a society's present and its future. For example, arguments over education spending, low-cost higher education, and new highways essentially are arguments over how best to invest in the state's future.

Where Budgeting Begins: The Economy

To best understand the politics of budgeting in California, we need first to ask, Where does the revenue come from? In short, the basic source of public revenue is the economy. When Americans think of "the economy," they tend to think in national terms; yet there are 50 interdependent state economies making up the whole. The health or vitality of California's economy is directly related to the revenues available both to the state government and to the state's local governments.

ECONOMIC DIVERSITY

Historically, California's diverse and resilient economy has been one of its strengths, heralding the state as a place of opportunity for all comers. As we noted in Chapter 1, modern California possesses a balanced economy consisting of numerous sectors: service occupations, retail, agriculture, tourism, manufacturing, and a plethora of "high-tech" activities such as computers, communications, and financial services. California's modern, $1.5 trillion economy is both industrial and post-industrial—noted for innovation, sophistication, new ideas, new products, and the new jobs that follow. Over the years, California's economy has been stimulated by discoveries of gold and oil, agricultural mass production, automobile manufacturing, defense spending, the aerospace industry, and in recent decades, the computer revolution. Also, international investment and foreign trade have contributed to making California's the sixth largest economy in the world.[2]

TODAY'S CHALLENGE: A TWO-TIER ECONOMY

Two aspects of California's economy ultimately affect the budget process. *First, California's bad times and good times seem to be either very bad or very good.* During California's early 1990s recession, California's unemployment rate was twice that of the nation's. Several hundred thousand jobs disappeared or exited the state. Given the number of military installations and defense contractors in California, when the federal government cut defense and aerospace funding, it further wounded California's economic base. By the late 1990s, California's economy was booming—as was state budget revenue—but that was followed by another economic downturn in 2001 and 2002. Even prior to the terrorist attacks of September 11, 2001 state revenues plummeted due to depressed foreign trade, rising unemployment, and steep declines in the U.S. stock market. Economic volatility leads to budget volatility as policymakers agonize over ways to cut spending or raise revenue. Budget volatility also stems from the fact that, compared to other states, California has increasingly depended on the unstable income tax and less so on the more stable property tax.

Second, the economic good times are not equally good for all Californians. As we noted in Chapter 1, there is in fact increasing socioeconomic fragmentation; income inequality is on the rise in California. In a technology-driven economy, many Californians are prospering beyond their wildest dreams, while others (immigrants, the poor, the unskilled, and the uneducated) have fallen behind. The reasons are clear. Compared to whites, California's Hispanic and African American workers earn lower wages due to lower levels of education and the poorer paying jobs that result.[3] In other words, a rising tide does not necessarily lift all boats. As you will see, California's *two-tier economy* has profound implications for budget making. Those who fall behind increasingly rely upon tax-funded welfare assistance, medical care, and housing.

CALIFORNIA'S LOCAL ECONOMIES

In Chapter 10, we noted the rich diversity of communities and local governments in California. There is also a rich diversity of local economies, which constitute the whole we call "the California economy." While some economic trends affect all communities in the state, these local economies vary enough to create their own opportunities and challenges for state and local policymakers. Some communities depend largely on only a few sources of income—tourism, agriculture, a dominant regional shopping mall, or even a single prison. Others remain militarily dependent; for better or worse, their destiny is tied to federal defense spending. Logging communities in Northern California depend on the vagaries of the construction industry. Silicon Valley communities are home to both successful technology firms and failed "dot-com" Internet firms. Large cities are so diverse, troubles in one economic sector are largely compensated for by growth in other sectors. Consider Los Angeles. Today, the city's economic growth is fueled by small, minority-owned manufacturing concerns. Collectively, these companies have made the Los Angeles region the nation's second largest manufacturing center. According to political scientist Fernando Guerra, "The ability of the [Los Angeles] economy to remake itself is amazing."[4] Local economies that are balanced and growing provide both needed jobs and needed revenue for local governments.

The Budget Process

Whatever the state of the economy, California policymakers must agree to budgets every year. *The budget process is the institutional framework within which budget decisions are made.* We will discuss some basic features of the process in California, the various constraints on it, as well as budgeting at the local level.

HOW CALIFORNIA BUDGETING WORKS

Although California's budget process is quite complicated, three features of it deserve special attention. It is incremental throughout, highly bureaucratic in the planning stages, and leadership-dominated in the later stages.

The Role of Incrementalism

California's budget process is *incremental*. In other words, specific agencies request increased funding for one *fiscal year* (July 1 to June 30)

based on whatever was allocated the previous fiscal year. To look ahead, agencies look back. In the "fat" years, when revenues continually grow, incrementalism makes budgeting easy. There is little incentive to ask whether an agency, service, or program is still needed. From the early 1950s to the present, the state budget grew steadily from $1 billion to nearly $110 billion—a reflection of California's economic and population growth. In the "lean" years, when revenue growth declines, incrementalism no longer works, and the potential for political conflict and gridlock increases dramatically. When revenues do not match desired expenditures, agencies accustomed to incremental growth can face less money than in the past. At minimum, they must settle for status-quo budgets.

The Role of the Executive

The governor and the bureaucracy dominate the planning stage, which takes about 18 months to complete. For example, the formal process to build the 2005–2006 budget (July 2005 to June 30, 2006) began early in 2004, as agency budget planners developed spending estimates. Negotiations between the governor's office, agency staff, department heads, and the Department of Finance (DOF) take nearly a year. According to political scientist Richard Krolack, this is when DOF "earns its reputation as the most powerful department in state service."[5] The end product is a budget the governor submits to the legislature by January 10, 2005. Incrementalism dominates the bureaucratic process. Projecting revenue is largely a guessing game as DOF officials must estimate future growth based on current trends, such as job growth and economic productivity. They may be on target; maybe not. At this stage of the process, career administrators provide continuity, given the comings and goings of their appointed bosses and elected officials, and form alliances among California's many interest groups. Masters of incrementalism, they can provide the most plausible reasons for retaining or increasing any agency's funding base.

The Role of Leadership

A third feature of California budgeting is that the external part of the process is leadership-dominated. When the governor submits the "budget" to the legislature, lawmakers actually receive several documents: The *Governor's Budget Summary* (a document highlighting the governor's own priorities); the actual *Governor's Budget* (a large phone book-sized document); a *Salaries and Wages Supplement*; and the budget bill itself (listing each expenditure line-by-line). The process is leadership-dominated in that these bills are submitted only to the two fiscal committees—the Assembly Budget Committee and the Senate Budget and Fiscal Review Committee. Standing policy committees (i.e. Education) are not directly involved. The two fiscal committees divide into subcommittees (such as Education and Health and Welfare) to study in depth portions of the overall budget. The Legislative Analyst's Office issues two reports: a comprehensive *Analysis of the Budget Bill* and a briefer *Perspectives and Issues* report. These reports sometimes challenge the governor's own budget assumptions (for example, what to expect in state revenues or federal aid). During legislative consideration, the governor proposes revisions, the most notable being the *May Revision*. Included may be new spending priorities and, more important, updated revenue estimates. Depending on the economy, these revenue updates may represent bad news (revenues even less than anticipated) or good news (revenues greater than original estimates). In 2002, the shortfall was $11 billion *more* than four months earlier; in 2005, revenue was $4 billion more than anticipated. Good news or bad, the May Revision highly impacts budget deliberations.

Although budget disagreements occur annually, some budget years move along more smoothly than others. In some years, the full fiscal committees vote on their respective budget bills and send them on to the floors of each house well before state-imposed deadlines. In the past, garnering the required two-thirds vote in each house (27 in the Senate and 53 in the Assembly) has taken as little as an hour. Now it takes months. A conference committee hammers out differences, allowing time for floor votes before the constitutional deadline of June 15. The governor is supposed to sign the budget before July 1, the first day of the new fiscal year. Once the Budget Act is passed, *trailer bills* follow. These 16 bills implement the budget by specifying exact taxes, fee increases, and spending formulas in broad policy areas such as education or transportation.

In the event this process breaks down, the *Big Five* (the governor, Assembly speaker, Senate president pro tem, and minority leaders in both houses) meet behind closed doors to hammer out compromises necessary to achieve the required two-thirds vote in each house. This group is designed to force budget decisions when protracted stalemates seem likely. In 2004 it intervened when deliberations at the committee level produced gridlock.

Although the state's budget process is dominated by a relatively small number of legislators, recent budget deadlocks can be traced to larger forces. As we noted in Chapter 7, newer legislators (Republicans and Democrats) have been more partisan and often more determined to have a budget voice on the floor. With majorities numbering less than two-thirds, achieving that percentage of votes is increasingly difficult. Even the Big Five have been ineffective at producing annual budgets on time. One 1990s budget impasse lasted so long (a record 65 days after the July 1 deadline) that the state began paying its bills in IOUs (registered warrants). Missed budget deadlines are common but not particularly disruptive to average Californians.

The final, approved budget consists of three types of funds. The general fund is the largest and finances the bulk of ongoing state programs. Special funds encompass revenues for which spending is restricted by law such as transportation and the state's new Tobacco Settlement Fund (California's share of tobacco-related litigation). Bond funds consist of bond revenues used for capital outlays and other projects. Together, these funds support nearly 170 different departments and agencies as well as local governments and individual Californians.

CONSTRAINTS ON THE PROCESS

In 1987, the *Economist*, a British periodical, carried an article entitled "The State That Tied Its Own Hands,"[6] referring to the budget constraints faced by California policymakers. Little has changed over the years. Here, we describe six of those constraints.

The Two-Thirds Problem

California's Constitution requires a two-thirds vote of the entire legislature to pass the whole budget. Only three other states impose this *two-thirds requirement.* As we have noted, this extraordinary majority has been difficult to achieve in recent years because of partisan friction, less than two-thirds majorities, and lack of shared budget priorities. These trends are amplified in revenue-lean years. Several reform groups suggest that the state budget be enacted by simple majorities of both houses (21 in the Senate and 41 in the Assembly).[7] The voters seem to think otherwise. They rejected a 2004 proposal to reduce the two-thirds requirement to 55 percent.

The Annual Budget Myth

The California Constitution also requires the governor to submit a budget each year, but there is nothing sacred about annual budgets. Long-term economic, social, and political trends (all of which affect budgeting) ignore arbitrary calendars. Economic and business cycles can last for many years. An approved budget on any July 1 is merely a primitive and temporary snapshot of the state's economy, its tax policy, and its expenditure choices. One-year budgets encourage California policymakers to "cook the books" through arcane budget maneuvers, lending the appearance of a balanced budget. The California Constitution Revision Commission recommended that a two-year budget be adopted (four years in the case of capital outlays).[8] Some California cities and several other states already do so.

Cruise Control Spending

One constraint, which we call *cruise control spending*, has to do with the relatively automatic nature of many spending decisions. For example, large portions of the budget are spent on *entitlements*—those payments to individuals who meet eligibility requirements established by law. CalWORKs (California's major welfare program) and Medi-Cal (California's version of federal Medicaid for the poor) are entitlement programs. As caseloads grow, so does spending. Other increases are based on the growth of certain populations (school-aged children and prisoners). Cruise control spending is also evident in cost of living adjustments—COLAs. This spending technique gives eligible groups *automatic upward adjustments* in the funding they already receive, such as welfare payments or state employee pension increases. Yearly adjustments by policymakers easily become yearly expectations by recipients. Due to all these "uncontrollables," the legislature and the governor have full discretion over only a small portion of the state budget.

Narrow Spending

Another constraint is the tendency to restrict spending by creating narrow categories of funded activity, called *categorical spending*. In education alone, there are well over 100 separate funding pots from special education to addressing the needs of poor students to training algebra teachers. Each category alone has merit and a constituency willing to defend it from cuts or elimination. As one legislator put it, "Over time, I think we went crazy. Every special interest that had a little idea decided to categorize."[9] These programs persist despite the fact that they tend to perpetuate obsolete programs, foster spending disparities, and resist fiscal accountability.

Third Rail Issues

"Touch it, you die!" *Third rail issues* refer to politically volatile issues that policymakers avoid, fearing voter wrath. Until recently, the federal Social Security and Medicare programs have illustrated this phenomenon. In California, Proposition 13 has been a third rail issue. Because it has become such an anti-tax icon, California lawmakers usually hesitate to make even needed reforms. One notable exception was the 2000 passage of Proposition 38, an initiative backed by then State Senator Jack O'Connell. It lowered the threshold for voter approval of local bonds from two-thirds to 55 percent, making it easier to build local schools.

Ballot-Box Budgeting

The initiative process is also an important sacred cow in California. It has given voters greater control over controversial issues and, to the consternation of many Sacramento policymakers, control over budgeting as well. This phenomenon, called ballot-box budgeting, has impacted the budget process in three ways. *First,* some initiatives have fundamentally restructured state and local relationships. For example, Proposition 13 cut property taxes so severely that the state government "bailed out" cities, counties, special districts, and schools with surplus revenues. Greater aid meant greater control, which local governments feel even today. As we noted in Chapter 10, school districts are now heavily dependent on state support.

Second, some initiatives and propositions have furthered the practice of *earmarking* (restricting certain revenues to certain purposes). For example, in 2002, voters approved Proposition 42, a constitutional amendment that required all gasoline sales tax revenues be spent on mass transit, roads, and highways. On occasion, voters will even approve tax increases if they are connected to (or earmarked for) perceived needs or desired benefits. For instance, Proposition 10 (1998) increased cigarette taxes to fund early childhood development programs. When earmarked revenues (fees to hunt and fish) are embedded in the State Constitution, changing them is unlikely. Over 20 percent of California's general fund is earmarked. While policymakers criticize this practice, earmarking will likely continue. It encourages voters to fund programs they regard as beneficial and provides a stable revenue stream for many programs requiring such stability (such as long-term highway and mass transit investments).[10]

Third, some initiatives effectively restructure the budget process by reordering spending priorities. In effect, voters set parameters within which elected budgetmakers must work. For instance, Proposition 98 (1988) has had the most profound impact on overall state spending priorities. This constitutional amendment requires that no less than 40 percent of the state general fund be spent on school districts and community colleges. It also requires that if the legislature pumps more than that into education, the new total becomes a new guaranteed funding base. All state education (K-14) spending now revolves around these requirements, unless they are suspended due to fiscal emergency. This protects education when revenue lags but also can be perceived as a spending maximum when more than 40 percent is needed.

Fourth, voters affect budgeting by readily approving bond measures that fund singularly worthy projects but encumber the state with cumulative long-term debt obligations. Elected officials themselves recommend borrowing as Arnold Schwarzenegger did with Propositions

CARTOON 11.1   California in a corner

Question: If you were the governor, what would you recommend to offset the limitations imposed by ballot box budgeting?

Source: 1993 Paul Duginski.

57 and 58 in March 2004. The revenues from those voter-approved bonds were to help fill short-term revenue shortfalls while policymakers pursued more permanent budget solutions. Most bonds are single purpose in nature. For example, in the fall of 2004 voters approved Proposition 71, which authorized the issuance of $6 billion in general obligation bonds to pioneer stem cell research.

The result of all these constraints has been what one editorialist called a "fiscal pretzel." Policymakers find themselves negotiating merely at the margins of $100–plus billion budgets. Although anti-tax crusaders Howard Jarvis and Paul Gann are gone, the initiative process gives voters awesome powers to make complex taxation and spending decisions. They also tend to paint policymakers into a corner in terms of budget flexibility (see Cartoon 11.1)

LOCAL BUDGET PROCESSES

Given the diversity of local governments in California, we can make only broad generalizations about how they raise and spend money. *First*, as we noted, local revenues depend on a host of factors including the nature of the local economy. The more diverse the economy, the more stable will be a community's revenue base. *Second*, local budgeting parallels state budgeting in many respects. California local governments normally utilize the same July 1 to June 30 fiscal year timetable. With some exceptions they, too, use annual budgets. The responsibility for budget leadership is executive in nature. During a four-to-six-month process, budget responsibility falls to city managers, county administrative officers, special district managers, and school superintendents along with their fiscal staffs.

Third, the public is largely apathetic. Duly advertised budget hearings are often sparsely attended. Proposition 13 effectively eliminated the need for local governments to set property tax rates; as a result most voters lost interest in the subject. Exceptions include local interest groups such as chambers of commerce, taxpayer groups, or recipients of local grants. *Fourth,* the local budget process is at the end of a "fiscal food chain." The federal and state governments respectively monopolize the income tax and the sales tax. What is left for California's local governments? The answer is the property tax, assorted "nickel-and-dime" taxes, fees, and aid from governments higher up the chain.

Given the dependence of local governments on the state, gridlock at the state level jeopardizes budget making at all levels. Because of parallel fiscal years, local governments build budgets only guessing as to what the state will do. Since the "locals" depend on state aid, their budgets are "held hostage" until the state budget is adopted. School districts are in a real bind. They must make mid-summer budget decisions using the previous year's attendance figures and estimates regarding next fall's enrollment, all the while closely watching the state budget process.

Types of Revenue

If a budget is the premier public policy statement, what can be said of the money raised to fund it? *Revenues are by-products of other policies and ultimately mirror society's values.* In this section, we describe major revenue sources used by California state and local governments. Each has its defenders and critics based on the following criteria.

Equity

Fairness or equity generally refers to citizen ability to pay a particular tax. Not all taxes are alike in this regard. A *regressive tax* is one where the effective tax rate falls as taxable income rises; it imposes a greater burden on lower than upper income groups. A flat sales tax disproportionately burdens the poor, who must spend a greater percentage of their incomes to pay it. A *progressive tax* rate increases according to one's ability to pay, such as an income tax with many rates pegged to income. California's overall tax system is both progressive and regressive; the income tax is progressive whereas sales and property taxes are regressive. In the end, tax equity depends on one's income level. While affluent Californians indeed contribute heavily to state and local treasuries, the poorest families pay out a greater portion of their income in taxes than do wealthy families. For example, the lowest 20 percent of California households pay 11.3 percent of their income in state and local taxes. The top 1 percent pay only 7.2 percent.[11] In recent years, the meaning of equity has come to include the "benefit principle" (those who receive benefits from government should pay for those benefits). State park campsite fees utilize the benefit principle.

Yield

Another criterion is yield, the amount of revenue collected given the effort required to collect it. From the government's perspective, the sales tax is the easiest to collect—retailers actually do it. The property tax is more cumbersome to collect, especially if people appeal their assessments. The state income tax is much more cumbersome to collect for both government and taxpayers. Parking ticket fines have been so hard to collect, California occasionally sponsors amnesty programs, allowing people to pay fines without late penalties.

Certainty

Will revenues be steady, regardless of economic or other conditions? Or are they uncertain and unpredictable? Consumption taxes, such as the sales tax, are considered elastic, and therefore unstable. During a recession, people tend to spend less and therefore pay less sales tax. In recent years, California's income tax revenues have become quite volatile, matching the gyrations of the stock market. On the other hand, the property tax is usually very stable and dependable.

Accountability

In a representative democracy, this criterion suggests taxes should be explicit, not hidden. California indexes the personal income tax to make it less hidden. That is, the tax is adjusted each year by the rate of inflation to prevent taxpayers from being pushed into higher tax brackets without a real increase in income. Prior to indexing, taxes "increased" without taxpayers realizing it. At the local level, many taxes such as assessments are relatively hidden.

Acceptability

A final criterion asks whether a particular tax is generally acceptable to the citizenry. True, everyone complains about taxes but some sources of revenue are more politically acceptable than others. For example, many nonsmoking Californians readily support higher taxes on tobacco products. Obviously, smokers find those taxes less acceptable. Although many Californians feel their overall taxes are too high, information in "Are Californians' Taxes Too High" suggests that most California taxes are not, compared to other states.

MAJOR STATE REVENUES

California's revenue system is a patchwork of taxes that were put into place during the 1930s. Experts regard the structure as complex and incomprehensible to average Californians. Specific revenues described below are found in the pie chart found in Figure 11.2.

Personal Income Tax

The largest source of state revenue is the personal income tax. Adopted in 1935, it largely parallels the federal income tax: taxpayers pay at different rates based on wages, salaries, stock options, and other forms of income. The state's standard rates range from 1 to 9.3 percent.

Are Californians' Taxes Too High?

Although many Californians think their taxes are much too high, compared with other states California ranks in the middle on many taxes and near the bottom on still others. When state taxes are measured relative to personal income, this is how California ranked in 2003,

Sales taxes	27
Alcohol	39
Tobacco	32
Gasoline	44
Personal income	8
Corporate income	6
All taxes collected	14

Note: Rankings represent taxes collected per $1,000 of personal income in the 50 states not including the District of Columbia.

SOURCE: California. Budget Project.

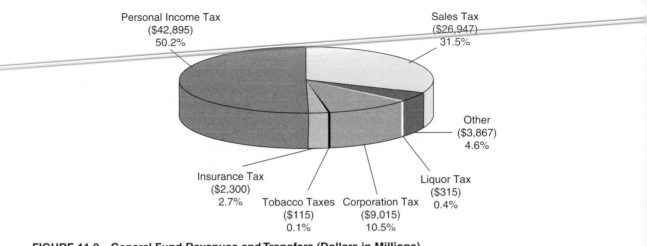

FIGURE 11.2 General Fund Revenues and Transfers (Dollars in Millions)

Source: Governor's Budget, Budget Summary 2005–2006, California.

Question: If your intent as a legislator was to cut taxes in general or for specific groups, how might this graph inform you?

In 2004, voters approved Proposition 63, which established a 1 percent surcharge on taxable incomes over $1 million to be spent on mental health services. It takes only $38,000 in annual income for an individual to reach the 9.3 percent rate; $52,000 for heads of households. Hostility to the income tax is commonplace and in fact there is an estimated gap of $6 billion between what Californians owe and what they pay. Californians are not hostile to raising taxes on others. One survey suggested that 69 percent of Californians would support raising the income tax top rates on the wealthy.[12] All in all, the income tax constituted about 50 percent of the state's 2005–2006 general fund.

Sales Tax

The second largest source of state revenue is the sales tax. Constituting over 31 percent of the 2005–2006 state general fund, it began in 1933 at a modest 2.5 percent tax on retail sales subject to the tax. The current statewide rate is 7.25 percent, including 2.25 percent for local government activities. Because it is inherently regressive, some necessities, such as food, pre-

scription drugs, and utilities are not taxed. In addition, voters in numerous counties and cities have approved sales tax "add-ons" to fund local transportation or other projects. The actual effective sales tax is as high as 8.5 percent (San Francisco), making California's one of the nation's highest.

The state's sales tax is fraught with loopholes and dichotomies—a testimony to good intentions and interest group clout. Numerous exemptions provide "targeted tax relief" to a variety of sales ranging from farm harvesting equipment to horseracing breeding stock to movies rented by theaters. One of the biggest exemptions today is the state's refusal thus far to tax Internet sales, depriving the state of billions of dollars in revenue.[13]

Corporate Taxes

California businesses pay a variety of taxes. The Bank and Corporation Tax is levied on all corporations doing business in the state. The rate is 8.84 percent of profits earned in California. There are two kinds. A franchise tax is imposed on corporations for the privilege of doing business in California. The corporate income tax is levied on those businesses outside California that derive income from California sources. A controversial unitary tax is levied on corporations based on income earned outside of California. Financial institutions including banks pay an additional 2.0 percent of income in lieu of personal property and local business taxes. The politically powerful insurance companies pay only a 2.35 percent tax rate on insurance premiums sold. Insurance taxes constitute only 2.7 percent of the 2005–2006 general fund; bank and corporation taxes 10.7 percent. Businesses and corporations can claim numerous deductions not available to individuals; in some cases, these breaks are so generous that some businesses and corporations pay little if any taxes to the state.

Excise Taxes

Numerous other taxes complement these larger sources of revenue. Excise taxes are assigned to particular items when they are made, sold, transported, or consumed. For example, California taxes tobacco products, alcoholic beverages, horse racing, and gasoline. They resemble sales taxes but are levied separately. Historically, California's "sin" taxes on tobacco and alcoholic beverages have been relatively low due to interest group pressure. Yet voters have approved several propositions significantly increasing the tax on tobacco products. The tax on cigarettes now stands at 87 cents per pack. Taxes on alcohol depend on the beverage but are quite low. For example, while the sales tax on spirits is $3.30 per gallon, the tax on beer and wine is only 20 cents per gallon. Traditionally, "sin" taxes were considered a dependable, albeit small, source of revenue. Small indeed. They amount to only 5 percent of the 2005–2006 general fund. Because smoking and alcohol consumption have declined somewhat in recent years, analysts predict this source of revenue will decline as well.

The excise tax on motor fuels (mostly gasoline and diesel fuel) is added to the regular sales tax plus substantial federal excise taxes, all of which are included in the retail price at the pump. Gas stations collect it and motorists rarely think about it. California's gas tax was raised to 18 cents per gallon thanks to Proposition 111 in 1990. Even that amount may be inadequate. With the notable exception of sport utility vehicles (SUVs), newer fuel-efficient cars consume less gasoline than their older "gas-guzzling" counterparts. Their owners pay less gas tax in the process. Experts think that basing the tax on the price of a tank of gas, not the number of gallons in the tank, would make the tax more inflation-sensitive than it is now. The gasoline tax is regressive, as are most excise taxes. Experts believe that the poor pay a greater share of their income in gasoline taxes than do the wealthy, but fewer of them drive.

The Lottery

Joining many other states, Californians approved a statewide lottery in 1984. To sell voters on the idea, one-third of the proceeds were earmarked for education. Nowadays, 52 percent of each lottery dollar goes to winners, 35 cents to education, 7 percent to ticket sellers, and 6 cents to administrative costs. Although participation in the lottery is purely voluntary, it is more regressive for the poor who participate than for the more affluent. As a source of state revenue, the lottery is small, unpredictable, inefficient, and, to some, ethically dubious. It amounts to roughly 2 percent of all K-12 spending in the state.[14] Revenues ebb and flow as gamblers tire of old games and no winnings. As a result, lottery officials must constantly advertise and "prime the pump" with new games. How inefficient is it? Former superintendent of public instruction Bill Honig once estimated that it took "1,450 Lottery tickets to buy one microscope for a high school chemistry class."[15] Furthermore, what about

Photo 11.1   Lottery Fever
Californians scoop up tickets for an $800 million Super Lotto jackpot. Despite the publicity, hype, and news accounts of such games, lottery revenues are only a small portion of all California state revenues. Question: Should public officials encourage gambling as a way of raising funds?

ethics? Should the state encourage chronic gamblers and thereby profit from their behavior? Should the real odds of winning (upward of 20 million to 1 with Lotto) be publicized alongside the hype? (See Photo 11.1.) Ethics aside, California seems addicted to the lottery, as are the 30-some other states that have it. Just as the lottery has cut into horse racing revenue, expanded Indian casinos may well cut into lottery proceeds.

Debt

Some government policies require more money than current revenues can provide. Adding a

new state park, prison, office building, or state university campus takes huge sums for land acquisition and construction costs. These capital improvements are normally funded through external borrowing. Although the State Constitution limits the debt the legislature can incur, it places no such limits on the voters. Therefore, when policymakers need to borrow for capital improvements, they seek voter approval to issue bonds. Why borrow? The rationale is that long-term financing pays for projects used and enjoyed by future generations. When the state borrows money, it issues bonds that are purchased by investors. The wording of the bond tells the investor its worth, the interest rate to be earned, and when the bond can be redeemed.

Two types of bonds are used in California: *general obligation* and *revenue bonds*. General obligation bonds are backed or secured by the "full faith and credit" of the state, meaning general revenues paid by taxpayers. They finance projects that do not in and of themselves produce revenue, such as schools, prisons, and freeways. Revenue bonds are backed by the future revenue generated by the facility being financed. "Lease purchase" bonds can be paid from any source—the general fund or project-generated revenue—and do not require voter approval. In recent years, several toll road projects in California have been financed through these bonds assuming future tolls would pay back the bonds. Because revenue projections are only projections, interest rates on revenue bonds are typically higher than on general obligation bonds. In recent years, California voters have approved numerous general obligation bonds to fund rail transportation projects, school construction, prisons, and park acquisition. Although some voters oppose what they regard as excessive borrowing, bond approvals are understandable. Voters can anticipate tangible results without paying directly for them.

Just as families can incur too much debt, so can governments. How much is too much? Proponents of borrowing claim that it is the only effective and politically feasible way to finance needed public improvements in the Golden State. Given the mammoth size of California's economy, the state can easily afford substantial indebtedness. Furthermore, bonds arguably create needed jobs—a helpful boost during recessions or anytime for that matter. Opponents of borrowing claim that it inflates the real cost of capital projects because of the interest paid and gives voters the impression that they can get something for nothing.

Who is right? One authoritative answer comes, not from Sacramento, but from bond-rating services in New York City. When Standard and Poor's Corporation or Moody Investor Services say the state of California is borrowing too much, California's credit rating suffers. This effectively makes California bonds more risky and harder to sell. Reduced ratings also translate into higher interest rates the state must pay, and therefore higher project costs. Depending on economic conditions, budget difficulties, and borrowing trends, these services have both upgraded and downgraded California's credit ratings.[16]

What happens when state revenues drop but current-year expenses and spending demands do not? In times like these, the governor and legislature may "balance" budgets by borrowing from (some say "raiding") other public assets like teacher and state worker pension funds or other special funds. This short-term borrowing may last only one day (to cover cash flow) or more than a fiscal year (during economic recessions). These funds are so huge that borrowing from them is very tempting. For instance, Proposition 42, a 2002 measure supported by 70 percent of the voters, dedicated the state sales tax on gasoline to transportation funding. Nevertheless, in order to balance the 2004–2005 budget, Governor Arnold Schwarzenegger and the legislature treated $1.2 billion of that revenue as a loan to the state general fund. Borrowing from pension and special funds is usually paid back with interest.

Chronic borrowing to meet routine annual expenses is a sign of *structural deficits*, deficits that reflect dual commitments to (1) seemingly permanent spending patterns (legal and political) and (2) inadequate revenues to sustain that spending. Budget experts believe that these structural gaps can only be closed by long-term policies that increase revenues, decrease spending, or provide for a combination of the two.

LOCAL REVENUE

Traditionally, the property tax has been a distinctly local revenue source to pay for property related expenditures. California's *ad valorem* (based on value) property tax is primarily governed by the provisions in Proposition 13. As we noted in Chapter 4, it froze existing residential and commercial assessments at 1978 levels. Growth in that value, hence the tax, could not exceed 2 percent per year, no matter how high the actual value had risen. New construction and property sales would trigger a new assessment based on purchase price.

The property tax is generally considered regressive. Regardless of ability to pay, everyone pays the same rate assuming the same assessed value. True, wealthy people owning multimillion dollar mansions pay higher property taxes than those owning modest bungalows, but fixed-income or retired homeowners may be less able to afford the tax. Regressivity is most severe for renters, who pay the tax indirectly through their rents but enjoy none of the other financial benefits of home ownership. Proposition 13 shielded homeowners from hefty property tax increases as long as they did not move.

The revenue effect of Proposition 13 was a substantial cut in property tax revenue followed by increased aid from the state and higher local fees. Proposition 13 essentially restructured the fiscal relationship between local governments, notably counties and school districts, and the state.[17] But Proposition 13 illustrates a more general axiom regarding revenue in California local government: *Revenue strategies in California communities are first and foremost dependent on factors external to local decision making.* These factors include the state of the overall economy, federal and state aid, voter initiatives, and interest rates. For instance, during period of recession, people spend fewer dollars and therefore pay fewer sales taxes. Federal aid to local governments has dwindled in recent decades. Proposition 13 cut property tax revenue, leaving a multitude of local governments to divvy up what was left. When the Federal Reserve Board cuts interest rates, local revenues on deposit earn less interest.

Local governments have responded to these trends as best they can. As a group, California cities receive only 23 percent of their revenue from local property taxes and 32 percent from sales and use taxes. Increasingly, they depend on assessments, service charges, and miscellaneous fees to balance their budgets. Many cities have attracted large shopping malls, which generate voluminous sales taxes. They have also aggressively pursued user fees associated with particular services (such as land use permitting, swimming pool use, recreation programs, and bicycle licenses). Some fees serve no purpose but to raise additional income (such as cable television franchise fees and business licenses). Flat fees may be small but are still regressive in nature. How are these fees calculated? By using cost-allocation techniques, a swimming pool user fee may take into account not only lifeguard costs and heating bills, but also debt retirement and other administrative costs assigned to the pool.

California counties have also raised fees considerably for public health and environmental inspections and processing land use projects. In many counties, inspectors once seen only infrequently, now show up like clockwork, in part because of their fee-generating potential. On the whole, though, counties have proved less nimble in recovering from the long-term impact of Proposition 13. Most revenue-rich shopping malls are within cities, not unincorporated areas served by counties. They are also heavily dependent on the vagaries of state budgeting in order to administer state programs.

Like the state, local governments may borrow money for needed projects. Historically, this has been difficult due to the Proposition 13-required two-thirds vote of the people. In 2000, voters approved Proposition 39, which lowered this high threshold to 55 percent. Since then, numerous school bond measures have passed thanks to Proposition 39. One method of financing has sidestepped Proposition 13.

The Mello-Roos Community Facilities Act of 1982 allows local governments to establish community development districts and then tax land slated for development within those districts. Future property owners who had no say in the matter pay the taxes, which fund needed infrastructure improvements and public services.

If you think that local governments, especially cities, can creatively raise needed revenue at will, think again. Still another initiative has limited that ability. In 1996, voters approved Proposition 218—The Right to Vote on Taxes Act. It requires local governments seeking new or increased assessments to do three things: (1) specify how assessed properties will benefit, (2) assess rather than exempt other local government property, and (3) hold a "mail-in" election of all affected property owners. In 2001, the California Supreme Court allowed certain local fees to bypass 218 requirements.

Where the Money Goes

As the state of California and its communities divide policy responsibilities, spending policies result not only from clear policy choices, but also from incremental, historical decisions that develop their own political momentum. Because we devote the last two Chapters of this book to public policy specifics in the Golden State, we will only briefly survey state and local expenditures here.

STATE EXPENDITURES

Occasionally newspaper reporters uncover legislators' spending ideas: $2 million for a San Francisco aquarium, a $150,000 model curriculum on human rights and genocide, or $149,000 for a California trade office in Armenia. Although such projects may confirm voter suspicions about wasteful spending, they do not reflect where most state revenue actually goes. Note Figure 11.3. A staggering 93 percent of the 2005–2006 state general fund went to education, health and welfare, and prisons—the "Big Three" of state budgeting. This spending trio in California is quite typical of spending patterns in other states.

Education

Public education from kindergarten through community college consumes about 42 percent of the general fund; Proposition 98 requires a minimum of about 40 percent. Spending for education remains enrollment-driven. The school-aged population in California has been growing at a much faster rate than the general population. This requires more classrooms and more teachers in what will always be a labor-intensive government service. Higher education (including the University of California (UC) and the California State University system (CSU) consumes another 11.7 percent of the 2005–2005 general fund. State funding for community colleges is governed by the provisions of Proposition 98. After suffering spending cuts during the early 1990s recession, higher education spending has increased somewhat and stabilized. In turn the UC and CSU systems have agreed to larger enrollments and greater productivity.

Health and Welfare

Addressing the health and welfare needs of California's poor, aged, blind, and disabled claimed 31.2 percent of the 2005–2006 general fund. Caseloads have dropped somewhat in recent years due to job growth and welfare reform. Expenditures in this area largely represent direct payments to individuals (such as CalWORKs) and to providers of particular services (medical doctors and hospitals). Within this portion of the budget, costs for Medi-Cal (California's version of federal medical care for the poor or Medicaid) have soared in recent decades due to rising medical care costs and

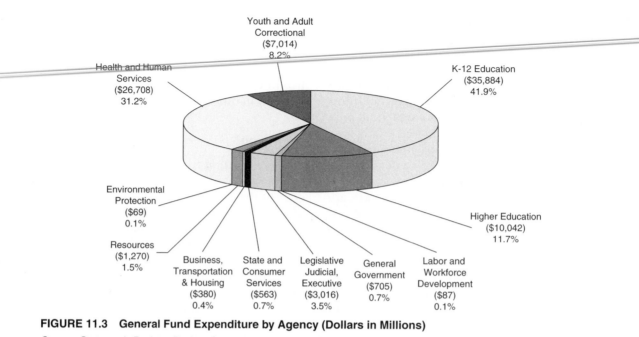

FIGURE 11.3   General Fund Expenditure by Agency (Dollars in Millions)

Source: Governor's Budget, Budget Summary 2005–2006, California.

Question: Aside from ideological concerns about the role of government, how does population growth affect the spending side of California's state government?

federal requirements to serve more medically needy groups. Even so, Medi-Cal caseloads have declined somewhat in recent years. Today, over 18 percent of Californians—about 6.5 million people—qualify for Medi-Cal in any given month. Chapter 13 addresses this major program in more detail.

Corrections

California's prison system consumed 8.2 percent of the 2005–2006 general fund—up from 3 percent in 1969–1970. This dramatic increase is the result of a combination of factors: rising crime rates, increases in crime-prone populations, and tougher sentencing policies (more prison time and less parole time). Increased sentences were partly mandated by Proposition 8, the 1982 "Victims' Bill of Rights." The state's Three Strikes law (see Chapter 9) also incarcerated more felons for longer periods of time. As a result, California's prison

population jumped from 35,000 in 1983 to more than 164,000 in 2005.

What Is Left

Traditional state operations (such as highways, environmental protection, resource management, business regulation, the state courts, and the legislature) plus tax relief receive the remaining 7 percent. Most of the executive branch agencies portrayed in Chapter 8 are funded from the thinnest slices in Figure 11.3. Efforts to balance state budgets by cutting these government operations will always have limited success since they constitute so little of the overall budget to begin with.

LOCAL EXPENDITURES

The two general purpose local government institutions in California are cities and counties. While California cities vary greatly in size and spending patterns vary, on average they spend their revenues accordingly:[18]

City Spending Category	Percentage
Public safety (police, fire, emergency)	25
Public utilities (water, gas, electric)	21
Transportation (streets, transit, airports)	16
Health (solid waste, sewers)	11
Community development (planning, engineering)	9
Culture and Leisure (parks, recreation, libraries)	9
General Government (legislative, management, legal)	9

Individual cities can vary substantially from these averages primarily due to their size. Generally speaking, the smaller the city, the less likely it will be to manage utilities, airports, museums, hospitals, and mass transit systems. Controlling for size, cities, unlike counties, can pick and choose many of the services they wish to provide.

California counties present a much different spending picture. For the most part, this is because counties deliver services on behalf of the state. As noted below, the two largest spending commitments are on public assistance and public protection. Public assistance includes welfare, social services, general relief, care of wards of the court, and veteran services. By far the largest expenditure in this area is the CalWORKs program. Public protection includes the local courts, sheriffs' departments, jails, and fire protection. Local court systems are the most expensive item in this area. The counties' health and sanitation responsibilities include public health, medical care, mental health, drug and alcohol abuse services, and sanitation costs. Other spending categories include general government (county boards of supervisors and administrative offices), roads, education administration, recreation programs, cultural facilities, veteran

memorial buildings, and interest on county indebtedness:[19]

County Spending Category	Percentage
Public Assistance	33
Public Protection	29
Health and Sanitation	18
General Government	10
Public Ways and Facilities	4
Education, Recreation, Cultural and Debt Service	5

The Need for Budget Reform

In reviewing the politics of budgeting in California, we see diverse interests confronting rather rigid political structures and economic trends. As Richard Krolack has put it, "California's budget is a complex process with many nuances and intangibles."[20] That said, three patterns of budgeting in California emerge:

1. *California budgeting is cyclical.* It heavily depends on the health of the state's economy. When the economy is growing, the budget pies grow as well. In these fat years, more revenue is available for all manner of policies and programs; tax cuts are even possible. When the economy is stagnant or in recession, the opposite is the case. In these lean years, programs and expectations must be cut or scaled back.

2. *California budgeting is group-differential*—that is, it treats different groups in different ways. Consider the combination of all California taxes. The total tax burden on Californians is a function of how progressive or regressive different taxes are. Income taxes are highly progressive; sales, excise taxes, and property taxes are regressive. In general, *higher income Californians benefit from the state's tax policies.* Although they pay high amounts of income taxes, the wealthy

can take advantage of numerous tax credits and deductions to offset their tax liabilities. Lower income families pay lower income taxes but are hit hard by regressive sales, excise, and property taxes. As we see more fully in Chapter 13, *lower income Californians benefit from the state's spending policies*, especially in the areas of health and human services. They also have access to relatively low cost higher education at the state's community colleges.

3. *California budgeting needs reform.* Today, California's budget process itself seems to please no one. The California Constitution Revision Commission called it "crippled" and "dysfunctional." The California Citizen's Budget Commission claims that "the budget process falls far short of today's needs." The California State Association of Counties calls a budget-related issue—the fiscal relationship between the state and local governments— "fundamentally flawed." A chorus of reform groups (including the California Governance Consensus Project, the Commission on Local Governance for the 21st Century, the Speaker's Commission on State and Local Government Finance, and the Governor's Commission on Building for the 21st Century) have recommended fundamental changes in the budget process. The following major reforms have been proposed:

• Use multiyear strategic planning to frame budget decisions

• Introduce multiyear budgets

• Require simple legislative majorities to pass budget bills

• Ensure prudent reserves for "rainy day" budgets

• Limit borrowing to cover budget deficits

• Keep the local property tax local

• Stabilize and simplify local revenues and state/local fiscal relations.[21]

In addition to these reforms, Governor Arnold Schwarzenegger proposed that there be across-the-board spending cuts when "fiscal emergencies" are declared. Critics of that idea contend that such indiscriminate cutting does not recognize the value of many programs and the need for some spending increases even in years when spending outpaces revenue.

Conclusion: The Cost of Diversity

At the outset of this chapter, we noted that a budget is a government's premier policy statement. In a representative democracy, it seems to say, "These are the things that we, the people, want to do as a society—both today and on behalf of future Californians." The consensus assumed in that statement seems missing from contemporary budget politics. State and local budget makers may epitomize fiscal gridlock to many Californians, but they are not the root cause of the problem. The true cause of annual budget struggles stems from economic change, population growth, group competition, and partisan conflict.

In a sense, budgeting in California puts dollar signs on "the politics of diversity." To the extent the tax system benefits the rich, it benefits only one segment of Californians. To the extent state expenditures benefit the poor (public assistance, Medi-Cal), the middle class (higher education, highways), the wealthy (tax credits and low corporate taxes), or particular interests (farmers, renters) they divide 35 million Californians into groups. To the extent the budget process itself divides power, fragments decision making, encourages group competition, and incurs gridlock, it exhibits hyperpluralism. This is all the more true when California voters wrest budget decisions from elected budget makers—"ballot box budgeting."

A budgeting expert once described California's operating budget as a "commitment to caring for people,"[22] and that is still largely true. The continuation of that commitment seems to be at issue. The foremost budget question Californians and their policymakers will need to address is this: How can the state and its communities agree on budgets in an age when societal and therefore political consensus is lacking and quite possibly unachievable? The alternative is "every group for itself" in the nation's largest and most diverse state.

KEY TERMS

two-tier economy   (p. 226)

fiscal year   (p. 227)

incrementalism   (p. 227)

May Revision   (p. 228)

Trailer bills   (p. 228)

Big Five   (p. 228)

two-thirds problem   (p. 229)

cruise control spending, entitlements   (p. 229)

third rail issues   (p. 230)

ballot box budgeting   (pp. 230–231)

earmarking   (p. 230)

regressive and progressive taxes   (p. 232)

general obligation and revenue bonds   (p. 237)

structural deficits   (p. 237)

REVIEW QUESTIONS

1. Describe the general characteristics of public budgets.
2. How do state and local economies affect state and local budgets?
3. How does the California budget process work? What constrains the process?
4. Using various criteria to evaluate taxes, describe the major sources of state and local revenue in California.
5. Describe the Big Three of California spending. How do cities and counties spend their revenue?
6. How does budget policy in California describe the "cost of diversity" and reinforce the theme of hyperpluralism?
7. Which budget reforms do you think are the most necessary?

WEB ACTIVITIES

California State Department of Finance (www.dof.ca.gov).

This agency advises the governor on the annual budget and makes available numerous documents on past and current state budgets and the state's economy.

Legislative Analyst's Office (www.lao.ca.gov)

This site provides nonpartisan, authoritative analyses of the state budget and other policy issues.

Advocacy Groups
California Budget Project (www.cbp.org)

This group advocates fiscal equity and fairness in California.

California Taxpayers Association (www.caltax.org)

This organization's mission is to "protect taxpayers from unnecessary taxes."

INFOTRAC® COLLEGE EDITION ARTICLES

For additional reading, go to InfoTrac® College Edition, your online research library, at http://www.infotrac.thomsonlearning.com

Fire with Fire; California's New Budget

Schwarzenegger's No-Tax-Increase Vow Alters California Budget Debate

Growing Economy Will Not Bail Out California's Budget

NOTES

1. Aaron Wildavsky, *The New Politics of the Budgetary Process* (Glenview, IL: Scott, Foresman and Co., 1988), 2.

2. Legislative Analyst's Office, *CAL FACTS: California's Economy and Budget in Perspective* (Sacramento: Legislative Analyst's Office, 2004).

3. Deborah Reed and Jennifer Cheng, *Racial and Ethnic Wage Gaps in the California Labor Market* (San Francisco: Public Policy Institute of California, 2003).

4. Quoted in Steve Scott, "The Morphing Economy," *California Journal* 28 (July 1997), 15.

5. Richard Krolack, *California Budget Dance: Issues and Process*, 2nd ed. (Sacramento: California Journal Press. 1994), 49.

6. "The State That Tied Its Own Hands," *The Economist* 304 (July 11, 1987), 30.

7. California Citizens Budget Committee, *A Twenty-First Century Budget Process for California* (Los Angeles: Center for Governmental Studies, 1998).

8. California Constitution Revision Commission, *Final Report and Recommendations to the Governor and the Legislature* (Sacramento: California Constitution Revision Commission, 1996), 10.

9. Quoted in Deb Kollars, "A Labyrinth of Spending: Special Programs Have Grown into Vast Bureaucratic Jungle," *Sacramento Bee*, February 2, 2003.

10. See Donald R. Winkler and Jeffrey I. Chapman, "Earmarked Revenues and Fiscal Constraints," in John J. Kirlin and Donald R. Winkler, eds. *California Policy Choices, Vol. 6* (Sacramento: University of Southern California School of Public Administration, 1990).

11. California Budget Project, *Who Pays Taxes in California?* (Sacramento: California Budget Project, 2005). Available at www.cbp.org/.

12. Mark Baldessare, *PPIC Statewide Survey: Special Survey on the State Budget* (San Francisco: Public Policy Institute of California, 2005), 3.

13. Kathleen Les, "California is No Leader in the Hunt for an E-Tax Solution," *California Journal* 32 (February 2001), 16–20.

14. For more on the state lottery, go to www.calottery.com/. This official Web site includes considerable data on the lottery's operation and its funding of public education. Critical views are absent.

15. Quoted in Michelle Quinn, "The Lottery Lemon: Have Californians Soured on Their Games of Chance?" *California Journal* 22 (December 1991), 571.

16. To locate current ratings, go to www.treasurer.ca.gov/ratings/.

17. Michael A. Shires, John Ellwood, and Mary Sprague, *Has Proposition 13 Delivered? The Changing Tax Burden in California* (San Francisco: Public Policy Institute of California, 1998).

18. State Controller, *Cities Annual Report, Fiscal Year 2001–2002* (Sacramento, California: California State Controller, 2004).

19. State Controller, *Counties Annual Report, Fiscal Year 2001–2002* (Sacramento: California State Controller, 2004).

20. Richard Krolack, *California's Budget Dance*, 111.

21. See *Dollars and Democracy: An Advocates Guide to the California State Budget Process* (Sacramento: California Budget Project, 1999).

CHAPTER 12

Policies Stemming from Growth

In Brief

Many state and local policies in California stem from the state's incessant population growth. Chapter 12 frames the issues of water, housing, transportation, and the environment in terms of the growth that makes them policy problems in the first place.

For decades, policymakers not only accommodated existing growth, they "built" a California that would actually encourage future growth. A political division of labor made new development relatively painless. Local govern-

ments approved individual projects, while the state provided the infrastructure required. As growth continued, so did its negative impacts. The result was reduced public support for the policies and taxes that had made growth possible. Political pressures in recent years have pitted Californian against Californian: farmers and city dwellers over water, new and old residents over housing, freeway drivers and mass transit advocates over traffic gridlock, and environmentalists and business over pollution.

Many of these policy problems stem from basic assumptions deeply engrained in California and national politics: that water is "free," housing is a private sector activity, widespread car ownership is a given, and government is responsible to clean up private sector–generated pollution. Recent attempts to solve these policy problems have included market approaches to water availability and environmental pollu-tion, plus modest public investment in rail transit. Affordable housing will likely remain an elusive goal. Policymakers have focused more on building the infrastructure needed to accommodate growth than on controlling the growth itself. In a diverse and hyperpluralistic state, this may be all policymakers can do or hope to do.

Introduction: Growth in California

In a public television documentary on the habitat of the bald eagle, narrator George Page declared, "California is where America meets its limit, a fitting place to realize that growth cannot extend itself forever. Growth itself has its limits." Many Californians would agree. In their view, the state's *quality of life* is gradually being undermined by the very growth that had sustained it for so many years. Ominous warning signs abound: the prospect of chronic water shortages, air quality improvements offset by still more cars, traffic gridlock in metropolitan areas, fertile farmland giving way to housing subdivisions, shopping malls, and pockets of smog throughout the Golden State.[1]

This chapter discusses growth and its ramifications in the Golden State. Numerous policy issues important to Californians, such as housing, transportation, water, and environmental pollution are rooted in population growth. We will look at the nature of California's growth, how specific growth-induced problems are addressed, and the efforts to manage growth itself. The central question is this: *How do California policymakers accommodate continual and inevitable growth without (1) degrading various qualities of life sought by diverse groups and (2) endangering the state's once-pristine environment?* This question brims with conflict ranging from the highest levels of state government down to interneighbor disputes over lifestyles, cars, noise, and fences. It also reflects the inability of a complex, fragmented, and hyperpluralistic political system to address, solve, or even keep pace with the problems that stem from growth.

An undercurrent in this chapter deals with evolving and diverse notions of what "quality of life" means. From the problematic neighbor who defines this term differently than the rest of the block to state and local debates on the subject, "quality of life" has come to represent alternative perspectives on what living in California was, is, and should be like. In the decades to come, as Californians become more numerous, culturally diverse, and politically divided, competing qualities of life will haunt, challenge, and elude policymakers.

WHY CALIFORNIA GREW

In California's history, population growth has resulted from a host of factors in and out of government. California boasted a favorable climate and scenic environment in which to live, work, and play. Gold Rush miners inundated parts of California, while others were lured by savvy marketing efforts of the state's railroads, citrus growers, and real estate entrepreneurs. Local governments boosted their own locales while state government accommodated the pro-growth interests of the railroads and other industries. World War II brought increased federal spending and wartime employees to

California. Growth-hungry city officials encouraged and enabled military-related growth.[2] After the war, military bases remained open and military spending continued.

California developed a de facto pro-growth policy in the postwar period. A statewide water system, new highways, and a complex master plan for higher education set the stage for future growth while accommodating growth pressures at the time. These bipartisan efforts, supported by business and labor, created not only a physical infrastructure to support more households, but also a social infrastructure to support people's own rising expectations. A new statewide political consensus viewed growth as positive and beneficial. In addition, national policies in effect subsidized growth in California by helping to fund the Central Valley Project (a massive water project) and the state's interstate highway system. During this pro-growth era, new housing kept pace with population growth. Much of it was suburban, low in density, and relatively cheap, considering the high demand for it. Necessary infrastructure (roads, highways, water projects, sewer systems, and schools) was funded through generous federal subsidies, state bonds, and growing general fund revenues. For decades, accommodating growth was relatively painless and uncontroversial.

THE DRUMBEAT OF GROWTH

Although rates of population growth in California fluctuate, this can be said: The state's long-term growth has been and will continue to be steady, if not relentless. California's 2004 population of 36,591,000 is only one aspect of the state's growth challenge. The state's compound annual growth rate in the last 50 years has been more than twice the national rate. In 1940, California's population was 5.2 percent of the nation's; by 2004, it was 12 percent; by 2025 it will be 15 percent. At current rates, the state will add 4 million people—the size of Los

Angeles—every six years. That translates to one new Californian nearly every minute.

Growth rates vary within California. In recent years, California's inland counties have experienced the highest population growth rates. Here growth was due to natural increases, urban and suburban "flight" (people fleeing crime and congestion), and an influx of retirees. But in terms of absolute population increases, the largest numbers have been in the coastal and near-coastal counties of California including Los Angeles, San Diego, Orange, San Bernardino, and Riverside counties. The U.S. Census Bureau projects a population of 50 million by 2025—a 68 percent increase since 1990. In that span of time, California growth will far outpace even other high growth states (Figure 12.2).

The impacts of all this growth have concerned many Californians. Beginning in the 1960s, some questioned how long rapid growth could continue without threatening the state's quality of life.[3] By the 1970s, the dominant growth consensus began to crumble. Why? First, California's political leaders sought to downsize government's role in fostering the state's growth. Governor Ronald Reagan (R, 1967–1974), while not objecting to growth itself, opposed the "big government" that growth made possible. His successor, Jerry Brown (D, 1975–1982), reduced infrastructure investment, especially in highway construction and large water projects.

Second, economic restructuring altered the prospect of unlimited growth without apparent cost. California's heavy manufacturing base declined, as did growth in personal income. So did taxpayer willingness to fund more public improvements. Proposition 13, which substantially cut property taxes in 1978, reinforced this unwillingness. It also cut funds local governments relied upon to provide the infrastructure required by new development. Instead, developers were charged for infrastructure costs, which, of course, were passed on to new home owners. Pressure to develop farmland

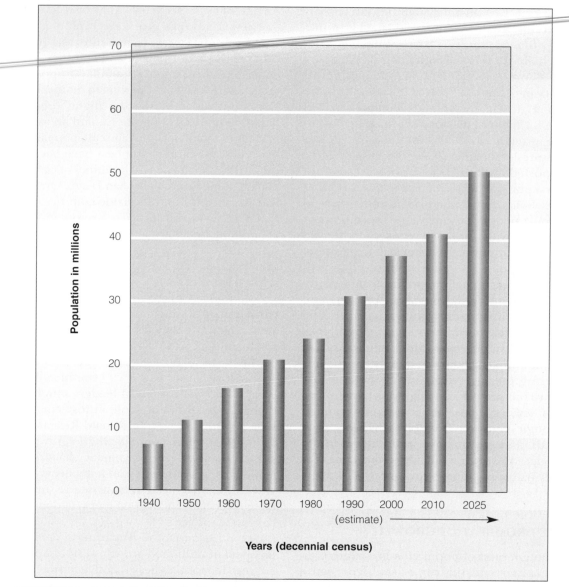

FIGURE 12.1   Population Growth Chart

Question: Are these population growth projections inevitable? Are they outside the purview of government control?

Source: California Statistical Abstract and the U.S. Census Bureau.

near cities grew. As one Lompoc, California, farmer put it: "I could make a whole lot more money growin' condos than farming." As environmental public awareness increased, development in ecologically sensitive areas (such as waterfronts, flood plains, and estuaries) became politically unacceptable. Voters approved the Coastal Act of 1972 to limit coastal development where land use demand always exceeded supply. By the late 1990s, almost

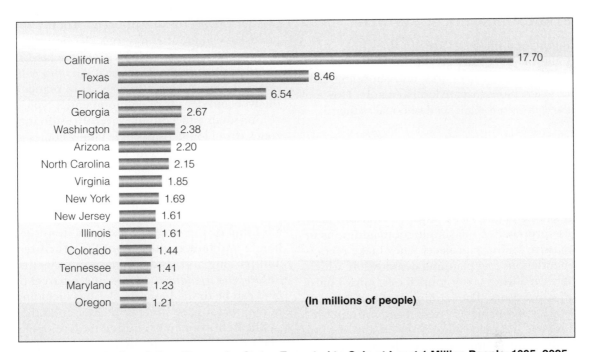

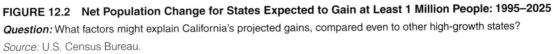

FIGURE 12.2   Net Population Change for States Expected to Gain at Least 1 Million People: 1995–2025

Question: What factors might explain California's projected gains, compared even to other high-growth states?

Source: U.S. Census Bureau.

two-thirds of Californians felt the state should restrict development, protect open space, and discourage high growth levels.[4]

Third, settlement patterns fed a popular desire to limit growth. Although California was not as densely populated as New Jersey (217 versus 1,134 people per square mile in 2003), Californians *perceived* they were overcrowded. This was because most of them lived in the state's coastal or near-coastal counties. Indeed, 58 percent of the state's population in 2003 lived in only six of 58 counties (Los Angeles, San Diego, Orange, Alameda, Santa Clara, and San Bernardino). In recent years, the highly developed coastal strip has both lengthened and thickened. An urban corridor now extends from Santa Barbara to Ensenada, Mexico—arguably the nation's first bi-national megalopolis. Furthermore, development has

moved inland in the three largest metropolitan areas (San Francisco, Los Angeles, and San Diego). Today, "edge cities" mix high-density commercial, professional, and residential uses while creating environmental impacts often beyond the control of any single government. The Los Angeles Basin boasts 26 such edge cities, the largest concentration of them in the nation.[5] These growth patterns result in some of the nation's costliest housing and busiest freeways.

Noncoastal Californians are becoming concerned as well. Residential and commercial development is gradually invading the state's, indeed the nation's, most productive agricultural areas. In fact, eight of California's 17 fastest growing counties are in the Central Valley, the oblong bowl stretching from Redding to Bakersfield.[6]

STRUCTURING LOCAL GROWTH

Population increases are not the whole story. Californians equate "growth" with new housing projects, industrial parks, and shopping centers—decisions that are local in nature. How are these decisions made, and who makes them?

The Structure of Planning

Cities and counties have planning or community development departments staffed by professional planners. They process various land use proposals, from simple room additions to massive multiuse projects. They make recommendations to a planning commission, which in turn advises a city council or county board of supervisors. They comment on the overall merits of a project, assess its environmental impact, and place conditions on approval to reduce those impacts. At both levels, public hearings allow citizens to comment on the project. After a project is approved, a developer must begin construction within a certain time period. During construction, numerous inspections make sure a project conforms to the many building standards and conditions placed on it. Developers pay *impact fees* to "mitigate" the impacts of development—new roads, water systems, sewers, even schools—costs once borne by taxpayers.

Tools Planners Use

A wide variety of policies govern project approvals. For instance, each California community has a state-required *general plan* or overall blueprint for the physical development of the area. Such plans contain general goals for future development, zoning maps, and other maps projecting future development. These documents must contain various "elements" or chapters addressing land use types, traffic circulation, housing, conservation, open space, and safety. General plans do not determine or

predict when growth will occur. Timing depends on economic conditions, developer initiative, and decisions by local governments.

Other planning tools abound. A *zoning ordinance* divides an area into districts to regulate the type and density of development. A typical zoning map will contain several residential zones (from low-density single family homes to high-density condominiums or apartments) as well as commercial areas, manufacturing areas, parks, open space, and other uses. The ordinance also establishes minimum lot sizes, setback rules (distances between a structure and a lot line or the street), maximum densities, height and bulk requirements for structures, and parking and landscaping requirements. *Subdivision regulations* dictate how a parcel of land can be divided into smaller lots including minimum lot sizes, street standards, and other public improvements required of developers. Planners also make use of statewide *uniform building codes,* which regulate the physical components of construction (roofing, heating, electric wiring, ventilation, sanitation, and earthquake resistance). Relatively new *planned unit developments* (PUDs) integrate many of these tools for housing developments or more complex projects. They allow developers to be more innovative and grant local officials more flexibility and control.

These policies do not necessarily appease residents who adamantly oppose particular projects under any circumstances or the overall momentum of growth in their communities. How do local officials address these concerns? First, they can control the timing of development by imposing temporary building moratoria or annual housing quotas. The Northern California city of Petaluma pioneered the quota concept. Second, the zoning ordinance can also be modified through "downzoning" (reducing legally allowed building densities on undeveloped land). Because downzoning in effect spreads development across more land, ironically it results in more traffic congestion, not less.

NO-GROWTH POLITICS IN CALIFORNIA

Opposition to development in California has mounted in recent decades. Two trends illustrate this phenomenon: a greater sensitivity to quality of life concerns and the rise of a no-growth movement in California.

Quality of Life Concerns

Numerous public opinion surveys have tracked a growing concern about development and its impacts. In a 2001 poll, 60 percent of California adults thought their communities were growing rapidly. They thought that the negative consequences of rapid growth included traffic congestion, high housing costs, urban sprawl, loss of open space, and pollution. Given population projections (45 million Californians by 2020), 82 percent predicted that, by 2020, the Golden State would be a less desirable place to live.[7]

The Rise of the Slow-Growth Movement

Voicing these concerns, various groups and individuals across the state have advocated various growth control measures. They have included requiring developers to fund infrastructure improvements, reducing zoning densities, prohibiting development on agricultural and rural land, purchasing open space, and subjecting development decisions to city- or county-wide voter approval. Some of these no-growth or controlled-growth policies are enacted by city councils and county boards of supervisors, but a growing number of such policies have been enacted through land use initiatives, a practice dubbed "ballot box planning." Some initiatives address growth in general while others seek to veto a particular project, such as a new Wal-Mart store. While critics decry the shortcomings of these initiatives, they do give voice to local slow-growth sentiments and provide a check on local planners and developers.[8]

What explains this desire to limit growth? Several factors emerge. First, urban Californians

indeed experience daily the impacts of growth; the freeways they ply daily seem more like parking lots. They view once-pristine open space now covered with housing tracts and shopping centers. Ironically, in some communities, no-growth views are shared even by newcomers (see Cartoon 12.1). Second, many Californians seem ambivalent regarding growth. They may favor the idea of affordable housing but oppose its actual construction in their communities. In one survey, two-thirds of respondents believed low-density family housing should be encouraged yet also believed suburban sprawl is a very or somewhat important problem in their region.[9] Third, opposition to growth often centers around specific projects close to home. Typical controversies involve *LULUs* (locally undesirable land uses) such as landfills, toxic cleanup sites, drug abuse centers, and many traffic-generating projects. Even places of worship and schools may be opposed as LULUs. Downtown merchants may oppose the development of competing shopping malls, warehouse retailers, and factory outlet stores. Individual home owners may fear the potential loss of property values. Common strategies used by *NIMBYs* ("not in my back yard" opponents) may include circulating anti-development petitions, packing public hearings with project opponents, placing initiatives on the ballot, and filing lawsuits. In religiously diverse California, not even churches are exempt. Complaints often center around incompatible design, increased traffic, and city hall concern over property tax losses. For example, one city council rejected a new Hindu temple after neighbors complained it would attract more Hindus to the area.

Water: Making Growth Possible

One way or another, a variety of public policy issues can be traced to the drumbeat of growth in California. Some policies have made growth feasible, such as the provision of water throughout

CARTOON 12.1   When I first moved here

Question: Do you recognize the attitude portrayed in Lewis's cartoon?

Source: Eric G. Lewis.

the state. Other policies such as housing, transportation, and environmental protection address the impacts of growth. In this chapter we explore several growth-related issues, but water comes first for a very simple reason: Increasing the supply of water and moving it around has been a necessary prerequisite to California's growth. Water drew people to the state and determined where they would settle.

California is really two states divided by water: Northern California has it, and Southern California wants it. Yet, in a sense, all of California is semi-arid. In response, California policymakers have always assumed that *water not used by people is water wasted*—an assumption that defies the state's physical geography. Rain and snow are more frequent and plenti-

ful in Northern California. As a result, the Sacramento-San Joaquin Delta region has been called "the great Central Valley mixing basin where a hundred rivers become one."[10] Once an inland sea, it now is a labyrinthine estuary of sloughs, waterways, and levees that channel drinking water to over half the state's population. In contrast, Southern California claims only 2 percent of the state's natural water supply. But that never stopped its impulse to grow. Southern California possessed an asset of its own: a pleasant climate. Several mountain ranges plus gentle coastal breezes protected Southern California from the heat and grit of the desert interior, creating a Mediterranean climate. The only resource missing was water. But as novelist Edward

Abbey observed, "There is no lack of water [in the desert], unless you try to establish a city where no city should be."[11]

STORING WATER

One marvel of California water is how it is stored for later use. California winters can be wet, but not all winters are equally wet. California endures cycles of wet years and droughts, which can be terrifying (see California Voices). Winter precipitation is saved in three great storage systems, two of which are nature's own. First is the Sierra Nevada snowpack. Some of the world's heaviest snowfall can occur in the Sierras, creating a year-round source of runoff water. Second is the state's underground water basins or aquifers (the airspace in soil and geologic formations displaced by water). Groundwater accounts for one-third of California's water supply. A third storage system is artificial, consisting of numerous reservoirs—surface lakes created by damming rivers and

capturing run-off from adjacent mountain ranges. Such reservoirs dot the California landscape. These three storage systems face dangers from both periodic drought and incessant population growth. During droughts, the Sierra snowpack becomes depleted, forcing overreliance on the other two storage systems. Reservoirs lose water to evaporation and become choked with silt. When California's aquifers are pumped excessively, "overdrafting" occurs. This not only lowers the water table but allows agricultural chemicals to invade rural aquifers and salt water to invade coastal valley aquifers. Groundwater overdrafting is increasing but largely unregulated.[12]

MOVING WATER

Some say California water is never where you want it, when you want it. But Californians were never deterred by that fact. As water law developed, so did various water rights. If you lived on top of or adjacent to a source of water, it was

CALIFORNIA VOICES

Steinbeck on California Water

The water came in a 30 year cycle. There would be five or six wet and wonderful years when there might be 19 to 25 inches of rain, and the land would shout with grass. Then would come six or seven pretty good years of 12 or 16 inches of rain. And then the dry years would come, and sometimes there would be only seven or eight inches of rain. The land dried up and grasses headed out miserably a few inches high and great bare scabby places appeared in the valley. The live oaks got a crusty look and the sagebrush was grey. The land cracked and the springs dried up and the cattle listlessly nibbled dry twigs. Then the farmers and the ranchers would be filled with disgust for the Salinas Valley. The cows would

grow thin and sometimes starve to death. People would have to haul water in barrels to their farms just for drinking. Some families would sell out for nearly nothing and move away. And it never failed that during the dry years the people forgot about the rich years, and during the wet years they lost all memory of the dry years. It was always that way.

Question: To what extent does Steinbeck's observation explain actual water policy and politics in California?

SOURCE: John Steinbeck, *East of Eden* (New York: Viking Press, 1952), 5–6.

yours (*riparian rights*). If you were the first to find or "create" a source of water, it was yours (through *prior appropriation*). If you used someone else's water with their knowledge, it was yours (*prescriptive rights*). Combined, these rights encouraged the movement of water throughout the state. California's earliest water projects were localized irrigation systems consisting of earthen dams and even hand-dug canals and ditches. In time, these efforts were dwarfed by four immense projects that would forever change the face of California: the Owens Valley and Colorado River Projects, the Central Valley Project, and the State Water Project. The politics behind these projects reminds one of Mark Twain's observation: "In the West, whiskey is for drinking, water is for fighting." As we survey these projects, as portrayed in Figure 12.3, remember that water is measured in acre-feet. An acre-foot is the amount of water needed to fill one acre to a depth of one foot, enough to supply two urban households.

Water for Los Angeles

The City of Angels' unquenchable thirst began in the late 1880s. Through civic boosterism, Los Angeles's population was booming, but a lengthy drought left city officials and business interests desperate. Combining controversy and intrigue, Los Angeles interests quietly purchased land in the Owens Valley east of the Sierra Nevada range. The goal? To divert the Owens River through 233 miles of aqueducts, tunnels, and pumping stations. In 1905, the *Los Angeles Times* audaciously announced the news: "Titanic Project to Give the City a River."[13] Drought-panicked Los Angelenos approved the bond measures required to build the Los Angeles Aqueduct. The project created one prerequisite to future growth—*surplus water* (more than people immediately needed). But tapping the Owens Valley was not enough, not for Los Angeles. Fueled by now-permanent growth, more bond

issues, a cooperative federal government, and the belief that anything was possible, the city proceeded to harness the Colorado River. The Hoover Dam, completed in 1941, channeled the Colorado River to Los Angeles via a maze of dams, canals, tunnels, reservoirs, and pumping stations. In addition to water, this project created a second prerequisite to urban growth: *electrical power*. The Metropolitan Water District of Southern California was formed to build and operate the project. In concert with cities, counties, and other water districts, this giant water wholesaler became and remains a Southern California growth machine. Northern Californians tend to criticize L.A.'s thirst, but they have played the same game. In 1913, San Francisco dammed up the Tuolumne River inside Yosemite Park (over naturalist John Muir's objections), establishing its own permanent water supply. Because it "created" more water than it could ever use, the city was able to sell surplus water (60 percent of total supplies) to other Bay Area communities—spurring *their* growth.

Central Valley Project

In contrast to Southern California, the state's heartland is laced by two sizable river systems, the Sacramento and the San Joaquin, plus their tributaries. As crops replaced native grasses and national markets replaced local ones, valley farmers yearned for a steady, weatherproof water supply. As in Los Angeles, a lengthy drought forced political action. In the case of the valley, underground overpumping provided the impetus for the 1931 State Water Plan. The 1936 Central Valley Project (CVP) was an effort to implement the plan. The U.S. Bureau of Reclamation assumed control after the state failed to finance it, and the bureau has run it ever since. The largest federal water project in the country, the CVP consists of an intricate network of rivers, dams, aqueducts, and power plants stretching nearly 500 miles from Shasta Dam in the north to

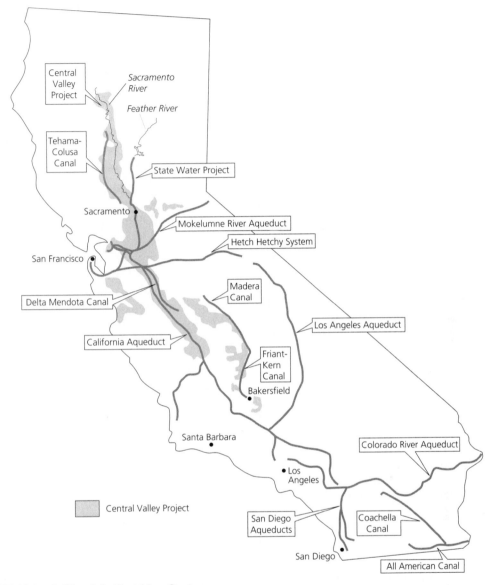

FIGURE 12.3 California's Plumbing System

Bakersfield in the south. It supplies about 20 percent of California's developed water and at heavily subsidized rates. According to one report, the average price for irrigation water from the CVP was less than 2 percent of what Southern Californians pay for drinking water.[14] Cheap, plentiful, agricultural water has skewed its uses. One single crop, alfalfa, consumes more water than the residents of Los Angeles and the Bay Area *combined*.

State Water Project

These projects did not end the political battles over water. California's postwar growth continued unchecked. Conflicts rose between urban and rural users, irrigation and flood control interests, and a confusing patchwork of water agencies. No single state agency had the power to referee this hyperpluralistic water anarchy. In the 1950s, a new Department of Water Resources published the California Water Plan, a visionary document detailing the State Water Project (SWP). It clearly recognized Californians' penchant to live where water is scarce. A massive bond measure to fund the plan barely passed in 1960, thanks to overwhelming support in Southern California. Its first project was the Feather River Project, which "tamed" the flood-prone Feather River at Oroville and moved its water through the Delta and further south via the California Aqueduct. The project moves water a total of 700 miles through 19 reservoirs, 17 pumping stations, eight hydroelectric power plants, and about 660 miles of open canals and pipelines. Of the contracted water supply, 70 percent goes to urban users and 30 percent to agricultural users.

In the 1980s, another north/south water battle focused on the Delta region. The trick has always been to use and move Delta water without allowing seawater to intrude and endanger farmland. To solve this problem, the California Department of Water Resources proposed a "peripheral canal" to channel fresh water east of the Delta and directly into the California Aqueduct. After years of study, the legislature approved the project in 1980. An anti-canal referendum drive was launched by two strange political bedfellows: environmentalists concerned about the Delta's ecology and large-scale farmers upset at probable water price hikes. In 1982, California voters defeated the canal project by a two to one margin; Northern Californians by a nine to one margin.

RECENT WATER DEVELOPMENTS

Continuous population growth matched every large-scale water project in California. But the public's willingness to build endless dams, canals, and reservoirs has waned. Education, transportation, health, and welfare needs have competed for tax dollars. Furthermore, environmental groups, convinced that curtailing surplus water would slow growth, fought additional water projects.

In recent years, several changes in water policy have occurred. First, many water districts have initiated mandatory rationing (during droughts) and permanent water conservation. Second, some communities sought alternatives to traditional water sources. Some built desalinization plants, converting sea water into potable water. To be sure, "desal" is expensive drought insurance, costing more than $1,000 per acre-foot—five times more than water from traditional sources. Others began to reclaim waste water for irrigation and other nonpotable purposes. Third, a 1992 federal law required California to consider the needs of threatened fish populations, namely salmon and smelt. Future water allocations from the CVP would have to reflect the respective needs of farmers, city dwellers, and fish. This law allows surplus agricultural water to be sold ("transferred") to urban users during draughts. These new marketing approaches recognize water as a precious commodity, not a free resource for the taking.[15] Fourth, the state resolved to restore the integrity of the Sacramento-San Joaquin River Delta. A federal-state partnership (CALFED) was formed to balance the needs of a water-consuming public and the ecological needs of the Delta itself.[16] Fifth, once disinterested segments of the population have begun to pay attention to water issues. For example, the Latino Issues Forum has identified and publicized particular water issues that impact Latino communities such as pesticide-contaminated drinking water and the lack of Latino representation on California's water policy boards. The chronic issue that faces all Californians is simply a supply and demand problem. Water planners predict that by 2020 the state will experience water deficits from 2 million to 8 million acre-feet.

Housing: For Many, the Impossible Dream

If providing water to a growing and thirsty state seems challenging, consider the Golden State's version of the American Dream—owning a home. Here we consider the challenge of providing adequate, affordable housing for all Californians.

THE CALIFORNIA DREAM

Although home ownership has been an enduring American value, it acquired a semi-rural dimension in California. According to state librarian emeritus Kevin Starr, "At the core of the [California] dream was the hope for a special relationship to nature."[17] In terms of housing, this meant a single-family, detached home with landscaped front, rear, and side yards, and plenty of privacy. The ideal was a residential suburb, far from the congestion, filth, and heterogeneity of the central city.

With the blessings of local government, single-family developments spilled across the landscape. The gridiron plan (resembling a checkerboard), considered efficient by American developers, left little room for common community uses such as neighborhood parks. This dispersed, low-density pattern occurred in California just when the automobile industry itself was expanding. Affordable cars became necessities as Californians consumed one housing tract after another, well away from where they worked. Retail businesses and even factories followed homeowners to suburbia as well. In the process, the idealized rural

lifestyle became increasingly elusive, as if just beyond the next golden hill.

In recent decades, the California middle-class "dream house" has become ever larger—featuring several baths and a bedroom for each family member. More cars per household required ever-larger garages. Census figures revealed that, in 2003, an enormous 38 percent of the nation's million-dollar homes were in California. The public rarely opposes upscale housing, and local officials often respond approvingly.

HOUSING POLICY AS "FILTER DOWN"

Although the federal Housing Act of 1949 envisioned "a decent home and suitable living environment for every American family," governments (federal, state, and local) have not, nor ever will, build much housing. True, federally guaranteed mortgages have helped promote middle-class housing and some publicly owned rental housing exists. But for the most part, it is a private sector activity. California's "policy" has largely mirrored the nation's: *Build housing for the haves and their housing will filter down to the have-nots. Filter down policy* assumes that, as people on the upper rungs of the economic ladder move up to better homes, the ones they vacate will be made available to those on the lower rungs. Private builders propose and construct the housing, and private lenders finance its purchase. Local governments determine and enforce development standards. A smattering of government aid assists a small percentage of the have-nots in their quest for housing.

Does filter down work? Yes, if there is equilibrium between the supply of housing and the demand for it. But this equilibrium has been rare in California due to several factors. First, developers gravitate to housing local governments will approve. Community resistance to multi-family rental units and the prospect of larger profits skew developers toward lower density, more expensive single-family homes. Locally imposed "pay to play" impact fees may add tens of thousands of dollars to the cost of a house. Second, interest rates affect housing costs. When interest rates are relatively low, as they were in the 1990s and early 2000s, more families can afford to buy homes. When they are high, as they were in the late 1970s and 1980s, fewer families qualify. Finally, California's constant population growth keeps demand for housing high, even when economic conditions retard construction or put home loans out of reach. This results in residential overcrowding, home sharing by both families and individuals, and an inability for some to move.

There is both good news and bad news in these housing trends. The good news is that home ownership has increased among California's ethnic groups. The largest gains in the last decade were among Latinos.[18] The bad news is that California still lags behind 48 other states in rates of home ownership. Simply put, demand outpaces supply. Given current population growth, about 220,000 housing units are needed each year; only 170,000 are in fact built. The greatest shortfall has been in multifamily housing. Because the provision of housing is heavily influenced by the private sector and local governments, state and federal policies can only do so much. The state's housing element law requires local governments to specify how and where they will locate their "fair share" of affordable housing. Many local governments resist complying with this law.

AFFORDABILITY

Of the housing units built in the Golden State, many are unaffordable to average Californians. In 2003, eleven of the twenty least affordable communities in the United States were in California. Understandably, many of those are along California's enviable coast but even more affordable Central Valley communities are considered relatively expensive compared to other regions in the United States, especially in the Midwest and the South. As a consequence,

only 18 percent of California households could afford a median-priced home in 2004.

Why is California housing so expensive? First, there is a shortage of appropriately zoned land where people want to live, especially along California's coast. This has forced many who work in coastal cities to move inland, driving upward home prices in those areas. Second, many slow or no-growth groups resist the construction of new housing in their communities. Some disfavor housing on flat land (because agricultural land needs preservation) *or* on hillsides (because of fire and flooding dangers). Third, many city officials believe housing does not generate enough property taxes to pay for the services it requires. They prefer sales tax–laden retail uses (such as auto malls and shopping centers) that require minimal public services. As noted earlier, this has been called the "fiscalization of land use." Fourth, local residents in some communities have been downright hostile to affordable housing, especially apartment buildings. This "drawbridge mentality," as planners call it, inhibits elected officials from approving such housing. This phenomenon spans the state and the consequences are dire. Nearly 40 percent of all California households are renters; that figure jumps to 55 percent for Latino and African American households. Many of these renters find their housing costs rising faster than their incomes which in turn requires them to spend an ever greater share of their incomes on housing. This pattern affects not only the poor but also middle-class Californians.[19]

What will it take to build more affordable housing in California? First, Proposition 13 formulas need to be modified so that more property tax revenues stay in the communities that generate them. For example, local governments could swap half their sales tax revenues for property taxes that are currently commandeered by the state; this would reduce at least some of the fiscal bias against housing development. Second, the state could award housing bonuses to local governments that

PHOTO 12.1 Stuck in traffic

Heavy traffic on the Harbor Freeway in downtown Los Angeles looks increasingly familiar to urban Californans.

Question: In what ways do urban patterns in California worsen traffic conditions?

meet ambitious affordable housing goals. Third, greater state-level investment in infrastructure such as road improvements would offset at least some of the local impacts of new housing and arguably some of the community opposition to housing rooted in infrastructure concerns.[20]

Transportation: Stuck in Traffic

A 1993 movie, *Falling Down,* portrayed a California motorist losing control while sitting in noisy, sweltering Los Angeles traffic. Today, we might call it a case of "road rage." Although these instances are rare, consider this. Today, Californians spend more than 300,000 hours

per day in traffic jams (Photo 12.1). Freeway speeds are slowing, and, on many urban freeways, the "rush hour" itself has disappeared into a cloud of heavy traffic—all day, every day. Bus and rail transit riders are not exempt from traffic delays. In fact, simple door-to-door commute times are shorter for automobile drivers than for public transit users.

THE PROBLEM

Although traffic congestion is easy to see and experience, it is a very complex policy problem. Three factors help explain why.

Personal Choice

Californians, as other Americans, love their automobiles. Before widespread car ownership,

259

streetcars and trolleys augmented walking, and living "in town" was actually desirable. The automobile essentially reversed those preferences. The automobile symbolized American individualism and personal choice. As a 1926 *Los Angeles Times* editorial put it, "How can one pursue happiness with any swifter and surer means than the automobile?" In modern times, acquiring one has become a rite of passage to adulthood. For many California college and university students, "wheels" are as fixed an expense as tuition, room, board, and books.

There is no escaping the congestion that results from these personal choices. Given the proliferation of car ownership, one household may claim at least one vehicle per driver. People can feel the impact. Once-picturesque residential streets are lined bumper- to- bumper with cars, more than city hall planners ever anticipated. Lengthy commutes may be the logical extension of personal choice in individualistic California. In this view, the "jobs/housing imbalance" (as urban planners call it) is really a rational choice tradeoff between relatively short commutes and affordable but distant housing.

Urban Development Patterns

Personal choice affects traffic, but so does the legacy of urban development in California. Cities dispersed as waves of newcomers arrived. Massive highway projects linked downtowns with the suburbs. These highways once accommodated the growth of suburban commuters, but no more. Even those who found jobs closer to home discovered local surface streets as clogged as the freeways. Urban and suburban sprawl has permeated California.

Environmental Effects

California's motor vehicles do more than create congestion. Consider smog. The chief component of smog is ozone (which occurs when hydrocarbons and nitrogen oxides react to sunlight). Nitrogen oxide forms during the combustion of fossil fuels. California's combination of climate and terrain creates what the Air Resources Board calls "Mother Nature's perfect smog chamber." Long before statehood, Native Americans called the Los Angeles Basin the "Land of a Thousand Smokes." California smog reaches farther than most people realize. Central Valley smog can affect Sequoia seedlings in the high Sierras and Southern California smog can reach Arizona's Grand Canyon. Vehicle smog is acute for several reasons. First, while California is only average among the states in automobile ownership, the sheer volume of vehicles—gasoline and diesel—makes California's air among the nation's dirtiest. Second, California's older vehicles can emit twice the pollution of newer cars. There have been some public efforts to buy up the worst offenders to cut smog levels.

Did You Know ... ?

Registered vehicles in California outnumber registered drivers. In 2005, there were more than 20 million licensed drivers in California, but there were more than 26 million vehicles (including automobiles, trucks, and motorcycles).

SOURCE: California Department of Motor Vehicles (www.dmv.ca.gov/).

Smog is only one vehicle-related culprit. Automobile contaminants (oil, grease, antifreeze, and small tire particles) wash into streams and waterways. According to one study, auto pollution rivals industrial waste as a danger to San Francisco Bay.[21] Traffic noise, fumes, and road dust are also major problems. The ribbons of freeways that snake through metropolitan areas create major noise pollution for nearby residents. The health effects can be severe. According to the Environmental Working Group, more than 9,300 Californians die each year by exposure to airborne particulate matter—more than by car accidents, homicides, and AIDS combined. Furthermore, this type of pollution affects the poor and non-Anglos more than affluent or white communities.[22]

CALIFORNIA'S TRANSPORTATION POLICIES

Few public policies boil down to one sentence; California's transportation policy largely does. *Historically, California's transportation policy has been to accommodate the automobile.* Local governments typically approved traffic-generating developments and provided the local streets required. Large-scale state and national highways and the interstate system were shared responsibilities, but the primary policymaker was the state of California. For years, even the agency titles (Highway Commission and Division of Highways) belied a policy bias. In 1923, a two-cent per gallon gasoline tax was established to finance this policy of accommodation. In the late 1940s, a new building program began to which was added the interstate system in the 1950s. Opposition to more freeways rose on occasion. San Francisco voters rejected them in 1964. In the 1970s, Governor Jerry Brown wanted to change the state's emphasis from highways to mass transit. Yet demand for highways continued and, by the 1990s, the renamed Department of Transportation (Caltrans) was understaffed, underfunded, and

backlogged with unfinished projects. While highway capacity increased by only 4 percent in the 1980s and 1990s, California's population grew by 50 percent. The result? Compared to other states, California ranks near the bottom in per capita highway spending.

Recent developments suggest some change in transportation policy. First, California voters have demonstrated some willingness to improve the state's transportation infrastructure. In 1990, a slim majority approved a gas tax increase (Proposition 111) and a mass transit bond measure (Proposition 108). But voters turned down additional bond and gas tax measures in 1992 and 1994. At the local level, voters in more than 20 counties have approved sales tax add-ons for city and county road improvements. Some counties have used these funds to complete projects the state once funded exclusively or to repair earthquake damage. In the late 1990s, Caltrans was able to work on a backlog of previously approved highway projects.

Second, a 1989 law permitted Caltrans to build toll roads—quite a departure for a state traditionally wedded to *free*ways. Toll roads, a given in many states, are a point of contention in California. For example, recently built toll roads in Orange County have been controversial. While easing some traffic congestion, these roads use so-called value pricing, which inflates tolls considerably during rush hours. Critics have called them "Lexus lanes." Despite a host of financial and jurisdictional problems, others defend toll roads as an important, if partial, answer to the backlog of state road projects.[23] Third, efforts have begun to improve rail transit throughout California. Residents and tourists alike are familiar with BART, the Bay Area Rapid Transit system that links San Francisco with its suburbs. In more recent years, several commuter rail systems have linked outlying suburbs to Los Angeles, San Jose, and other cities. Planners also envision a high-speed rail system connecting San Diego, Los Angeles, the Bay Area, and Sacramento.

Such a rail corridor would reduce air travel and airport-related automobile traffic. At present, the Los Angeles/Bay Area air corridor is the most highly traveled in the nation.[24]

Energy and Environment

California's population growth has severely impacted the state's quality of life in two broad areas: energy and environment. Energy policies address the oil, natural gas, and electricity demands of a complex, energy-hungry economy and the lifestyles of nearly 37 million residents. Environmental policies address the impacts of economic and population growth on the quality of the state's water, air, land, and natural resources.

ENERGY

The electricity crisis of the early 2000s highlighted a host of energy-related concerns. Californians suffered both spiraling electricity prices and infuriating gaps in service—brownouts and blackouts. As the British journal, *The Economist,* put it, "One of the wealthiest regions in the world is on the brink of an energy crisis of third-world proportions. How did California come to this?"[25] The answer to that question lies in a confluence of public policies and events—electricity's version of the perfect storm. The key decision was the passage of Assembly Bill 1890, a 100-page law that sought to replace a patchwork of regulatory practices with an open-market approach.[26] Electricity generation did become more competitive, but other developments worsened the situation:

• Wholesale energy prices floated freely while policymakers froze retail prices.

• No new power plants were built to replace old plants and meet increased demand.

• Stable long-term energy contracts were disallowed.

• Energy generators and traders (like the infamous Enron Corporation) "gamed" the system by withholding capacity to spike short-term prices.

• Encouragement of energy conservation was neglected.

• The two largest public utilities became insolvent, requiring state aid to avoid bankruptcy.

In short, California's approach to deregulation failed. To many, the outcome was as much a debacle as a crisis—a bitter lesson in how *not* to deregulate. In response, Governor Gray Davis and the legislature offered still more reforms, including these: (1) using public funds to bail out financially strapped public utilities, (2) selling energy bonds to repay state costs, (3) renegotiating costly energy contracts, (4) streaming the construction of new power plants, (5) encouraging consumer conservation, and (6) researching alternative energy resources (such as solar and wind). In 2004, Governor Arnold Schwarzenegger called for a modest, more cautious return to deregulation in order to insure affordable yet stable electricity supplies. Energy experts advocate a pragmatic mix of strategies to craft a crisis-proof energy policy.[27]

ENVIRONMENT

Continued efforts are also under way to address environmental pollution in the Golden State. In one respect, California's population growth adds nearly 2,000 new "polluters" daily. But population is only one part of the equation. The development of new technologies (silicon chips, synthetic materials, and industrial processes) also adds new toxins to the environment. The long-range impact of environmental pollution may well be global warming—the *greenhouse effect*. This is caused by a buildup of gases that allow the heat of the sun to penetrate the atmosphere but prevent it from escaping. If this problem is as serious as some scientists claim, a permanent warming trend would raise ocean levels (inundating California's coastline), threaten the ozone layer (worsening the state's already high skin cancer rates), alter plant growth patterns (endangering the agricultural base of the state), and diminish the Sierra winter snowpack (reducing California's water supply).[28]

The short-term impact of environmental pollution is more immediate and visible. A derailed train spills chemicals into a scenic river, destroying all manner of life in its path. Residents near toxic waste dumps trace their illnesses to those dumps. Beaches are plagued or even closed by untreated sewage, elevated bacteria levels, storm runoff, and oil deposits. The California Air Resources Board indicates that more than 90 percent of Californians breathe unhealthy levels of at least one air pollutant during some part of the year. The most vulnerable residents—children, the elderly, and those with respiratory problems—may be advised to stay indoors on "smog alert" days.

News accounts and the prospect of continued population growth well into the twenty-first century gives environmental concern a sense of urgency.[29] In what seems like an uphill battle, California policymakers now rely on four separate but interrelated approaches to environmental pollution. All are based on a fundamental truth: *The private sector largely creates pollution, but it is government's responsibility to eliminate it.*

Regulate It

One traditional approach has been to issue regulations, set standards, and order offenders to comply. Sometimes called *command and control,* this approach has been implemented by numerous agencies. For example, the legislature periodically authorizes the Air Resources Board to set emission standards for various types of vehicles and to establish deadlines for compliance. Because California represents 13 percent

of the automobile market nationwide, these regulations spur manufacturers to innovate and seek more fuel-efficient hybrid and fuel cell technologies.[30] The Integrated Waste Management Act required that 50 percent of the state's solid waste be diverted from landfills by the year 2000. In response, local governments required trash haulers to provide recycling opportunities. Some regional agencies have also used the regulatory approach. The South Coast Air Quality Management District has issued tough regulations requiring emission reductions from autos and stationary sources such as power plants and industrial sites. Although the command and control approach seems heavy-handed, it has fostered new recycling techniques and some new products (unleaded gasoline, methanol, recyclable plastic).

Move It

Another "solution" to pollution in California has been to send it somewhere else. Indeed, by the late 1980s, more than 30 other states were receiving toxic waste from California. In recent years, such exports have slowed. Ironically, strong environmental laws in California make intrastate waste disposal difficult and costly. Where it is feasible, large amounts of waste have been stored near poor, ethnic minority communities, a practice sometimes called "environmental racism." NIMBYism has discouraged siting new toxic waste facilities most anywhere. With nowhere to go, many toxins are simply stored in garages, warehouses, and factory yards.

Price It

A recent development in environmental protection has been a market-based approach. For example, by determining a price or market value for nitrogen oxide, government can create incentives for companies to offset existing sources of smog when plants expand. Also, cities place a "price" on automobiles when they charge high fees for all-day downtown

PHOTO 12.2 Farming the wind

These wind turbines near Palm Springs serve the Los Angeles Department of Water and Power. Given recent energy woes, farming the wind and sun may become more attractive.

Question: If cleaner sources of energy cost a bit more (as they did in the 1990s) would you be willing to pay the added cost?

parking. At some point, some drivers may consider cheaper, cleaner alternatives such as mass transit, ridesharing, biking, walking, or telecommuting from home. Pricing incentives assume a partnership between the private and public sectors, but this is just beginning in California. And the state's environmentalists remain uneasy when they hear terms like "emission reduction credits."

Replace It

One last approach has been to replace fossil fuels and hydroelectric power with renewable sources of energy such as solar, wind, geothermal, biomass, and small-scale hydropower (see Photo 12.2). In the past, "green power" was not attractive to utility companies because it cost more to produce and was less predictable (due to cloudy days and sporadic winds). State tax credits in the 1970s and early 1980s provided tax incentives to develop some renewables (solar power, for example). Today, technological advances such as fuel cells, lower operating costs, and reaction to the electricity crisis are making these energy alternatives both competitive and attractive in environmentally conscious California.[31]

Conclusion: A New Growth Policy for California?

California has experienced phenomenal growth throughout its history. A generalized pro-growth consensus among policy leaders aided post-World War II growth. Population growth continued unchecked, local governments readily approved commercial and residential development, and the state provided the necessary infrastructure. Notable were vast water projects, highways, and a comprehensive education system. By the 1960s and 1970s, concerns about too much growth were raised. Development sprawled across the landscape, an automobile-dominated transportation system seemed to choke on itself, smog was a permanent reality in much of California, and news of environmental damage was commonplace.

Growth as a potent issue has an ebb and flow quality to it. By the late 1980s, concern over growth in California entered the mainstream of California politics. Governor Pete Wilson, Assembly Speaker Willie Brown, other legislators, interest groups, and academic think tanks were simultaneously discussing the issue and proposing various reforms.[32] But California's economic recession in the early 1990s consumed political attention in Sacramento; in later years, education and energy seemed to supplant growth as dominant issues. Yet the drumbeat of population growth fuels most other issues in the state.

To the extent policymakers consider various "solutions" to the problem, they will likely include the following ideas.

A Statewide Growth Strategy

You may have been impressed with the number of agencies at all levels that address land use, water, housing, transportation, and environmental protection. This jurisdictional fragmentation can and does result in policy conflict. For example, some policies (such as building more freeways) encourage automobile use at the expense of mass transit. Building more housing may conflict with the protection of open space. One solution would be a comprehensive, future-oriented statewide growth strategy. Such a strategy would both control growth itself and accommodate growth that cannot be controlled. So far, policymakers have been unable to do either very effectively. Then-Governor Gray Davis laid out the challenge: "As California moves into the 21st Century we face the dual problem of preserving the schools, highways, bridges, water systems, and housing of today while also planning and building new facilities for a growing population. There is no choice: we must maintain our current capital investments—"infrastructure"—and make new investments."[33] In the years since, the state's budget woes have resulted in an infrastructure deficit that grows each year. One report by the California Infrastructure Coalition sums up the current state of affairs—*Infrastructure in California: Overburdened, Outdated, and Overlooked.*[34]

Controlling California's population growth itself is a much more difficult challenge. It seems to be treated as a given that policymakers can do little about. After all, in a diverse, representative democracy, how does government tell families to have fewer children? How does a mere state barricade an international border? In light of private property rights, how do local officials tell people they cannot build houses on land zoned for that use? No wonder policymakers are at best ambivalent about population growth control.

Rethink Home Rule

Under the engrained doctrine of home rule, local governments can and should make their own decisions about growth. Yet this approach ignores the impact that decisions in one community may have on its neighbors. Interjurisdictional turf battles may result, but managing regional growth does not. Proposed solutions to the home rule "problem" include giving greater land use authority to existing councils of governments (COGs), establishing still larger superagencies to manage regional growth, and reducing the power of single-purpose, single-minded agencies that focus exclusively on water, air quality, or transportation. Progress on this front is slow.

Defiscalize Development

In the current "do-it-yourself" era of American federalism, local governments have depended less on the state and federal governments to subsidize local growth and its infrastructure. This trend, coupled with Proposition 13, compelled local officials to approve projects that pay more in taxes than they consume in services (for example, shopping centers). In turn, communities compete to attract such projects while shunning less lucrative ones (for example, low-income housing). Numerous reform groups now seek "smart growth" strategies that manage, steer, and coordinate land use decisions while decoupling them from their revenue impacts.

Reduce Population Growth

At the center of the issues discussed in Chapter 12—land use, water, housing, transportation, energy, and environment—is, and will continue to be, population growth. One grassroots lobbying organization, Californians for Population Stabilization (CAPS), addresses that issue head on. They point to high fertility rates within the state and "over-immigration" to the state—noting that California is growing as fast as Mexico. CAPS urges more family planning, strict immigration controls, and other policies to protect what they consider to be a quality of life enjoyed by all Californians. Some of these ideas are controversial because they challenge behavior deeply rooted in the state's diverse ethnic and cultural groups. They may also seem heavy-handed, elitist, and reactionary. Yet any growth management efforts that ignore population growth itself will likely miss the mark in California.

KEY TERMS

quality of life   (p. 246)

impact fees   (p. 250)

general plan, zoning ordinance, subdivision regulations   (p. 250)

uniform building code   (p. 250)

PUDs   (p. 250)

NIMBYs and LULUs   (p. 251)

riparian rights, prior appropriation rights, prescriptive rights   (p. 254)

filter down policy   (pp. 257–258)

fiscalization of land use   (p. 258)

greenhouse effect   (pp. 262–263)

command and control   (p. 263)

REVIEW QUESTIONS

1. Why did California grow and why does it continue to do so?

2. Describe land use politics at the local level.

3. Explain the rise and meaning of California's no-growth movement.

4. Delineate the major components of California's plumbing system.

5. What is the California Dream and to what extent do filter down policies fulfill it?

6. Explain California's ongoing relationship with the automobile.

7. Outline the major approaches to environmental pollution in the Golden State.

8. To control the impacts of growth in California, what has been recommended and what do you recommend?

WEB ACTIVITIES

Business, Transportation, and Housing Agency
(www.bth.ca.gov/)
This state mega-agency provides links to a number of data-rich agencies dealing with housing and transportation.

California Environmental Protection Agency
(www.calepa.ca.gov/)
This is a similar umbrella agency with links to boards dealing with air, water, and solid waste pollution.

California Futures Network
(www.calfutures.org/)
This broad-based coalition encourages land use policies that are fiscally, socially, and environmentally sound.

INFOTRAC® COLLEGE EDITION ARTICLES

For additional reading, go to InfoTrac® College Edition, your online research library, at http://www.infotrac.thomsonlearning.com

Housing, Population Statistics Reveal Ongoing Divisions in State

Taking Its Toll

In Fish vs. Farmer Cases, The Fish Loses Its Edge

NOTES

1. A summation of this concern can be found in Nancy Vogel, "Is California Bursting at the Seams?" *California Journal* 22 (July 1991): 295–299.
2. Roger W. Lotchin, *Fortress California, 1910–1961: From Warfare to Welfare* (New York: Oxford University Press, 1992).
3. Examples include Raymond Dasman, *The Destruction of California* (New York: Macmillan, 1965) and Samuel E. Wood and Alfred E. Heller, *California Going, Going . . .* (Sacramento: California Tomorrow, 1962).
4. Californians and the Land, "Polling Audit: Urban Sprawl in California," (1997) located at www.calfutures.org/ITNpolling.html/.
5. See Joel Garreau, *Edge City: Life on the New Frontier* (New York: Doubleday, 1991), especially chaps. 8 and 9 on Southern California and the Bay Area, respectively.
6. Eric Bailey, "More People Headed Inland," *Los Angeles Times,* December 31, 2001.
7. Mark Baldessare, *PPIC Statewide Survey: Special Survey on Growth* (San Francisco: Public Policy Institute of California, May 2001).
8. See William Fulton and Paul Shigley, "Land-Use Woes Hit Home," *California Journal* 31 (December 2001): 50–53 and Richard Taylor, et al. *Ballot Box Planning: Understanding Land Use Initiatives in California* (Sacramento: Institute for Local Self Government, 2001).
9. Mark DiCamillo and Mervin Field, *The Field Poll,* Release #2045 (May 15, 2002).
10. Erwin Cooper, *Aqueduct Empire* (Glendale, CA: The Arthur H. Clark Company, 1968), 202.
11. Edward Abbey, *Desert Solitaire* (New York: Simon and Schuster, 1968), 126.
12. Noel Brinkerhoff, "Who's Minding the Aquifer?" *California Journal* 32 (July 2001): 16–21.
13. Quoted in Norris Hundley Jr., *The Great Thirst: Californians and Water, 1770s–1990s* (Berkeley, CA: University of California Press, 1992), 148.
14. *California Water Subsidies* (Washington, D.C.: Environmental Working Group, 2004). Available at www.ewg.org/reports.
15. Noel Brinkerhoff, "Water Marketing: Let's Make a Deal," *California Journal* 30 (August 1999): 12–17.
16. Steve Scott, "Restoring the Delta," *California Journal* 28 (May 1997): 36–43.
17. Kevin Starr, *Americans and the California Dream, 1850–1915* (New York: Oxford University Press, 1973), 417.
18. Ann Martinez, "Minorities Make Gains in Owning Homes," *San Jose Mercury News,* August 8, 2001.
19. For more on this rental dilemma, see *Locked Out 2004: California's Affordable Housing Crisis*

(Sacramento: California Budget Project, 2004). Available at www.cbp.org/.

20. Reid Cramer, "The Crumbling California Dream: Erecting Structural Changes to Solve California's Housing Crisis," *California Journal* 36 (January 2005), 25–28.

21. Olszewski, Lori, "Autos Attacked as Major Water Polluter," *San Francisco Chronicle,* August 20, 1991.

22. Available online at www.ewg.org/.

23. Jenifer B. McKim, "For Whom the Road Tolls," *California Journal* 32 (June 2001): 46–50.

24. For more on transportation issues, see Sigrid Bathen, "Gridlock . . . and Beyond," *California Journal* 29 (November 1998): 36–39.

25. "California's Power Crisis," *The Economist* (January 20, 2001): 57.

26. For an overview of this deregulatory effort, see Steve Scott, "California's New Electric Bill," *California Journal* 27 (November 1996): 9–13.

27. Charles J. Cicchetti, Jeffrey A. Dubin, and Colin M. Long, *The California Energy Crisis:*

What, Why and What's Next (Hingham, MA: Kluwer, 2004).

28. On this last impact, see Edie Lau, "Sierra Will Be Hit Hard by Warming, Study Says," *Sacramento Bee,* June 4, 2002.

29. Tom Knudson, "Is It Too Late to Save California?" *California Journal* 26 (April 1995): 18–21.

30. William J. Kelly, "Getting Bigger and Better," *California Journal* 34 (February 2003), 6–10.

31. Peter Asmus, "California's Energy Legacy: A Desperate Innovator," *California Journal* 32 (January 2001): 16–21.

32. An excellent survey of earlier reforms is John D. Landis, "Regional Growth Management," in John J. Kirlin, ed., *California Policy Choices, Vol. 8* (Sacramento: University of Southern California School of Public Administration, 1992).

33. *Governor's Budget Summary, 1999–2000* (Sacramento: Governor's Office, 1999), 21.

34. Accessed at www.calinfrastructure.org/.

CHAPTER 13

Policies Stemming from Diversity

In Brief

In Chapter 13, we consider the cultural diversity of California and its impact on five policy areas: abortion, education, higher education, social programs, and immigration. Policy conflicts in these areas are struggles among competing groups—cultural hyperpluralism and ensuing political conflict seem best to describe this state of affairs.

Many of the policies described in this chapter reflect several patterns in politics: *client,*

entrepreneurial, interest group, and *majoritarian.* In California, as elsewhere, the issues of abortion and gay rights mirror a diversity of values and fundamental disagreements over what constitutes personhood and marriage. Public education (K–12) must deal with population growth, ethnic diversity, social change, and variable funding. Education reforms are frequent, and they vary in effectiveness. Multicultural politics is evident even in textbook adoptions and testing. California's Master Plan for higher education promises affordable access to colleges and universities for all qualified Californians, yet observers wonder if it will be able to handle future demands.

California's array of social programs serve a growing, diverse population, many of whom do not fully participate in the political process. Programs to alleviate poverty involve all levels of government and are aimed primarily at the "deserving poor." In terms of medical care, state-regulated private insurance and Medi-Cal cover many Californians, at dramatically rising costs. Yet many working Californians are both uninsured and uncovered by government assistance. The worst-off seem to be the deinstitutionalized mentally ill, some of whom are homeless. Last, California's policies toward immigrants, especially illegal ones, have become increasingly restrictive and, to some, mean-spirited.

These are the challenges facing an emerging multicultural democracy—one depicted by population growth, cultural diversity, and group conflict.

Introduction: The Challenge of Diversity

At a neighborhood forum, residents complained about disruption caused by Latino immigrants: cars sitting in front yards, chickens clucking, parks commandeered by soccer players, *ranchera* music day and night. "It's a different culture, a different breed of people. They don't have the same values. You can't get together with them. It's like mixing oil and water." Were these the words of a reactionary white suburbanite? No, they were spoken by the president of an African American homeowners association in South-Central Los Angeles.[1] They illustrate the most profound, long-term challenge facing the Golden State: building a multiracial, multicultural society that is at peace with itself. In terms of the nation's motto, *E Pluribus Unum* (out of many, one), the likelihood of California's political system forging an *unum* out of a *pluribus* is an open question. There never has been one monolithic culture in California, but even the myth of one is diminishing. Politically speaking, the notion of an overarching public interest—what founder James Madison called "the good of the whole"—seems increasingly elusive in California.

California is at a major juncture in its political development, a time when the broad forces of growth and diversity are colliding and will likely change how politics is done. In Chapter 12, the policy issues of water, housing, transportation, and pollution were used to explain the larger question of population growth and its consequences. Chapter 13 examines the issues of abortion, gay rights, education, welfare, health, and immigration to emphasize the larger topic of cultural diversity and its consequences.

Cultural diversity is nothing new in California's political development. Historically, minority cultures were either extinguished or separated from the larger society. In the 1500s, a Spanish culture largely replaced California's Native American culture through disease and conquest. Mexicans subsequently dominated the region of California until the mid-1800s. The discovery of gold brought white settlers from other U.S. states and Europe. Historians refer to this influx of non-Hispanic whites as the "Americanization" of California. These settlers intermarried widely, creating a dominant culture—a process sociologists call *cultural amalgamation*. For much of California's history as a state, Euro-Americans have been the dominant cultural group. At times, they discriminated against Chinese and Japanese immigrants as well as against African Americans and Latinos, enforcing a *cultural separatism*, often through housing segregation. The dominant pattern in modern times has been *cultural assimilation;* to "succeed," minority groups need to adopt the practices and characteristics of the "host" society.[2]

According to demographer Leon Bouvier, by the early-1900s, a two-tier pattern in California was evident: "a melting pot among the majority people of European ancestry, and cultural separation for non-white minorities."[3] Civil rights legislation in the 1960s and widespread immigration by nonwhite minorities from Latin America and Asia in the 1980s and 1990s began to change that pattern. From 1975 to 1994, California absorbed 38 percent of immigrants legally entering the United States (600,000 out of 1.6 million). It also became home to 53 percent of the 3 million immigrants granted amnesty under the 1986 Immigration Reform and Control Act. By 2005,

well over 2 million illegal immigrants resided in California.

As the white majority in California continues to shrink in size (see Figure 13.1), the traditional idea of assimilation into a "majority" culture begins to lose meaning. In a growing number of California cities, no ethnic group constitutes a majority. What California now faces is *cultural hyperpluralism:* various ethnic, racial, religious, and other groups rejecting the idea of "one people," elevating the importance of group identity, and competing among themselves for scarce public resources. "Balkanization" has been used to describe California's emerging society and the politics that mirror it. Madison's warnings about factions, those groups he viewed as "adverse to the rights of other citizens, or to the permanent and aggregate interests of the community" ("Federalist, No. 10"), seem as relevant today as ever.

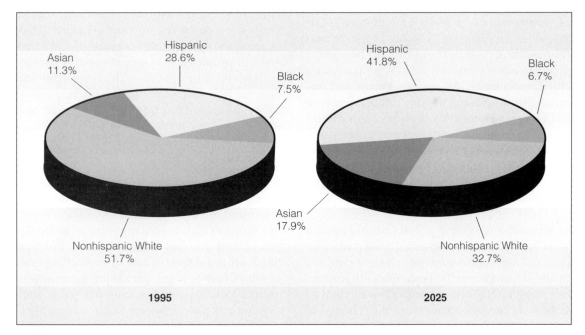

FIGURE 13.1 Where California Is Headed

Question: To what extent do you see these changes taking place today?

Cultural hyperpluralism goes beyond ethnicity. It is also evident in a variety of policy conflicts involving educational and lifestyle issues. Sociologist James Davison Hunter describes these conflicts as "political and social hostility rooted in different systems of moral understanding."[4] According to this perspective, a number of policy debates in California and the nation (such as abortion, gay rights, and certain educational policies) can ultimately be traced to differing views of moral authority. The goal of opposing groups is not peaceful coexistence but winning a war of values.

California Policy as Group Struggle

Political scientists consider groups (economic, social, racial, religious, or otherwise) highly important in the policy process. According to political scientist James Q. Wilson, politics involves a struggle between groups or coalitions of groups over the perceived benefits and costs of particular policies. Wilson suggests that four political patterns help explain how many groups coalesce around various policy issues: client, entrepreneurial, interest group, and majoritarian. To varying degrees, all four emerge in California politics. Yet these patterns cannot be rigidly applied to each and every public policy. Although some issues may not fall squarely into just one category, they do help explain how people perceive policy—perceptions that change over time.

1. *Client Politics.* Client politics occurs when a small group stands to benefit from a particular policy. The costs of such policies are paid for by the larger society. Two examples are instructive. One is federally subsidized water rates to California farmers. Farmers are the "clients" in this case. Nonfarming Californians pay higher rates or higher taxes to make those subsidies possible but are either unaware they are doing so or do not much care. Another example would be the state's two failed voucher initiatives (Propositions 174 and 38). One reason they may have failed was that voting majorities (69 and 71 percent, respectively) perceived that vouchers would unacceptably benefit a particular client group—private school parents. Several Indian gaming measures (Propositions 5 and 1A) have furthered the goal of self-sufficiency for the state's Native American tribes but two others (Propositions 68 and 70) have sought to limit the impact and expansion of gaming in California.

2. *Entrepreneurial Politics.* In this pattern, coalitions form around a relative handful of individuals (policy entrepreneurs) who claim to speak for a much larger number of people. They strive for policies that would presumably benefit the "silent majority" while imposing costs on some small group. California entrepreneurs rarely succeed in Sacramento, but they are remarkably successful in qualifying and passing initiatives. In 1978, Paul Gann and Howard Jarvis sponsored Proposition 13, the famous property tax cutting measure. They claimed to represent all "overtaxed" Californians and promised that only the state's bureaucrats would suffer the costs. In 1998, actor and director Rob Reiner qualified and campaigned for Proposition 10, a tobacco tax increase that now funds local-level child development programs and antismoking efforts at the expense of California smokers.

3. *Interest Group Politics.* This pattern represents the pushing and pulling of competing, organized interests. It occurs when one group or coalition stands to gain from a particular policy and another stands to lose. Political battles may be fought not only over material benefits (such as tax breaks or government grants) but also over less tangible goals (such as political power, social status, or cultural dominance). To be sure, these groups represent the immediate interests of their members, but they may also reflect attitudes and opinions

in the larger political culture. Although these groups are familiar with the ways of Sacramento, they also use the initiative process. In 1993 and 2000, the California Teachers Association spent millions to defeat voucher activists. Recent elections have pitted Indian casinos against Las Vegas casinos and tobacco companies against antismoking interests. In the Capitol legislative process, opposing interest groups face off over gun control, abortion, educational testing, affirmative action, and a host of lesser known issues.

4. *Majoritarian Politics.* This coalitional pattern occurs when a large majority of people believes they will benefit from a particular policy and are willing to shoulder the costs of that policy. Historically, some of California's most ambitious policies could be characterized as majoritarian. For instance, the state's highway system benefits millions of motorists who in turn pay gas taxes. California's growing prison system benefits (protects) the law-abiding majority who support it through the state's general fund. Public education, too, is a majoritarian policy. Most school-aged Californians (more than 6 million) attend publicly funded schools. Majoritarian education policy extends through the community college system with its open admissions policy. As access narrows progressively to California State University (CSU) and the University of California (UC) because of entrance requirements and space limitations, higher education to some people seems less "majoritarian" than it has been or ought to be.

Social Issues: Abortion and Gay Rights

Some public policy issues do not involve large expenditures of public funds. They cannot be viewed as government programs, run by permanent state agencies. Unlike the annual state budget, they do not consume vast amounts of policymaker time. Yet they stir human emotions, produce conflict, and divide Californians unlike most other public policies. We call these policies *social issues.* Here we focus on the two most familiar ones—abortion and gay rights.

ABORTION

Abortion is one of the most controversial political issues for both the nation and for California. In the Golden State, the controversy actually preceded the U.S. Supreme Court's famous decision in *Roe v. Wade* (1973), which established a woman's right of privacy relative to giving birth. Before the 1960s, abortion in California was relatively rare and largely illegal. Prosecutions were rarer still, because it was assumed physicians knew best what to do. During the 1960s, legislation was introduced to legalize what many doctors were already doing—performing abortions to protect the life and health of the mother. As medical procedures improved, the woman's health became a less important justification for abortion. In 1962, publicity surrounding a pregnant woman who had taken the drug Thalidomide, plus a rubella epidemic, heightened public awareness of the philosophical issues involved. Was a damaged life still worth living? Few Californians had bothered to ask that question before. Physicians no longer controlled the abortion issue when the general public began asking what being a "person" really means.

In 1967, the Therapeutic Abortion Act (the "Beilenson bill") clarified abortion practice in the Golden State. Allowable reasons for an abortion were expanded to some extent, but physicians would still be "in charge." The impact of the Beilenson bill was stunning, immediate, and surprising to many. Between 1968 and 1972, California abortions increased by 2,000 percent (from 5,000 to more than 100,000 annually). A law intended to simply codify existing practice was perceived to allow abortion

TABLE 13.1 California Voters and Abortion

In respect to the issue of abortion, do you favor laws that would make it more difficult for a woman to get an abortion, favor laws that would make it easier to get an abortion, or should no change be made in existing laws?

Make abortion easier to obtain	Make no change	Make abortion harder to obtain	No opinion
26%	45	22	22

Source: The Field Poll (June 4, 2004), 2.

on demand, before *Roe v. Wade* nationalized the controversy. The Beilenson bill and the *Roe* decision unleashed two grassroots movements, each supporting a conflicting fundamental right—the right to terminate a pregnancy versus a right to be born.[5] The political divide between these two movements is deep and wide. One group calls the unborn fetuses; the other, babies. Even group labels are politicized. According to one side, those calling themselves "pro-choice" are actually pro-abortion. According to the other side, self-described "pro-life" groups are not only anti-abortion, they are anti-choice. See Table 13.1 for a snapshot of voters' opinions on abortion in the Golden State.

Much is at stake for both sides. In 2000 abortions in California numbered about 236,000—18 percent of the national total. Abortion rates have been declining nationwide and in California for several years. Several recent U.S. Supreme Court cases, *Webster v. Reproductive Health Services* (1989) and *Planned Parenthood v. Casey* (1992), while not overturning the right to an abortion, upheld a number of state restrictions on its use. In effect, this moved the political war over abortion to the states. In California, the battle is waged on several fronts. The first is among policy-makers and the interest groups that influence them. In Sacramento, interest groups such as the California Pro-Life Council and the California Abortion Rights League have lined up predictably for or against Medi-Cal funding of abortions for the indigent. In some years, the California legislature has denied Medi-Cal funding for abortions, but the courts have regularly overturned such restrictions. A second front has been in state courts. For example, in 1997, the California Supreme Court on a four to three vote struck down a never-enforced law requiring teenage girls to obtain parental or judicial approval for an abortion (*American Academy of Pediatrics v. Lungren*).

A third front has involved protest activity. In the 1990s, the anti-abortion group Operation Rescue organized clinic protests and blockades as well as harassed clinic doctors and employees. Increasingly, these tactics were countered by pro-choice demonstrators. Occasionally, violence or vandalism has occurred. In recent years, several court cases have limited the ability of pro-life groups to block access to abortion clinics. Abortion protests have become less frequent as anti-abortion activists focus more on counseling and abstinence education.

A fourth front has been the court of public opinion. In recent years, a majority of California voters have reflected a pro-choice sentiment. As Table 13.1 suggests, about 26 percent favor making abortion easier to obtain, 45 percent support current policy, and 22 percent support making abortion harder to obtain. Other polling data suggest that support for abortion rights declines the longer a woman is pregnant. A majority favors parental consent for teenage abortions but also supports late-term abortions if the mother's life is in danger.[6]

To sum up, California's political climate today is largely pro-choice. California Democrats, who are more pro-choice than Republicans, control the legislature. Recent governors (Pete Wilson, Gray Davis, and Arnold Schwarzenegger) have been pro-choice. Even pro-life Republicans have been tempted to downplay the issue in recent elections. This climate is supported by the state constitution's explicit right of privacy (Article I, Section 1). Although this provision was not passed with abortion in mind, it does provide a vehicle to defend abortion rights in California courts. Yet, it appears that either extending or curtailing current abortion rights will not draw majority support.

GAY RIGHTS

As with abortion rights, advancing the rights of California's homosexuals and lesbians has been waged on several fronts. The most visible one has been at the ballot box. As you recall from Chapter 4, Proposition 22 was a 2000 initiative that amended the state's Family Code by adding this simple statement: "Only marriage between a man and a woman is valid or recognized in California." More than 60 percent of the voters agreed with that statement. Today, the vast majority of states and the federal government refuse to recognize same-sex marriage. Recent public opinion polls suggest the views of Californians are more conflicted or nuanced than the stark results of Proposition 22 would imply. While 25 percent of Californians oppose either same-sex marriage or civil unions for gays, 38 percent support civil unions only, and 32 percent believe that gays should be allowed to legally marry.[7] They are also evenly split on whether or not there should be an amendment to the U.S. Constitution that would recognize only heterosexual marriage and that would prevent states from legally recognizing same-sex marriages.

A more successful policy front for gays has been the legislative process. For example, in 2001, Governor Gray Davis signed landmark legislation that granted "domestic partner" benefits to same-sex couples and heterosexual senior partners who register as such with the state. Among other provisions, AB 25 allows partners to make medical decisions for incapacitated partners, sue for wrongful death, adopt a partner's child, and will property to a partner. Interest group opponents included the Campaign for California Families and the

Traditional Values Coalition; proponents included the California Alliance for Pride and Equality. Both sides used family values arguments. Opponents claimed the bill "cheapened every marriage in the state" while Davis himself said the bill was about "responsibility, respect, and most of all about family."

Gay rights have also advanced at the local level. By the early 2000s, eight counties and 29 cities had passed ordinance barring discrimination against gays. These rights vary from place to place, but they include public and private employment, public accommodations, education, housing, and lending practices. A number of cities including San Francisco and Oakland now require all private sector suppliers to grant domestic partner benefits in order to obtain city business. That said, local governments may not alter the state's policy on marriage itself. In 2004, the California Supreme Court ruled that the granting of over 4,000 marriage licenses to same-sex couples in San Francisco was "void and of no legal effect" due to Proposition 22. On all these fronts, the overall issue stirs heated debate and highlights fundamental cultural divisions in the state.[8]

Education: Coping with Growth and Diversity

Unlike abortion, education is a public service deeply rooted in California's political history. Yet the state's educational system faces unprecedented challenges. In 2003–2004, the state's 9,230 public schools in 1,059 school districts served 6.3 million students from kindergarten through high school. About 600,000 students attended private schools and thousands more are homeschooled or partly homeschooled in conjunction with public and private schools. In fiscal year 2005–2006, the state provided about 53 percent of K–12 funding, local taxes 27 percent, and federal funds 13 percent. Once the envy of the nation, one challenge after another now faces California's educational system, including enrollment growth, ethnic diversity, and social change.

PRESSURES ON EDUCATION

Pressures, many of which are external to the educational system itself, buffet California educators and students alike. Here we consider enrollment growth, ethnic hyperpluralism, social conflict, and funding challenges.

Enrollment Growth

The sheer growth of California's school-aged population is by far the most profound challenge. Historically, education enrollments have reflected a boom-or-bust pattern. Enrollments surge and slow based on birth rates and immigration. Some classrooms that were jammed with Baby Boomers in the 1960s stood empty in the 1970s. During the 1980s, demographers detected another boom they think is long-term in nature. In 2000, enrollments reached 6 million. In the decade from 2000 to 2010, a projected 50,000 students will be added to California K–12 schools *each year*. To provide for these students alone would take 1,700 new classrooms. This growth, coupled with efforts to reduce class size in the lower grades, has created a massive and urgent need for added classrooms, new schools, and more teachers.

Ethnic Hyperpluralism

The ethnic composition in California's public schools has been shifting for some years and will continue to do so well into the twenty-first century. Ethnic and cultural hyperpluralism are increasingly the norm. Consider Table 13.2. No single

ethnic group constitutes a public school majority. Latinos will continue to be the most rapidly growing group. Diversity is more than ethnicity, as language differences illustrate. Statewide, about 25 percent of K–12 students (1.6 million) are English learners (EL). That is, they are not proficient enough in English to succeed academically in mainstream English programs. Of Hispanic K-12 students, 48 percent are English learners, a challenging statistic for districts with high numbers of such students. While Spanish is the stereotypical first language for many students, it is by no means the only one. The state Department of Education "Language Census" records nearly 60 major languages present in California schools—more than in all of Europe.

For many years, educators dealt with this language diversity by offering bilingual education. EL students were taught in both their first languages and in English, with the goal of making them proficient in English. Meeting the goal was a challenge. Many non-English speakers enter California schools at all grade levels, bringing a variety of language "readiness" with them. Growing frustration with the results of bilingual education resulted in the passage of Proposition 227 in 1998. It required all instruction to be in English unless parents objected. It also allowed EL students

TABLE 13.2 Public School Diversity in California

	1987–1988	1997–1998	2007–2008*
Latino	30.1%	40.4%	49.8%
White	50.0	38.8	29.8
Black	9.1	8.6	7.5
Asian	7.3	8.2	8.6
Filipino	2.1	2.4	2.6
American Indian	0.8	0.6	0.7
Pacific Islander	0.5	0.6	0.7

*Projected.

Source: California Department of Education and the Demographic Research Unit, California Department of Finance.

Question: To what extent are these trends evident in your community?

to participate in sheltered English immersion programs for a maximum of one year.

Social Conflict

Broader social changes affecting all segments of society have introduced new levels of conflict in California schools. Two-income parents, single parents, child abuse, parental neglect, and poverty have changed the very mission of public schools. Teachers are not only educators but also disciplinarians, surrogate parents, counselors, social workers, detectives, and nurses. Problems stemming from gangs, gang attire, graffiti, guns on campus, and drug use are increasingly routine. California's schools are becoming more hyperpluralistic as students emphasize their own differences and identities based on race, ethnicity, income, gender, sexual orientation, and religious faith. In the late 1990s, some high schools experienced a rise in extracurricular ethnic clubs. Some students and educators worried that such clubs would foster intergroup tension, not just intragroup pride.[9]

The Funding Challenge

In absolute numbers, California spends far more on education than any other state, almost $61 billion in 2005–2006. Yet in terms of per-pupil, state-only spending, California's numbers are less impressive. In 2003–2004, New York spent $12,059 per pupil; California spent only $7,692. The United States average was $8,204. Those numbers ranked California twenty-fifth in such spending. Compared to other states, California has seen both better and worse days. In 1964–1965, it ranked fifth in per pupil spending; in 1992–1993, it ranked forty-second.

Education spending in California results from numerous pressures involving court decisions, statewide propositions, enrollment growth, and substantive education policy-making.

1. A decades-old state Supreme Court case has partially influenced the direction of state spending. In *Serrano v. Priest* (1971), the Court ruled that a wide variation in per pupil spending between districts was unconstitutional. Although the legislature has sought to equalize funding since 1971, interdistrict inequities continue to exist. Furthermore, affluent districts are able to raise substantial amounts of additional revenue from parents, booster clubs, and foundations—belying the notion of equal funding.[10]

2. California voters have made numerous decisions directly relating to education funding. As Figure 13.2 suggests, these actions have ranged from tax cuts to funding guarantees and massive bond measures.

3. Enrollment growth drives increased education spending. Because the state provides per-pupil funding based on average daily attendance (ADA), the addition of each new student triggers another $7,300 or more annually in education spending.

4. Education and other policy reforms create pockets of education spending. For instance, the state's class size reduction program required startup funding for additional teachers and classrooms. Welfare reform obligated the state to provide on-site child care so that schools and community colleges could provide job training programs.

EDUCATION REFORM

The challenges of enrollment growth, diversity issues, and funding pressures have led to a number of education reforms in California. By the late 1990s, reform efforts took on a sense of urgency. Three areas of education reform reflect both current education trends and the politics of diversity in the state.

Improving Quality

Given the diversity of California students, educational performance is a constant challenge. California Department of Education statistics

Year	Policy	Effect
1978	Proposition 13	Cut property tax base of education and shifted weight of education funding to state
1984	Proposition 84	Established a state lottery with 34 percent of ticket sales dedicated to education
1988	Proposition 88	Guaranteed that K–12 education would receive no less than 40 percent of annual general funds spending
1998	Proposition 1A	Provided a record $6.7 billion in general obligation bonds for K–12 school and classroom construction

FIGURE 13.2   How Voters Affect Education Spending

Question: To what extent *should* voters affect complex education spending decision in California?

are telling. Although dropout rates have declined and some test scores have improved, only 69 percent of California's ninth-graders graduate with their classes. After years of disappointing results, test scores in reading, math, language, and spelling have recently improved, especially in the lower grades. Nonetheless, only 29 to 33 percent of California students are considered "proficient" or better as English readers. Those who score poorly on such tests tend to be economically disadvantaged and/or English learners.

Efforts to improve educational quality in California are nothing new. The 1983 Hart Hughes Educational Reform Act increased high school graduation requirements and provided for longer school days and school years. The 1992 Charter Schools Act allowed the creation of parent-, teacher-, or community-established schools that would operate independent of many state and local regulations. In 1996, after experiencing some of the highest student–teacher ratios in the nation, California launched a dramatic class size reduction program. In kindergarten through third grade, class sizes would be limited to 20 students. The results were immediate and mixed. While

teacher morale and classroom manageability increased, so did local costs and shortages of classroom space, and credentialed teachers.[11] In the late 1990s, new reforms included the monitoring of individual school performance, a required high school exit exam, peer assistance for teachers, various awards and incentives, and new reading programs.

Dissatisfied with state-level reforms, Congress passed the *No Child Left Behind Act* (NCLB) in 2001. This was President George W. Bush's signature education policy aimed at improving educational quality. The law requires schools to (1) give standardized English and math tests annually from third through eighth grades and (2) increase the number of students scoring high enough to be labeled proficient. As with other states, California must set annual improvement goals and publicly identify districts and individual schools in need of improvement.

Improving Accountability

The politics of diversity is not limited to funding and reform issues. It also includes how students, schools, and even textbook publishers are held accountable for educational success. Textbook publishers must heed California's massive Education Code and work within a variety of frameworks (general curricular goals) and content standards (detailed subject specifications for each grade level). These standards guide local school districts on what to teach and publishers on what to write. For each grade level and subject area, the California Department of Education approves lists of textbooks from which local school districts can choose. Publishers must address questions like these: Should textbooks reflect America's European heritage versus the experience of "marginalized" groups—Latinos, African Americans, gays, and women? Should reading texts be literature-based, phonics-based, or both? Are mathematics texts error-free and user friendly? Do history and civics texts adequately communicate the multicultural past and present of the nation and of California?

Student and school accountability centers around testing. As educators well know, testing itself can raise as many problems as it purports to solve, leading some to conclude "the perfect test" is an oxymoron. Accordingly, dissatisfied policymakers move from one statewide test to another or from one testing approach to another. In 1993, the California Learning Assessment System (CLAS) replaced traditional multiple-choice achievement tests. The questions on the CLAS tests assessed the reasoning behind student answers in reading, writing, and mathematics—and that was the problem. Critics complained that the test invaded student privacy and exposed pupils to controversial issues such as unwed motherhood. In its place, the Department of Education chose the Stanford-9 test to initiate its new Standardized Testing and Reporting (STAR) Program for grades 2 through 11. In addition, the *No Child Left Behind Act* mandates its own testing expectations.

The policy challenge with frameworks, standards, and tests is never-ending. One problem stems from educational policy fragmentation, frequent policy changes, and lack of policy coordination. Local educators often complain that the state adopts new standards and employs new tests without aligning new textbook and curricula materials accordingly. Furthermore, they argue that a greater emphasis on testing skews academic objectives and fosters a "teach to the test" mentality in the schools. Other questions arise over the testing of English language learners. If the same test is given to all students, including EL students, does that penalize those students and those districts with high EL enrollments? Is it then fair to compare and rank all California schools without regard to language, income, and other social variations among them? The NCLB law simply adds another layer to this dilemma.[12]

Improving Choice

One approach to improving education policy in California is to improve educational choice. Many parents desire choice as a matter of principle; some school reformers claim it would encourage competition between schools, resulting in educational improvement statewide. The most radical proposals have involved school vouchers. Proponents of such voucher plans have argued that, because public schools are wasteful and overly bureaucratic, parents deserve a choice of schools. Furthermore, competition from voucher-funded private schools would force public schools to improve. Opponents have feared that vouchers would drain public education budgets and allow private schools to deny access to poor families and "problem" students—the physically impaired, English learners, or low academic achievers. California voters overwhelmingly rejected two such voucher plans in 1993 and 2000. The latter, Proposition 38, would have provided state-funded, tax-free grants of about $3,000 to children in private and parochial schools, including nontraditional programs.

While California voters have definitively rejected vouchers, less radical "managed choice" options are available. Charter schools have provided educational alternatives for relatively few Californians. In addition, state law now allows intra- and interdistrict transfers. In other words, students may attend public schools elsewhere in their districts or in other districts, for example where their parents work. Magnet schools attract students from across districts by offering specialized courses or approaches. The state's class size reduction program appeared to have lured some private school families back to the public schools. Smaller student–teacher ratios is what they had sought when they exited public schools in the first place. The NCLB law empowers parents to seek out more successful schools if their own neighborhood schools are low-performing ones. Yet this promise of choice may be a ruse if nearby schools or entire districts are also underperforming or are too overcrowded to accept NCLB refugees.

In one sense, these choice-oriented policies reflect the popularity of "market" approaches to public services generally. But in another sense, they reflect a disintegration of majoritarian policymaking in education. Is education still a majoritarian investment into which all Californians contribute and from which all equally benefit? What we do know is that education policy seems to be increasingly client- or interest group-based. General taxes still fund education, but the product itself is increasingly differentiated or fragmented. The problem is particularly dire for low income, minority school children, where substandard school facilities are the norm. Evidence ranging from dilapidated classrooms and the absence of college preparatory courses to sub-par graduation rates among certain minorities has prompted some analysts to label California's education system a "two-tier" one—dividing students into the educational haves and have nots. In response to a class action lawsuit, the state has vowed to rectify at least some of the quality disparities that now characterize public education in California.[13]

Higher Education: An Uncertain Future

Historically, Californians have taken pride in their institutions of higher education. But population growth, increased cultural diversity, and chronic underfunding have raised some profound issues for the state's colleges and universities. Students and faculty know the symptoms of the problem only too well. Fees are raised, courses are cancelled, graduation plans are delayed, and needs outpace revenues. For many public university students, a four-year baccalaureate degree is largely a myth. How have these pressures come about?

THE MAJORITARIAN IDEAL

Like other western states, California lacked a significant private college sector in the decades following its statehood. In its place, the state developed a comprehensive public system of higher education, featuring high quality and open access. Initially, the Organic Act of 1868 created the University of California. Later, state teachers colleges and junior (or two-year) colleges were added. Concurrently, numerous private colleges and universities were established with little state attention or help. Anticipating an enrollment surge by Baby Boomers in the 1960s, the legislature passed the Donahoe Higher Education Act of 1960—commonly called the *Master Plan for Higher Education.* According to a legislative report, what began as a modest agreement between educational institutions evolved into a "world-renowned social compact" articulating a bold vision for the future.[14]

The plan did three things. First, it prescribed enrollment parameters for each level. UC would admit students from the top 12.5 percent of high school seniors; CSU (formerly the teachers colleges) would admit the top one-third; and the community college system (formerly the junior colleges) would admit any student capable of benefiting from instruction. Low fees and no tuition would provide ready access to the academically qualified at UC and CSU, although admission to any particular campus was not guaranteed. Second, the Master Plan assigned different missions to each level. UC would emphasize research, graduate programs, and offer doctoral degrees. CSU would focus on liberal arts teaching and professional education through the master's degree. Community colleges would provide standard college courses for transfer to four-year institutions, plus vocational and technical training. The transfer function was to be paramount. Third, the Master Plan created governance structures to operate each sector and to resolve the inevitable turf battles that would occur.

The entire system grew beyond all projections in the decades that followed. Today, the overall system encompasses a huge complex of campuses throughout California. UC consists of nine general campuses and one health science campus enrolling more than 205,000 full-time equivalent (FTE) students. The ninth campus is UC Merced, which opened in 2005; it was the first new UC campus in four decades. CSU consists of 23 campuses and six off-campus centers enrolling 332,000 students. The state's 109 community college campuses and other sites enroll 1.6 million full- and part-time students. California's 227 independent colleges, universities, professional schools, and other specialized campuses enroll another 233,000 students. Although the "privates" produce only a quarter of the state's baccalaureate degrees, they produce nearly half of the master's and doctoral degrees, and over 70 percent of the professional degrees.

RETHINKING THE PLAN

In recent years, revenue shortfalls and ensuing budget deficits have hit higher education's share of the state budget. University and college administrators have responded by authorizing significant budget cuts and sizable fee increases. Students have grumbled, protested, and transferred to community colleges, private colleges, or even to out-of-state public universities. Community college fees have also increased during this period. The students least able to absorb these increases have dropped out of college altogether. How much longer could these systems tolerate both enrollment and funding pressures? Begun in 1999, a joint legislative committee partnered with numerous educators to consider a new master plan more in keeping with the modern challenges facing both K-12 and higher education in California.

Policy discussions in recent years have focused on three interlocking issues: access, growth, and pricing. First, access is an especially sensitive matter for California's college-bound minorities. They embrace the original vision of ready access and large public subsidies, arguing that some minorities, especially low income ones, are more likely than whites to drop out when fees increase dramatically. This trend only exacerbates an existing dropout problem among minorities that is usually attributed to social alienation on California campuses. In 1999, Governor Gray Davis proposed and the UC Board of Regents approved a new rule extending UC eligibility to the top 4 percent of students at each high school, whether or not they were in the top 12.5 percent of all California high school seniors. Eligibility, though, does not guarantee admittance. Due to budget constraints, the UC system was unable to accept all qualified applicants in 2003, the first time that happened in 40 years. Clearly, resolving larger access issues would require more campuses, classrooms, courses, and funding to match.

Second, rethinking California's commitment to higher education comes when the state is facing major population growth (see Chapter 12). Each system needs several new campuses to accommodate current and future growth, but planning has been marred by competition for scarce budget dollars. Since UC, CSU, and the

California Community Colleges (CCC) are running out of physical space to serve more students, suggestions for coping with anticipated growth include new campus construction, year-round instruction, greater on-campus efficiencies, increased private college aid, and more online (Internet) coursework. Some administrators characterize these efforts as providing "authentic access"—not merely admission but real access to courses needed by students in order to graduate in a timely manner.

Third, many policymakers and educators continue to support low fees for the public campuses, but critics question the practice. Given the personal benefits of a tax-subsidized degree, they think that today's students should pay a greater share of their own education than their predecessors did. Such increases could be offset by greater financial aid to the most needy students.[15] To be sure, public higher education in California is a relative bargain compared to similar institutions elsewhere (see Figure 13.3). That is, for the students. Aside from fees, taxpayers fund a significant share of overall higher education costs. Opponents of higher student fees point to the continued need for access in a time of population growth, growing numbers of price-sensitive minority students, and the relatively high total costs of attending college in California, including living expenses. The fundamental challenge for policymakers is this: Public higher education in California is an increasingly scarce resource, belying its historic mission of affordable education for all qualified students.[16]

DIVERSITY ON CAMPUS

If those issues were not enough, consider the challenge of achieving diversity on California's campuses. In some respects, college campuses have always been considered laboratories for thinking through and acting out trends in the larger society. Idealists have thought that these places should model "correct" behavior for the larger society in such areas as race rela-

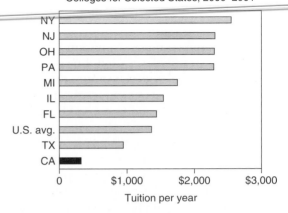

Average Annual Tuition at Public Two-Year Colleges for Selected States, 2000–2001

FIGURE 13.3 Higher Education Fees
Average Annual Tuition at Public Two-Year Colleges for Selected States, 2000–2001
Source: Public Policy Institute of California 2004.

tions and civilized speech. Given the ethnic and cultural hyperpluralism in California, it is only natural that this hyperpluralism would be felt on campus—and so it has. In the process, California's college and university campuses, public and private, are both modeling societal ideals and mirroring the difficulties inherent in reaching them.

On campus, diversity issues include the students themselves and the subjects they study. Efforts to diversify California student bodies have been a partial success. The community colleges are the most ethnically diverse; UC and the private institutions are the least diverse. At one time, California's public colleges and universities used affirmative action to increase minority enrollments. This practice encouraged efforts to recruit, admit, and enroll students from underrepresented backgrounds (such as race and ethnicity). Although the U.S. Supreme Court, in *Bakke v. Regents of the University of California*, rejected hard and fast numerical quotas for admitting minorities, they did laud the general goal of diversity. In 1995, the UC Board of Regents ended affirmative action in UC admissions. Minority applications fell but only temporarily. In 1996, voters approved Proposition 209, which banned racial and other similar preferences in all state programs, including higher education. On appeal, the federal courts affirmed 209. Despite these setbacks, student bodies are more diverse now than they were decades ago. Diversifying California's professorate has been more challenging. The California Post Secondary Education Commission reports that, despite recent progress, higher education faculties are much less diverse than the students they teach.[17]

Campuses have also offered more diversity-related courses and course content, including multiculturalism, gender bias, and other topics. Some campuses have separate majors addressing Latino, African American, or women's studies. General education requirements have become more inclusive, including the addition of multicultural courses and nonwestern perspectives in civilization courses. There have also been some efforts to diversify personnel appointments—from top governing boards to faculty members.

Increasing diversity on California's college and university campuses has not been an easy process, as the debate on affirmative action attests. Even on numerically "diverse" campuses, self-imposed segregation in co-curricular activities tends to isolate different ethnic and racial groups. Conflict also abounds over political ideology, leading to concerns over political correctness or indoctrination by some or the lack of speech sensitivity or civility by others.

Social Programs

The Golden State has a long history of social programs that cushion the impact of life's slings and arrows. For example, California's workers' compensation system (to assist injured employees) dates back to the Progressive era. Still other programs are a legacy of the New Deal in the 1930s and the War on Poverty in the 1960s. Like other states, social programs in California are a jerry-built arrangement of multiple agencies and financial partnerships spanning every layer of the federal system. In child-care services alone, nearly 50 programs are administered by 13 California agencies. A patchwork of social programs reflects the different times in which they were enacted, mixed priorities, and approaches plus some measure of ambivalence toward those in need. In fact, the history of social policy typifies *ambivalent benevolence*—on one hand, a caring concern for California's "truly needy" and, on the other, a reluctance to reward those who seemingly prefer "handouts" to honest work.

Taken together, California's social programs consumed more than 31 percent of the state's general fund for 2005–2006. When combined with federal funds, nearly $70 billion is devoted to the broad areas of health and welfare. In recent decades, this share of the budget has grown due to high birth rates among the poor, high levels of immigration, high divorce rates, and federal mandates.

Who are California's poor? Roughly 13 percent of all Californians are poor. Poverty rates are especially high for children (17 percent), foreign-born Hispanics (24 percent), and female-headed households (30 percent). Contrary to popular impressions, most poor families are employed. Where do they live? The highest rates of poverty occur in the San Joaquin Valley and the lowest rates are in the San Francisco Bay Area.[18]

WELFARE POLICY

Programs to help the poor are deeply rooted in perceptions about the poor. Americans perceive the poor as either deserving or undeserving. The *deserving poor* or truly needy are poor presumably through no fault of their own. Children, the blind and disabled, the laid-off unemployed, and the elderly fall into this category. The *undeserving poor* include unemployed able-bodied adults, especially men, the "lifestyle" poor or unemployed, and abusers of drugs and alcohol. Presumably these individuals have chosen their lot in life, and the personal consequences are not society's fault or responsibility. California's policies toward those in need combine these two perceptions. The largest programs target needy families, children, those who are elderly or disabled, and other adults.

1. *Families.* California's major program to aid needy families is *CalWORKs* (California Work Opportunity and Responsibility to Kids). This program implements the federal Temporary Assistance to Needy Families (TANF) program that, under welfare reform, replaced the old Aid to Families with Dependent Children (AFDC). It provides time-limited assistance (food and shelter) to eligible families in times of crisis. The state's 58 counties administer the program. In 2005–2006, a monthly cash grant for a family of four ranged from $768 to $806. For those families that tend to fall in and out of poverty, there is a cumulative five-year limit on aid. Recipients must participate in job skills training and various work activities with the goal of becoming permanently self-sufficient. Due to a booming economy in the late 1990s, CalWORKs caseloads dropped as employable and newly trained clients found work but have leveled off since then. In 2005–2006, an average of 473,000 Californians per month received CalWORKs support. Is the program working? Well, yes and no. According to one study, many families have moved off the welfare rolls and into jobs. But for many, their paychecks provide little more than what they received from welfare. While many have stayed off welfare, they continue to need "transitional benefits" such as food stamps and Medi-Cal.[19]

In addition to CalWORKs, the federal food stamp program provides nutritional assistance to eligible low-income families. Recipients receive coupons that can be used like cash at participating grocery stores. In recent years, nearly 2 million Californians received food stamps worth roughly $200 per household per month. While that seems like a large number of recipients, only 39 percent of eligible Californians were receiving food stamps in 2003, placing California dead last among the 50 states in rates of participation.

2. *Children.* Obviously, children benefit if a parent qualifies under CalWORKs. Benefits include not only monthly cash assistance but publicly funded child care while parents work or receive training. But there are a plethora of other programs to help California's high-risk children. The Child Protective Services program intervenes when there is evidence or suspicion of in-home child abuse or neglect. The state's Out-of-Home Care System places more than 74,000 such children with relatives, foster families, or group homes. The Cal-Learn program assists pregnant and parenting teenagers to obtain high school diplomas or the equivalent. The Child Support Enforcement Program locates and requires noncustodial parents to pay court-ordered child support. In 2004, several billion dollars in such payments went to nearly 800,000 California families.

3. *Seniors and Disabled.* A variety of programs also assist the elderly and disabled. Some of them are separated from the largest federal programs, Social Security and Medicare. People 60 years or older may receive continuing care at state-approved facilities. In-Home Supportive Services provides a variety of services to help seniors, the disabled, or blind remain in their homes. The federal Supplemental Security Income (SSI) program is part of Social Security. It provides monthly cash aid to 1.2 million aged, blind, and disabled Californians who meet the program's income and resource requirements. California augments the SSI payment with an SSP (State Supplemental Payment) grant. SSI grants range from about $800 for a single person to $1,400 for aged and disabled couples. The blind receive somewhat more.

4. *Other Adults.* What about those adults who are not covered by the programs just described? Several programs exist for them. The Adult Protective Services program assists elderly and dependent adults who are functionally impaired, unable to meet their own needs, or are victims of neglect or abuse. Lastly, the state's Refugee Settlement Program helps refugees from other countries who locate in California become self-sufficient.

HEALTH POLICY

As Americans grow in number and live longer, medical care becomes a major policy issue at both the state and federal levels. Crises such as AIDS (acquired immune deficiency syndrome) also impact an already stressed health care system. Unlike welfare policy, health policy commingles the public and private sectors, both in terms of care and funding. The "medical industrial complex," consisting of medical professionals, hospitals, and insurance companies, dominates the system. Two simple truths govern the politics of health care. First, costly medical care does not necessarily equal good health; being healthy has a great deal to do with heredity, lifestyle, social conditions, and physical environment. Second, health services (both public and private) involve a vast transfer of wealth. In the public sector, this means in effect transferring resources from higher income (less needy) to lower income (more needy) Americans. In private sector health care, it means transferring resources from the healthy to the sick and those who care for them. Although taxes and insurance premiums fund medical care in these two sectors, people rarely receive in care exactly what they have "paid" in taxes or premiums. Redistributing health dollars in both private and public sector is a fact of life.

California's approach to aiding the sick is multifaceted and increasingly expensive and includes three broad approaches: private insurance, Medi-Cal, and deinstitutionalization.

Private Insurance

In the United States, our health care system depends heavily on private insurance. Traditionally, state-regulated insurance companies paid doctors on a *fee-for-service* basis. Each medical procedure had a price, and insurance companies unquestioningly paid whatever it was at the time it was rendered. Increasingly, insurance companies and doctors have been moving to *managed care:* networks of doctors and hospitals providing comprehensive services for a predetermined price. In recent years, about two-thirds of California's nonelderly have been covered by employer-provided or privately purchased health insurance. What about the rest? In 2004, about 6.5 million Californians—over 20 percent of the non-elderly population—had no health insurance of any kind, ranking the state fourth from the bottom in the percentage of residents without health care. Roughly a third of those uninsured Californians qualify for Medi-Cal or Healthy Families, two major state programs. The rest are workers and their dependents whose employers provide no private health insurance (a common practice in agriculture, construction, retail, and small businesses), but who earn too much money to qualify for publicly funded care—the working poor. Lack of health insurance disproportionately affects Latinos. Nearly 32 percent of Latinos under the age of 65 lack health insurance, and most noncitizen Latinos work in low-wage jobs or for small companies that offer no coverage.

For years, people would lose their insurance if they switched jobs, were laid off, or were found by a new insurance carrier to have a "pre-existing condition" such as AIDS or cancer. Although Congress passed legislation in 1996 guaranteeing the portability of health insurance coverage for those who lose or leave their jobs, that law does not help those who lack insurance in the first place. California voters rejected two measures—Propositions 166 (1992) and 72 (2004)—that would have required many employers to provide basic insurance for all full-time and some part-time workers. In 1997, California partly filled this chronic insurance gap with "Healthy Families," a program offering low-cost insurance coverage for the children of uninsured workers who earn too much to qualify for Medi-Cal. The plan covers usual health, dental, and vision needs. In 2004, this program stood to benefit about 732,000 children.

Medi-Cal

California's version of the federal Medicaid program for low-income individuals is called *Medi-Cal.* Medi-Cal pays for two types of care—core and optional services. Federally required core services include access to physicians and nurses, hospital care, laboratory tests, home care, and preventative services for children. Federal matching funds are available for any of 34 optional services such as hospice care, adult dentistry, and chiropractic services. As part of Medi-Cal, California funded nearly 54,000 abortions in 2002. CalWORKs and SSI/SSP recipients, qualified expectant mothers, and poor children automatically receive Medi-Cal benefits. Other low-income people qualify but pay for a portion of their medical care.

Medi-Cal spending generally increases or decreases in response to economic trends, various eligibility expansions, and state-imposed cost controls on health care providers. In 2004, nearly 7 million Californians qualified for Medi-Cal in any given month. In an effort to control spiraling costs, California has encouraged Medi-Cal beneficiaries to select managed care plans and providers. By 2002, almost half had done so. In recent years, the state has reduced the number of optional Medi-Cal services it is willing to fund.

What about health care for California's large immigrant population? Are they deserving or undeserving of Medi-Cal support? This has been the subject of protracted political debate and numerous legal challenges. Many Republicans in Congress and in California's state government have tried to curtail welfare, health care, and other benefits for both legal and undocumented immigrants. Many Democrats have fought to retain those services, notably Medi-Cal. While California's legal immigrants still qualify for regular Medi-Cal, the controversy has confused and puzzled many immigrants. Fearing bureaucratic hassles or immigration troubles, they avoid the public programs available to them, such as Healthy Families. Said one: "I know it will cause trouble for me when I apply for [immigration] papers for my family."[20] Where do these families turn when sick or injured? In addition to financially strapped emergency rooms, they may seek out bogus doctors, "back room" clinics, smuggled drugs, home remedies, or at best, low-cost community clinics.

In short, California's health care system is in trouble. Public spending on health care is enormous due to the growth of needy populations, the rising costs of health care for everyone, and prior spending commitments when there were revenue surpluses. Given its portion of the budget, health care is a likely target for spending freezes or budget cuts to counter revenue shortfalls. All the policy choices seem painful. Eligibility and program cuts threaten the "social safety net" for millions of the state's most vulnerable residents. Cuts in provider reimbursements threaten the already fragile finances of many hospitals and clinics, forcing some to turn away Medi-Cal patients or even close their doors. In fact, nearly half of all urban physicians in California already refuse such patients due to below-cost reimbursements from the state. Policy analysts believe nothing short of a health care overhaul is needed to address this problem.[21]

Deinstitutionalization

A much less discussed health care approach in California has been the *deinstitutionalization* of the mentally ill. Historically, psychiatric patients were placed in institutions, apart from

PHOTO 13.1   Homeless in Santa Barbara

society and family. Prior to the 1960s, California had a reasonably progressive and balanced approach, including prevention and early intervention in mental cases. But in the 1960s, two trends merged. First, Governor Ronald Reagan persuaded the legislature to reduce funding for mental health programs and shift them to the counties. Second, mental health professionals embraced a new treatment philosophy that placed mental patients in communities, not institutions. Neighborhoods and families would help "mainstream" the mentally ill. In California, these forces converged in the Lanterman-Petris-Short Act of 1968. In effect a civil rights law, it made the confinement of unwilling mental patients exceedingly difficult.

Ironically and even tragically, many mental patients were victimized by this "reform." A decade later, Proposition 13 cut revenue for just the mental health programs these people needed. Furthermore, the ideal of community-based treatment fell far short of expecta-

tions. Anticipated community-based mental health centers never materialized. Many former mental patients did not return to families or live in group homes—they became homeless. Indeed, thousands of California's homeless population have disabilities, mental illness, or other health problems. Many call jail home because without close supervision or daily medication they lose control and commit crimes. Shelters, low-cost hotels, and other "transitional housing" accommodate only a fraction of California's homeless.

In communities across California, the homeless problem represents a clash of civic values—compassion for those in need versus the impulse to protect property values, tourism, and business interests. As a result, some California communities try to criminalize homelessness, prosecuting them for loitering, squatting, unauthorized camping, and panhandling. To one Santa Cruz homeless person, "It looks like they push the homeless around to satisfy the people with money."[22]

Immigration:
Conflict over Newcomers

Commenting on his move from Fresno, California, to Turner, Maine, Mexican national Francisco Guzman reflected, "It's a different life than in a place like California, where sometimes it feels like Mexico."[23] Exactly. Mr. Guzman's observation is at the core of California's conflict over newcomers. On one hand, California's surging Latino population does give at least certain locales a "Mexican" flavor. On the other hand, some Californians argue that California feels *too much* like Mexico. In the early 2000s, nearly 27 percent of all Californians were born outside the United States, and the largest single source was Mexico.

At several points in Chapter 13, we have discussed the impact of immigrants on various public policy issues facing the Golden State. In Chapter 2, it was suggested that California's political development is, in part, the story of state-building through domestic migration and foreign immigration. Today, the result is the development of a culturally diverse and increasingly hyperpluralistic state. In Chapter 3, California's proximity to Mexico and the Pacific Rim was described as an ongoing policy challenge. California's location results in significant foreign immigration, which in turn affects politics. It is therefore fitting to revisit the challenge of immigration as we conclude this book.[24]

FEDERAL POLICIES, CALIFORNIA IMPACTS

Immigration is and always has been a federal matter. As we noted earlier, the history of immigration policy in the United States has been a flower petal policy—"Now we need you, now we don't." The ebb and flow of this policy was predictable. When the nation needed cheap labor only immigration would supply, federal rules were relaxed, quotas were increased, and large numbers of immigrants were allowed entry.

When economic recessions periodically occurred, the flow of immigration was staunched, and immigrants already here were subject to abuse. This pattern has occurred time and time again.

The 1980s brought some changes to this pattern. A robust economy resulted in massive illegal immigration. Waves of undocumented people came to California to join their friends and kin already here. The then Immigration and Naturalization Service (INS) was relatively helpless to stop the flow. Only 14 miles of the U.S./Mexico border were relatively secure, and Border Patrol agents seemed hopelessly outnumbered. The Immigration Reform and Control Act of 1986 (IRCA) used a "carrot and stick" approach. On the one hand, it granted amnesty to illegal immigrants already in the United States, including 1.6 million living in California. On the other, it provided sanctions for those employers who knowingly hire illegal immigrants. In recent years, the INS instituted Operation Gatekeeper in an effort to make the California/Mexico border more difficult to cross. This program has curbed illegal crossings to some extent.

Over the years, the impacts of federal immigration policies on California have been substantial. We have already noted the vast numbers of English language learners in California's public schools. In recent years, one in seven state prison inmates have been undocumented persons. Another 14,000 are housed in county jails. The IRCA requires federal reimbursement for these incarceration costs, but California receives substantially less than full reimbursement.[25] President George W. Bush has proposed eliminating that obligation entirely, due to federal border enhancements. Other policies are impacted as well. Because U.S.-born children of illegal immigrants are by definition American citizens, they qualify for Medi-Cal, welfare, and other state-funded benefits if they are poor.

In 2005, President Bush reiterated his proposal to create a temporary worker program for current illegal immigrants, including over 2 million residents in California. Supporters of this initiative believe it is a realistic response to the economic needs of the American economy and the aspirations of those it would cover. Critics, including many fellow Republicans, contend that it is amnesty in disguise, a program that would encourage still more illegal immigration as potential workers enter the states in hopes of qualifying under its provisions.

CALIFORNIA'S IMMIGRATION "POLICY"

In recent decades, pressures mounted for California policymakers to "do something" about illegal immigration, even though it is a federal responsibility. A 1993 *Los Angeles Times* poll revealed that 86 percent of Californians believed that it is a major or moderate problem. In fact, 52 percent thought that *legal* immigration should be reduced.[26] Ten years later, over 80 percent of voters in California's recall election thought that stopping illegal immigration was extremely, very or somewhat important (40, 26, and 18 percent respectively).

California's approach to immigration has been both reactive and proactive. Reactive policies are in response or opposition to some condition or trend. Ballot initiatives can be reactive in tone, purpose, and content. For example, in 1994 Proposition 187 attempted to deny publicly funded services (education, health, and welfare) to illegal immigrants. It would have required public school officials to survey their students and report to the state the legal status of their families. A federal judge declared 187 to be an unconstitutional infringement on federal immigration responsibilities. Governor Gray Davis decided not to appeal that decision, finding the educational provisions of 187 draconian: "I personally will never be a party to an effort to kick kids out of school."[27] In recent years, the state legislature granted drivers licenses to illegal immigrants but reversed course after the recall of Governor Gray Davis. In 2005,

the U.S. Congress effectively preempted the whole issue by rendering such licenses useless for typical identification purposes.

Other approaches to immigration have been more proactive and less initiative driven. That is, policymakers have sought to accommodate high levels of immigration and/or cooperate with the federal government in controlling those levels and the costs associated with them. These efforts have included:

- Improving the reading performance of all California school children, not just that of English language learners

- Allowing some undocumented students to attend the University of California by paying low in-state tuition rather than nonresident tuition

- Seeking higher federal reimbursements for the costs of incarcerating undocumented felons

- Encouraging Border Patrol efforts to staunch the flow of illegal immigrants across the California/Mexico border

California's efforts to control immigration and its impacts reflect a fundamental political debate over the future of the state—what it is and is becoming. What we do know is that California never was a melting pot but rather a stew pot. Today, there are simply more ingredients than ever before, including the sheer growth of the state's foreign-born population in recent decades (see Figure 13.4). Immigration policy arguments now seem to center around the ingredients themselves. Will new and different ingredients enrich the whole stew, stand distinctively alone, or be left out of the recipe altogether?

Conclusion

California's size and cultural hyperpluralism affect its politics and policies in some profound ways. Many policies mirror the pushing

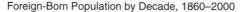

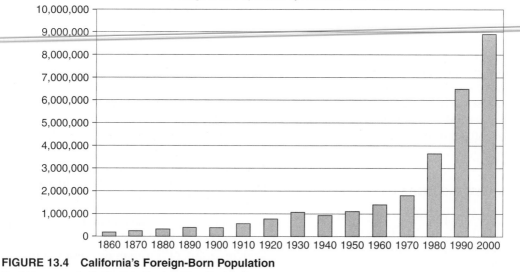

Foreign-Born Population by Decade, 1860–2000

FIGURE 13.4 California's Foreign-Born Population
Rapid Increase in California's Foreign-Born Population
Source: 2000 Census Supplemental Survey. Reprinted from Public Policy Institute of California, 2004.

and pulling of various interest groups based on ethnic, gender, class, lifestyle, or religious differences. Some majoritarian policies (those paid for and benefiting the larger society) seem to be splintering into interest group and client policies, contests between relatively narrow factions in society.

Examples abound in California. Abortion policy is essentially a continuing struggle among diverse values and contrary views over moral authority and the meaning of personhood. Education policy is more a conglomerate of contests over how best to address enrollment growth, ethnic diversity, and social change as well as ways to improve educational funding and academic quality. Higher education faces a crossroad as competing interests reconsider a social compact called the Master Plan. The caseload and spending growth of California's social programs reflects a subtle rivalry between California's taxpayers and tax

spenders, a contest exacerbated by sluggish economic growth. California's efforts to control the impacts of large-scale immigration reflect a growing concern over how diverse Californians are and are willing to be.

As the Golden State begins a new century, the broad forces of growth and diversity promise to challenge the state's political system as never before. Forging a new multicultural democracy will be painful and controversial, straining both government institutions and policymakers at the state, regional, and local levels. Given demographic and economic trends, multicultural democracy in California will also strain public budgets to their limits as demands for more spending by some groups confront demands for less spending by others. The old Chinese curse, "May you live in interesting times," seems particularly suited to modern California politics.

KEY TERMS

cultural amalgamation, separatism, and
   assimilation   (pp. 270–271)

cultural hyperpluralism   (p. 271)

client, entrepreneurial, interest group, and
   majoritarian policies   (pp. 272–273)

No Child Left Behind Act   (p. 278)

Master Plan for Higher Education   (p. 280)

ambivalent benevolence   (p. 283)

deserving and undeserving poor   (pp. 283–284)

CalWORKs   (p. 284)

fee-for-service and managed care   (p. 285)

Medi-Cal   (p. 286)

deinstitutionalization   (pp. 286–287)

REVIEW QUESTIONS

1. Describe Wilson's categories of public policy used in this chapter.
2. Why is there so little common ground among foes on the abortion issue?
3. Describe the pressures facing K–12 education in California.
4. To what extent and why is the Master Plan in trouble? How might that be evident in your own experience?
5. Survey California's array of social welfare programs and describe the pressures on each of them. Which Californians are easiest and hardest to help and why? Who are the deserving and undeserving poor?
6. What can California policymakers realistically do about immigration to the state?

WEB ACTIVITIES

California Department of Education
(www.cde.ca.gov)
This site contains a wealth of data on virtually every aspect of K–12 education policy in California.

California Post Secondary Education Commission
(www.cpec.ca.gov)

A good source of higher education enrollment data, diversity issues, and links to all public and private campuses in California.

California Department of Social Services
(www.dss.cahwnet.gov)
Provides complete descriptions of most major social service programs offered or funded by the state.

Bureau of Citizenship and Immigration Services
(www.immigration.gov)
Now part of the Department of Homeland Security, this agency website features immigration statistics relative to California and elsewhere.

INFOTRAC® COLLEGE EDITION ARTICLES

For additional reading, go to InfoTrac® College Edition, your online research library, at http://www.infotrac.thomsonlearning.com

Gays Advance in California

State Curriculum Standards and the Shaping of Student Consciousness

Illegal Immigration to California Comes with a $10.5 Billion Price Tag

NOTES

1. Quoted in Frank Clifford, "Tension Among Minorities Upsets Old Rules of Politics," *Los Angeles Times*, August 11, 1991.
2. These terms were used by Milton M. Gordon in his seminal work *Assimilation in American Life: The Role of Race, Religion and National Origins* (New York: Oxford University Press, 1964).
3. Leon Bouvier, *Fifty Million Californians* (Washington, D.C.: Center for Immigration Studies, 1991), 56.
4. James Davison Hunter, *Culture Wars: The Struggle to Define America* (New York: Basic Books, 1991), 42.
5. More detail on the early years of California abortion reform can be found in Kristin Luker, *Abortion and the Politics of Motherhood* (Berkeley: University of California Press, 1984), chap. 4.

6. Mark DiCamillo and Mervin Field, *The Field Poll* (May 8, 2002, and June 4, 2004).

7. *Los Angeles Times Poll*, April 26, 2004.

8. For a status report on gay rights in California, see Bill Ainsworth, "Next Step: Equality," *California Journal* 35 (January 2004), 6–10.

9. Diane Seo, "As Ethnic Clubs' Popularity Rises, So Do Tensions," *Los Angeles Times,* May 12, 1996; see also Louis Sahagun, "Diversity Challenges Schools to Preserve Racial Harmony," *Los Angeles Times,* February 14, 1999.

10. Doug Smith, "Funding and Fairness Clash in Public Schools," *Los Angeles Times*, February 16, 1999.

11. For more on teacher shortages, see Emelyn Rodriguez, "The Search for Qualified Teachers," *California Journal* 32 (August 2001): 10–17.

12. For a review of these testing issues, see Sylvia Fox, "Testing, Anyone?" *California Journal* 32 (September 2001): 32–36.

13. Sigrid Bathen, "The Mississippification of California Schools," *California Journal* 35 (September 2004), 10–16.

14. *Master Plan for Higher Education in Focus: Draft Report* (Sacramento: Assembly Committee on Higher Education, April 1993), 2.

15. Patrick Murphy, *Financing California's Community Colleges* (San Francisco: Public Policy Institute of California, 2004).

16. Pam Burdman, "Low Income, High Ed," *California Journal* 35 (June 2004), 20–24.

17. Online at www.cpec.ca.gov/secondpages/stat0204.asp/

18. Deborah Reed, "Recent Trends in Income and Poverty," *California Counts*, Vol. 5, No. 3, February 2004.

19. Thomas MaCurdy, Grecia Marrufo, and Margaret O'Brian-Strain, *What Happens to Families When They Leave Welfare* (San Francisco: Public Policy Institute of California, 2003).

20. Quoted in Louis Freedberg and Sabin Russell, "Immigrants' Fears of Leaving Children Without Insurance," *San Francisco Chronicle*, January 15, 1999.

21. Stephen Robitaille, "A System on the Brink," *California Journal* 35 (March 2004), 8–13.

22. John Johnson, "The Mean Streets of Santa Cruz," *Los Angeles Times,* February 3, 2002.

23. Quoted in Patrick J. McDonnell, "Mexican Arrivals Seek New Frontiers," *Los Angeles Times*, January 1999.

24. For more on immigration in California, see Jack Citrin and Andrea L. Campbell, "Immigration: California Tomorrow," in Gerald C. Lubenow and Bruce E. Cain, eds., *Governing California: Politics, Government, and Public Policy in the Golden State* (Berkeley: Institute of Governmental Studies, 1997), 267–296.

25. Dana Wilkie, "Who Pays for Jailing Illegal Immigrants," *California Journal* 34 (July 2003), 20–23.

26. Daniel Klein, "Majority in State Fed Up with Illegal Immigration," *Los Angeles Times*, September 19, 1993.

27. Quoted in Dave Lesher, "Davis Won't Follow Prop. 187 on Schools," *Los Angeles Times*, May 21, 1999.

Photo Credits

Index